SHAKESPEARE, ALCHE
CREATIVE IMAGI

CW01081641

Shakespeare's Sonnets and *A Lover's Complaint* constitute a rich tapestry of rhetorical play about Renaissance love in all its guises. A significant strand of this is spiritual alchemy: working the 'metal' of the mind through meditation on love, memory work and intense imagination. Healy demonstrates how this process of anguished soul work – construed as essential to inspired poetic making – is woven into these poems, accounting for their most enigmatic imagery and urgency of tone. The esoteric philosophy of late Renaissance Neoplatonic alchemy, which embraced bawdy sexual symbolism and was highly fashionable in European intellectual circles, facilitated Shakespeare's poetry. Arguing that Shakespeare's incorporation of alchemical textures throughout his late works is indicative of an artistic stance promoting religious toleration and unity, this book sets out a crucial new framework for interpreting the 1609 poems, and transforms our understanding of Shakespeare's art.

MARGARET HEALY is Reader in English and Director of the Centre for Early Modern Studies at the University of Sussex. She teaches many aspects of Renaissance literature, and is particularly interested in the cultural history of the body and the interfaces among literature, medicine, science and art. She is the author of *Fictions of Disease in Early Modern England: Bodies, Plagues and Politics* (2001) and *Richard II* (1998), and the co-editor of *Renaissance Transformations: The Making of English Writing 1500–1650* (2009). She edits the new British Medical Journal, *Medical Humanities*.

SHAKESPEARE, ALCHEMY AND THE CREATIVE IMAGINATION

The Sonnets and *A Lover's Complaint*

MARGARET HEALY

CAMBRIDGE
UNIVERSITY PRESS

CAMBRIDGE
UNIVERSITY PRESS

University Printing House, Cambridge CB2 8BS, United Kingdom

Published in the United States of America by Cambridge University Press, New York

Cambridge University Press is part of the University of Cambridge.

It furthers the University's mission by disseminating knowledge in the pursuit of education, learning and research at the highest international levels of excellence.

www.cambridge.org
Information on this title: www.cambridge.org/9781107637740

© Margaret Healy 2011

First published 2011
First paperback edition 2014

A catalogue record for this publication is available from the British Library

ISBN 978-1-107-00404-7 Hardback
ISBN 978-1-107-63774-0 Paperback

Contents

Illustrations

Acknowledgements

This project would certainly have been very much longer in coming to fruition without the generous support of the Leverhulme Trust. I am grateful to the Trust for granting me a Research Fellowship throughout 2008, enabling me to research and write this book.

I would like to thank Michael Schoenfeldt for inviting me to contribute a chapter to the Blackwell *Companion to Shakespeare's Sonnets* (2007), which encouraged me to try out some initial ideas that have formed the kernel of this book. I would also like to acknowledge the valuable input of Helen Hackett, Tom Healy, Michael Schoenfeldt and an anonymous reader, who read earlier versions of this book and provided important feedback. Members of the London Shakespeare Seminar, particularly Eric Langley, Russ McDonald and Susanne Scholz, have commented helpfully too. At Cambridge University Press, my editor, Sarah Stanton, and the production team – notably Rebecca Taylor, Rosina Di Marzo and my copy-editor, Caroline Drake – have been encouraging and supportive throughout the process. Special thanks are certainly due to those students, postgraduates and colleagues in the Centre for Early Modern Studies at the University of Sussex whose enthusiasm for discussing Renaissance literature, alchemy and the creative imagination has spurred me on, convincing me that I am not alone in my preoccupations. I am indebted to Tynan for crucial insights that have emerged during our stimulating walks, while the importance of Tom Healy's constant encouragement, warmth and sense of humour goes without saying.

A note on the texts

All references to Shakespeare's *Sonnets* and *A Lovers Complaint* are to Colin Burrow (ed.), *The Complete Sonnets and Poems* (Oxford: Oxford University Press, 2002). Throughout my text I have used the original 1609 quarto versions of the titles. *Shake-speares Sonnets* suggests the playful character of the sequence, conveying a hint of the Herculean task confronting the poet, while the absence of an apostrophe in *A Lovers Complaint* appropriately allows the possibility of one and/or multiple lovers, capturing the poem's chemical fluidity.

After a first full note, all references to primary works are given in parentheses in the text of the book. Where citations are from early printed books, the original spelling and punctuation have been preserved, although the short 's' has in all cases been substituted for long, and omitted letters from contractions and suspensions have been inserted. Any emphases in early books are indicated by italics in my transcription.

All references to Shakespeare's plays are to *The Complete Works*, compact edition, general editors Stanley Wells and Gary Taylor (Oxford: Clarendon Press, 1988). Unless otherwise stated, all biblical references are to the 1599 Geneva Bible, facsimile edition (Ozark, Mo.: L. L. Brown Publishing, 1995).

The following editions of frequently cited sources are used throughout the book:

Brian P. Copenhaver, *Hermetica: The Greek 'Corpus Hermeticum' and the Latin 'Asclepius' in a New English Translation* (Cambridge: Cambridge University Press, 1992)

Marsilio Ficino, *Commentary on Plato's Symposium on Love (De amore)*, trans. Sears Jayne (Dallas, Texas: Spring Publications Inc., 1988). This work is cited throughout the text as *De amore*, with page number.

The Letters of Marsilio Ficino, trans. Language Department, School of Economic Science, London, 7 vols. (London: Shepheard-Walwyn Ltd, 1975–)

Michael Maier, *Atalanta Fugiens*, in *Atalanta Fugiens: An Edition of the Fugues, Emblems and Epigrams*, trans. from Latin by Joscelyn Godwin, with an Introduction by Hildemarie Streich (Grand Rapids, Mich.: Phanes Press, 1989)

Paul Eugene Memmo (trans. and Introduction), *Giordano Bruno's The Heroic Frenzies* (Chapel Hill: The University of North Carolina Press, 1964)

Sir Philip Sidney, *An Apology for Poetry* (1595), in G. Gregory Smith (ed.), *Elizabethan Critical Essays*, 2 vols. (Oxford: Oxford University Press, 1904), vol. I

Frank Whigham and Wayne A. Rebhorn (eds.), *The Art of English Poesy by George Puttenham: A Critical Edition* (Ithaca and London: Cornell University Press, 2007)

Introduction

No study abounds in the marvellous like that of metallurgy, and no
other branch of science presents us at every turn with such totally
unexpected, and in many cases inexplicable, results. The old idea of
the transmutation of metals was, no doubt, induced by some of these,
and is not merely an idle dream of the alchemist . . . Certain forms of
lead and copper, pure though they be, oxidize with great rapidity in
air . . . Ingots of tin . . . have fallen into powder; and many metals,
including iron, on being released from an amalgam of mercury, are left
in such an extraordinary state that they take fire . . . The presence of
the vapour of iron shows that the metal is an important constituent of
the sun and of most of the heavenly bodies.

(*Ironwork*)[1]

Metallurgy is a science of extraordinary wonder and unpredictability, closely
associated with the sun and the 'heavenly bodies' even at the turn of the
twentieth century when the above study was written.[2] The transformation of
base substances dug out of the bowels of the earth into metal of value, of dull
blackness into a spectrum of colour and polished brightness through fire and
chemical reactions, is magical and captivating. It is not surprising, therefore,
that at certain periods in history the 'marvellous' metallic stuff that dreams are
made of, together with the fiery craft of its transmutation, has taken a
powerful grip on the cultural imagination; in Western Europe the
Renaissance was one of these, the nineteenth century another.

Such times allow the apprehension of a metallic-mineral mind in which
ores retrieved from the deep, dark seams of unconsciousness can be brought
to light, purified and burnished and in which fusions of opposites can occur
with chemical happenings that produce radically new things. The
Renaissance associated this with divine inspiration, while the Romantic
period spoke of genius. As Esther Leslie's *Synthetic Worlds* so perceptively
describes, at these dynamic moments productive synergies occur between
previously separated and antithetical areas of experience:

I

[A 'mineral'] consciousness was present in nineteenth-century Germany, when an arc was made between a subjective and romantically accented study of nature and significant technical and scientific discoveries. The Romantic ... philosophy of nature ... presupposed dynamism, dialectic, animated nature and empathy between humans and nature ... In such a cosmos, magical exchanges occur between humans and minerals, spirits and matter, poles and forces. In such a vision all is alive ... subject to change and movement ... nature is an animated unity.[3]

In the nineteenth century, as in the Renaissance, this was a poetic, philosophic and scientific synergy in which humans, nature and the cosmos were one thing – a mystical unity. As a cultural theorist of modernity, Leslie positions Marx, Engels, Walter Benjamin and Theodore Adorno in the foreground of an unravelling tale of 'chemical–poetic encounters' prompted by Goethe and the German mystics, but for those of us who work in earlier centuries the story must emphasize the particular fusions of beliefs and discourses that began under the aegis of Marsilio Ficino and Pico della Mirandola in the fifteenth-century Florentine academy and which reached a high-water mark in England in the middle of the seventeenth century.[4]

My book traces the development of alchemical–aesthetic interactions through the Renaissance, demonstrating that at least by the time his 1609 volume of poetry was published, Shakespeare subscribed to a powerfully transformative chemical vision in which working the 'metal'/'mettle' of the mind had strangely literal, uncanny, as well as important theosophical implications. Indeed, it is significant that 'metal' as a substance and 'mettle' as 'a quality of disposition or temperament' were not distinguished by spelling in this period.[5] Donne alluded to divine 'metal' work in his sermons, as on Easter Monday 1622: 'God can work in all metals and transmute all metals: he can make ... a Superstitious Christian a sincere Christian; a Papist a Protestant.'[6] Indeed, the famous line 'Batter my heart, three person'd God' is charged with such metalwork meaning.[7] Speaking of the Psalms he declared that in the production of 'all Metricall compositions ... the whole frame of the poem is a beating out of a piece of gold'.[8] In this scheme, God is the 'maker' par excellence, purifying souls by holy alchemy and – as we shall see – late sixteenth-century poetic treatises urged earthly makers to imitate the divine example, particularly taking note of David's Psalms and Solomon's *Song of Songs*.

Shakespeare engages overtly with the discourse of alchemical soul work and making in lines such as Henry V's 'There is some soul of goodness in things evil, / Would men observingly distil it out' (IV. i. 4–5) and more seriously playfully in Sonnet 114:

> Or whether shall I say mine eye saith true,
> And that your love taught it this alchemy?
> To make of monsters, and things indigest,
> Such cherubins as your sweet self resemble.   (Sonnet 114)[9]

Granted, alchemy was (and remains today) a perfect metaphor for talking about the operations of the transforming imagination. However, as this book demonstrates, in a culture that was increasingly construing the mind and body in chemical terms, these lines are freighted with more than simply metaphorical import. This 1605 passage from a medical text describing the potential for purification and thus transmutation of the metallic 'little world' of man is illuminating: 'In man (which is a little world) there lye hidde the mynes of imperfect metals, from whence so many diseases do growe, which by a good faithful and skilful Phisitian must be brought to Gold and Silver, that is to say, unto perfect purification' (Thomas Tymme, *Chymicall Physicke*).[10]

In fact, alchemical language pervades Shakespeare's sonnets, but because we no longer imagine ourselves in this way, and are unfamiliar with chemistry's archaic lexicon, we tend to dismiss such gems as 'Pluck the keen teeth from the fierce tiger's jaws, / And burn the long-lived phoenix in her blood' (Sonnet 19) as richly imagistic but probably devoid of significance beyond rhetorical flourish. For understandable reasons Shakespeare's modern editors tend to glide past, leaving unglossed, baffling phrases such as 'blunt thou the lion's paws' and the oddly vampiric, 'Thou art the grave where buried love doth live, / Hung with the trophies of my lovers gone' (Sonnet 31).[11] Similarly, as we shall see, Shakespeare's choice of the analogy of the 'dyer's hand' in relation to the craft of poetry emerges as far from random when we learn that George Ripley, one of the most important alchemical writers published in the late sixteenth century, declared 'At the dyers craft you may learne this science.'[12] Even the eerie, frequently remarked upon, burgeoning 'babe' (Sonnets 60, 115, 126, for example) – 'this stillborn, ancient babe' in Joel Fineman's words – who wanes and grows becomes explicable in the alchemical context.[13] Indeed, the extent to which the linked discourses of metallurgy and alchemy had penetrated the understanding of the creative making mind by the turn of the seventeenth century has been seriously neglected by Shakespearean scholars and Renaissance studies more generally. My book occupies this inviting intellectual space.

Most critics would agree that *Shake-speares Sonnets* and their surreal companion piece in the 1609 quarto, *A Lovers Complaint*,[14] together constitute a rich tapestry of rhetorical play and textual allusion about Renaissance love in all its guises. The majority would be perplexed, however, by my hypothesis that a significant and colourful strand of this, hitherto unravelled, is spiritual alchemy: a 'deep brained' activity aimed at purifying and ordering the malleable mineral mind through meditation on love, memory work and intense imagination.[15] Indeed, as we shall see throughout this book, Shakespeare's sonnets often strive to blur distinctions between secular and spiritual domains, refusing binaries. Thus, for example, memory images of the lovely boy ('Mine eye hath played the painter, and hath stelled / Thy beauty's form in table of my heart', Sonnet 24), and working the mind by meditation on them ('then begins a journey in my head / To work my mind', Sonnet 27) during 'sessions of sweet silent thought' (Sonnet 30), constitute a 'zealous pilgrimage' (Sonnet 27) which has the potential to be spiritually uplifting. 'Sweet love remembered' can transport the poet 'from sullen earth' to sing 'hymns at heaven's gate' (Sonnet 29). Such spiritual 'wealth' is worth more than that of 'kings' and restores 'losses' (Sonnets 29, 30): it has soul-regenerating effects. This intense headwork is given pronounced alchemical expression in the strangely gothic Sonnet 31 alluded to above, which contains the extraordinary image of a 'grave' (symbolic of the contemplating mind in alchemy) whose epicentre is the beloved, 'hung' with accumulated memory seals of 'precious friends' now deceased – 'the trophies of my lovers gone' (Sonnets 30 and 31). This is serious play at its most profound. As the following chapters explicate in detail, the soul's renewal through a repetitive process of memory work and meditation is symbolized by the growing 'babe' of love, whose eerie haunting of the sonnets perplexes critics, as Fineman's words above suggest. The triumphant moment of spiritual alchemy is the rebirth of the soul with heightened powers of perception, the key symbols of which are the philosopher's child and the phoenix.

This book demonstrates, therefore, how a recognizable process of soul regeneration, construed as essential to inspired poetic making and dependent upon divine as well as secular love, is inscribed in these interlinked poems, accounting for some of their most cryptic lines, odd obsessions (with 'time' and 'store', for example), their 'aggressive impatience, intensity, and concentration', 'sustained momentum', and urgency of tone.[16] It therefore proposes a new understanding of Shakespeare's 1609 volume of poetry – of both *Shake-speares Sonnets* and *A Lovers Complaint*. In its concluding chapter, it sheds a little more light on that other mysterious Shakespearean concoction, 'Let the bird of loudest lay' (or 'The Phoenix and Turtle') suggesting that here, as in his other works, we

can locate a turn-of-the-seventeenth-century 'chymical' poetics of religious toleration. Along the way too, though far more allusively, it illuminates how thinking alchemically, and thus transformatively, played an
important part in the English Renaissance's wider ferment of creativity.[17]
Here my insights are supported by eminent intellectual historians such as
Paulo Rossi, Charles Webster and Allen G. Debus, who have long been
stressing the crucial role of alchemy and mystical science in the apocalyptic
and millennial mentalities associated with the rise of experimental science
in the seventeenth century.[18]

Shakespeare's sonnets have a marked tendency to produce antithetical
critical responses. One major scholarly dividing line, for example, is whether
or not Shakespeare ordered his sonnet collection himself and saw the 1609
quarto through the press; related to this – and currently very topical – is *A
Lovers Complaint* a foreign interloper inserted by a roguish publisher (yet
with Shakespeare's name printed at the top of its first page) or Shakespeare's
own, rather perplexing creation?[19] The majority of recent editors including
Katherine Duncan-Jones, Colin Burrow, John Kerrigan and Helen Vendler
have argued in favour of the volume being organized by Shakespeare prior
to publication – although many of the sonnets were obviously written and
circulated among his 'private friends' far earlier – and that, bearing so many
resemblances (in terms of style, themes and diction) to the late plays,
especially *Cymbeline*, the conjoined *Complaint* is most likely to be by
Shakespeare too.[20] My book provides new evidence to support the latter
view: the allegory of alchemical process woven so dexterously throughout
the 1609 poems strongly suggests that Shakespeare exercised considerable
control over the first edition, and it is reasonable to assume that he would
have desired his volume of ground-breaking lyrics about love and the
process of poetic making to leave the press 'in his owne name'.[21] If the
1609 text was pirated or corrupted he surely would have objected and
countered with his own volume. As far as we know he remained remarkably
silent.

But there are other very pronounced critical binaries that might be
productively mediated by an understanding of alchemy. The author of
Bawdy and Soul (2003) notes, for example, that recent work, drawn to the
sexual implications of the lovely boy sonnets, has tended to divide between
readings 'exclusively along homosexual lines' and 'strictly platonic' alter-
natives.[22] Equally, there are frequent adamant assertions that Shakespeare is
not a Neoplatonist – presumably because he is too preoccupied with
material bodies and sex.[23] Such assessments construe Neoplatonism along

scholastic Petrarchan lines: as the unconsummated desire of a male subject for a rather remote, beautiful female object; desire that should lead upwards to the divine. But what if Shakespeare was involved, in the manner of John Donne, in redrawing the creative lines of Petrarchanism ('Love must not be, but take a body too', in 'Aire and Angels', line 10, p. 22)? As we shall see, theosophical alchemy's central thrust was, in fact, to unite all contraries and thus to eradicate troubling binaries. After all, in their own way Neoplatonism and early Petrarchan poetry had radically recast Platonism to avoid Christian embarrassment about love between men. Philosophical and religious movements are 'contingent constructions' responsive to cultural currents; they are not set in stone.[24]

Less divisive are the debates about the orthodox religious content of the sonnets. With few exceptions, critical opinion over the past few decades has seemed remarkably united in finding Shakespeare's sonnets 'strikingly secular' (Richard Strier), 'explicitly and insistently secular' (Duncan-Jones), 'without mediation or qualification of any Christian kind' (Douglas Trevor).[25] However, Heather Dubrow finds that 'some of the poems resemble an internalized meditation' and Helen Vendler, too, describes the 1609 poems as 'inward, meditative and lyrical' but emphasizes that the 'speaker of Shakespeare's sonnets scorns the consolations of Christianity – an afterlife in heaven for himself, a Christian resurrection of his body after death ... The sonnets stand as the record of a mind working out positions without the help of any pantheon or any systematic doctrine.'[26]

Nonetheless, Vendler provides us with a characteristically brilliant reading of the sonnet that most critics regard as a religious interloper in a secular sequence – Sonnet 124 – in terms of Platonic form. Indeed, assessments of the sonnets as un-Christian leave us with a pronounced problem: how do we then explain the liturgical prayer (even The Lord's Prayer in Sonnet 108) and biblical echoes that pervade the sonnets and which Vendler, Duncan-Jones and Kerrigan (to name but three influential editors) have been so astute at detecting and glossing? Of course, secular work can absorb biblical echoes without becoming religious. However, Shakespeare's sonnets seem to go beyond this: as has been recently foregrounded, several of Shakespeare's sonnets appear to dialogue with the Geneva Bible marginalia – annotations that were meant for private religious meditation.[27] And then there are those constant allusions to the Trinity – 'In this change is my invention spent, / Three themes in one, which wondrous scope affords' – which at times merge with the Platonic insistence on 'Fair, kind and true' (Sonnet 105). The overriding impulse has been to read such incursions into extreme secularity ironically – wicked Will is simply 'trafficking in words' and being shockingly blasphemous.[28]

Although broadly adhering to this view, Thomas Roche's voluminous and erudite study, *Petrarch and the English Sonnet Sequences*, injects a note of caution: 'we have not yet learned the rules of the game … and we still need to know more about the meaning of individual words. Historical criticism has foundered in the cul-de-sac of biography without adequate sociological or religious information or interest.'[29] In addition he, like Alastair Fowler, is convinced that a divine mathematics pervades the sonnet sequence, but while Roche reads this as intentional irony Fowler is notably less convinced, recalling C. S. Lewis's view that 'the greatest of the sonnets are written from a region in which love abandons all claims and flows into charity'.[30] Is it conceivable that Shakespeare would have expended so much intellectual energy devising and inscribing a highly complex divine geometry into his sequence simply to be outrageously blasphemous? This does not square with the mentality of the poet that we uncover in his other works. But editorial accounts that simply dismiss the numerology in the sequence as critical fantasy – 'ingenious eyes can see a lot in numbers' – fail to satisfy, too, because the reader is then left wondering why the sonnets themselves draw attention to their number-play, even giving instructions:[31]

> In things of great receipt with ease we prove
> Among a number one is reckoned none.
> Then in the number let me pass untold,
> Though in thy store's account I one must be. (Sonnet 136, 7–10)

Why is 'one … none' and why on earth should we count Sonnet 136 out? What is 'thy store's account'? Again, reading alchemically offers insights: as we shall see, divine geometry was an integral part of the alchemical *opus* or 'work'.

Shakespeare may be playing games with us but equally we critics play games and take liberties with Shakespeare's enigmatic sonnets, as James Schiffer foregrounds: 'what is obvious to one serious critic is not to another. Each uses internal evidence to support his reading, and each is highly persuasive. All that is missing in their strong analyses is the admission that their theories are built in speculation rather than fact.' Schiffer makes a timely and welcome plea for 'agnostic tolerance' and the eschewing of 'dogmatism'.[32] In 1961 the Oxford scholar J. B. Leishman gave book-length voice to an issue that for him was puzzling in the extreme and which he, for one, was not prepared to resolve by merely papering over the critical cracks: 'Although Shakespeare never employs Platonic or transcendental language one cannot but feel that his love immeasurably transcends its immediate object ... Behind many ... of his great affirmations one is aware of an immense weight of conquered negation, but who can say precisely what it was that he had to overcome?'[33]

He found the 'religiousness' of so many of Shakespeare's expressions of love comparable only with the religious poetry of Donne, Herbert and Vaughan and he recalled how Herbert had 'dwelt on the possibility and desirability of writing a kind of religious love poetry'. He concluded, 'we should be content to regard [Shakespeare's] ... whole collection, especially those addressed to the friend', as being, like Herbert's *The Temple*, 'a picture of many spiritual conflicts', of many 'trials and testings of Shakespeare's love and faith', and as a reflection of his 'inner weather' over a period of perhaps as much as ten years.[34] Only this could account for the tone and substance of sonnets like 'Poor soul, the centre of my sinful earth' (Sonnet 146) and 'If my dear love were but the child of state' (Sonnet 124). Thus for Leishman the 1609 poems both eschewed transcendental language and were deeply religious. In fact, if we refuse selective readings that block out obstacles to a coherent vision, the constant drawing together of antitheses (like biblical echoes and erotic desire) in Shakespeare's sonnets (antithesis is their major figure as Vendler foregrounds) inevitably produces paradoxes that modern readers find unsettling and perplexing.[35] What on earth was the bard up to merging religion with sex?

There is, I suggest, another way of encountering this apparent critical bind. It involves trying to find out more 'about the rules of the game' (as Roche phrased it) and its lexicon around 1600; investigating what 'Neoplatonism' might have meant to Shakespeare and his 'private friends';[36] and probing the particular philosophic-aesthetic climate that gave birth to the 1609 volume. As Kerrigan suggests, 'Shakespeare's audience had a framework for reading it' – one that we have lost.[37] My book, historicized and interdisciplinary in its approach, attempts to reconstruct this aspect of the mentality of Shakespeare and his contemporaries. It argues that, while being seriously playful throughout, the literal surface meanings of the sonnets and *Complaint* are designed to lead the uninitiated astray while an alchemical allegory inscribes alternative or additional meanings. A contemporary *Lexicon of Alchemy* (1612) is helpful here:

Language: In the writings of Hermetic science, the Philosophers never express the true significance of their thought in the vulgar tongue, and *they must not be interpreted according to the literal sense of the expression*. The sense which is presented on the surface is not the true sense. They discourse in enigmas, metaphors, allegories, fables, similitudes, and each philosopher adapts them after his own manner. (Martin Rulandus, *A Lexicon of Alchemy*, 1612, my emphasis)[38]

As an elite theosophical language that prized its coterie exclusivity, Hermetic alchemy spoke in enigmas, metaphors, allegories, and fables – this was serious play for a charmed circle of initiates. But for the modern reader the problem of understanding is compounded by alchemy's archaic language – by its virtually dead sign system. It is small wonder in this context that such an astute decoder of language as Inga-Stina Ewbank finds it necessary to observe that 'it is not so much that Shakespeare lacks a language for the self as that contemporary critical language cannot get a purchase on the Sonnets'.[39] She finds Joel Fineman's sophisticated Lacanian reading of the sonnets' 'new poetics of the person' (which asks 'is Shakespeare Freudian?') anachronistic and therefore unconvincing.[40] Religion and the soul are, indeed, remarkably absent from Fineman's brilliant discussion of subjectivity in the sonnets.

It would seem that our modern theoretical vocabularies are not quite up to the task of unravelling all the fascinating dimensions of the early modern psyche. My book will demonstrate how the lost lexicon of late sixteenth-century European alchemy, with its pronounced discourse of love and soul work, and its explicit sexual symbolism, facilitated Shakespeare's inscription of an interior drama of a desiring mind involved in poetic creation. Its synthesizing philosophy prompted him also continually to unite contraries – crucially, to draw down the spirit into embodied subjects that have sex. I would like to suggest that where we, peering through our post-Cartesian precision lenses (and firmly ensconced behind modern disciplinary fences) find troubling divisions and incompatible binaries, Shakespeare's 'private friends', reading through blurred alchemical spectacles (and striving for unity), undoubtedly encountered productive fusion. They saw and read differently and relished the interpretive challenge of enigmas. Indeed, 'darke sayings' and 'Parables' were closely linked to divine teaching in this period. As Michael Schoenfeldt has pointed out, John Donne articulated at length in a sermon 'his admiration for Jesus' particularly strategic use of such obscurity':

when it is said, *They were astonished at his Doctrine, for his word with Power* [Luke 4.32], they refer that to this manner of teaching, that hee astonished them with these reserved and darke sayings, and by the subsequent interpretation thereof, gained a reverend estimation amongst them . . . For those Parables, and comparisons of a remote signification, were calld by the Jews, *Potestates,* Powers, Powerfull insinuations. (*Sermons*, vol. VII, pp. 315–16)[41]

Contextualized studies such as this one, which has even required the reclamation of a lost lexicon, certainly do not emerge out of the ether, and my book is heavily indebted on nearly every page to Lyndy Abraham's magnificent *Dictionary of Alchemical Imagery* (1998). It is also informed by her pioneering examination of poetic alchemy in *Marvell and Alchemy* (1990) and that of Charles Nicholl in *The Chemical Theatre* (1980) and Stanton J. Linden in *Darke Hierogliphicks* (1996) and *Mystical Metal of Gold* (2007). John S. Mebane's *Renaissance Magic and the Return of the Golden Age* (1989) has been a treasure trove of knowledge, as has Stanton J. Linden's *The Alchemy Reader* (2003) and the publications of the intellectual historian, Charles Webster.[42] The debt of all of us to the extraordinary research of Dame Frances Yates into the humanism of the Florentine and Parisian academies and the Neoplatonic, Hermetic contexts of literary production in late sixteenth-century Europe almost goes without saying. Although Yates' formidable scholarship has been much critiqued over recent decades (not always positively), its intellectual range and insights remain astonishing.[43] Her work on Shakespeare's late plays, Nicholl's and Linden's on *King Lear* (as well as Jonson, Donne and Herbert), and Mebane's on *The Tempest*, has reassured me that I am certainly not alone in finding alchemy in Shakespeare but the discovery of a significant alchemical thread woven throughout the 1609 quarto is my own.[44]

This is a particularly timely moment to re-engage with the debates surrounding the culture of Renaissance alchemy spearheaded by Yates in the 1960s and 70s. Over recent decades considerable advances have been made by intellectual and cultural historians and historians of science into the understanding of the alchemical mindset and the role of esoteric mysticism in the rise of experimental science in the seventeenth century.[45] The revelation that several leading mathematicians and scientists of the period including figures such as Newton and Boyle were keen alchemists has reshaped the contours of the way in which the story of the scientific revolution can be told.[46] The past two decades, too, have seen important reassessments of a key figure in the history of English alchemy, John Dee (culminating in 2009 in a major conference to mark the quartercentenary of Dee's death), with this noted practitioner emerging less in his former guise as a maverick magus and conjuror of angels and more as one of the most original yet pragmatically minded thinkers of his day.[47] Along with John Dee, alchemy and its close associate natural magic increasingly wear respectable faces.[48] There is mounting evidence too (and growing scholarly opinion across a range of disciplines) that the early modern 'art' had pronounced spiritual/psychic dimensions as well as being early chemistry – something which has not always been understood or acknowledged.[49] A willingness among researchers in recent years to cross subject (and geographical) boundaries that would have made little sense four hundred years ago, and to contribute to multi- and interdisciplinary forums, has greatly enhanced our understanding of this particularly complex and multi-faceted intellectual field.[50]

The literary studies by Mebane, Abraham, and Linden have incorporated crucial elements of this knowledge as it has become available, while at the same time extending our awareness of the range of authors and texts engaging with Hermetic philosophy. But there have been important developments in literary critical perspectives that have lent impetus to this particular project. Since the 1980s, with the advent of new historicism and cultural materialism, studies of Shakespeare have understandably tended to be dominated by previously neglected topics such as gender, race, power relations, sexualities, homoeroticism and the pursuit of modern subjectivities. However, this critical landscape has been reconfigured in recent years to encompass a range of important earlier concerns. The publication of Ewan Fernie's *Spiritual Shakespeare* (2005) has served to rekindle interest in the spiritual dimension of Shakespeare's work, while research into Renaissance discourses of 'amity', such as Laurie Shannon's *Sovereign Amity* (2002), is promoting a re-evaluation of late sixteenth-century Neoplatonism and male friendship in relation to the sonnets.[51] John Manning's masterful re-assessment of emblem book culture (2002) – helpful for our understanding of alchemical emblems – has been a welcome addition too. Also, there is a significant, steadily rising re-engagement with the early modern preoccupation with the formal elements and spatial patterns of poetry – areas shunned as retrograde and inward-looking for several decades.[52] Meanwhile, literary historians – notably Sharon Achinstein and Elizabeth Sauer (2007) – have made notable interventions in the wider field of religion and literature that are helping us to conceive of a poetics of religious toleration in this period.[53] This project intersects with all these (re)emerging critical fields.

The readings of the sonnets found in this book are by no means intended to be exhaustive or to efface competing interpretations. While my particular desire is to foreground the alchemical making mind at work in these poems, in the spirit of James Schiffer's inclusiveness, I would like to stress that Shakespeare's richly complex 1609 volume of poetry invites multiple and even contradictory readings; indeed, it is as though – in the spirit of alchemical philosophy – the poems and the volume are constructed to eschew dogmatism. A multiplicity of critical voices (not always in unity) is the inevitable outcome of this – toleration is important.

My approach in this book marries a precise historicism with formal concerns in the belief that the most productive studies today refuse any artificial cleavage between the two. Chapter 1 is devoted to setting out the alchemical-hermetic contexts that are crucial to understanding their significance to Renaissance literature and culture. Chapters 2 and 3 unravel the alchemical thread and uncover the divine geometry in the lovely boy sonnets and in the dark lady sequence. Chapter 4 analyses *A Lovers Complaint* as an alchemical coda to the sonnets that climaxes in an allegory of the Passion. These chapters adopt an intertextual methodology, tapping liberally into the rich seam of alchemical writings circulating in early modern England. Crucially, they analyse the cultural productions (including architecture, pendants, masques and poems) contemporary with *Shake-speares Sonnets* that demonstrate the pervasiveness of this particular theosophical system in the early seventeenth century. Drawing on devotional, philosophical and literary treatises, Chapter 5 serves to amplify the relationships among inner looking, alchemy and the creative imagination in the early seventeenth century. Chapter 6 draws the study to a close by briefly widening the lens of this book to explore the cultural work performed by the alchemical mindset and its discourses around 1609, when *Shake-speares Sonnets* was published. In the process it discusses the significance of my findings for Shakespearean studies more generally, arguing that Shakespeare's interweaving of alchemical process and textures throughout his works – especially the later plays and poems – is indicative of a self-conscious artistic stance, promoting religious toleration and unity. By restoring alchemy and its literary productions to their rightful place in English studies, I demonstrate that far from being a marginal preoccupation of madmen, fools and covetous types (such as we find in contemporary satire, notably Jonson's *The Alchemist*), alchemy was a serious practical as well as a philosophical and spiritual pursuit without which the particular creative ferment associated with the Renaissance would probably not have happened.[54]

In the first half of the seventeenth century 'an arc' was indeed made between the study of internal nature (the soul) and that of external nature; Hermetic alchemy's influence extended far beyond the realm of soul remaking and creative writing. In fact, it was one of the founding fathers of the Royal Society for the promotion of science, Elias Ashmole, who put together the largest seventeenth-century collection of English alchemical texts. *Theatrum Chemicum Britannicum* (1651) advertises itself as containing 'severall Poeticall Pieces of our Famous English Philosophers, who have written the Hermetique Mysteries'. It is clear from Ashmole's preamble that plumbing the depths of Hermetic 'learning' was never easy:

Past Ages have like Rivers conveied to use, (upon the floate) the more light, and Sophisticall pieces of Learning; but what were Profound and Misterious, the weight and solidity therof, sunke to the Bottome: Whence every one who attempts to dive, cannot easily fetch them up: So, that what our Saviour said to his Disciples, may . . . be spoken to the Elected Sons of Art; Unto you it is given to know the Mysteries of the kingdome of God: but to others in Parables, that seeing they might not see, and hearing they might not understand.[55]

Enveloped in dark 'Parables' and relishing its exclusivity even at the height of its appeal, knowledge of the 'Angellicall Stone' or alchemist's gold was surely destined for obscurity: what was the mysterious 'Stone'? The poem that was allotted primacy of place in Ashmole's collection riddlingly declares:

> It was never for Mony sold ne bought,
> By any Man which for it hath sought,
> But given to an able Man of grace,
> Wrought with great Cost.[56]   (Norton, *Ordinall of Alchimy*)

This is an 'art' to attain the pearl of great price, spiritual 'gold' or the inner Christ, and amongst Ashmole's contemporaries in the Royal Society it was also associated with a quest to find a universal medicine to cure all 'ills' produced by the Fall – a golden drug for a restored golden age.[57] Nevertheless, as the same alchemical treatise conveys so clearly, the chemical art had negative associations:

> Some People would not have it cauled Holy,
> And in this wise thei doe replye,
> Thei say how Painims maie this Arte have,
> Suche as our Lord will never save:
> For their wilfull fals Infidelitie.
>
> (Norton, *Ordinall of Alchimy*, p. 13)

'Painim', like 'Infidel', signified 'a non-Christian', chiefly 'a Mohammadan or Saracen' in this period.[58] Could it be that the hasty comment – 'What a heap of wretched Infidel Stuff' – scrawled at the end of a first quarto of *Shake-speares Sonnets* is an angry response to the pronounced alchemical (and therefore 'Infidel'-tinged) trajectory of Shakespeare's 1609 collection of poems?[59] Was our 'dyers hand' considered indelibly stained with an Islamic tint by at least one early reader? It is time to find out more about this tantalizing 'Arte'.

CHAPTER I

Alchemical contexts

Since what Alchymia is, and what its composition is, your Latin world does not yet know, I will explain in the present work.

(Robert of Chester, 1144)[1]

Knowledge of the ancient art of alchemy appears to have filtered into Europe in the twelfth century through Latin translations of Arabic texts such as Robert of Chester's *Liber de compositione alchemiae* (*Book of the Composition of Alchemy*). Moorish Spain, and especially the intellectual centre, Toledo, served as the major distribution point for the accumulated knowledge of the Islamic alchemists who had added their distinctive imprint to the wisdom of sages practising and writing in China, India, Egypt and Greece. Closely associated, therefore, with Islam's incursions into Christendom, alchemy was bound to be regarded with suspicion in Europe. Yet this perceived origin also prompted admiration. For one thing, Eastern metallurgy, and other crafts dependent on sophisticated techniques of practical chemistry, such as glass-making, dyeing, tinting and goldsmithery, were the envy of the Western world.[2] Indeed, alchemy's particularly close association with metallurgy led the historian of chemistry John Read to propose that the art sprang up among the 'skilled metal-workers of the Middle East, possibly in Mesopotamia, whence it spread westwards to Egypt and Greece, and eastwards along the caravan routes to India and China'.[3] Others, noting the presence of similar alchemical practice and philosophy in these diverse cultures and encountering the legends surrounding the art in India and China about knowledge of alchemy coming from across the seas, speculate about a more mysterious shared origin – namely Atlantis, the advanced civilization lost to the sea but memorialized by Plato's *Timaeus* and *Critias*.[4] It is interesting in this respect that Francis Bacon called his utopian fable about a hidden island community of industrious experimental scientists *New Atlantis*.[5] Whatever its ultimate source, alchemy appears to have taken its name from the black soil of Egypt, which for many make it the most likely candidate for primacy: 'al Khem', the country of dark soil, was the ancient name for Egypt.[6]

It should be emphasized, however, that by the Middle Ages there was not one alchemy but several, with distinctive as well as overlapping traditions: in the manner of all belief systems, alchemy was culturally constructed.[7] Importantly, alchemies shared a holistic view of the Universe: a cosmology in which a complex network of correspondences and sympathies connected lower and higher worlds (astrology helped to interpret these), and the earth and the heavens and all were caught up in a constant flow of transforming energy (known as 'chi' in China). External nature (the outer environment – the macrocosm) and internal nature (body, soul and spirit – the microcosm) were construed as one thing, alive and growing. In this world view, metals and minerals were gestating inside the womb of the earth, slowly moving towards the perfection of gold and the skilled alchemist was simply harnessing energy and speeding up this natural process through the art of fire and pain-staking labour over retorts and furnaces. Crucially, it was imagined that if external nature could be purified and brought to perfection through practical, exoteric alchemy ('outer work'), internal nature could be likewise transformed through esoteric or 'inner work' – 'working the metal of the mind'.[8] The latter was believed to be achieved through ascetic techniques including, most significantly, the repetition of meditative exercises involving intense imagination. The alchemical adept had to purify himself internally before he could proceed to the successful completion of outer work: the divine spark within had to be nurtured and developed, the 'gross' body converted to the 'subtle' body. There was no major bifurcation between matter and spirit in most alchemies – rather, there were degrees of airiness and subtlety or denseness and heaviness. Rejecting a philosophy of warring polarities that can never be harmonized, alchemy strove to fuse and balance all apparently contrary forces, which were imagined predominantly as male and female principles that needed to be united through repeated 'conjunctions'; this is one reason why images of sexual 'copulation' abound in alchemical poetry and emblem books.

In China, inner alchemy shared many aspects of Taoism, including the pursuit of longevity and immortality and the belief (at least from the sixth century) in two sides of the self – 'yin' and 'yang' – which had to be harmonized: a lighter, clearer, higher soul identified with male energy called 'yang' and a lower, darker, denser opaque feminine soul called 'yin'.⁹ Receptive, creative 'yin' had to be clarified and mastered, while 'yang' had to be further purified, and both aspects of the soul had to be repeatedly fused and balanced to achieve wholeness. Indian alchemy, like the Chinese version, had a pronounced metaphysical leaning and particularly favoured the use of explicit sexual symbolism to represent the repeated 'copulations' taking place inside the furnace of the head. From at least the tenth century, Indian alchemy was an aspect of Tantra, a sect of Hinduism in which male Shiva and dark, mysterious, creative female Shakti correspond closely to the gendered energies encountered as 'yang' and 'yin' in Taoism. Indeed, in both Taoist and Tantric alchemy, skilfully directed sexual impulses – construed as going with the flow of nature – were embraced as enhancing spiritual progress.¹⁰ Adepts of both Taoism and Tantra strove for spiritual purification and inner unity, with Tantric alchemists having as their goal nothing less than 'the bodily transformation of the living practitioner into a perfected immortal' – a god.¹¹ As this brief outline suggests, there was undoubtedly a continuous exchange of ideas regarding things alchemical between India and China and the Middle East; well-established trade routes helped facilitate this.

If Egypt gave alchemy its name, it was also associated with its legendary founding father, the thrice great, Hermes Trismegistus, 'identified with Thoth, the Egyptian god of revelation and wisdom'.¹² Thought to have been active around the time of Moses, he was a priest-philosopher-king closely connected with the dissemination of Egyptian religion but also with formulating the alphabet and teaching natural philosophy as well as law and the arts. The latter made Hermes a good candidate for his eventual evolution into a likeness of the Roman god Mercury, whom we shall repeatedly encounter in Renaissance masques (especially those of Ben Jonson). The 'sons of Hermes', alchemical adepts, based their art on thirteen precepts that were said to have been inscribed in Phoenician characters on the 'Tabula Smaragdina' or 'Emerald Tablet' either taken from the tomb of Hermes by none other than Alexander the Great or removed from his hands, after death, by Abraham's wife, Sarah.¹³ As might be anticipated, the 'Emerald Tablet' has a pronounced mystical aura: the first precept states, 'That which is above is like to that which is below, and that which is below is like to that which is above, to accomplish the miracles of one thing', the second talks of 'the contemplation of one' and another promises, 'Thus thou wilt possess the glory of the brightness of the whole world, and all obscurity will fly far from thee.'¹⁴

These phrases are continuously reiterated in subsequent alchemical texts but echoes of them can be found in orthodox Christian writings too. Although the extent to which Trismegistus' philosophy of 'one' permeated the Christian humanist mindset in the Renaissance has been particularly illuminated by the pioneering work of Frances Yates, the Hermetic texts themselves (which are available in a modern scholarly edition) remain largely shunned by literary critics as marginal occult ephemera.[15] Their centrality to Renaissance humanist culture – foregrounded in relation to Pico della Mirandola in Jacob Burckhardt's monumental *The Civilization of the Renaissance in Italy* – certainly needs to be re-stressed, but equally their 'occult' character, which has tended to be overemphasized and misrepresented, should be reduced.[16] As this book argues, Shakespeare's refrain on 'one', 'To one, of one' (Sonnet 105) requires reconsideration from the Hermetic perspective. Here, for example, is the Protestant Philippe Du Plessis Mornay on 'one God' and Hermes, as translated by Sir Philip Sidney: 'Mercurius Trismegistus, who (if the bookes which are fathered upon him bee his in deede, as in trueth they bee very auncient) is the founder of them all, teacheth everywhere, That there is but one God ... which hath universall power of creating all things ... That unto him alone belongeth the name of Father, and of Good.' [17]

Du Plessis Mornay (who notably dissociated himself from all forms of magic) was certainly impressed by elements of Hermes' writings, the small body of which is now known as the *Hermetica*, consisting of the Greek *Corpus Hermeticum* and the Latin *Asclepius* (which was available throughout the Middle Ages).[18] They take the form of dialogues between teacher and pupil, Hermes and his son Tat and Hermes and his student Asclepius, for example. In fact references to these, especially to the *Asclepius*, occur in the writings of several church fathers, including Lactantius, Augustine and most notably Thomas Aquinas, who seems particularly to have embraced alchemical thinking.[19] Trismegistus even appears in gigantic form on the grand black and white mosaic pavement of Sienna Cathedral, which declares, 'Hermes Mercurius Trismegistus Contemporaneus Moyses' (*c.* 1480). As we shall see, the work of the Florentine Academy did much in the fifteenth century to establish Hermes as a prophet of pristine religious wisdom.

It seems, therefore, that this ancient sage was far from being construed as a dodgy occult interloper into Christianity – on the contrary, in fifteenth-century Italy he was on a par with Moses. How could this be? Unbeknown to Florentine commentators, the bulk of Hermetic texts were actually written in the early Christian era, undoubtedly by Neoplatonists.[20] This meant that they caught the fifteenth-century renewed tide of enthusiasm for Platonism and the mystical-spiritual religion encountered in them not only chimed sufficiently well with orthodoxy (having been written by Christians) but seemed to many to be relatively free from the corruptions and antagonisms of latter-day religion – here was a new route to truth.[21] To intellectuals centred in the Florentine academy, crucially Marsilio Ficino, Hermeticism's stress on one religion and on inner purification and spirituality provided a peaceful-seeming contrast to the strife and factionalism they were witnessing around them.[22] To many then, Hermes Trismegistus with his Egyptian religion appeared a credible exponent of the true religion before Christ and the wellspring of all philosophy: Ficino described him as the 'first author of theology' while, almost two centuries later, Henry Vaughan's rendering of *The Chymist's Key* (1657) declared, '*Hermes*, the Father and the Prince of all true and loyall Philosophers'.[23]

A sticking point for some in the Western Church, however, was undoubtedly the unsettling knowledge that the Hermetic writings had permeated the West (and eventually Renaissance humanism) infused with the culture of the Turks. When Muslim forces conquered Egypt in the seventh century, Hermeticism, as embellished by early Christian Neoplatonists, together with its science of alchemy, had been given a substantial intellectual boost – indeed, 'it was in the Islamic world that alchemy reached its fullest flowering'.[24] The invaders were impressed with the wealth of Alexandrine scholarship and Hermetic teaching, which fitted well with the Islamic doctrine of 'oneness of existence'.[25] Alchemy was apprehended as a sacred science because it confirmed the Oneness of the Universe and Alexandrine Hermetic manuscripts were translated into Arabic along with many other esoteric philosophical texts and conveyed throughout the Islamic world, often via the great centre of learning around 750, Baghdad. *The Book of Ways* (847) describes 'unprecedented comings and goings' between scholars from Babylonia, Syria, Egypt and Spain in this particular intellectual melting pot.[26]

One of the first recorded Islamic alchemists was the prince Khalid ibn Yazid (660–704), who forged his reputation in Damascus in Syria. Legend has it that he fled the corruptions of court life determined to pursue alchemical studies by surrounding himself with Greek and Coptic scholars from Egypt. A Christian alchemist called Morienus also contributed to this project and Khalid and his accolites are said to be responsible for translating a vast range of alchemical, medical and astronomical writings into Arabic, including his celebrated *Paradise of Wisdom*, reputed to comprise no fewer than 2,315 verses. Another attributed to him was *The Booke of the Secrets of*

Alchimie, and this was published in London in 1597 in *The Mirror of Alchimy* – a digest of basic alchemy – as by 'Galid the sonne of Jazich' ('translated out of Hebrew into Arabick, and out of Arabick into Latine, and out of Latin into English'), along with the *Smaragdine Table of Hermes Trismegistus* and works by the English medieval alchemist, 'the Thrice-Famous and Learned Fryer' Roger Bacon.[27]

The most famous Muslim alchemist, Jabir ibn Hayyan (eighth or ninth century AD), much alluded to in Medieval and Renaissance alchemical texts, was a Sufi – a member of a belief system infused with Neoplatonism and Hermeticism, that gave precedence to heart as opposed to cerebral knowledge, and that used meditation, prayer, exercises and dance to reach internal perfection and ecstatic union with God.[28] Jabir advocated laboratory experimentation and had a particular love of Pythagorean numerology; he believed that sacred geometry used as a focus of meditation could enable the adept to access the world of eternity. While a triangle symbolized harmony, the square denoted stability, and the circle everlasting life. In later alchemical textbooks, as we shall see, the frequent image of a triangle circumscribing a square and a circle conveyed Jabir's idea that these shapes represent the same unity and are therefore capable of transmutation into one another, like base metal into gold – they are essentially One. Jabir became known to the medieval West as Geber and a work attributed to him called *Summa Perfectionis Magisterii* (*Summary of the Perfection of the Mastery*), but which may well have been written by a Christian alchemist in Moorish Spain, was the most significant medieval alchemical treatise and one of the first to emerge from the printing presses in 1485.[29] Some modern commentators distinguish between the Arabic body of texts – the *Corpus Jabirianum* – and 'Geber's' medieval Latin works.[30] The latter expound the familiar coupling between sulphur (male principle) and mercury (female principle) encountered in later alchemies, deal with furnaces and other equipment and detail the major steps in the preparation of the Stone. They certainly give the impression that exoteric and esoteric alchemies flourished together in Islamic culture.

The intellectual melting pot of medieval Moorish Spain facilitated, too, the intermingling of Jewish philosophy, including Cabala, with other traditions. Martin Ruland's *Lexicon of Alchemy* (1612) defined Cabala in particularly intriguing terms:

Cabalistic Art is a most secret science which is affirmed to have been made known in a divine manner to Moses at the same time as written law; it reveals to us the doctrine of the Messiah of God; it constitutes a bond of friendship between angels and men who have been instructed in it; and it gives knowledge of all natural things. It also illuminates the mind with a divine light; and drives all darkness there from ... The true Cabal has its foundation in the Holy Scriptures.[31]

It seems that Cabalists shared much with other alchemists; indeed, the Zohar even echoes *The Emerald Tablet* at points: 'Everything which is on the earth is also up above ... Everything is connected and united together.'[32] The Cabala was distinctive in its assertion of the importance of love in the universe – something that we find in abundance in later alchemies: 'if we are good, the flow of love increases; if we are evil, the severity of judgement grows'. Humans can activate love in the universe by loving God and others and immortality is sought through inner distillation, as part of a process in which humans strive with God 'to restore the original universal harmony'.[33] Cabalistic ideas such as the latter (returning the corrupt world to its former perfection) were crucial to the growth of experimental science in seventeenth-century England – Francis Bacon was certainly sympathetic to them.[34]

As we have seen, therefore, while alchemy most simply conceived was the art of transformation through purification techniques, alchemies themselves, together with the tightly interlinked philosophy of Hermeticism, were constantly transforming through a multiplicity of inheritances, infiltrations and cross-fertilizations. In the Graeco-Egyptian era the art was infused with a liberal dose of Pythagoreanism and Platonism; subsequently early Christianity left its mark on the Hermetic writings; while theosophic alchemy was evolving simultane-ously in the Hebraic context too. With the Arab conquest of Alexandria in the seventh century, an impressive injection of Islamic culture over subsequent centuries led to a very hybrid alchemy in 'infidel' costume eventually encountering Christian Europe in the Middle Ages.

EAST MEETS WEST

The learned facilitator of this cultural encounter – the Archdeacon of Pamplona, Robert of Chester – notably translated the Qur'an as well as books of algebra and alchemy from the Arabic.[35] Following the appearance of his *Liber de compositione alchemiae* (1144), which intro-duced Morienus and Khalid to the West, other Latin translations rapidly followed and alchemical ideas and symbolism began to enter discussions in the encyclopaedic works of Thomas Aquinas, Roger Bacon and Raymond Lull.[36] Alchemical practitioners were clearly active in England in the thirteenth and fourteenth centuries, and Geoffrey Chaucer's satirical *Canon's Yeoman's Tale* leaves us in no doubt that they were not only regarded with suspicion but were also considered fair game for burlesque literary treatment (but then so were physicians and lawyers). As the quote from Norton's *Ordinall* discussed in the Introduction suggests, European alchemists had to steer a very careful path indeed to avoid being daubed with a derogative 'Painim' brush or tainted by accusations of greed.[37] So how did serious English alchemists themselves construe their art – what were they doing and seeking?

Two fifteenth-century works, *The Compound of Alchymie* (1471) penned by George Ripley, Canon of an Augustinian Priory in Bridlington, Yorkshire, and *The Ordinall of Alchimy* (1477) by Thomas Norton, wealthy businessman and Privy Councillor, were regarded as key alchemical treatises (both take the form of long poems) throughout the early modern period. Ripley's was the most famous; his manuscript went into print in 1591 and was one of a clutch of alchemical treatises published that decade to meet a new thirst for alchemical knowledge (the famous *Mirror of Alchimy* appeared in 1597). As Deborah E. Harkness's *The Jewel House* describes, late Elizabethan London was bristling with budding students of nature, including fledgling chemists labouring over smoky backstreet furnaces.[38] Written in deliberately obtuse doggerel verse, Ripley's *Compound* nevertheless works hard to convey the seriousness of its quest and its religious orthodoxy: it concludes, for example, 'kepe thy Secretts in store unto thy selve; / And the comaundements of God looke thou fulfill'.[39] I say quest, because it describes the alchemical work as a journey – a foray into a Philosophical castle of secret wisdom. The adept has to pursue his work through twelve gates: the twelve stages of the *magnum opus*. These 'gates' are described in turn as 'calcination' (the reduction of a solid to powder), 'solution' (the solid is rendered liquid and returned to the first matter of creation – *prima materia*), 'separation' (the breaking apart of the four elements), 'conjunction' (the joining together of opposite properties in a 'chemical wedding'), putrefaction (the nadir of the journey entailing 'paines by heat' and 'darkness of purgatorie withouten lights' eventually leading to the matter turning as 'black as a crowes bill'), 'congelation' (the stone is now congealed and white), 'cibation' (a process of fortification), and, finally, 'sublimation', 'fermentation', 'exaltation', 'multiplication' and 'projection'. The last five mysterious processes serve to deliver from the castle stronghold 'the Red Man and his White Wife' – the perfect Stone.[40] The whole *opus* is

construed as a turning of 'the Wheele of our Philosophie' – the alchemical
process is notably circular 'work'.

Cutting through Ripley's imposing terminology, it would seem that, in
brief, applying heat by means of a furnace, the alchemist dissolves, disinte-
grates and 'kills' the substance in his flask and then resurrects and unites it
again in altered, purified form. However, in spite of Ripley's liberal deployment of terms that sound to the modern ear as though they should be
associated with practical 'chymistry', the *Compound* reads more like a
philosophical tract with pronounced spiritual implications than a chemical
recipe book. If anything, the treatise of Ripley's alchemical disciple Thomas
Norton, which ostentatiously declares itself 'A Booke of secrets given by
God; / To men Elect' – those who love justice with 'spotles-Minde' – serves
to deepen this sense of a frustratingly vague divine 'Art' (Preface, sig. C2r).[41]
Indeed, at points the project described in the *Ordinall* appears to have more
to do with creative art than with chemistry. Nevertheless, in Lauren
Kassell's study of Simon Forman, we discover at least one serious 'chymist'
and medical practitioner in 1590 taking pains to copy Norton's *Ordinall*
from a borrowed manuscript circulating among his friends and neighbours.[42] Ashmole clearly thought highly of it too, seeing fit to position
this work before Ripley's in his important collection. A closer scrutiny of the
treatise is in order.

Norton certainly anticipates his readers' frustration:

> All *Masters* that were of this Soleme worke
> They made their bokes to many Men full derke,
> In Poyses, Parables, and in Metaphors alsoe,
> Which to Schollers causeth peine and woe.   (p. 8)

As a 'Master' himself, he is revelling in his own paradoxes and obscurities – a
feature, as he suggests, of most alchemical works. To write clearly would be to
reveal the secrets of the holy 'science' (p. 15) to unworthy, covetous fools –
'Gebars Cookes' (p. 103) seeking only to make silver and gold from lead 'for
Mony, Cupp or Ring' (p. 13). This is not, he repeatedly insists, the goal of
'holy Alkimy', which 'treateth of a precious Medicine' (p. 20), a red 'elixir'
that is achieved, at great cost, by a painful, dangerous 'Pilgrimage'-like
journey (p. 105). Indeed, the devil is constantly peering over the alchemist's
shoulder, eager for signs of 'Haste . . . Despaire . . . and . . . Deceipte' (p. 30).

Warnings aside, *The Ordinall* gestures towards two puzzling 'Materialls'
resembling 'Mother and . . . Childe' – but 'one' not 'two' – 'apt for
Generation' (pp. 41, 44). The two must be repeatedly joined in unexpected,
intriguing ways:

Now to *Conjunction* let us resorte,
And some wise Councell therof reporte:
Conjoyne your elements *Grammatically*,
With all their Concords conveniently:
Whiche Concords to healpe a Clerke,
Be cheefe Instruments of all this worke. (p. 59)

Joyne them also in *Rhetoricall* guise,
With Natures Ornate in purified wise.
Joyne them together also *Arithmetically*,
By suttill Numbers proportionally,
Wherof a little mention made ther was,
When Boetius said tu numeris elements ligas.
Joyne your Elements *Musically*,
For two causes, one is for Melody;
Which there accords will make to your mind.
With *Astrologie* joyne Elements also,
To fortune their Workings as theie go. (p. 60)

Grammar, rhetoric, arithmetic, music and astrology are integral elements of Norton's alchemical process and the 'chiefe Mistres' of this science-art (he conjoins the two in this important couplet) is 'Magick Naturall' (p. 61). We seem to be in the laboratory of the creative mind here with brain, especially 'Imagination', as the best 'Instrument' (pp. 97, 96). This is hinted at, too, by the *Ordinall*'s discussion of the best furnaces for the 'Arte': a new one has been discovered by the author, which has 'secreate Power with study sought' that 'with greate Cost was dearly bought' (an allusion to Christ's crucifixion and the redemption) but which cannot be 'formed in Picture' (p. 97).

With conjunction of the 'foure Elements' (p. 61) successfully achieved, a process of 'digestion' – decomposition by heat – begins, and now the alchemist must be hyper-alert to the colour, taste and smell of the mixture in his flask so that he can 'temper' it accordingly by adding its contrary. When the stone has passed through a spectrum of colour changes ('All Colours be made which your Eyen sees', p. 66), but crucially from black to white to red, it is cooked to perfection and 'transubstantiation' – a significant choice of word – has been achieved. Norton describes the colouration process as 'Intellectual': 'For then worketh inward heate naturall, / Which in our substance is but Intellectual' (p. 61). It also involves a moral challenge, 'All proude appetites to equalitie to bringe' (p. 67), and 'good odour' (p. 71) indicates success, 'stinking' the opposite (p. 69). The Stone grows like 'to Man' and has a 'Nativity' (pp. 86, 81) yet the end product is an 'Elixir' of

'Water' that can 'fier ... abide' – a 'Quintessence, the fift thing' (p. 71). We might briefly reference here that Shakespeare's sonnet sequence has a mysterious 'babe' that grows and that the final sonnet registers fiery water ('Love's fire heats water', line 14).

Is Norton's elusive *Ordinall* outlining a process of chemistry, or creativity in the arts involving imagination (hence the grammar, rhetoric, music), or an inner spiritual process? Actually, such a question misses the crucial point: in alchemy's holistic view of the universe, disciplinary boundaries as we know them today are irrelevant; categories of knowledge and experience have to be construed in much more fluid, interchangeable terms. The student of alchemy Thomas Rainold optimistically extolled the virtues of this refreshing 'science' in 1551, declaring that in his lifetime God had aroused many 'excellent virtuous witts' so that 'science wil be so renuid, refreshed, and purged, that thei which hitherto have boren al the bruit, & have obtained al autorite, wil leese a greate portion of there creadit'.[43] Certainly in 1590s London, when it was so much in vogue, alchemy was both practical science with a growing pharmaceutical and medical wing, and esoteric philosophy-religion.[44] It was a way of thinking about the world:

> Holi Alkimy:
> A wonderfull Science, secrete Philosophie,
> A singular grace & gifte of th'almightie.
>
> (Norton, *Ordinall*, p. 13)

It is noteworthy, however, that Ashmole regarded Norton's treatise as 'much more curious in the studies of Philosophy than others'.[45] Alchemy's late fifteenth-century philosophical turn had undoubtedly been encouraged by the Florentine Academy's marked shaping influence, in particular by the endeavours of Marsilio Ficino (Angelo Poliziano and Pico della Mirandola were two other key figures) under the auspices of the Medici family.[46]

HERMETICISM AND RENAISSANCE HUMANISM

Poised prominently in a niche in Florence Cathedral, rests a bust of Marsilio Ficino (1439–99) fingering his translation of the works of Plato in such a manner as to evoke his playing of a lyre – the instrument of Orpheus that he is said to have mastered so brilliantly. Ficino was once Canon of this cathedral (as well as philosopher, physician to the Medici and musician) and when he preached there large congregations are said to have gathered, mesmerized by his sermons as if by Orpheus' instrument.[47] In his time he was designated the second Orpheus (and he regarded Orpheus as the second Hermes) and was renowned as a 'doctor of soul' – a metaphysician resembling a type of early psychologist. Although a priest, Ficino was also a noted critic of church practices and he was not afraid of writing to leading clergy, including the Pope, reminding them of their obligations. Crucially, he urged that a heightened inner spirituality was needed to purge the Church of its corruptions, and all his writings effectively cohere around man's central goal of returning to his divine source through 'moral conduct', love and contemplation.[48] Love-Christ, through transforming himself into a man, had made this return or 'ascent' possible:

Let him [man] revere himself as an image of the divine God. Let him hope to ascend again to God, as soon as the Divine Majesty deigns in some way to descend to him. Let him love God with all his heart, so to transform himself into Him, who through singular love wonderfully transformed Himself into Man.[49]

Ficino was well placed to preach this spiritual message because he was the age's major translator of the Greek works of Plato, Plotinus and Zoroaster, the *Hymns* of Orpheus and the *Hermetica*, which together teach that the individual soul is immortal and divine – a concept of major importance to Renaissance thinking and achievements. As Frances Yates points out, 'the Florentine Academy included NeoPlatonism with Platonism and did not make the modern distinction in the use of these terms. Plotinus, Proclus, Porphyry, Jamblichus, Pseudo-Dionysius are for Ficino simply "Platonici".'[50] Though the Platonism or Neoplatonism of the Florentine academy was distinctive, it also derived from medieval philosophical and religious thinking (including, notably, Macrobius, Boethius, St Augustine and Pseudo-Dionysius). This philosophical synergy is frequently termed 'syncretism' in recognition of its multiplicity of origins.[51] Ficino and his noted follower Pico della Mirandola successfully convinced their peers in the Florentine academy and beyond that 'lawful philosophy is no different from true religion; and lawful religion no different from true philosophy' developing the understanding that Hermes Trismegistus was the single source of Judaic religion and Greek philosophy.[52] Ficino declared in *The Christian Religion*:

Divine Providence does not permit any part of the world at any time to be completely without religion, although it does allow rites to differ. Perhaps variety of this kind is intended ... God prefers to be worshipped in any manner, however unfittingly ... than not to be worshipped at all through pride.[53]

In Ficino's scheme, non-egotistical religious love was more important than doctrinal religion (we might simply recall at this point the mysterious line in *A Lovers Complaint*, 'Religious love put out religion's eye', line 250), and Orphic Hymns, Greek myths and Platonic dialogues were envisaged as allegorically encoding the wisdom of the ancient sage of Egypt. Thus he could declare: 'To the Egyptian priests medicine, music and the mysteries were one and the same study. Would that we could master this natural and Egyptian art as successfully as we tenaciously and wholeheartedly apply ourselves to it!' (*Letters* 1: 5, p. 40).

Ficino's *Commentary on Plato's Symposium On Love* (also known as *De amore*) is effectively a Christianized rendering of Plato infused with his own highly syncretic brand of philosophy, which embraced Orphism, Hermeticism and Neoplatonism, elements of Pythagoreanism, and Cabalism – it is, as its modern translator points out, best understood as a 'compilation of ideas about love'.[54] Ficino's *De amore* was written in Latin in 1469 and circulated in manuscript form (becoming a favourite in European courts) before being published in Latin with Ficino's *Works of Plato* in 1484.[55] According to Frances Yates, Sir Thomas More's humanist circle was 'deeply read' in Ficino and his associates in the Florentine academy, most notably Pico della Mirandola.[56] A new French translation of *De amore* by Guy Le Fèvre de la Boderie (associated with the French Academy) was published in 1578; further, Pico's *Commento* (1486) on Benivieni's poetic adaptation (in 154 sonnets) of *De amore* circulated widely in late sixteenth-century England (again, in a new French translation). George Puttenham's library notably contained works by Ficino, Pico della Mirandola and even texts attributed to Hermes Trismegistus.[57]

As I demonstrate throughout this book, Shakespeare's sonnets (like Spenser's *Hymns*, Chapman's prefaces to his translations of the Greek myths, late Elizabethan court entertainments, Jonson's masques and *The New Inn* and the marginalia to Gabriel Harvey's treatise on divine madness) are illuminated by Ficino's treatise on love. Shakespeare would not have needed to borrow Ben Jonson's copy of *De amore* (which Jonson used extensively in *The New Inn*) to be aware of much of its content or indeed that of the gist of Ficino's more esoteric theological texts.[58] Indeed, an allegorical court entertainment of 1581, *The Fortress of Perfect Beauty*, in which the queen was identified as the 'heavenly Venus', is obviously informed by *De amore*, as was Castiglione's *The Courtyer*, Englished by Sir Thomas Hoby (available from 1561). Most significantly, however, Ficino's published *Letters* were widely available in England, and these offer a highly digested, accessible rendering of Ficinian philosophy. Ficino wrote and published them himself, even selecting the title for each letter, with this dissemination function in mind.[59] Among his learned correspondents was the Dean of St Pauls, John Colet (1466–1519), whom he addressed as 'beloved' and, on the basis of library catalogues, Sears Jayne describes the *Epistolae* as 'relatively popular' in sixteenth-century England.[60]

One particular 'love letter' to Ficino's 'unique friend', prefacing the holograph copy of *De amore*, is worth quoting at length:

Marsilio Ficino to Giovanni Cavalcanti: A long time ago, dear Giovanni, I learned from Orpheus that love existed, and that it held the keys to the whole world; then from Plato I learned the definition of love and its nature. But what power and influence this god has, had lain hidden from me until I was thirty-four years old, when a certain divine hero [his friend Cavalcanti] glancing at me with heavenly eyes, showed me, by a certain wonderful nod, how great the power of love is. Being in that way fully informed, as it seems to me about amatory things, I have composed a book *On Love*.[61]

This desiring relationship (characteristically extravagantly expressed) is not about sex (and other letters make this clear, notably 1: 47), it is rather the spur to intellectual 'procreation' and spiritual growth – to its author's 'return' to his divine source. In Letter 42 Ficino describes how where 'the single ray of the one God . . . shines more clearly, it especially attracts the man who is watching'; he is set on fire by desire and the soul 'as by a hook' contemplates the divine and in a frenzied state, 'becomes God' (1: 42, pp. 84–5). In many ways the letters convey the practical application of *De amore*'s philosophy by charting Ficino's own intellectual and spiritual illumination, which is stimulated by the desire for beauty and truth (discovered in Ciceronian-style friendships) and achieved through love, contemplation, music (especially playing the lyre), study and the maintenance of an ethical code of 'justice'.

Artistic pursuits, the 'making' of beautiful things, especially poetry, music, painting and architecture, were also crucial to Ficino's scheme for spiritual progress. Letter 88 describes 'Divinity of soul from invention', while *De amore* declares: 'love is the creator and preserver of all things and the master and lord of all of the arts' (p. 97). For him it was the contemplative mind, stirred by beauty, engaged in 'intellectual procreation' and filled with divine light, which produced significant art forms. 'Divine ecstasy and frenzy' that 'arises through the eyes' was construed as essential to invention inspired by 'ideas' – 'the models of all things' in the divine mind but also accessible in the purified individual soul ('On divine frenzy', 1: 7, pp. 41–8). The process of perfecting the psyche (inner nature) was construed by Ficino both as a form of alchemical sublimation and as soul-tuning; his understanding of Orphism was crucial to the latter and indeed to Renaissance humanism's high evaluation of Orphic Hymns and myths. Indeed, the first three operas of the seventeenth century took as their subject Orpheus and his lost love, Eurydice.[62] The myth of this shaman-type god-musician who visited the land of the dead to bring back his lost love is frequently interpreted allegorically in the Renaissance as the pursuit, through deep soul-searching and much pain and suffering, of lost wisdom. The quest for enlightenment entails, therefore, loss, death and eventual rebirth – the same ritual cycle as alchemy.

Renaissance Orphism requires amplification not least because it part-nered spiritual alchemy in this period. The Neoplatonist Proclus had declared, 'All Greek theology is the offspring of the Orphic mystical doc-trine', while Porphyry named him 'the oldest and foremost of all theolo-gians' and St Augustine said Orpheus 'predicted . . . truth of the Son of God or the Father'.[63] Orpheus is the 'poeta theologus' of Ficino's world: the first poet to soften the hearts of beastly people and lead them to civilization; it is his beautiful voice, his eloquence that the devout Christian must combine with wisdom in seeking true, uncorrupted religion. Orpheus is appre-hended as one in a chain of *prisca theologia* stretching from Hermes Trismegistus, Moses, Zoroaster, Solomon to Orpheus, Pythagoras, and Plato.[64] He thus links the Greek and Hebrew worlds, and in the *Argonautica* (alluded to in Ficino's *De amore*) Orpheus sings to the heroes the story of the Creation of the world 'following the theology of Hermes Trismegistus': 'he [Orpheus] placed chaos before the World, and located Love in the bosom of that Chaos, before Saturn, Jove, and the other gods' (*De amore*, pp. 37–8). Love is the light glimmering in darkness that the Renaissance 'maker' must kindle, copying the divine 'maker's' powers of invention, imposing form on chaotic matter:

The mind is turned toward God in the same way that the eye is directed toward the light of the sun . . . The eye, at first dark, like Chaos, formless, loves the light while it looks towards it; in so looking, it is illuminated; in receiving the ray, it is informed with the colors and shapes of things. (*De amore*, p. 39)

Legend has it that the lyre was given to Orpheus by Mercury and sub-sequently to Pythagorus: with its seven strings mirroring the seven planets it symbolized the harmony of the spheres and mathematically the intervals of the Orphic lyre are the structural basis of the visible universe and the human soul.[65] The aim of Ficino's own frequent hymn singing, lyre playing and contemplative techniques (much alluded to in his *Letters*) was to prepare his *spiritus* to receive an influx of *spiritus* from an astral body. The one most frequently invoked is the Sun (which was the visible image of God for Ficino). This was a crucial part of his scheme of 'natural magic' but also of caring for soul, hence his designation as 'doctor of soul'. Importantly, he praised the 'higher' senses – sight and hearing – because it is through these that we 'hunt beauty', 'which appears in sounds and bodies', and 'as if by means of certain footprints' man can 'track down the beauty of the soul' (*De amore*, p. 42) – beautiful male bodies are a pathway to beautiful souls. Music is particularly efficacious and his letters reveal the 'sweet solace' he associated with his lyre and singing (not unlike Queen Katherine in Shakespeare's *Henry VIII*): 'Now, my Foresi, just after I had written farewell, I rose to my feet, and hastened to take up the lyre. I began to sing at length from the hymns of Orpheus. Get up yourself . . . take up the lyre, that sweet solace of labour.'[66] As we shall see, Ficino's re-formulations of Orphism and Platonism were to exert a crucial shaping influence on Renaissance aesthetic theory as developed by subsequent generations in the Florentine and Parisian academies, but Ficino's translations of the Hermetic writings were also to have a profound impact on scientific and medical culture.

When a collection of short Greek texts – part of the *Corpus Hermeticum* – came to light around 1460, Cosimo de Medici ordered Marsilio Ficino to interrupt his studies of Plato and set to work translating these. Ficino readily complied and in 1471 he published them together with his commentary as the *Book on the Power and Wisdom of God, Whose title is Pimander*. The latter proved immensely popular, undergoing sixteen editions prior to 1500; by the middle of the sixteenth century it had been published in two dozen editions and stimulated vernacular versions in French, Dutch, Spanish and Italian; we know it was accessible in England in 1520.[67] Ficino was unaware that the pronounced Platonic influences he found in the Hermetic writings derived from their having actually been penned in the third or fourth century AD rather than in ancient times. Although this was established by the scholar Isaac Casaubon in 1614, Hermetic philosophers 'ignored the evidence' and the *Hermetica* continued to be influential throughout the seventeenth century.[68] Indeed, the *Hermetica*'s footprints can be ascertained in a wide range of late sixteenth- and seventeenth-century writers and thinkers, among them Philippe Du Plessis Mornay, George Puttenham, Christopher Marlowe, Sir Philip Sidney, Giordano Bruno, Shakespeare, Francis Bacon, John Donne, Henry Vaughan, John Milton and the heroes of science, Isaac Newton, Robert Boyle and Johannes Kepler.

As the names of these latter three might suggest, Hermeticism captured the Renaissance imagination for another crucial reason – its immense concern with the secrets and powers of nature. Undoubtedly Francis Bacon found this passage – a dialogue between Hermes and his pupil Asclepius – particularly inspiring:

> Pure philosophy that depends only on reverence for god should . . . wonder at the recurrence of the stars, how their measure stays constant in prescribed stations and in the orbit of their turning; it should learn the dimensions, qualities and quantities of the land, the depths of the sea, the power of fire and the nature and effects of all such things in order to commend, worship and wonder at the skill and mind of god. (*Asclepius*)[69]

According to the *Hermetica*, the book of nature was, in effect, a second work of divine revelation (after Holy Scripture) and the devout Renaissance philosopher was thus duty bound to study the works of nature and seek out the treasures that became hidden after man's expulsion from the Garden of Eden. As Lauren Kassell's *Medicine and Magic in Elizabethan London* stresses, natural magic was not considered 'a perversion of religion' but rather 'a perfection of it' – this point is crucial.[70] In the Hermetic cosmology of the late sixteenth and early seventeenth centuries, the celestial bodies are a link between God and mankind (the doctrine of sympathy and antipathy): they are capable of infusing their powers into terrestrial matter (including the human mind); they possess divine efficacy, which the skilled natural philosopher might access. Processes such as alchemical distillation could eventually lead to the recovery of divine signatures. Francis Bacon described natural magic in the following terms: 'I . . . understand it as the science which applies the knowledge of hidden forms to the production of wonderful operations; and by uniting (as they say) actives with passives displays the wonderful works of nature' (*De Dignitate et Augmentis Scientarum*).[71] In this scheme of things, the scientist assisted the work of nature, encouraging her to yield her secrets, which gave him enhanced 'powers' that could be deployed, in Bacon's summation, to 'the effecting of all things possible'.[72]

This audacious belief was underpinned by a heightened confidence in human potential that was also supplied in swathes by the *Hermetica*:

> A human being is a great wonder, a living thing to be worshipped and honored: for he changes his nature into a god's, as if he were a god . . . He cultivates the earth; he swiftly mixes into the elements; he plumbs the depths of the sea in the keenness of his mind. Everything is permitted him. (*Asclepius*, p. 69)

Such a heroic conception of man certainly captured the Renaissance imagination; indeed, we might think of Marlowe's Icarus-winged notorious 'overreacher', Faustus. Hamlet's famous words seem to resonate, too, with those of Hermes in *Asclepius*: 'What a piece of work is man! How noble in reason, how infinite in faculty, in form and moving how express and admirable, in action how like an angel, in apprehension how like a god . . . the paragon of animals!' (*Hamlet*, II. ii. 305–9).[73]

Hermeticism was a liberating, motivating vision that seemed to offer a way back into Eden – a divinely sanctioned method of recapturing golden worlds. In this philosophy, man's immortal component is highly creative and he can purify and regenerate his soul, letting in more divine light and 'consciousness', and thereby enhancing his ability to manipulate and control the powers of nature: 'Eternity's understanding . . . is a consciousness gained from the sensible world, from which its quality can be discerned' (*Asclepius*, p. 87). It was humankind's privileged, central position in the universe that enabled humans to interpret the forms in inner and outer nature, uniting the intelligible and physical aspects of the cosmos, using art to better nature. Crucially, as we shall see in Chapter 5, it was the aspect of the human soul known as 'Fantasy' that was key to this purification process. Through Christ's Incarnation as 'universal Humanitas' man had the unique ability to bring things to perfection and to regenerate the fallen world.[74]

Some Renaissance thinkers, notably Pico della Mirandola in his *Oratio*, had stretched this liberating and shape-shifting thinking to extremes that a more conservative figure like Sir Francis Bacon would probably not have been happy to endorse:

Who does not wonder at this chameleon which we are? Or who at all feels more wonder at anything else whatsoever? Not unjustly did Asclepius the Athenian say that humanity was symbolized by Proteus in the secret rites, by reason of our nature sloughing its skin and transforming itself; hence metamorphoses were popular among the Jews and the Pythagoreans.[75]

For Pico, man was a protean 'molder and maker' of himself; he could degenerate into a 'brute' or become 'divine' according to his will and actions.[76] As Jacob Burckhardt recognized (while acknowledging the 'peculiar philosophy of Pico'), this was the lofty myth that facilitated the birth of Renaissance man – 'it may justly be called one of the noblest bequests of that great age'.[77]

This immensely liberating conception of Protean man had been given a seal of divine approval by the *Hermetica* – man as Maker in God's likeness was capable of accessing special powers and transforming himself and his environment ('God is maker of the world and all it contains, governing all things along with mankind, who governs what is composite.' *Asclepius*, p. 72). It must be conceded, however, that this wisdom – termed a 'sacred survival of better times' by Francis Bacon – remained suspect for some: original sin and Calvinistic predestination did not sit easily with notions of man's divinity, his perfectability, or with his capacity to shape the world.[78] At the very least the upsurge in science was deeply unsettling – 'And new Philosophy calls all in doubt' proclaimed John Donne ('First Anniversary', line 205).[79] Shakespeare's Prospero is in fact an Asclepian-type Magus with powers to manipulate his world, producing harmony out of discord, but he notably ends his magic and begs for mercy when this is achieved – he knows when to stop. Like Prospero, real Hermetic philosophers recognized that they were treading a very narrow path of respectability and even committed ones like the Anglican Henry Vaughan registered unease about the extensive 'rifling' of Nature's 'secrets' that natural magic involved:

> I summon'd nature: peirc'd through all her store,
> Broke up some seales, which none had touch'd before,
> Her wombe, her bosome, and her head
> Where all her secrets lay a bed
> I rifled quite . . .   ('Vanity of Spirit', lines 9–13)[80]

Anxieties aside, the rape of nature had begun in earnest and while Bacon took care to dissociate himself in print from extremists who saw Nature as a 'courtesan for pleasure', others, like Hugh Plat – a much more hands-on scientist – appeared to revel in the plunder: 'I may happily be encouraged to pry a little further into Nature's cabinet, and so to disperse some of her most secret jewels'.[81] By 1600 London was bristling with natural philosophers;[82] furthermore, alchemical, Paracelsian medicine – closely affined to Hermeticism – had become so established in England that it was competing with Galenism.

ALCHEMICAL MEDICINE AND SCIENCE

In the sixteenth and seventeenth centuries alchemical medicine was closely associated with its Swiss founding father, Theophrastus Bombastus von Hohenheim (1493–1541), commonly known as Paracelsus.[83] This radical physician presented traditional humoral cosmology with the most serious challenge to its authority that it had encountered since its inception.[84] As Paracelsus's words reveal, he sought deliberately to overturn the learning of the 'high colleges' (universities), instituting a new system of physic that required divinely inspired physicians and knowledge based on 'shoebuckle' experience and arcane wisdom. He confidently proclaimed:

I will let Luther defend his cause, and I will defend my cause . . . this I shall do with the help of the *arcana* . . . / It was not the constellations that made me a physician: God made me . . . my shoebuckles are more learned than your Galen and Avicenna, and my beard has more experience than all your high colleges.[85]

His pamphlets became an important vehicle for anticlericism and for obvious reasons he was sarcastically dubbed the Luther of medicine.[86] Paracelsus's view of the world was deeply mystical and, like the chemical physician who developed his theories in the seventeenth century, Jean Baptista van Helmont (1577–1644), he considered himself a prophet sent by God to recover the 'pristine',[87] uncorrupted knowledge possessed by Adam before the Fall. The English Paracelsian R. Bostocke's *Auncient and Later Phisicke* (1585) argued that Plato had followed the 'Priestes of Aegypt' in subscribing to 'chymicall' as opposed to 'heathenish Physick' and that Paracelsus had simply revived the ancient, purer form of medicine.[88]

Arcane wisdom, according to Paracelsus, could not be 'copied from books' (p. 56). Access to divine secrets had to be learned first through consulting the cabala (p. 133) and subsequently through the intensive study of nature which involved travelling (hence the 'shoebuckles'), alchemy ('the art which makes the impure into the pure through fire', p. 143) and magic ('Magic has power to experience and fathom things which are inaccessible to human reason.' p. 137). As in Hermeticism, the mysteries of the firmament were revealed through an intuitive interaction between the 'light' of nature and the 'light of man' (pp. 43–4) and all this was dependent on the Holy Ghost: 'the Holy Ghost and nature are one . . . each day nature shines as a light from the Holy Ghost and learns from him, and thus this light reaches man, as in a dream' (p. 181).

The cosmos articulated in the writings of Paracelsus and his followers was intensely integrated, unified and activated through spirit: 'Matter was at the beginning of all things, and only after it had been created was it endowed with the spirit of life, so that this spirit might unfold in and through the bodies as God had willed' (p. 15). It was an enchanted Hermetic place in which each individual had an animal body of earth and water and a spiritual body of fire and air 'and both are one, and are not separated' (p. 18). Furthermore the heavens, earth and man were all composed of three minerals – 'mercurius, sulphur, and sal' (mercury, sulphur and salt) – and were only distinguished by the form in which they manifested themselves – 'for they are only ONE thing, ONE being' (pp. 18–19). Bostocke declared emotively for his English readership that while Paracelsian medicine was 'founded upon the Centre of unity, concord and agreement', with the end of bringing the sick person 'to unity in himself', the false 'phisicke . . .commonly used [Galenism] . . . is founded upon a false center . . . For it consisteth in dualitie, discord and contrarietie. It maketh warre and not peace in mans body' (*Auncient and Later Phisicke*, sig. BIr). 'Consent and agreement' not 'Monomachie' had to be maintained between 'Sal, Sulphur and Mercury' (p. 69). Harmony, extreme unity and spirituality were the hallmarks of the Paracelsian medical schema which was notably born out of the religious instabilities and German peasant wars of the 1520s.

Elizabeth I's surgeon, William Clowes, was renowned for his use of 'chymical' remedies and increasingly physicians practised a hybrid Galenic-Paracelsian form of physic utilizing a growing spectrum of mineral 'cures'.[89] The practitioners Thomas Moffet (a respected member of the prestigious College of Physicians) and John Hester championed Paracelsian methods and one of its major exponents, the alchemist Robert Fludd, far from being considered an irrational medical maverick, was deemed sufficiently mainstream in the first decade of the seventeenth century to be admitted into the College of Physicians and was subsequently four times elected as its censor. The French Paracelsian, Théodore Turquet de Mayerne, was court physician to James I and then Charles I and went on to become Oliver Cromwell's doctor; Paracelsian surgeons seem to have been particularly favoured by Parliamentary troops in the English civil wars.[90] Significantly, within two decades of his death Paracelsus had been listed by a Strasbourg scholar as one of three important innovators of his time: 'Martin Luther in religion, "Theophrasto" in medicine, and Albrecht Durer in the visual arts'.[91] Ole Peter Grell maintains that today in German-speaking areas in particular 'more people are likely to have heard of Paracelsus than any other medical figure in history, including . . . Hippocrates and Harvey'.[92] His reputation has fared less well in English-speaking countries but his status as an accomplished practitioner and innovator is currently being recuperated; it is no longer so surprising to discover that an image of Paracelsus accompanies those of Copernicus and Tycho Brahe in the Bodleian Library reading room.[93]

It appears that Hermeticism's chemical dream of refinement, protean change, and golden worlds was firmly embedded in the English psyche and it was to have far reaching effects on the material world – effects that its first peace-seeking Florentine exponents could never have anticipated. The

Hermetic-alchemical mindset fuelled frightening visions of fiery apocalypse in the seventeenth century such that the diarist John Evelyn (not a noted fanatic) imagined the distillation of the saints into clouds before the 'dreadfull Conflagration of this present Earth' – he was fascinated by chemical explosions – while Joseph Glanvill frightened his associates with prophecies of the world 'enveloped in a ball of fire'.[94] But it also underpinned the aspirations of those who founded the Royal Society for the promotion of science in the Restoration years and who were seeking to create a millennial utopia – a New Jerusalem. It is no coincidence that the blueprint for this institution (as Thomas Sprat's *History of the Royal Society*, 1667, confirms) was Francis Bacon's utopian fable *New Atlantis* in which the scientists of Salomon's House bear a strong resemblance to Hermetic philosophers avidly pursuing nature's secrets for the betterment of mankind.[95]

In fact, in the middle of the seventeenth century and through to the 1680s, far from declining as the 'scientific revolution' advanced apace, the publication of alchemical and Hermetic texts reached its zenith.[96] Further, scholars in recent years have been uncovering the substantial alchemical beliefs and activities of those renowned scientists Newton and Boyle: the mystical mentality of alchemy can no longer be dissociated from seventeenth-century advances in science.[97]

THE PHILOSOPHER'S STONE AND SPIRITUAL STORE

As Charles Webster has described at length in his *Great Instauration*, in the middle of the seventeenth century a vigorous search was on for a philosopher's stone in the form of an elixir – a medicine that could cure all diseases and help remake a utopian world. Paracelsian millenarian expectations had certainly encouraged this quest. The poet Henry Vaughan, a Royalist, defended 'Hermeticall Theory' against 'malicious despisers of true knowledge' declaring, 'For my owne part, I honour the truth where ever I find it, whether in an old, or a new Booke, in Galen, or in Paracelsus.'[98] However, his translation of *Hermeticall Physick* (1655) argues:

The Hermetic Phylosophy layes open the most private and abstruse closets of nature, it doth most exquisitely search out and find out the natures of health and sickness, it provides most elaborate and effectuall Medicines, teacheth the just Dose of them, and surpasseth by many degrees the vulgar Philosophy . . . it doth much exceed and outdo the Galenicall Physick. (p. 550)

This treatise is careful to distance itself from those 'who know onely to distil a little water from this or that Herb' and certainly from those 'Sophisters and Imposters' 'who seeke to extract from other things by their sophistical operations a great treasure of Gold, which onely nature can supply us with' (p. 550). Meanwhile, a key founding member of the Royal Society, Elias Ashmole, declared that the pursuit of the 'Angelicall Stone ... The Food of Angels ... The Tree of life' was 'not any wayes Necromanticall, or Devilish, but easy, wonderous easy, Naturall and Honest'.[99] Hermes himself had abjured 'other Stones' (material riches in the form of gold, silver and gems):

> After Hermes had once obtained the knowledge of this Stone, he gave over the use of all other Stones, and therin only delighted: Moses and Solomon [together with Hermes were the only three that] excelled in the knowledge therof, and who therewith wrought Wonders. (*Theatrum Chemicum Britannicum*, sig. B2r)

Solomon had long been appropriated as an alchemist by Hermetic philosophers, and this is why Joseph Hall's commentary on the *Song of Songs* (1609) interprets 'this whole Pastoral-marriage song' as an alchemical allegory 'where the deepest things of God are spoken in riddles'.[100] The *Song* is an allegory about the 'blackish, and darke of hew' Church or soul which is rendered white by 'Salomons Divine Arts' gleaned from a 'profounde' understanding of nature. Hall's commentary unravels the kernel of the song's riddle as 'Blessed is the man that findeth wisedome, and getteth understandinge: the merchandise thereof is better then the merchandise of silver, and the gaine therof is better then golde' (p. 24). The philosopher's stone here ('the merchandise') is divine wisdom and purification of the soul and of the true Church and the vehicle for Solomon-Christ's message is, notably, an erotic love story.

I will return to the Song of Solomon in Chapter 3. I wish merely to pause here and note that in the troubled erotic love story conveyed by Shakespeare's sonnet sequence, 'store' (one of the meanings of which is 'merchandise') is one of the most mysterious and frequently reoccurring words:

> Let those whom nature hath not made for store,
> Harsh, featureless and rude, barrenly perish.   (Sonnet 11)

> As truth and beauty shall together thrive
> If from thyself, to store thou wouldst convert.   (Sonnet 14)

> The sea, all water, yet receives rain still,
> And in abundance addeth to his store.   (Sonnet 135)

> Though in thy store's account I one must be.   (Sonnet 136)

What 'store', whose 'store' is this? We might recall the alchemist Ripley's final lines, 'Kepe thy Secretts in store unto thyselve'; in the poem *Cantilena* he declares: 'What Man is he will slight so Rich a Store, / As drowns the very thought of being Poore?'.[101] Further, in Henry Vaughan's poem *Vanity of Spirit* we discover a poet-philosopher 'rifling' nature's 'store' (line 9). The word occurs particularly frequently in Hermetic contexts. The accumulation of Shakespearean 'stores' seems to reach a climax in Sonnet 146 (a sonnet which is so difficult to explain in a sequence that is understood as entirely secular) in which a choice is foregrounded between 'store' with 'outward walls so costly gay' – material riches – and spiritual 'store' associated with immortality; indeed, a lexicon of 'spiritual accounting' pervades the sequence ('What acceptable audit canst thou leave', Sonnet 4).[102] Sonnet 146 declares:

> Then, soul, live thou upon thy servant's loss,
> And let that pine to aggravate thy store;
> Buy terms divine in selling hours of dross;
> Within be fed, without be rich no more.   (Sonnet 146)

Significantly, in the Hermetic ascent 'evil strivings after wealth' must be conquered.[103] Thus Henry Vaughan's poem on this topic concludes railing against 'Fortune': 'Then leave to Court me with thy hated store, / Thou giv'st me that, to rob my Soul of more' ('The Importunate Fortune', lines 109–10). In Shakespeare's Sonnet 146, too, the poet-speaker's 'soul-store' appears to win. As we shall see, it is through intellectual memory's 'stored up treasures' that spiritual capital is accrued.

SERIOUS PLAY, SOUL WORK AND ALCHEMICAL EMBLEM BOOKS

Remember that most men, and above all great men, transact their business affairs lightly and as it were in play: whilst their pleasures and pastimes they perform as serious matters, setting about them with a most attentive mind. (Antoine de Baif, 'Dedication to Joyeuse, Les Mimes', 1581)[104]

It is impossible to acknowledge the layers of philosophical and religious meaning at play in *Shake-speares Sonnets* and *A Lovers Complaint* without first apprehending Renaissance humanism's supremely important linked notions of *serio ludere* (serious play) and of veiling 'truths' from common eyes. These techniques were particularly favoured by the Platonic academies in Italy and France where Ficinian Hermeticism was developed in relation to aesthetics. As Yates points out, the Florentine and French academies were connected by the patronage of the Medici family – by Cosimo and Lorenzo

in Italy and by Catherine de'Medici in France – and this inevitably
facilitated intellectual exchange. Antoine de Baif was the founder of the
Academie de Poesie et de Musique – the first French academy to be officially
instituted by royal decree and which nurtured Pierre de Ronsard and the
famous Pleiade.[105] Here Ronsard developed a poetic method informed by
Hermeticism of 'hiding the truth of things' ('veiled statements of truths of
moral and natural philosophy which harmonized with Christian doctrine')
in poetry, myth and image.[106] Of course, *serio ludere* had a noted English
heritage too – Thomas More was a master of Lucianic-style serious play and
interestingly he, like Colet, was 'deeply read' in Ficino and Pico della
Mirandola.[107] As early dialogues between Ronsard and Baif reveal, these
two figures, like More and Colet, discussed a wide range of philosophical
and religious issues, straying widely from the purely 'literary'. At the heart of
Baif's *Academie*'s philosophy from the 1560s was a pronounced Hermetic
yearning to bring multiplicity into unity: to unite the warring church
factions into one universal religion; to this end, Protestants and Catholics
would meet together to sing and play in Orphic harmony.[108]

Frances Yates draws attention to one particular creation of the French
academy artists as an example of 'pleasure' as 'serious matter' for 'attentive
minds': a court entertainment, the *Ballet Comique de la Reine* (1581).[109] This
is a play with music and dance (not dissimilar in its combination of artistry
to later English court masques) that stages what might be described as an
externalized theatre of the mind with a Hermetic plot. Its allegorical meanings are printed with the text so we know much about how Renaissance
initiates construed it. At its centre is 'natural man' who is personified as
Circe – the famous enchantress with her magic wand who has the power of
transforming men into beasts. Circe, daughter of male Sun and female
Ocean, is an embodiment of 'natural man' because she combines heat and
moisture (the substances of creation, productive of birth, decay and metamorphosis); 'she' is the instinct for sexual excess and debauchery in man
which needs to be restrained. The *Ballet* also features Ulysses and his
companions, who are actually personified powers and faculties of the soul
and senses. Ulysses must order and control these faculties so that they are
not transformed into beasts by Circe. This is a familiar Renaissance 'myth'
and, as I shall demonstrate in Chapter 3, its basic structure informs
Giordano Bruno's sonnets and haunts Shakespeare's sequence, too, but in
a more subtle, veiled form. It is also the driving myth underpinning many
late sixteenth-century Hermetic emblem books since alchemy is a process
whereby man purifies and orders his internal 'nature'. It is important to note
that female Circe in the alchemical formulation is not an 'other' to man but

an integral, fertile aspect of 'natural man'; through combining and balancing male and female energies the artist attains wisdom and emotional
harmony and maximizes his creative powers. This is why the historian
John Read defines alchemy as pre-psychology as much as pre-chemistry.
The operations of the 'Great Work' were often compared to the tasks of
Hercules; while Ulysees, the wanderer, was construed by alchemists as an
'adept who "errs in divers ways until he reaches the desired goal"; the
fruitless efforts of Penelope, who unwove by night that which she had
woven by day, were viewed as an image of the abortive labours of the
uninformed seekers after the Stone'.[110]

The famous Renaissance philosopher and personal physician to Rudolph II,
Michael Maier (1568–1622), produced several beautifully engraved volumes
which explicated classical mythology alchemically, as in the above formulations. He was a friend of Robert Fludd and we know that he came to London
to learn English in the early seventeenth century so that he could translate
Thomas Norton's *Ordinall* into Latin.[111] Maier, like Ficino, was a physician of
soul, but he particularly delighted in 'serious play', which involved veiling
alchemical truths in striking and frankly odd visual emblems. This fashion had
been set in train by the uncovering of a Greek translation of an Egyptian work
in 1419 that was thought to explain the hidden Hermetic wisdom of Egyptian
hieroglyphs – *Hieroglyphica*. It was printed by Aldus in 1505 and translated
into Latin and the European vernaculars. Its success prompted the Emperor
Maximilian to have himself depicted by Albrecht Dürer in 1515 covered
in bizarre 'hieroglyphs' containing veiled meanings accessible to only the
learned about his fame, wisdom and magnificence (*The Triumphal Arch of
Maximilian*). The same vogue for secret subtleties initiated by *Hieroglyphica*
and the French Academy's preoccupation with Hermetic Neoplatonism
prompted the publication of two important French works: *Le Songe de
Poliphile* (1546, 1553, 1561) and in 1600 an enhanced translation of it called
*Le Tableau des riches inventions couvertes du voile des feintes amoureuses, qui sont
representees dans le Songe de Poliphile desvoilees des ombres du songe et subtilment
exposees par Beroalde* by François Beroalde de Verville.[112]

As Stanislas Klossowski de Rola explains, Beroalde dedicated his work
'To the Beautiful Spirits who shall arrest their gaze upon those projects
of serious pleasure'. He proceeds to praise the author of *Poliphile* who

Follows the manner of the Ancients who veiled any kind of philosophical truth
with certain agreeable figures which attracted men's hearts, either to detain them
upon the husk of what offered itself, or to strive to open that which hid the inner
beauty in order to enjoy it, thus both pleasing the vulgar and satisfying those
desirous of perfection.[113]

1 Title page, *Le Tableau des riches inventions*, by François Beroalde de Verville.

Beroalde's words deliver us into the midst of the intellectual climate that nurtured Shakespeare's 1609 volume of poetry. On the title page of Beroalde's *Le Tableau des riches inventions* (Paris, 1600) (see Fig. 1), for example, we find a lion with its paws cut off, (recalling Shakespeare's enigmatic line, 'Blunt thou the lion's paws'), an eagle (symbol of mercury), a fire sprouting a tree of life topped by a phoenix (philosopher's stone), an hour glass (indicating the need for both time and patience in alchemical 'work'), and myrtle branches growing in all directions, signifying that the origin, cause and end of all things is Love.[114] Lovers kissing, copulating, dying in a fire and rising anew as one hermaphrodite are the key recurring 'amorous deceits' of these turn-of-the-century alchemical volumes. The significance of these motifs, and particularly of the alchemical hermaphrodite in relation to Shakespeare's 1609 poems, will be elaborated in Chapter 2.

Paging through the vivid imaginative landscape of the beautifully engraved alchemical emblem books of the late sixteenth and seventeenth centuries reveals the appeal of this richly symbolic art to Renaissance wits in pursuit of new invention. Some of these volumes even present the stages of the *opus circulatorium* (the circular work) in the form of theatrical scenes complete with audiences; others take the form of allegorical romances. Their arcane imagery certainly opens a window of understanding onto some of Shakespeare's most obscure lines and makes sense of the Pythagorean geometry, with its divine implications, that many scholars have found in Shakespeare's sequence but are at a loss to explain in the context of an entirely secular sequence.

The alchemical soul work uncovered in Michael Maier's volumes helps particularly to illuminate the intellectual-cultural milieu that inspired them. Maier's generous prefaces and explanations assist the 'liberally educated' reader's task of decoding the riddles and of apprehending what Maier described as 'a chaste virgin behind a lattice' – chemistry, whose secrets had to be concealed (veiled in rhetorical colours) from fraudulent eyes.[115] The 'Preface to the Reader' accompanying *Atalanta Fugiens* (1618) declares:

Now for the cultivation of the intellect, God has concealed infinite arcana in nature, which like the fire that is struck from flint can be extracted and put to use by innumerable arts and sciences. The secrets of Chemistry are not last among these, but the first and most precious after the searching out of divine things: not in the hands of those wandering deceivers and pseudo-chemical frauds ... but in those of higher skills, liberally educated and born to investigate greater things that are most subtle, august, sacred, rare and abstruse, thus to be comprehended by the intellect ... rather by profound contemplation after reading the authors and comparing them with one another and with the workings of nature, than by sensible operation or manual experimentation, which is blind without previous theory. (p. 101)

Chemical philosophy involves eliciting nature's divine secrets, reading and comparing authors and examining these in relation to nature and through 'profound contemplation', only then followed by 'manual experimentation'. The combined spiritual, philosophical, and practical dimensions of the art of alchemy are beautifully captured by the title-page illustration of Maier's *Tripus Aureus* (1618) (see Fig. 2). *Atalanta Fugiens* is actually an aid to 'profound contemplation' comprising:

New Chemical Emblems of the Secrets of Nature, Adapted partly for the eyes and intellect in figures engraved on copper, with legends, Epigrams and notes attached, partly for the ears and the soul's recreation with about 50 musical fugues in three voices, of which two are set to a simple melody suitable for singing the couplets, to be looked at, read, meditated, understood, weighed, sung and listened to, not without a certain pleasure. (title page)

This is deeply serious play that engages the higher senses pleasurably in order to cultivate intellectual 'health' and spiritual 'treasure':

> I've shown them to your senses, that your mind
> May grasp the treasures that lie hid therein.
> You can have wealth, or Medicine of health.
>
> (*The Author's Epigram*, p. 97)

2 Title-page illustration, Esoteric and exoteric alchemy, Michael Maier, *Tripus Aureus*.

The organizing myth of *Atalanta Fugiens* is rendered alchemically by Maier:[116] fruit can grow from trees, minerals in the bowels of the earth, in deepest winter we can grow leaves and flowers from the cut branch of an apple tree; so in chemistry things can regenerate. Nature's cycles of sunrise and sunset, of birth, growth, decay and death inform every level of alchemical thinking; it is this primordial creative, transformative power that the alchemist must harness and profitably utilize. Atalanta (the fugitive substance female Mercury) is the beautiful fleet-of-foot princess who outran all her suitors except Hippomenes (male sulphur), who caught her by casting three golden apples in her path. After the two marry and copulate in the Temple of Cybele they are transformed into lions just as sulphur and mercury conjoin in the glass vessel to form the regenerative royal red tincture. The fifty 'three-voiced' fugues (two in strict canon and a third constant apple melody which has been identified as the 'Christe eleison' of Gregorian Mass IV), are a key facet of this harmonizing soul work, or 'medicine'.[117] The repetition and monotony of the fugues appear to create and maintain a mood suitable for deep contemplation, for conjoining and balancing antithetical energies and principles in the soul, helping to facilitate the ordering of internal nature – the chaotic mass of *prima materia* or *pia mater* upon which 'sweet' form must be imposed according (as we shall see in Chapter 2) to 'measure, and number, and weight', Wisdom 8:1. In Maier's fugues the divine spark of light, hidden but waiting to be retrieved and developed in all created things, is present in the constant 'Christe eleison' voice of the Golden Apple, which stabilizes and unites the conflicting opposites.[118]

The number three is highly significant in *Atalanta Fugiens*, as in most alchemical works, representing the Holy Trinity; body, soul and spirit; and mercury, sulphur and salt. There are three key stages of the process that will be further illuminated in relation to Shakespearean alchemy in subsequent chapters: the *Nigredo*, the *Albedo* and the *Rubedo*, and the aim of the alchemical process is to unite the material, spiritual (or psychic) and cosmic worlds. The entire alchemical *opus* is represented in Emblem 21 (see Fig. 3) geometrically as the three-sided triangle circumscribing a square and circle:

> Around the man and woman draw a ring,
> From which an equal-sided square springs forth.
> From this derive a triangle, which should touch
> The sphere on every side: and then the stone
> Will have arisen. If this is not clear,
> Then learn Geometry and know it all.
>
> (*Atalanta Fugiens*, p. 147)

3 Illustration accompanying Emblema XXI, 'Around the man and woman draw a ring . . . square . . . triangle'. Michael Maier, *Atalanta Fugiens*.

The message is clear: there can be no alchemy without some knowledge of divine geometry (as the renowned adept Geber had foregrounded) and three is a key number in this scheme.

It is not difficult to understand why twentieth-century psychoanalysis, notably the Jungian variety, found much in alchemical volumes such as Maier's that seemed analogous to its own psychic integration processes. For example, the analyst Hildemarie Streich found in the alchemist's *Nigredo*, the phase of insight into 'the dark subconscious shadow-area of the psyche'; the next phase of development, corresponding to the whitening *Albedo* stage of alchemy, she explains as a recognition of one's dark side, especially the female side in man and the masculine side in woman; while the triumphant alchemical *Rubedo*, which brings the sunrise, corresponds to the phase of treatment in which 'the person undergoing the process changes to a mature

EMBLEMA III. *De secretis Naturæ.*

Vade ad mulierem lavantem pannos, tu fac similiter.

EPIGRAMMA III.

ABdita quisquis amas scrutari dogmata, ne sis
   Deses, in exemplum, quod juvet, omne trahas:
Anné vides, mulier maculis abstergere pannos
Ut soleat calidis, quas superaddit, aquis?
Hanc imitare, tuâ nec sic frustraberis arte,
Namque nigri fæcem corporis unda lavat.

C 3   Si

4 Emblema and Epigramma III, 'Go to the woman washing sheets, and do likewise'.
Michael Maier, *Atalanta Fugiens.*

personality conscious of his responsibilities and aware of experiencing
the deeper connections of existence'.[119] Interesting as these analogies
may be, my purpose in this book is not to delve further into modern
appropriations of alchemy but rather to try to understand early modern

5 Illustration accompanying Emblema XXXIII, 'The Hermaphrodite needs fire'. Michael
Maier, *Atalanta Fugiens*.

alchemical writings and pursuits on their own terms, and these centre, significantly differently, on soul work, religion and natural philosophy. Renaissance alchemical books certainly look backwards as much, if not more, than they anticipate the future, and if we neglect that past, raiding it only for elements which, on the surface, seem interesting for us today, we run the danger of losing crucial insights into the rich complexity of our heritage.

The stages of the *opus* (the alchemical work or circle) traced in *Atalanta Fugiens* are recognizable from the pages of medieval treatises, and aphorisms from Hermes' *Emerald Tablet* emerge in the songs of the fugues and in the emblems. While the modern mentality seeks to know if this strange hybrid volume is a recipe book for spiritual or for practical chemistry, it is most likely that (in true Hermetic spirit) it sought to guide both esoteric and exoteric practices simultaneously, denying

6 Illustration accompanying Emblema XXXIV, 'He is conceived in the bath and born in the air'. Michael Maier, *Atalanta Fugiens.*

distinctions. It is the excellent, if bizarre, engravings produced by Théodore de Bry (see Figs. 3, 4, 5 and 6) and their philosophical commentaries that makes this a very different, much more sophisticated alchemical textbook than its late medieval forbears.

As Joscelyn Godwin's study points out, the engravings of *Atalanta Fugiens* confirm that Maier had an appetite for the 'marvellous, the arcane, the weird and wonderful'; this undoubtedly had something to do with them being aids to memory fixing and recall.[120] He certainly had a sense of humour: here we find images of incestuous copulation; a *rebis* born from a mountain and hermaphrodites ('Don't spurn the dual sex, for male and female, / One and the same, will give the king to you', Epigram 38, p. 181); a king whose virile member has been lost at sea (Epigram 44, p. 193); and another sitting in a bath 'Swollen with bile ... cruel and severe', while dew washes his melancholy away (Emblem 28, p. 161). Esoteric advice is rendered in oddly domestic scenes such as a woman doing the laundry:

> Let one who loves to study secret dogmas
> Not fail to take up every helpful hint:
> You see a woman, washing stains from sheets,
> As usual, by pouring on hot water?
> Take after her, lest you frustrate your art,
> For water washes the black body's dirt.
>
> (Epigram 3, p. 111; see Emblem 3, **Fig.** 4)

Alchemy's laundry and washing motifs are, as I shall demonstrate in Chapter 4, particularly important for understanding strange Shakespearean images in the 1609 poems (notably in *A Lovers Complaint*). While in Emblem 42 a goggle-eyed philosopher carrying a candle lamp follows personified Nature's footprints closely through a moonlit landscape seeking to dispel darkness, the epigram urges 'Let Nature be your guide, and with your art / Follow her closely' (p. 189).

ALCHEMICAL CENTRES

Maier's alchemical soul work had been nurtured at the court of Rudolph II, where he was a practising physician in the years prior to 1612; but do we have any evidence that this brand of Hermetic philosophy penetrated far outside the confines of that noted esoteric community? Crucially, could its influence at the turn of the seventeenth century have extended as far as London, where Shakespeare was writing? Lyndy Abraham provides a detailed account of the comings and goings of alchemists based in intellectual centres traversing Europe at this time: alchemical research was flourishing in Paris, Strasbourg, Tübingen and Frankfurt (where the renowned publisher of alchemical books, Johann Theodor de Bry had his workshop), in Prague, Cracow and Pozsony in Hungary, and in Moscow and at Laski's estates (he was Dee's patron) in Poland. There is certainly sufficient evidence to support the claim of the intellectual historian R. J. W. Evans that 'alchemy was the greatest passion of the age in central Europe'.[121] Three noted English practitioners, John Dee, Edward Kelly and Edward Dyer, spent lengthy periods at Rudolph's court at Prague, where they lived royally, making 'projections' and rubbing shoulders with the famous alchemists Oswald Croll, Heinrich Khunrath, Ruland the Elder and Maier. At home in Mortlake, Dee created his own intellectual centre, which boasted a vast library (containing a particularly impressive collection of alchemical treatises), laboratories and frequent court visitors including Robert Dudley Earl of Leicester, Fulke Greville, Sir Philip Sidney and Mary Herbert, Countess of Pembroke, who constructed her own alchemical laboratory at Wilton. Peter French suggests that in the 1580s Dee's Mortlake base resembled the earlier Florentine academies and emulated the More–Colet circle, looking forward to the English Royal Society.[122] Queen Elizabeth employed Dee's polymath talents at court but she had a personal alchemist, too, Cornelius de Lannoy. Indeed, as we shall see in Chapter 3, court propaganda radiated from the fantasy of Elizabeth as both divine alchemist and philosopher's stone: the Phoenix ushering in a new golden age of purified religion.

But there were other English alchemical centres: Gresham College in London was one and Raleigh's Durham House another. Raleigh's 'set' included figures such as the 'wizard Earl', Henry Percy, Ninth Earl of Northumberland (whose own library boasted a fine collection of alchemical volumes),[123] and the mathematician Thomas Harriot, who had tutored Sidney's brother Robert as well as Raleigh. From 1603 to 1616 Raleigh was imprisoned in the Tower where, according to its Lieutenant in 1606, he conducted his experiments in an old hen house in the garden converted to a still house.[124] In 1607 Harriot set up his own alchemical laboratory in the grounds of Northumberland's Sion House. Both these locations are associated with literary visitors, including John Donne, George Chapman and Christopher Marlowe.[125] In the early decades of the seventeenth century the Bishop of Worcester's home, Hartlebury Castle, established itself as a significant site of alchemical practice and, later, an important circle grouped around Samuel Hartlib and the famous 'Invisible College'.[126]

It would seem, then, that at least from the 1580s and 90s, Hermetic alchemy was firmly ensconced in London and particularly around Elizabeth's court; this is substantiated by the Records of Gray's Inn printed in 1688, which give an account of the Christmas revels of 1594 including an anonymous entertainment (in which, it has been speculated, Francis Bacon may well have had a large hand) known as the *Gesta Grayorum*. This is part of the speech of 'The Second Counsellor, advising the study of philosophy' to Henry Prince Purpoole:

I . . . will wish unto your Highness the exercise of the best and purest part of the mind, and the most innocent and meriting conquest, being the conquest of the works of nature; making this proposition, that you bend the excellency of your spirits to the searching out, inventing, and discovering of all whatsoever is hid and secret in the world; that your Excellency be not as a lamp that shineth to others and yet seeth not itself, but as the Eye of the World, that both carrieth and useth light. Antiquity, that presenteth unto us in dark visions the wisdom of former times, informeth us that the [governments of] kingdoms have always had an affinity with the secrets and mysteries of learning.

'Salomon' is listed among the notable beacons of natural knowledge of former times and then the text details the equipment needed to uncover Nature's secrets: 'The fourth such a still-house, so furnished with mills, instruments, furnaces, and vessels, as may be a palace fit for a philosopher's stone. Thus, when your Excellency shall have added depth of knowledge to the fineness of [your] spirits and greatness of your power, then indeed shall you be a Trismegistus.'[127] This court entertainment does, indeed, read like a Baconian-inspired forerunner of *New Atlantis* and the latter, we should recall, provided the blueprint for the Royal Society.

It is noteworthy that *Gesta Grayorum* was staged in the same year (1594–5) that Sidney's *Apology for Poetry* was published (written *c.* 1583) and six years after George Puttenham's *The Art of English Poesy* (1589): as we shall see, both these works incorporate elements of alchemical philosophy into their deliberations on poetics. Contemporary accounts of Sir Philip Sidney's links with Dee's intellectual circle render this unsurprising. Thomas Moffett's biography of Sidney (written to be presented to William Herbert but not published until 1652) records: 'Led by God, with Dee as teacher, and with Dyer as companion, he [Sidney] learned chemistry, that starry science, rival to nature.'[128] In the same year (1583) that Sidney was translating his friend Du Plessis Mornay's *The Trewnesse of the Christian Religion* and writing his influential *Apology for Poetry* (*Defence of Poesy*), he certainly visited Dee, who numbered among his distinguished guests at that point the notorious Italian Hermeticist Giordano Bruno, who spent three years in England (between 1583 and 1586), having fled persecution in Italy and following a controversial sojourn in Paris.[129] Frances Yates has described Bruno as the 'last link in the chain by which the Platonic tradition can be traced up to, and including, the age of Shakespeare'.[130] Bruno clearly found Sir Philip a sympathetic figure: he dedicated several of his philosophical works to 'the Most Illustrious Sir Philip Sidney', including *De gli eroici furori* (*The Heroic Frenzies*, 1585) – a hybrid collection of sonnets, verbal emblems, mottos and commentaries. A copy of Bruno's book annotated in Henry Percy's hand can still be found in the library at Petworth House today. Bruno is a fascinating figure who, among other things, pitted his wits against the weight of prevailing University Aristotelianism. He preached Copernicanism and inveighed against dualism with its doctrine of warring contraries expounding, in its place, the Platonism of Nicholas de Cusa (active in the fifteenth-century Florentine academy) with its 'coincidence of opposites': 'all opposites are united in their infinite measure, so that which would be logical contradictions for finite things, can exist without contradiction in God'.[131] In this scheme, paradoxes and contradictions are fusions of two extremes into a harmonic one and the driving force for this conjunction is love/ desire (this is, of course, the philosophy of late sixteenth-century Hermetic alchemy with its symbolic 'copulations', 'chemical weddings' and 'marriages'). In line with this, Bruno promulgated the belief that the revival of Egyptian religion, as expounded in the writings of Hermes Trismegistus, especially the *Asclepius*, offered a way of reuniting Catholic and Protestant Christendom and returning religion to its pristine state; a focus on universal love was key to this regenerative spiritual alchemy.[132]

John Dee appears to have shared this belief and desire for religious unity: 'a betterment of our life. . . piety, and . . . the practicing of peace and charity towards our neighbours'.[133] As demonstrated earlier, Du Plessis Mornay, too, appropriated the fabled 'Mercurius Trismegistus' in the service of the 'one God . . . which hath universall power of creating all things . . . [the] Good'.[134] A year before Sidney's translation of Mornay (completed by Arthur Golding) was published in 1587 the first English version of the popular, encyclopaedic *French Academie* by Pierre de la Primaudaye (which went through multiple editions between 1586 and 1618) appeared in London bookshops, its 'Epistle Dedicatorie' praising 'the pleasant walkes of this Platonicall academy & schoole of Morall Philopsophy'. John Erskine Hankins has helpfully demonstrated the numerous echoes and resonances from la Primaudaye in Shakespeare's works.[135] It is this European-wide fashionable intellectual environment which fostered court productions like the *Gesta Grayorum* and which led Francis Bacon to commend James I in 1605 as 'invested of that triplicity which in great veneration was ascribed to the ancient Hermes; the power and fortune of a King, the knowledge and illumination of a Priest, and the learning and universality of a Philosopher'.[136] It also informed influential European late sixteenth-century and seventeenth-century poetic treatises; indeed, the extent to which Hermetic alchemy shaped English Renaissance poetic theory with its pronounced discourse of poet as inspired 'maker' has been seriously underestimated.

ALCHEMY AND POETIC THEORY

A poet . . . is both a maker and a counterfeiter: and poesy an art not only of making, but also of imitation.

And this science in his perfection can not grow but by some divine instinct – the Platonics call it *furor* – or by excellence of nature and complexion, or by great subtlety of the spirits and wit, or by much experience and observation of the world and course of kind, or, peradventure by all or most part of them. (Puttenham, *The Art of English Poesy*, 1589)[137]

Onely the Poet, disdaining to be tied to any . . . subjection, lifted up with the vigor of his owne invention, dooth growe in effect another nature, in making things either better then Nature bringeth forth, or, quite a newe, formes such as never were in Nature . . . Her world is brazen, the Poets only deliver a golden. (Sir Philip Sidney, *An Apology for Poetry*, 1595)[138]

Christopher Marlowe's first strutting Tamburlaine notably praised 'the heavenly Quintessence' that poets

Still
From their immortall flowers of Poesy,
Wherin as in a myrrour we perceive
The highest reaches of a humaine wit.[139]

Again employing alchemical imagery, the later writer John Cleveland declared, 'Verse chymically weeps; that pious raine / Distill'd with Art, is but the sweat o' th' braine.'[140] These poets' words, I wish to suggest, conveyed far more than simply a string of beautiful images to the ears of intellectual wits among original audiences and readers. This was a remarkable phase in the history of poetic theory in which the technique of writing was understood to involve 'distillation' ('still') and intellectual memory images ('immortal flowers'), and both were essential ingredients of an aesthetics of 'chymical making' in which the poet's heightened imaginative powers rendered him especially close to the divine Maker – he could even become, as we shall see in the pages of this book, an *alter deus*.[141] As Puttenham's *Art of English Poesy* and Sidney's *Apology for Poetry* reveal, by the late sixteenth century poetic theory and Hermetic 'chymistry' had become thoroughly intertwined.

Puttenham is probably thinking not only of Hermes Trismegistus – 'the holiest of priests and prophets' in his estimation (1, 8, p. 112) – when he utters these words, but also about his successors in a chain of prophets (including Orpheus, Homer, Plato and Virgil) who encoded 'holy mysteries' into their writings:

Poets therefore are of great antiquity ... And so were the first priests and ministers of the holy mysteries ... and in continual study and contemplation, they came by instinct divine, and by deep meditation and much abstinence (the same assubtiling and refining their spirits) to be made apt to receive visions both waking and sleeping, which made them utter prophecies. (Puttenham, *Art of English Poesy*, 1, 3, pp. 96–7)

'Study', 'contemplation', 'deep meditation', the 'assubtiling and refining their spirits' are aspects of the craft of inner alchemy which, as I shall demonstrate at length in Chapter 5, was construed as producing an especially finely honed eye of the mind, able, in a state of ecstatic *furor*, to link up with the Divine Mind – crucial to prophetic visions and the production of textual and (eventually) actual golden worlds. Following the model of God, the divine alchemist, the poet can regenerate and 'mend Nature' (inner and outer) and thus help reverse the ravages of the Fall. This philosophy underpins Milton's assertion, 'the end then of Learning is to repair the ruines of our first Parents by regaining to know God aright, and out of that knowledge to love him, to imitate him, to be like him' and Donne's in his famous sermon cited earlier in which God is an alchemist.[142] Wondrous transmutations could be achieved through working the metal of the mind-soul and 'metall'/'mettle' work was crucial to creativity: 'for man is but his mind, and as his mind is tempered and qualified, so are his speeches and language ... and his inward conceits be the metall of his minde'.[143] Thus you could judge the purity and subtlety of a man's soul by his writing.

Henry Reynolds' poetic treatise, *Mythomystes* (1632), registers the growing urgency associated with the 'refining' process as the seventeenth century increasingly experienced the tensions and divisions (indications of a corrupt world) that heralded the mid-century turmoil:

Wee live in a myste, blind and benighted; and since our first fathers disobedience poisoned himselfe and his posterity, Man is become the imperfectest and most deficient Animall of all the field; for then he lost that Instinct that the Beast retaines ... What concernes him now so nearly as to attend to the cultivating or refining, & thereby advancing of his rationall part, to the purchase & regaining of his lost felicity? And what meanes to conduce to this purchase can there bee, but the knowledge first, and love next ... of his Maker, for whose love and service he was only made. (*Mythomystes*)[144]

For Reynolds, the route to regeneration is clear: we must 'search for the knowledge of the wise and hidden wayes & workings of our God's hand-maid, Nature' and search the myths of the old poets to uncover veiled wisdom (p. 165):

So *Orpheus* within the foults and involvements of fables hid the misteries of his doctrine, and dissembled them under a poeticke maske, so as who reades those hymnes of his will not believe any thing to bee included under them but mere tales and trifles. Homer likewise, by the same mouth positively averred to have included, in his two Poems of Iliades and Odisses, all intellectual contemplation. (*Mythomystes*, pp. 156–7)

Reynolds reads the Greek myths in the manner of Maier, as allegories and riddles of abstruse Hermetic-alchemical knowledge (pp. 170–1). Intriguingly in this system the 'beautifull Ganimede they [the ancient poets] sing of'– the startlingly lovely boy who charmed Zeus and was transported up to heaven from where he sprinkles the earth with rain – becomes none other than 'the contemplation of the Soule, or the Rationall part of Man' and this is 'so deare to the God of gods and men, as that it raiseth it up to heaven, there to powre out to him (as they make him his cupbearer) the soveraigne Nectar of Sapience and wisdome' (*Mythomystes*, p. 152). Meanwhile, the key Orphic romance becomes an allegory of lost knowledge of divine Pythagorean mathematics:

And I am fully of opinion . . . that the Poets generally-sung fable of *Orpheus*, whom they faigne to have recovered his *Euridice* from Hell with his Musick, that is, Truth and Equity from darkenesse of Barbarisme and Ignorance with his profound and excellent Doctrines; but that in the thicke caliginous way to upper-earth, she was lost againe, and remaines lost to us that read and understand him not, for want merely of the knowledge of that Art of Numbers that should unlocke and explane his Mysticall meanings to us. (*Mythomystes*, p. 159)

Reynolds traces a line through 'those old wise Ægyptian Priests', who searched out 'the Misteries of Nature (which was at first the whole world's only divinity)' and recorded them in 'certaine marks and characters of things . . . which markes they called Hieroglyphicks or sacred gravings . . . and in mysticall riddles', through Homer (who 'included, in his two Poems of Iliades and Odisses, all intellectual contemplation', pp. 156–7), Pythagoras and Plato to the Renaissance 'Picus' – Pico della Mirandola. Importantly, he maintains that it is crucial that these 'high and Mysticall matters should by riddles and enigmaticall knots be kept inviolate from the prophane Multitude' (p. 156). Renaissance alchemy certainly prized its elitism and enigmatic riddles. No wonder, then, that Sidney tantalizingly claimed in his poetic treatise, 'these arguments wil by fewe be understood' (*Apology*, vol. 1, p. 157) – they were accessible only to a charmed circle of initiates, those, we might assume, like Shakespeare's 'private friends' (alluded to by Meres) who had privileged access to his 'sugred Sonnets'.[145] Or, indeed, like the 'Sometime . . . blusterer, that the ruffle knew / Of court, of city' – the 'reverend man' who haunts the pages of *A Lovers Complaint*, listening, and apparently trying (in the same manner as its baffled readers) to decipher the meaning of the 'afflicted fancy' before him who is notably tearing up letters 'sealed to curious secrecy' (see lines 57–70, 49). Coterie poetry demanded active readers with privileged knowledge; its difficulty and exclusivity was part of its appeal.

As we shall see throughout this book, within the Hermetic-aesthetic scheme the poet is the mercurial conjoiner of antitheses, his 'strong imagination' is the 'glue' linking earth and heavens through a tissue of metaphors and networks of correspondences. Thus, in Theseus' words:

> The poet's eye, in a fine frenzy rolling,
> Doth glance from heaven to earth, from earth to heaven,
> And as imagination bodies forth
> The forms of things unknown, the poet's pen
> Turns them to shapes.   (*A Midsummer Night's Dream*, v. i. 12–16)

This is why Gabriel Harvey refers to the 'stirring witt' of the poet as a 'quintessence of quicksilver' and proclaims particularly of 'Petrarcks verse': it is that of 'a fine lover, that learneth of Mercury to exercise his fairest giftes in a faire subject, & teacheth Wit to be inamored upon Beautye, as Quicksilver embraseth gold ... [and] to make arte more excellent by contemplation of excellentest Nature'.[146] While the 'good poet' spends much time in 'sollid contemplative studies' (inner alchemy), his opposite, the producer of 'ingenious Nothings', is likened to one of Geber's cooks 'that the world swarmes with ... like sophisticate alchemy gold' (*Mythomystes*, pp. 154–5) – false fool's gold. For the 'good' philosopher harnessing the 'divine power of the spirit' in alliance with 'imagination', passionate extremes are contained by the sonnet's 'closes' and 'wrought into an Orbe of order and forme' which is pleasing to 'nature':

For the body of our imagination being as an unformed *chaos* without fashion, without day, if by the divine power of the spirit it be wrought into an Orbe of order and forme, is it not more pleasing to nature, that desires a certaintie and comports not with that which is infinite, to have these closes, rather than not to know where to end, or how farre to goe, especially seeing our passions are often without measure? (Samuel Daniel, *A Defence of Rhyme, c.* 1603)[147]

We might connect this 'orbe' with John Donne's 'well wrought urne' (line 33) of 'The Canonization', a poem much informed by the 'Phoenix riddle' – the alchemical philosopher's stone.

This is the intellectual climate that nurtured the sonnet sequences of Giordano Bruno and Sir Philip Sidney. It is unclear which collection was written first but Bruno's, *De gli eroici furori* (*The Heroic Frenzies*, 1585), alluded to earlier and dedicated to Sir Philip Sidney, is a densely theosophical work thoroughly informed by Hermeticism that proclaims itself modelled on Solomon's *Song of Songs* which, 'under the guise of lovers and ordinary passions contains similarly divine and heroic frenzies, as the mystics and cabbalistic doctors interpret' ('Dedication', p. 62). As I shall unravel in Chapter 3, Bruno read the *Song of Songs* as a veiled record of spiritual experience and, in his sequence, the nine 'blinded' lovers can be restored to sight only by the soul-regenerating cure of Hermes. Sidney's *Astrophil and Stella* is a very different, much more playful, traditional Petrarchan endeavour that, as we shall see in Chapter 5, appears to dialogue with the creations of the foremost poets 'making' under the auspices of the French Academy. Sidney certainly uses an abundance of alchemical imagery to describe Astrophil's unrequited desire for 'Phoenix Stella':

> When sorrow, using mine own fire's might,
> Melts down his lead into my boiling breast,
> Through that dark furnace to my heart oppressed
> There shines a joy from thee, my only light.   (Sonnet 108)[148]

Here the motifs of creative 'metall' work are used superficially as simple embellishment. Shakespeare does something extraordinarily novel and exciting: he takes us deep inside the shadowy alchemical 'making' mind – the poet's head becomes his theatre.

CHAPTER 2

Lovely boy

PART I LOVE, MARRIAGE AND ALCHEMICAL PROCREATION

A year before *Shake-speares Sonnets* was published, a highly popular book of love emblems was launched into the European marketplace – Otto Vaenius's *Amorum Emblematum* (Antwerp, 1608). This magnificent tri-lingual edition testifies to a fashion for 'erotic polyglottism' that reached its apogee in the first decade of the seventeenth century.[1] In his study of the emblem tradition, John Manning suggests that this and other works point to 'a whole linguistic universe ruled by Love' and characterized by 'interconnectedness' in the form of 'visual and verbal puns and textures'.[2] This was not restricted to emblem books: philosophical treatises, pub-lished letters, spiritual manuals, plays and poetry were among the texts participating in a web of cross-fertilizing conversations and tropes con-nected by love. To try to separate out sacred and profane love in this context – an exercise that modern commentators are prone to undertake – is a hazardous enterprise. George Herbert's wonderful poem 'Love III', in which Love-Christ is suggestively a prostitute while the poet-speaker is cast as a client, indicates that, in the first half of the seventeenth century, sex and the sacred could share the same poetic bed.[3] Certainly, the rhetorical vogue for playing seriously (*serio ludere*) frequently involved manipulating love in many guises and it is this cultural-aesthetic envi-ronment that gave birth to the sonnets' most highly charged erotic creations – lovely boy and black beauty. By resituating *Shake-speares Sonnets* firmly in the midst of the turn of the seventeenth-century 'theatrical erotomachia' – at the heart of which was a lexicon of Hermetic Neoplatonism – I aim to re-engage with the spiritual thread running through the sequence, dispelling the often reiterated myth about the entirely secular character of the sonnets.[4] This chapter dem-onstrates that the sonnet-speaker's plea – 'Let not my love be called

57

idolatry' (Sonnet 105) – deserves to be taken more seriously. It is with the alchemical 'conjunction' – or 'marriage' – that I begin.

The chemical marriage

Out of man and woman make a round circle … and you will have the philosopher's stone. (*The Rosary*)[5]

There is no term in more frequent use among the philosophers than is the word Marriage. They say that the Sun and the Moon must be joined in marriage together … The union between the Fixed and the Volatile, which takes place in the Vase by the intermediation of Fire. All seasons are fitting for the celebration of this marriage, but the Philosophers especially recommend spring as that period when Nature is most impelled to generation. (Ruland, *A Lexicon*, 1612)[6]

It is a commonplace of Shakespearean criticism that his sonnets begin rather oddly with the poet-speaker urging the beautiful youth to marry. There is, however, an important cultural analogue for this. Otto Vaenius's celebrated book of love emblems, which was notably dedicated to 'the most honorable, and woorthie brothers, William Earle of Penbroke, and Philip Earle of Montgomerie', opens with 'Cupids epistle to the yonger sorte' and the latter wittily deploys a key alchemical image to promote marriage and procreation:[7]

> Do all well know & fynd what thing it is to love,
> The Salamander doth not leave deer loves desire,
> Since I it do conserve with him admiddes the fyre,
> Behold the Sun and Moon, resembling man and wyf,
> How they remain in head in love and lasting lyf
> By whose conjunction all what men on earth do fynd,
> Are both produc'd & kept in nowriture & kind
>
> . . .
>
> What man then may hee seem which liveth still alone,
> Unjoyn'd unto a wyf which maketh two in one?[8]

In the alchemical lexicon, the Salamander is the sulphurous masculine seed of metals and as it burns in the alchemist's fire it multiplies or procreates.[9] The preface continues to urge its marriage theme with arguments that resonate with Shakespeare's sonnets – 'His being borne anew, hee in his children sees'; 'That him immortall makes, so that hee ever lives' – and familiar graphic warnings about the ageing process:

> When thy faire frilled heare set up and pleated brave,
> To greynesse shalbe turn'd, or that thow baldnesse have,

> When furrowes overspred the forehead of thy face,
> Then mayst thow rue thy yeares lost in sweet loves disgrace.

(Preface n.p.)

Among the themes expounded by the emblems that follow are 'love blyndeth' (pp. 60–1), 'love had never foul mistres' (p. 217), 'Love liveth by fyre' (p. 289) and 'loves fyre is unquenchable':

> No water slakes loves heat, but makes his fyre to flame,
> Cupids hart-burning fyre, makes water for to burne,
> By coldness hee doth cause encreasing heates returne.

(pp. 170–1)

These lines resonate with those of the *Song of Solomon* – 'Love is strong as death . . . a vehement flame. Much water cannot quench love' (Saloman's Song, VIII: 6) – which also reverberate in Shakespeare's final sonnet ('Love's fire heats water; water cools not love', 154).[10] In Vaenius's book, too, we find emblems celebrating friendship – 'one soul in two bodies', 'the end of love is that two might become one' and 'love is not perfect unless [directed] towards one' (pp. 2–3). God is Love, Cupid is a divine child, sometimes a distiller stoking secret fires of desire in this volume, in which Ciceronian friendship discourses, allusions to biblical texts, divine mathematics, the baroque fiery hearts of Counter-Reformation treatises of meditation, as well as occasional witty lasciviousness, converge around a Ficinian Neoplatonism rich with alchemical symbolism – the terrain of Shakespeare's much more complex sonnet sequence.

Read in this light, Shakespeare's first seventeen sonnets urging the youth to marry would not have seemed so strange around 1609: the preface to Vaenius's popular book – which linked marriage to the alchemical 'conjunctio' – had provided an accessible precedent for this. Neither would the poet-speaker's desire to become one with his male friend, linked to his claim in Sonnet 105 that his love is not idolatrous, have seemed as blasphemous to the sonnets' initial coterie readership as it does to some commentators today. 'A marriage of true minds' leading, ultimately, 'To one' (Sonnet 105) – God – is the suggested aim of the speaker's erotic relation with the beautiful youth.[11] This does not, however, imply the absence of same-sex desire or preclude a constant play of bawdy wit throughout the sonnets: ribald and spiritual meanings rub shoulders in the sonnets. However, in terms of the network of discourses in which the sonnets are operating, genital 'erections' should, by the stage of physical maturity, have been re-directed from men to women. Ficino's *De amore* is explicit on this point: 'It should have been noticed that the purpose of erections of the genital part is not the useless act of ejaculation, but the function of fertilizing and procreating; the part should have been re-directed from males to females' (p. 135).

Michel de Montaigne's widely read essay 'Of Friendship' is notably voluble on the distinctions between marriage 'concluded to other ends' and love between men:

> Friendship is enjoyed according as it is desired, it is neither bred, nor nourished, nor increaseth but in jouissance, as being spirituall, and the minde being refined by use and custome ... Concerning marriage besides that it is a covenant which hath nothing free but the entrance, the continuance being forced and restrained ... a match ordinarily concluded to other ends ... To speake truly ... the ordinary sufficiency of women, cannot answer this conference and communication, the nurse of this sacred bond. ('Of Friendship')[12]

Women are imagined as simply not up to the 'sacred' intellectual task: while marriage is necessary to produce material offspring, spiritual procreation is the sole preserve of men. Montaigne quotes Cicero, 'Love is an endevour of making friendship, by the shew of beautie' (vol. 1, p. 201) and proceeds, 'In the amitie I speake of, they entermixe and confound themselves one in the other, with so universall a commixture, that they weare out, and can no more finde the seame that hath conjoined them together' (vol. 1, p. 201). According to Montaigne, such intense desire to blend with a male friend feeds and 'refines' the soul; it is 'a general and universall heat' – a fire (vol. 1, p. 198). In the early modern period, male friendship discourses were a particularly rich site of creative improvisation and, at the turn of the seventeenth century, they were often erotic – an eroticism that could be heightened by a play of alchemical language which, while appearing overtly sexual (copulation and incest were, for example, alchemical terms), actually refers to the spiritual domain: 'the desire of a spiritual conception engendred in the beloved' (vol. 1, p. 200).[13] Montaigne had set a trend in this direction; his love for Etienne de La Boetie culminates in passionate copulation or spiritual union producing 'quintessence': 'It is I wot not what kinde of quintessence, of all this commixture, which having seized my will, induced the same to plunge and lose it selfe in his' (vol. 1, p. 202). In the same vein in 1588, Thomas Churchyard's *A Sparke of Friendship* declared, 'friendship is ... the onely true love knot, that knits in conjunction [a key alchemical term], thousands together'.[14]

As many scholars have noted in recent years, the humanists' rallying cry, *ad fontes* (back to sources), certainly meant – for some – an imitation of ancient Greek and Roman homoeroticism, as expressed in writing at least.[15]

We should recall at this point how the circulation of Shakespeare's sonnets was comparatively restricted ('among his private friends');[16] witty and erotic male friendship discourses would certainly have flourished within this coterie context and, furthermore, they were associated with pronounced literary experimentation. *Churchyard's Challenge* interestingly represents 'Minde', which collapses into 'Imagination', alchemically, as a type of fiery furnace, a conflagration that 'must needes burne or consume any thing that long remaines in it'.[17] These are, of course, also similar to baroque religious images (the fiery furnace of the heart-soul where memory images were once thought to reside) but they are being deployed here to pay homage to the imagination: 'A Man is but his Minde', *Churchyard's Challenge* proclaims (sig. G3v).[18] Such texts are illuminating of the immense intellectual excitement about mind and creativity that was flourishing in the closing decades of the sixteenth century, fuelled by the French academies' developments of Neoplatonism and by the faith increasingly being invested in the powers of the transformative alchemical mind.

There was another important continental precedent for the philosophical drift of Shakespeare's sonnets: the Italian poet Benivieni – a contemporary of Ficino in the Florentine academy – had adapted the substance of the latter's *De amore*, producing 154 sonnets known as *Canzona della Amore Celeste et Divino*. We know that Pico's commentary on these circulated in translation in French intellectual circles in the late sixteenth century (it was printed in 1572 and 1601), together with a new translation of Ficino's *De amore*;[19] certainly, the ferment associated with these reached England: as mentioned earlier, Ben Jonson owned a copy of the latter.[20] We have seen how Sir Philip Sidney incorporated alchemical motifs into his sonnets to illustrate his relatively conventional English Petrarchan conceits. The literary challenge for Shakespeare around 1600 was – as the poet repeatedly reminds us (in Sonnets 76 and 108, for example) – how to recycle the old words and tropes to create something new, and the combination of Ficinian Neoplatonism and spiritual alchemy – so closely linked to the operations of the creative imagination at this point – enabled him to do so.

His sonnets give us 'Mind' 'in character', and, as in Montaigne's *Essays*, it is a fragmented mind in motion seeking unity – growing, creating, transforming. Furthermore, the intertwined discourses of Ficinian Neoplatonism and alchemy enabled Shakespeare to create a heated emotional drama that focuses its lens out and in, up and down, on material and immaterial bodies or ones which seem to be both male and female at the same time. Chemical transmutations notably blur distinctions, refuse boundaries: alchemy's entire drive is to unite contraries, to make the material spiritual and the spiritual material, to link bodies with bodies, souls with souls, and heaven with earth – to strive for 'oneness'. This is why the 'conjunctio', 'chemical wedding' or 'marriage' (synonymous terms) is the key term in the alchemical process. It is also why Shakespeare's lovely boy is able, potentially, to be William Herbert or the Earl of Southampton; a distillation of many lovers, both male and female; an aspect of the speaker's mind and God; or a creative synthesis of them all. Indeed, the furnace of our poet's alchemical 'head' (another name for the distilling apparatus in alchemy) excels at distilling a quintessence of unity from multiplicity.[21] Sonnets 53 and 108 are particularly suggestive in this respect:

> What is your substance, wherof are you made,
> That millions of strange shadows on you tend?
>
> (Sonnet 53, 1–2)

> What's in the brain that ink may character,
> Which hath not figured to thee my true spirit?
> What's new to speak, what new to register,
> That may express my love, or thy dear merit?
> Nothing, sweet boy; but yet, like prayers divine,
> I must each day say o'er the very same,
> Counting no old thing old, thou mine, I thine,
> Even as when first I hallowed thy fair name.
>
> (Sonnet 108, 1–8)

Passages like this one from Sonnet 108 have been described as 'the idolatrous substitution of friend worship for Christian worship', but, read from within the philosophical contexts outlined above, friend worship is not distinct from divine worship.[22] On the contrary, it is *the* route to ultimate spiritual fulfilment – refinement of the soul culminating in 'oneing' with Christ. Undoubtedly, this is the inspiration behind the 'wondrous excellence' (6) and 'One thing expressing' (8) of Shakespeare's famously enigmatic Sonnet 105, which invokes the Trinity and begins 'Let not my love be called idolatry' (as though to head off misinterpretation of the sonnets through too literal reading). In fact, Shakespeare's first 126 sonnets inscribe the conjoining and procreative phase of this process as a heated drama taking place in the alembic of the poet-speaker's 'head' – the stage of the mind – and the alchemical *opus* always begins with 'marriage': 'Make a circle around man and woman, then a square, now a triangle; make a circle, and you will have the Philosopher's Stone' (see Fig. 3, Emblem 21, *Atalanta Fugiens*).[23]

We should recall that the whole operation of the alchemical *opus* was aimed at recapturing man's 'Adamic' undivided state of wholeness and this necessitated an initial 'conjunctio' of opposites – of male and female, Sol and Luna, Sulphur and Mercury, fixed and volatile, form and matter – through their dissolution and blending by fire in the alchemist's alembic or 'head'.[24] Metaphysically, the chemical marriage symbolized the union of male and female qualities to produce pure love – the new birth, the stone.[25] Furthermore, Ficinian Neoplatonism construed this as absolutely crucial to the artist's powers ('artists in all of the arts seek and care for nothing else but love').[26] The chemical 'marriage' was, as we have established, a key symbol of alchemy and, by commencing his sonnet sequence with a repetitive call to the male beloved to beget an heir through union with his female opposite, Shakespeare was undoubtedly signalling the alchemical trajectory of his sequence: a trajectory which is gradually reinforced through an accretion of suggestive images. The 'Rose' (emblem of the philosopher's stone – capitalized and italicized in the 1609 quarto as Dympna Callaghan points out),[27] 'flame' and 'fuel' of Sonnet 1, though conventional Petrarchan emblems of love, point the 'wise' reader in the right direction, but with the introduction in Sonnets 4 and 5 of the two most important protagonists (aside from the mercurial poet) in the 'theatre' of the alembic – Nature and Time – together with the striking image of the lover pent up and 'distilled' in a 'sweet … vial' in Sonnet 6 (recalling the surreal illustrations found in alchemical emblem books), any lingering doubts begin to disappear.

Furthermore, rhetorical and grammatical manoeuvres throughout the sonnets enact crucial alchemical 'conjunctios'. On the latter note, we should recall Norton's instruction, 'Conjoyne your Elements Grammatically'; 'Joyne them also in Rhetoricall guise' (*Ordinall*, pp. 59, 60) and ponder afresh Shakespeare's balanced antithetical lines and half lines, which work obsessively throughout the sequence to connect opposites and confound bifurcations: contraries meet to form one endlessly and often paradoxically in his sequence. As Helen Vendler has noted, antithesis is 'Shakespeare's major figure for constructing the world in the sonnets' and the poet allowed these 'to breed and bring to birth a third thing' – a very suggestive observation in relation to my alchemical reading of the sonnets.[28] We should consider, too, Shakespeare's frequent use of connecting figures such as *zeugma* (where a word common to two clauses is inserted in only one); and *hendiadys* (where two nouns are fused to produce a mysterious unity) and his apparent odd compulsion to use *chiasmus* – a figure much commented on by critics – which, as we shall see, in its forward and recursive, doubling back action, perfectly captures the rhythm of alchemical time ('time which gives, takes away'). Alchemical movement is notably not straightforward; rather, it flows forth and ebbs back: 'Like as the waves make towards the pebbled shore' (Sonnet 60, 1). As this sonnet suggests, any progress is hard won and precarious: 'And Time that gave doth now his gift confound' (8).

But, before I proceed further to unravel the alchemical thread woven with such skill throughout Shakespeare's richly textured sequence, the sonnets' pronounced eternalizing theme requires further consideration.

Progeny of the soul and immortality

What is the love of men, you ask? What purpose does it serve? It is the desire for procreation with a beautiful object in order to make eternal life available to mortal things. (Ficino, *De amore*, p. 130)

> And nothing 'gainst Time's scythe can make defence
> Save breed to brave him when he takes thee hence.
>
> (Sonnet 12, 13–14)

The speaker's quest to persuade his beautiful Muse to marry and beget a child seems to be flagging by Sonnet 12: we hear yet again that the 'wastes of time' loom unless the reluctant youth 'breed[s] to brave him' – to outdo personified Time with his scythe. Then a new theme interrupts the constant haranguing and a strange note of optimism emerges:

> But from thine eyes my knowledge I derive,
> And, constant stars, in them I read such art
> As truth and beauty shall together thrive
> If from thyself, to store thou wouldst convert.
>
> (Sonnet 14, 9–12)

This would be a conventional Petrarchan conceit if it were addressed to a female beloved, but it is not. In fact, Platonism re-engages here with homoerotic desire in a startlingly uncorrupted way – this is daring humanistic *ad fontes* and it is certainly a refreshing alternative to the remote woman worship we encounter in Sidney, for example. The above lines benefit from re-examination in the light of Diotima's instruction to Socrates rendered here by Ficino:

Then from that body of a younger man it shines out, especially through the eyes, the transparent windows of the soul. It flies onward, through the air, and penetrating the eyes of an older man, pierces his soul, kindles his appetite, then leads the wounded soul and the kindled appetite to their healing and cooling, respectively, while it carries them with it to the same place from which it had itself descended, step-by-step indeed, first to the body of the beloved, second, to the Soul, third to the angel, and finally to God, the first origin of this splendor. (Ficino, *De amore*, p. 126)

According to the guide Diotima, just as the human body can become pregnant, so the soul can procreate, and both are stimulated to childbearing by the incitements of love. But some, 'either by nature or by education, are better fitted for progeny of the soul than of the body, and others, certainly the majority, the opposite. The former follow heavenly love, the latter, vulgar' (Ficino, *De amore*, p. 135). Our poet-speaker seems to have been partly reflecting on such a division as early as Sonnet 11:

> Let those whom Nature hath not made for store,
> Harsh, featureless and rude, barrenly perish.
> Look whom she best endowed she gave the more,
> Which bounteous gift thou shouldst in bounty cherish.
> She carved thee for her seal.   (9–13)

'Seal' is an interesting word here because in the Renaissance it could denote a memory image, and inner, as well as outer, nature is being invoked in this context. Repeated calls for the well-endowed youth to marry appear to have fallen on deaf ears but all is far from lost. It seems that intellectual, heavenly procreation suggests itself to our philosophical poet: the vision of the beautiful youth affects his eyes, kindling his 'appetite', and pondering examples from nature provokes contemplation about memory, its enemy, Time, and a peculiar remedy, grafting:

> When I perceive that men as plants increase,
> Cheered and checked even by the self-same sky,
> Vaunt in their youthful sap, at height decrease,
> And wear their brave state out of memory;
> Then the conceit of this inconstant stay
> Sets you most rich in youth before my sight,
> Where wasteful time debateth with decay
> To change your day of youth to sullied night,
> And, all in war with Time for love of you,
> As he takes from you, I engraft you new.   (Sonnet 15, 5–14)

The youth's image is being newly 'engraft[ed]' but not – as editors usually suggest – solely in the speaker's lines; he is being inscribed and stored in memory too as a 'seal'. Hence by Sonnet 122 we hear:

> Thy gift, thy tables, are within my brain
> Full charactered with lasting memory,
> Which shall above the idle rank remain
> Beyond all date even to eternity.   (1–4)

Indeed, as we shall see in Chapter 5, without memory there can be no poetry, and it is through memory and the eye of the mind that the realm of eternal truths – 'Ideas' and heavenly 'store' – is accessed. The quest to achieve immortality is a constant theme of the sonnets, and memory is definitely implicated. Diotima's instruction to Socrates in the *Symposium* is helpful here. She explains that, when the senses together with the 'power of the soul' look at 'the images of bodies', it gives birth to representations 'like them but much purer still': this is called imagination or fantasy. These are stored in memory and

> By these the eye of the soul is often aroused to contemplate the universal Ideas of things which it contains in itself. And for this reason at the same time that the soul is perceiving a certain man in sensation, and conceiving him in the imagination, it can contemplate, by means of the intellect, the reason and definition common to all men through its innate Idea of humanity; and what it has contemplated, it preserves. (*De amore*, p. 115)

Crucially, intellectual memory is not mortal – it can be accessed by the soul after the body's death, but no new memories can be made without the body. The accretion of heavenly 'store', such as we encounter in Spenser's eulogy to Sidney – 'He now is dead, and all is with him dead, / Save what in heaven's storehouse he uplaid' (*The Ruines of Time*, 1591, lines 211–12) – requires considerable attention in life, then, if the bourn that we all have to cross at death is not to be a terrifyingly blank intellectual space.[29] In life, meanwhile, memory work can reconnect us with divine light and 'the One' – with the immortal inscriptions that are clouded, stained and unable to be clearly deciphered by the post-Fall eye of the mind. A passage in Mary Carruthers' seminal study of memory interpreting Thomas Aquinas' *socius'* description of Aquinas' spiritual ascent is illuminating; Carruthers explains: 'Desire begins the ascent to understanding by firing memory, and through memory's stored-up treasures the intellect is able to contemplate; the higher its understanding, the more desire flames in love as it both gets and gives more light.'[30]

As noted in my Introduction, 'store' is an unusually frequent word in the sonnets and in Shakespeare's time it had close associations with memory work: trained memory was a 'treasury', an 'orderly moneybag', a store of intellectual as contrasted with material wealth.[31] In Shakespeare true riches are memory seals 'imprisoned' in the heart ('chest'): 'So am I as the rich, whose blessed key / Can bring him to his sweet up-locked treasure' (Sonnet 52, lines 1–2). As we shall see in the second part of this chapter, the poet's 'eternal numbers' – his deployment of divine geometry – function in relation to achieving immortality.

DISTILLING BEAUTY

Blunting the lion's paws

Devouring Time, blunt thou the lion's paws,
And make the earth devour her own sweet brood,
Pluck the keen teeth from the fierce tiger's jaws,
And burn the long-lived phoenix in her blood.

(Sonnet 19, 1–4)

Shakespeare's Sonnet 15 has signalled that the memory's 'grafting' and preservation process is underway and Sonnet 19's accretion of bizarre symbols confirms that this is being envisioned and presented as an alchemical process. The alchemical book dedicated to 'serious pleasure' mentioned in my introduction, François Beroalde de Verville's *Le Tableau des riches inventions* (Paris, 1600) (see Fig. 1, p. 40), provides insight into Shakespeare's enigmatic Sonnet 19. We should recall that among other alchemical symbols on its title page we find a lion with its paws cut off, top left (symbol of sulphur, which has fixed volatile mercury); an eagle-phoenix (symbol of 'Philosophick Mercury'); a fire sprouting a tree of life (equivalent to the phoenix or philosopher's stone); an hour glass (indicating the need for both time and patience); and myrtle branches growing in all directions (signifying that the origin, cause and end of all things is Love).[32] Its author tantalizingly warns that its rich inventions are 'covered with the veil of amorous deceits'.[33] Lovers kissing, copulating, dying in a fiery conflagration and rising anew in one hermaphrodite form are the key recurring 'amorous deceits' of these alchemical volumes (see Fig. 5). As the scholar of Platonism, Ronald Gray, has highlighted, sixteenth-century alchemists thought nothing of combining explicit sexual images with Christian beliefs.[34]

Read against the backdrop of these engravings, even the surreal images of Shakespeare's particularly perplexing Sonnet 19 resonate with meaning. Time (who, as Saturn, devoured his own children) is being invoked to assist sulphur (the lion) in the process of fixing mercury. The tiger probably alludes to the acid added to the alchemist's alembic, which gradually 'loses its teeth' or abates as it aids the dissolution or devouring of the distinct, male and female raw 'materia' into a chemical soup from which the refined new hermaphrodite birth will emerge.[35] The poet is having immense fun here

playing seriously with these highly evocative arcane images; to try to pin
down the exact meaning of each of them is actually a rather foolish pursuit
(alchemical symbols are remarkably labile and ambiguous). In this context
they refer, of course, to psychic, imaginative transformations: the emblems
of exoteric alchemy are being deployed to figure an inner process. Together
they confirm that an *opus circulatorium* is in progress and through the poet's
mercurial mind (the adept's head is his 'still') he will 'distil' and thus
preserve 'beauty's pattern' for eternity – in intellectual memory and in his
verse. A successful alchemical *opus*, producing the quintessence, philosopher's stone, or phoenix was also imagined as a route to eternal youth:

The Adepts assure us that it is possible not only to prolong life, but also to renew
youth. To renew youth is to enter once again into that beautiful season when the
forces of our being were at the spring and freshness of early power. Paracelsus, by
means of his celebrated Mercury of Life, claimed to metamorphose an old into a
young man. (Ruland, *Lexicon*, p. 441)

To achieve his goal, the philosopher-alchemist had to imitate nature,
labouring, with her assistance, to distil and 'store' beauty's 'essence' because
the soul must be 'pregnant with ideal Beauty' before the secrets of the art
could be accessed.[36] This was a process that necessitated patience, time and
toil but which, paradoxically, was simultaneously opposed by Time
(Saturn) and his scythe. Saturn was also the base metal (the darkened
soul) from which gold was extracted. In order for beauty's essence to be
distilled, the beloved must, as Sonnet 5 rather disturbingly asserts, become
'A liquid prisoner pent in walls of glass' (the alembic) – the visual equivalent
of being locked in the poet's mind. The alchemist-poet – needing time but
at war with time – labours to 'give life' to his beloved in 'eternal lines'
(Sonnet 18) and 'flowers distilled' (Sonnet 5); the latter was a common term
for memory images.[37] In terms of the imaginative system of alchemy, the
chemical wedding does not necessitate a direct union, but is facilitated by a
third mediating principle – the mercurial poet – who 'ties the knot at the
wedding'.[38] With the fixing of volatile mercury in Sonnet 19, considerable
progress is signalled and the triumphant note of Sonnet 20 registers success:
'beauty' is now an alchemical fusion of male and female qualities. The
operations of the poet's 'head' have produced a hermaphrodite (also called
Mercurius in alchemy) – the wondrous master mistress of the poet's
'passion'/Passion. Both ribald and spiritual meanings are in play in
Sonnet 20: this constitutes, I wish to suggest, a hermeneutic contest over
ways of seeing; while the vulgar reader will only be aware of the erotic
inference, the tutored gaze of the philosopher will uncover greater riches.

MASTER MISTRESSES AND ALCHEMICAL HERMAPHRODITES

Then I have read somewhere, that man and woman
Were, in the first creation, both one piece,
And being cleft asunder, ever since
Love was an appetite to be rejoined.
                              (Jonson, *The New Inn*, 1629, III. ii. 78–81)[39]

While Duncan-Jones has presented a strong case for the identity of Shakespeare's lovely boy being William Herbert,[40] Colin Burrow has countered that, while Herbert seems the strongest candidate for the Bard's male muse, it would, nevertheless, have been 'audacious beyond belief' for a published poem by a commoner to address an earl as 'the master mistress of my passion'.[41] The identification of lovely boy with the Earl of Pembroke, or, indeed, with the Earl of Southampton should be ruled out if this was the case. But would it have been completely beyond the sixteenth-century pale for an aristocrat to be addressed, in print, in these terms? I wish to suggest not, but to justify this I must amplify a range of contexts that might make it conceivable for one of lovely boy's 'shadows' to be a respectable earl and positively male-female too.

I begin with the reflection, above, of Ben Jonson's character, Beaufort, in *The New Inn*. The myth of origins he alludes to, involving bisexual first humans, would have been commonplace to Renaissance wits. Plato's *Symposium* contains a graphic account of our former plenitude which, furthermore, is explained as the source of all human desire. Aristophanes describes three genders of duplex humans – male-male (born from the sun), female-female (from the earth), and male-female (from the moon) – who were all split in half lengthwise by Jupiter, as if with an egg cutter, because they got above themselves and vied with the gods (Ficino, *De amore*, pp. 71–2). Ever since their splicing humans have pursued their other half, so that they might become whole again; desire was construed by Plato in terms that are familiar to us today – as loss and absence, a yearning for wholeness. Ficino's commentary on Plato's *Symposium* gives a notably Christian gloss to this: the desire to make one out of two 'inspires the highest hope in us who worship God piously, that by restoring us to our former condition and healing us He will make us most blessed' (*De amore*, p. 72). In typical syncretist fashion, Ficino's text proceeds further to fuse Plato's myth with Christian ideas (possibly derived from Aquinas) by reading it allegorically: 'Men, that is, the souls of men, formerly, that is, when they are created by God, are whole, they are provided with two lights, one innate and the other infused, in order that by the innate light they may perceive inferior and equal things, and by the infused, superior things' (*De amore*, p. 73).

In keeping with the spirit of such myths, arrogance and hubris prevailed with unfortunate effects: these well-endowed souls tried to equal God and by doing so they turned themselves towards the innate light alone. Hence they became divided; they shut out the crucial 'infused splendor' (p. 73). All was not totally lost, however; with growing maturity some men are aroused by their innate light 'to recover, through the study of truth, that infused and divine light, once half of themselves, which they lost in falling' (p. 73). Of course Ficino, following Plato, linked this with love between men – the desire to conjoin or fuse with a male friend is a desire for wholeness, for union with the divine.

In the Hermetic text *Poimandres*, God the father or 'mind' is notably 'androgyne and existing as life and light' and his earthly progeny are androgyne too (though man has to work to rekindle both aspects of himself).[42] As Ruth Herbert's study of hermaphroditism describes, Judaism also imagined a bisexual divinity and, in late medieval and early modern representations, Christ was often feminized – Jesus as mother, for example.[43] Furthermore, the 'chymical' physician Paracelsus referred to Adam as 'the true Hermaphrodite'.[44] This is why the hermaphrodite is a symbol of the developing philosopher's stone in spiritual alchemy (see Fig. 5). Perfection, wholeness, nearness to Christ, *is* the man-woman in this context: the ideal being is an integration of the best male-female qualities. This understanding enables us to throw light on a rather strange episode in Sidney's *Arcadia*, in which Pyrocles dresses up as an Amazonian warrior and, furthermore, proudly sports a brooch depicting a womanish Hercules bearing Omphale's distaff and the motto, 'Never more valiant'. This is meant to provoke amusement, but while the foolish reader will merely laugh, the wise Renaissance mind will find serious truth here and endorse Pyrocles's assertion that virtue is incomplete unless it enshrines male and female qualities: this is an example of the 'delightfull' teaching that is construed by Sidney's *Apology* as the end of poetry.[45] There is a popular emblem book source for this representation: Georg Pictor had depicted a feminized Hercules as simultaneously 'Hercules Imago' and 'Palladis Imago' in *Apotheoseos* (Basel, 1558)– interestingly, alchemical lore construed Hercules as an alchemist.[46] It is notable, too, that Spenser's *Faerie Queene* makes extensive use of hermaphrodites to represent spiritual harmony.

Such understanding was not lost on Renaissance princes looking to boost their standing and convince of their divinity. Both the French king François I and his son Henri II had propaganda images made of themselves in which they appear as transvestites. In 1545 Niccolo Bellin da Modena pictured François I (looking pregnant but brandishing a sword and wearing a helmet) as Mars, Minerva, Diane, Love and Mercury (as the inscription confirms) – an alchemical fusion of plenitude in unity.[47] Notoriously, too, Elizabeth I favoured an androgyne master mistress outfit when she went to address her troops at Tilbury on the eve of the Spanish Armada (proclaiming, too, that she had 'the heart and stomach of a man') and, as a phoenix (one of the key symbols in her emblematic portmanteau), she was the hermaphroditic philosopher's stone embodied. If the queen found such representations appealing and decorous, why, then, should her earls not aspire to be apprehended and represented artistically (especially by the most noted poet-dramatist of 1609) as androgyne perfection, as God-like artist's muses?[48] This is the lens through which we should view the rather angelic portrait in Hatchlands Park, East Clandon, long taken to be that of an anonymous woman but identified in 2002 as the Earl of Southampton.[49]

Allowing ourselves to re-associate a homoerotic transvestite domain with the divine, the sacred with playful profanity, we re-engage with a Renaissance wit's mindset around 1600. It is then possible to concede that the 'master mistress' (sovereign mistress) designation could conceivably be decorous and flattering, especially to an earl like Pembroke, whose family were known for their alchemical pursuits. However, lovely boy has many shadows, many forms, material and ethereal, and it would be against the spirit of this alchemical sequence to try to stabilize him and tie his identity down. In Sonnet 20 with its proliferation of feminine rhymes he *seems* a virtuous, 'gilding' hermaphrodite: master mistress's 'gaze' – his eyes – can confer gold (spiritual, alchemical gold) on the onlooker and he controls all hues – all colours of the spectrum (encountered in the 'chymical' laboratory?). Thomas Norton's *Ordinall* describes a stage in the *opus* in which 'the foure Elements wisely joined be' so that 'Colours will arise towards perfection' (p. 61): colour transformations were crucial for assessing the progress of the work. 'Hues' undoubtedly refers to rhetorical 'colours', too, but it also has a pertinent archaic meaning. In earlier times 'hue' meant 'he, she, and they' – it was a gender blurring term – so Sonnet 20's construction, 'all hues ... controlling', suggests master mistress's ability to influence everyone through his powers of eloquence.[50] He is, as we shall see, a very mercurial entity indeed and he is inside (as well as possibly outside) the poet's head.

Death, sun, eclipses and triumph

The poet's imaginative 'womb' has given birth to a hermaphrodite; crucially, however, the *opus* has really only just begun: a procreative cycle is under way but much painful 'work' is necessary to bring this 'child' to maturity. Time that gives, takes away: the 'conjunctio' mediated by the alchemist is actually a curious deathly embrace – the beloved object must be conjoined, die and be resurrected again and again from the ashes of the adept's 'head' for the philosopher's stone to be brought to fruition. Spiritually, this meant that the 'substance' of the soul had to be repeatedly dissolved and crystallized anew through intense meditation and prayer: luminosity demanded the painful integration of all the dark impulses of the soul.[51] In the alchemists' language, the 'womb' of generation inevitably becomes a 'grave', 'tomb' or 'prison' of decay and the workman must proceed to grapple with the mental torments of 'hell' – the dark phase or *Nigredo* of the cycle. As the adept Artephius explains, this was an essential phase in the cycle of purification: 'that which does not make black cannot make white, because blackness is the beginning of whiteness and a sign of putrefaction and alteration'.[52]

Shakespeare's sonnets are dense with the melancholic symbolism of the *Nigredo*. A gloomy litany of 'darkness', 'ghastly night' (Sonnet 27); 'oppression', 'clouds', 'grief' (Sonnet 28), 'bootless cries' (Sonnet 29) and 'sorrows' (Sonnet 30) ensues, and this is closely associated with memory seals ('Mine eye hath played the painter, and hath stelled / Thy beauty's form in table of my heart', Sonnet 24), inner looking ('sessions of sweet silent thought') and working the mind (Sonnet 27). This is sometimes spiritually uplifting: the beautiful youth's 'sweet love remembered' can transport the poet 'from sullen earth' to sing 'hymns at heaven's gate' (Sonnet 29). Such spiritual 'wealth' (store) is worth more than that of 'kings' (material store) and restores 'losses' (Sonnets 29, 30); it has soul-regenerating effects. This intense headwork is given pronounced alchemical expression in Sonnet 31:

> Thou art the grave where buried love doth live,
> Hung with the trophies of my lovers gone.   (9–10)

The memory seal of lovely boy is now a distillation of all his former lovers. There is, as Burrow comments, something curiously 'resurrective' as well as 'vampiric' in the way life appears to have been made from buried former loves in Sonnet 31.[53] The alchemical imagination can open a window of understanding on to why this is the case. The 'grave' was the alchemist's vessel during the *Nigredo* and it was of course here that the lovers (male sulphur and female mercury) were 'imprisoned', burnt and purified. Inevitably, this involves loss, as only one androgynous body can be resurrected from the fire. Sometimes in alchemical texts (as in Mylius's *Philosophia reformata*, 1622) the dead bodies are macabrely pictured in a coffin or tomb. In terms of psychic alchemy this corresponds to a graphic location in the memory store, the site of 'seals' of distilled beauty, which, like jewels 'hung in ghastly night', are precious beacons of hope as the productive focus of intense meditation and imaginative activity, which are spiritually regenerative. The speaker's designation of his inventive 'brain' as both 'tomb' and 'womb' of generation for his 'in-hearsed' 'ripe thoughts' (Sonnet 86) is, thus, alchemically inspired. Indeed, Shakespeare had employed this trope very effectively in the prison scene in *Richard II*: Richard's brain-womb peoples his cell with 'A generation of still breeding thoughts' (v. v. 6–9).

Our poet's confrontation with the dark side of his psyche is fortunately, however, rewarded by periodic brief glimpses of unclouded light, and in Sonnet 33 the speaker signals his productive inner alchemy by drawing an analogy with 'heavenly alchemy':

> Full many a glorious morning have I seen
> Flatter the mountain tops with sovereign eye,
> Kissing with golden face the meadows green,
> Gilding pale streams with heavenly alchemy,
> Anon permit the basest clouds to ride
> With ugly rack on his celestial face,
> And from the forlorn world his visage hide,
> Stealing unseen to west with this disgrace:
> Even so my sun one early morn did shine
> With all triumphant splendour on my brow;
> But out alack, he was but one hour mine,
> The region cloud hath masked him from me now.
> Yet him for this my love no whit disdaineth:
> Suns of the world may stain, when heaven's sun staineth.

(Sonnet 33)

'Sun' here is celestial and a unity in multiplicity: the sun that shines, Christ, lovely boy and the burgeoning philosopher's stone; it/he is also simultaneously the speaker's soul. Through repeated operations of the *opus*, his soul is being purified and cleansed of 'stains' enabling the alchemist to recapture the 'infused splendor' (Ficino, *De amore*, p. 73) of God: hence, 'triumphant splendour' shines 'on my brow'. In fact, 'stain' had a precise alchemical meaning: it was the unclean matter of the stone, which had to be purified in the philosophical fire.[54] A passage in Ficino's *De amore* that uses the same sun, cloud and stain metaphors serves to clarify and amplify this spiritual layer of meaning:

Now you comprehend in a measure the beauty of God, which excels other beauties at least as much as that light of the sun itself, pure, single, and inviolate, surpasses the splendor of the sun dispersed through the cloudy air, divided, stained, and obscured. Therefore the source of all beauty is God. Therefore the source of all love is God. (*De amore*, p. 140)

God is love, beauty, the sun and when the soul is turned toward God and 'illuminated by His ray', then, Ficino explains:

By the splendor of that ray, its appetite is increased. The whole of that increased appetite reaches out to God. As it reaches out it receives form. For God, who is omnipotent, imprints on the Mind, reaching out toward Him, the natures of things which are to be created ... These forms of all things, conceived in that celestial Mind, by a certain fomenting of God, we do not doubt are the Ideas. (*De amore*, p. 38)

This process of re-illumination culminates in access to immutable 'Ideas' but, 'alack', our speaker's ray of hope lasts only briefly; clouds of sin rapidly gather to 'stain' the sun. The alchemical *opus* we are witnessing still has a very long way to go: an implementation of 'goodwill' or 'kindness' is essential to dissolve the 'stains' of 'self-will'.[55] Most editors see only the sinful 'stains' of a material beloved in the last lines, but since the friends are one we should not – unless we wish to read anachronistically – rupture them apart or drive a wedge between the material and spiritual domains. In Ficinian Neoplatonism Christ is the source of all love and beauty and it is through erotic attraction to a beautiful male friend that men seek spiritual purification and union with the divine: as our poet puts it in Sonnet 101, 'Both truth and beauty on my love depends'.

Our alchemist-poet continues to make slow, painful progress. In Sonnet 45 we find that the alchemist's elements have 'separated' (see Ripley's 'gates' in my Introduction): 'slight air' and 'purging fire' have been separated from earth and water. Eventually the 'blessed shape' of Adonis-Helen in Sonnet 53 is surely a 'triumph' of luminosity: perfect androgynous beauty is now 'stilled' and 'stored' – a 'trophy' to the alchemist's art. But, as we learn in Sonnet 54, distillation must begin again immediately and tinctured 'truth' is now the goal.

DISTILLING TRUTH

The mercurial sea

Like as the waves make towards the pebbled shore,
So do our minutes hasten to their end,
Each changing place with that which goes before,
In sequent toil all forwards do contend.
Nativity, once in the main of light,
Crawls to maturity, wherewith being crowned
Crooked eclipses 'gainst his glory fight,
And Time that gave doth now his gift confound.

(Sonnet 60, 1–8)

'Like as the waves make towards the pebbled shore / . . . Each changing place with that which goes before' (Sonnet 60), the progress of the alchemical *opus* always incorporates erosive movement and counter-movement – both loss and hard won gain – and the latter is paradoxically facilitated by and yet obstructed by time. This spiralling movement back and forth is symbolized by the entwined serpents of Mercury's caduceus. Shakespeare's metaphors are particularly appropriate because mercurial water was known as the 'sea' which dissolved the base metals and nourished the infant stone which 'crawls to maturity', continually set back by 'Crooked eclipses': phases of putrefaction and death which, negative as they may seem, lead to new understanding and thus to 'growth'. This 'fight' for 'glory' – 'Nativity' (birth of the stone) – necessitated extreme concentration and sustained toil, and Sonnet 60 brilliantly captures the intensity, working energy and excitement of an obsessed, brow-mopping scientist who feels he is at last gaining ground and bringing something truly momentous to fruition; Mary Shelley's Dr Frankenstein springs to mind. The analogy is more appropriate than it may seem for, as in Frankenstein's case, the moral status of the projected 'birth' is not guaranteed. Thus Sonnet 93 anxiously reflects, 'How like Eve's apple doth thy beauty grow, / If thy sweet virtue answer not thy show', and Sonnet 94, 'Lilies that fester smell far worse than weeds'. The lily, like the rose, was an emblem of the philosopher's stone.

The evil still and spiritual illumination

As the *opus* 'crawls' haltingly but progressively forth, the poet-alchemist's 'distraction', 'fears' and 'hopes' reach 'fever' pitch:

> What potions have I drunk of siren tears,
> Distilled from limbecks foul as hell within,
> Applying fears to hopes, and hopes to fears,
> Still losing when I saw myself to win?   (Sonnet 119, 1–4)

'Tears' are literally the drops of moisture that condense at the top of the still and rain down upon the blackened body lying at the bottom of the alembic, cleansing it of its impurities. The foul medicine produced by the 'evil still' seems to have worked, however, for the sonnet concludes on a positive note, affirming, in true Christian fashion, the value or 'gains' of suffering:

> O benefit of ill: now I find true
> That better is by evil still made better,
> And ruined love when it is built anew,
> Grows fairer than at first, more strong, far greater.
>   (Sonnet 119, 9–12)

Spiritual improvement consequent upon torturous inner alchemy is registered in these lines and confirmed by Sonnet 124. The poet's 'dear love'

>   was builded far from accident,
> It suffers not in smiling pomp, nor falls
> Under the blow of thralled discontent,
> Whereto th'inviting time our fashion calls.
> It fears not policy, that heretic,
> Which works on leases of short-numb'red hours,
> But all alone stands hugely politic.   (Sonnet 124, 5–11)

Constancy and simplicity are now the essence of the speaker's love, and by Sonnet 125 it is clear that the body of his beloved has merged, mysteriously, with that of Christ:

> No, let me be obsequious in thy heart,
> And take thou my oblation, poor but free,
> Which is not mixed with seconds, knows no art,
> But mutual render, only me for thee.   (Sonnet 125, 9–12)

'Oblation' is the sacramental bread and wine offering to God and 'mutual render' refers to Christ's crucifixion and the Redemption of mankind. The echo from Leviticus 1: 13 ('it is a burnt offering, an oblation made by fire for a sweete savour unto the Lord') in the earlier line, 'For compound sweet forgoing simple savour' (line 7), is significant in this context: alchemical purifications were, of course, brought about through 'fire'. Has distilled 'truth' been captured? Certainly, the poet's desire for his 'lovely boy' beloved merges with and is even obscured by meditations on divine love in this group of sonnets. To the 'sensual' he has, indeed, brought in 'sense', as he promises in Sonnet 35. It would seem that two of the 'trinity' of Platonic virtues might have been harnessed – beauty and truth. The third, goodness or kindness, is, in fact, the preoccupation of the culminating twenty-eight sonnets.

To establish whether truth has been distilled we need not only to consider the mysterious short Sonnet 126 in depth but also to unravel the complex numerology, music and geometry woven into the sequence. If, as I have been arguing, Shakespeare is dramatizing the process of spiritual alchemy from inside the head (in his 'deep-brained sonnets', *A Lovers Complaint*), we should anticipate 'Eternal numbers' – divine mathematics.

PART II 'SUTTILL NUMBERS': 'CONJUNCTIO' BY ARITHMETIC, MUSIC AND DIVINE GEOMETRY

> Joyne them together also *Arithmetically;*
> By suttill Numbers proportionally,
> Joyne your Elements *Musically,*
> For two causes, one is for Melody;
> Which there accords will make to your mind,
> The trewe effect when that ye shall finde.
> And also for like as *Diapson,*
> With *Diapente* and with *Diatesseron,*
>
> (Thomas Norton, *The Ordinall of Alchimy*, 1477)[56]

A lonely field in rural Northamptonshire is home to a very strange building that forces the onlooker to concede just what a bewildering and foreign place the past can sometimes seem. Built in the 1590s by Sir Thomas Tresham (1545–1605), this mysterious 'Lodge' is in the form of an equilateral triangle rising to three stories with three windows on each of its three sides (Fig. 7). Each face has three triangular gables, each bearing a pinnacle, and at the intersection of the roof is a curious three-sided chimney stack topped by a 'taper' (a diminishing pyramidal structure) rising to the sky. The latter clearly once bore smoke up to the heavens, achieved by an ingenious internal arrangement that carried the flue from the top-floor corner fireplace to the central chimney and required massive timbers to support the central stack. Directly below the gables is a frieze bearing an unbroken Latin inscription around the three, thirty-three-foot-long sides, each face bearing thirty-three letters

7 Rushton Triangular Lodge, view from the north-east.

(Let the earth open and bring forth a Saviour. Who shall separate us from the love of Christ? I have considered thy works, O Lord, and been afraid).[57] Above the entrance door on the south-east front are the words *Tres Testimonium Dant* ('there are three that bear witness', with a pun on Tresham's name).

Like Longford Castle (1591) in Wiltshire this is unmistakably a Trinitarian building with divine import.[58] The rest of its embellishments, however, prove far more elusive to the untrained modern eye. Each face is decorated with large symbolic numbers (for example, 9 and 3 on the north front), strange pictorial emblems, and further Latin inscriptions extracted from biblical texts. Among the emblems on the south-east chimney face is the sacred monogram HIS with a cross above and three nails below enclosed in an octagon. The other two chimney faces bear a square and a pentagon, each framing a further emblem. The words on the

central gables of the three walls read *Respicite, Non Mihi, Soli Laboravi*,
which, taken together, proclaim 'Consider that I laboured not for myself
only.' What does it all mean?

Tresham's puzzling structure requires further elucidation, but the two
points that should be stressed at this stage are, first, that its symbolic
numbers, geometry and emblems have biblical, Pythagorean and Platonic
significances – the philosophy underpinning its plan and aesthetics is truly
syncretistic – and, second, that it evidences a late sixteenth-century vogue
for divine mathematics, which also left its considerable stamp on the
period's poetry, and on the practice of spiritual alchemy too.[59] As
Thomas Norton's *Ordinall* reveals, the 'conjunctio' was understood to
necessitate 'suttil [subtle] Numbers' – with attention to 'proportion',
music and harmony. Thus in Michael Maier's Emblem 21 (Fig. 3) an
alchemist-geometer is featured inscribing a square, circles and a triangle
on a wall with the help of a large pair of dividers while various measuring
instruments, together with a sheet of paper covered with geometrical
shapes, litter the floor beside him.[60] Furthermore, we should recall that
a fugue (counterpoint, or the art of combining two or more independent
melodic lines) of three voices accompanies each of the fifty alchemical
emblems in Maier's book. Significantly, among Shakespeare's sonnets
there are several with musical emphases and, as we shall see, the sequence
features particularly elaborate spatial structuring devices. Indeed, the
latter caused Alastair Fowler to pause in his analysis of their complex
numerology in his groundbreaking study, *Triumphal Forms*, advocating
that Shakespeareans

pay more attention to the religious language that differentiates the Sonnets
of Shakespeare from most secular sonnets of his time, and perhaps to develop
C. S. Lewis's view that 'the greatest of the sonnets are written from a region in
which love abandons all claims and flows into charity ... This transference of the
whole self into another self without the demand of a return [has] hardly a precedent
in profane literature.'[61]

Fowler was unaware of the spiritual alchemy inscribed in Shakespeare's
sequence, but that a purely secular sequence should contain such complex
divine mathematics was perplexing, even paradoxical, and urged interpretive caution. While internal structuring devices and symbolic numbers tend
to get short shrift from modern scholars – busy eyes can see numbers
everywhere and attention to form smacks of outmoded and inward looking
'formalism' – they were an integral part of early modern religious-aesthetic
theory.[62] Yet the words of St Augustine (*The City of God*), who was such an

authoritative patristic voice for this period, should make us hesitate to pour scorn on numerology: 'The theory of number should by no means be contemned, for many passages of the Bible call the careful reader's attention to the fact that it ought to be highly esteemed; and not in vain is it said in the honour of God: But thou hast ordered all things in measure, and number, and weight.'[63] St Augustine's teachings contain numerous passages extolling the truth of numbers but in *On The Trinity* those who doubt their veracity and significance are particularly severely denounced: 'No sober person will decide against reason, no Christian against the Scriptures, no peaceable person against the church.'[64] In Augustine's view, it was unreasonable and akin to heresy to ignore numbers. But why were they so important?

St Paul's *To the Hebrews* 8: 5 is a crucial text in this regard: 'Who serve unto the paterne and shadowe of heavenly things, as Moses was warned by God when he was about to finish the Tabernacle, See, sayd he, that thou make all things according to the paterne, shewd to thee in the mount.' That 'paterne' was construed as the threefold principle.[65] If the world was ordered sweetly (*Wisdom* 8: 1) by 'measure, and number and weight', all acts of creation must imitate the godhead's divine arithmetic. The leading mathematician of the Elizabethan period, John Dee, reinforced this belief in the divine efficacy of numbers, stating in his influential preface to Euclid's *Elements* (1570), 'all thinges ... do appeare to be Formed by the reason of Numbers. For this was the principall example or patterne in the minde of the Creator'.[66] George Puttenham's *Art of English Poesy* similarly observed, 'It is said ... that God made the world by number' and described how 'poesy is a skill to speak and write harmonically; and verses or rhyme be a kind of musical utterance'.[67] The poet-musician Thomas Campion even composed a song in praise of the divine mathematician, which was published in 1601:

> Come, let us sound with melody the praises
> Of the kings king, th'omnipotent creator,
> Author of number, that hath all the world in Harmonie framed.
>
> (Poem XXI)[68]

By extrapolation, creating an 'Orbe of order and forme' (Samuel Daniel, *A Defence of Rhyme*) in one's sonnets, and in particular the ordering of a sequence with spiritual import, necessitated imitating the creative 'paterne' articulated in the Bible involving 'measure, and number and weight' (*Wisdom of Solomon* 11: 21).[69] But what exactly might this entail, and can we probe, further, the question of why the strategy of imitating God's 'paterne' was considered so mysteriously efficacious? To understand the divine science of numbers and its significance for aesthetics and soul regeneration we must trace its ancient roots.

According to Henry Reynolds' *Mythomystes* (*c.* 1633), 'The mysticall doctrine of Numbers, and what ever the Greeke philosophy had in it great and high, flowed all from the Institutions of Orpheus, as from their first fount'.[70] Citing 'Picus' – Pico della Mirandola – Reynolds further surmises that Pythagoras had the 'Theology of Orpheus as his coppy and patterne, by which hee formed and fashioned his philosophy' (p. 153). In his refusal to separate out pagan and Christian strands of thought, Reynolds is typical of early modern commentators: Orphism, informed by Egyptian wisdom, is thoroughly intertwined in his imagination with sixth-century BC Pythagoreanism and this is inextricable from God's 'patterne' (p. 153). Consequently, Reynolds concludes, 'Well might Plato ... affirme that, among all liberall Arts and contemplative Sciences, the most divine was the Scientia numerandi' (p. 158).

The central Pythagorean tenet was that number was the basic principle in the universe and that relationships among its constituents were determined by numerical ratios, thereby producing a structure of harmonious proportions.[71] One of the most accessible accounts of Pythagorean philosophy is this rather sceptical passage from Aristotle's *Metaphysica*:

The ... Pythagoreans applied themselves to mathematics, and were the first to develop this science; and through studying it they came to believe that its principles are the principles of everything. And since numbers are by nature first among these principles, and they fancied that they could detect in numbers, to a greater extent than in fire and earth and water, many analogues of what is and comes into being and since they saw further that the properties and ratios of the musical scales are based on numbers, and since it seemed clear that all other things have their whole nature modelled upon numbers, and that numbers are the ultimate things in the whole physical universe, they assumed the elements of numbers to be the elements of everything, and the whole universe to be a proportion or number.[72]

Pythagoreans believed that through self knowledge, strict bodily control and the study of arithmetic, geometry, music and astronomy the individual could achieve perfection. This is clearly the philosophy that informed St Augustine's numerical exegesis of the scriptures and which is thoroughly interwoven with his theology and aesthetics.

There is still, however, a crucial missing link in Augustine's hybrid philosophy and that is, of course, Plato. Imbued with the Pythagorean legacy, Plato's *Republic* had proclaimed that the study of arithmetic was crucial to men in the city not simply for practical reasons (namely, buying and selling and war) but because it facilitated 'the apprehension of the idea of the good', compelling the soul 'to contemplate essence'. It had the power to 'draw the soul to truth', producing a philosophical attitude of mind, 'directing upward the faculties'.[73] Meanwhile the *Timaeus* – which Augustine maintained was indebted to Mosaic narrative (*City of God*, VIII, ii) – set out an elaborate mathematical scheme known as the *Lambda* formula (two squared and cubed and three squared and cubed, both issuing out of the One) producing an emanation of triangles, whereby the universe was said to have been created.[74] Numbers thus bridged the gap between the world of forms and that of matter – they were an accessible route to knowledge of absolute truth. The 'shadowes of heavenly things' (*To the Hebrews* 8: 5) were observable in numerical patterns; geometry raised the soul to the perusal of eternal forms. Thus Augustine's *De Musica* taught that arithmetic, geometry, astronomy and music were sciences of number through which the mind was raised from the contemplation of 'changeable numbers in inferior things to unchangeable numbers in unchangeable truth itself'.[75] It now becomes clear why John Dee's preface to Euclid's *Elements* (1570) could claim that numbers were able to 'winde and draw' the reader into 'the inward and deep search and vew, of all creatures distinct virtues, properties, and *Formes*'.[76]

Numbers were not just beautiful and practically useful, then, they had spiritually uplifting, regenerative effects: the soul was numbers and through its strenuous ordering a return to Unity or the One might be achieved. The belief in the divine efficacy of numbers meant that scriptural numerology was commentated on and utilized throughout the Middle Ages. Dante favoured the three-in-one terza rima for obvious reasons and symbolic numbers often determined rituals: *The Myroure of oure Ladye* explains to its Brigittine nun readers why divine service is said seven times a day and why three psalms should be heard before the Bible lesson. The *Myroure* also foregrounds the importance of eight as a symbol of 'the endless joye. That all goddes chosen shall recyve at the last resurreccyon at the day of dome'.[77] The number seven ('plus or minus two units') was particularly important for ordering texts in 'chains' for memorization: this number was felt to be the limit of working or short-term memory – numerology was closely bound up with medieval mnemonic techniques.[78] Popular works by Macrobius and Boethius were crucial for disseminating knowledge about symbolic numbers. Macrobius's *Commentary on the Dream of Scipio* carefully explained to its readers that 'One is called *monas*, that is Unity ... the Supreme God' and even provided them with a simplified, Christianized and accessible version of the *Timaeus*'s complex *lambda* formulation:

It was by this number [7] first of all, indeed, that the world-Soul was begotten, as Plato's Timaeus has shown. With the monad located on the apex, two sets of three numbers each descended on either side, on one the even, on the other the odd: that is, after the monad we had on one side two, four, and eight, and on the other three, nine and twenty-seven; and the mixture arising out of these seven numbers brought about the generation of the world-Soul at the behest of the Creator.[79]

The science of numbers was, therefore, well established before the Florentine Neoplatonists revivified it in the light of Hermeticism. The significance of Augustine's formulations to both Ficino's and Pico's versions of Neoplatonism, and to the developments of their philosophies by the sixteenth-century French academies, has been stressed by Maren-Sofie Røstvig, who has demonstrated how, between them, Pico della Mirandola (*Heptaplus*) and his disciple Francesco Giorgio (*De Harmonia Mundi*) built on the legacy of classical, patristic and medieval numerology, incorporating Hermetic and cabalistic ideas and further Christianizing the *Timaeus*. In the Preface to *De Harmonia* (1525) Giorgio declared that his purpose was no less than to provide a 'unique and abridged road to perfection'.[80] He emphasized the regenerative effects of the science of numbers and their efficacy in unifying higher and lower regions: 'by the affinity of numbers these initiates could ascend from the lowest to the highest sphere, from the visible to the invisible'.[81] He foregrounded the geometrical and numerical proportions discovered in Hermes, Orpheus, Plato, Moses, Ezekiel, Daniel, St John, David and Solomon, singling out Ezekiel and John for special comment. He concluded that Ezekiel's vision of the divine chariot in twenty-eight verses meant that twenty-eight was a perfect number employed to depict a vision of perfection. The burning wheels of the chariot symbolized Christ and prophesized purification through fire at the Redemption. Similarly, St John's vision of the heavenly Jerusalem in twenty-seven verses was significant because it was the number of the deity, three, cubed.[82]

Importantly, the crucial books on numerology by both Pico and Giorgio – *Heptaplus* and *De Harmonia Mundi* – were translated into French by Guy Le Fèvre de la Boderie in the 1570s and became seminal texts in the context of the French academies. Guy Le Fèvre's prefatory chapters to his translation of Giorgio's Latin original describe how before proceeding to his work, the artist must 'penetrate to the archetypal pattern in the mind of the Deity'; this was achieved by the contemplation of things created by and 'en Dieu' (in God).[83] The artist must then proceed to apply that pattern (of the intelligible world) to his work. The artefact created would thus resemble a musical instrument that plays 'le soufflé & le vent de l'esprit de Dieu'.[84] Le Fèvre's accessible translation and interpretation of Giorgio's complex numerological scheme, served to circulate the message throughout late sixteenth-century European elite circles that the artist, in imitating God's creative process with numbers, was like a god (Julius Scaliger had designated the poet an *alter deus*) permitting privileged access to the divine.[85]

The study of arithmetic was undoubtedly given a boost by this; certainly, it encouraged the production of textbooks simplifying Pythagoras and Euclid for general audiences. Henry Billingsley's commentary to the 1570 edition of Euclid's *Elements of Geometrie* instructed, for example, 'A signe or point is of Pithagoras scholars after this manner defined: a point is an unitie which hath position. Numbers are conceaved in mynde without any forme & figure, and therefore without matter . . . place and position' (*Elements*, fo. 1). This is why one is no number in Pythagorean mathematics. According to this system, while two points define a line which has dimension, three points define a surface and four a volume – the tetrad – a crucially important building block in the Pythagorean scheme for the extended universe. Billingsley emphasized the significance of the five regular bodies – the Cube, Tetrahedron, Octohedron, Dodecahedron and Icosahedron – that 'containeth infinite secretes of nature' – and associated each with its traditional element: for example, 'the Pyramis, or Tetrahedron they ascribed to the fire, for that it ascendeth upward according to the figure of the Pyramis' (*Elements*, fos. 319v–320r). Both the tetrad and the decad were considered truly significant numbers: four represented the extended universe and ten its limit. Waxing lyrical about One, Three and Ten, Du Bartas proclaimed in 1605:

> Marke here, what figure stands for One, the right
> Roote of all Nomber; and of Infinite:
> Loves happiness, the praise of Harmonie,
> Nurcerie of All, and end of Polymnie:
> No Nomber, but more then a Nomber yet;
> Potentially in all, and all in it.
>   Heere now observe the Three,
> Th'eldest of Odds, Gods Nomber properly;
> Wherin, both Nomber and no-Nomber enter:
> Heav'ns deerest Nomber.

The Tenne, which doth all Nombers force combine:
The Tenne, which makes, as One the Point, the Line.[86]

Renaissance emblem books served further to circulate the wisdom and
mysticism attached to numbers. Vaenius's *Amorum Emblemata* (1608),
for example, contains an emblem of Cupid treading on a number board
(representing multiplicity) and holding up a card with a prominent
number one on it: love is not perfect unless it is directed at one.[87] His
later book of explicitly religious emblems makes it clear that One is
divine and perfect. By the turn of the seventeenth century the study of
numbers had, it seems, accrued a wide – albeit educated and elite –
following, and considerable symbolic import leading to exaggerated
claims which can only have increased the sales of textbooks such as
Thomas Masterson's (1595): 'Seeing God made, governeth, and main-
taineth all things in number, weight and measure, it is verie difficult for
man to know any thing certainly concerning the celestiall spheres, or
assuredly to speake and determine, of terrestriall and humane affaires,
without that excellent gift of God the science of numbers.'[88] By 1624
William Ingpen's *Secrets of Numbers* could even advertise itself on its title
page in grandiose terms as 'a key to lead a man to any doctrinall knowledge whatsoever'.[89] Meanwhile, for the poets, Michael Drayton
announced that the most important attribute of poetry was 'inchaunting
numbers' and urged the mysterious and powerful 'high Divinitie of
sound' and 'powerfull Number'.[90]

Viewed from the perspective of the 1590s, it is clear that Thomas
Tresham's Triangular Lodge was redolent with symbolism that might
have seemed commonplace and even rather overstated to educated, elite
spectators. While stressing Tresham's recusancy as the spur to his strange
building project, the English Heritage guidebook omits to tell modern
visitors that he owned an extraordinary library containing over twenty
books of architectural-aesthetic theory – classical, Italian and French –
probably the largest collection in England. The celebrated 'wizard earl',
Henry Percy, the Ninth Earl of Northumberland, possessed about twelve
on this topic, which was far more the norm among the intellectual elite.[91]
Further, Tresham was in communication with Robert Stickwell, a free-
mason architect-craftsman who was renowned for his intellectual aspirations.[92] He also seems to have consulted a Cambridge mathematician,
astronomer and astrologer, John Fletcher.[93] Given these associates and
Tresham's remarkable collection of books, we might expect the
Triangular Lodge to incorporate the latest aesthetic-religious principles.

In this extraordinary building Pythagorean, Platonic and biblical numerology and geometry combine with emblems and inscriptions producing a powerful Christocentric message about the Redemption echoed in the thirty-three-foot sides (Christ was thirty-three when he was crucified), urging the significance of the crucifixion and resurrection to the salvation of God's chosen. The sacred emblem on the south-east chimney face – HIS with a cross above and three nails below enclosed in an octagon – signifies regeneration.[94] Gazing upwards at the Pythagorean triangular chimney with its tapering tetrahedron issuing smoke, spectators might have been enthralled by the 'infinite secretes of nature' connecting the world of forms with that of earthly matter it was said to enshrine (Billingsley, *Elements*, fo. 320) and readily grasped the visualization of the scriptural prophecy (contained in Ezekiel's much-cited vision of the divine chariot) about purification through fire. Casting their eyes over the windows, they may well have deciphered the Pythagorean Tetractys incorporating a progression of one, two, three and four triangles and been alert to the presence of Plato's *Lambda* numbers.[95] The preponderance of threes associated with the structure is not surprising, three being, 'Heav'ns deerest Nomber', and conveniently resonating, too, with *Tre*sham's name. In conceiving in his mind and causing this 'Idea' to be materially embodied by his builder, Tresham was imitating the divine architect's creation of the universe which, according to the *Timaeus*, was based on an effusion of innumerable triangles. Numbers were the paradigms in the mind of the creative godhead and the building blocks of nature. By ordering his numbers 'sweetly' (Wisdom 8: 1), the earthly 'maker' could facilitate a spiritually regenerative process in himself but also in the observers of his work, hence the inscription: 'Consider that I laboured not for myself only.' The message of St Paul's *Epistle to the Romans* 1: 20 is crucial here: 'For the invisible things of him, that is, his eternall power and Godhead, are seene by the creation of the world, being considered in his works, to the intent that they should be without excuse.'

Ordering a piece of writing into a work of art by 'measure, number and weight' might involve arranging the parts into proportioned sections and/or securing equilibrium by organizing the same number of units each side of a mid-point, or disposing the units so that they form one of the ratios that achieve harmony. The ratio of the diapason (the eight) was construed as articulating absolute truth. Internal texture was important too: parts (such as lines or half lines in the case of poetry) might be balanced against parts and unified through various forms of linkage, including metrical and rhyme schemes. Dante's *Divina commedia*, for example, exhibits an elaborate symmetry with the point of his 'conversion' occurring in the central canto of the central book; while Petrarch plotted his love on the calendar of the Christian year. Edmund Spenser arranged the twelve eclogues of the *Shepheardes Calendar* around the twelve months and the far more complex structuring devices of his later works have been extensively demonstrated, notably by Alastair Fowler.[96] *The Faerie Queene*'s Una and Duessa are explicitly symbolic, in the light of Plutarch's pronouncement that because of its moving away from unity into multiplicity, 'the indefinite binarie, is the divell and evill'.[97] Drayton self-consciously used the 'grand climacteric' number sixty-three in arranging the 1619 edition of his sonnets – 'Idea, in sixty three sonnets' – sixty-three was construed as a critical stage of development for body and soul. Henry Constable and Giordano Bruno also used the number sixty-three symbolically in their sonnet collections, the latter to mark a crisis point in the spiritual journey of the nine men in *De gli eroici furori*, which will be discussed in the next chapter.

Sonneteers do seem to have been particularly self-conscious about their use of structuring devices and sometimes talked about their creations in architectural terms: in 'To the Reader' in the 1607 edition of his works Samuel Daniel likened himself to a 'curious builder' refurbishing the frame and rooms of his sonnets, while Drayton compared the final couplet of a stanza to an architectural base.[98] Of the stanza form in *The Baron's Wars* he declared, 'I chose this stanza, of all other the most complete and best proportioned, consisting of eight lines, six interwoven and a couplet in base.'[99] Henry Constable prefaces an arrangement of his sonnets with a significant description of 'The Order of the book', beginning: 'The sonnets are divided into 3 parts, each part containing 3 several arguments, and every argument 7 sonnets': three was divine and seven was considered 'immutable' (Pico's *Heptaplus* associates it with the creation of the world); there were seven numbers in the *lambda* series which formed the basis of the world soul.[100] There was an important precedent for this scheme: Pico's commentary on Benivieni's *Canzona della Amore Celeste et Divino* (printed in the 1572 and 1601 editions of Pico's works) demonstrates a numerological pattern using the triad and products of seven.[101] Røstvig has foregrounded how writers of romance epics involving the hero in moral and religious choices, especially the Choice of Hercules (for example, Tasso's Rinaldo and Spenser's Guyon) appear to have found numerological structuring devices particularly appropriate.[102] Sir Philip Sidney's *Astrophil and Stella* depicts such a choice and several scholars have described elaborate structural patterning here. Tom Parker has, for example, highlighted a harmonic scheme in *Astrophil and Stella* based on the number 108, which, he argues, was subsequently adopted by the Sidney circle poets: '108 may be considered to be a condensation of the Platonic construction of the soul of the world (the *lambda* pattern), and particular subdivisions of this number may render in linear fashion what to Plato was a three-dimensional scheme'.[103]

All these poets were clearly thinking in spatial ways about their poetry, employing an 'allegory by numbers' to link form with content.[104] None of the sonneteers of the turn of the seventeenth century, however, exhibits such a dazzling deployment of symbolic numbers and geometrical patterning as Shakespeare. This is not surprising on several counts: first, he is the only English poet to attempt to capture the process of inner alchemy in his sequence and – as we have seen – adepts insisted that 'subtill Numbers' were essential to the 'conjunctio' phase of the *opus*; second, and related to this, numerology is particularly evident in poetry dealing with 'creation . . . or with God's scheme for the redemption of man' – focal concerns of alchemy.[105] As the next chapter will demonstrate, too, a 'Choice of Hercules' scenario is played out in the dark lady section of Shakespeare's sonnets and that topos – with its moral-spiritual implications – is especially linked to structural patterning. Finally, though not least, the sonnets revel in their creative ingenuity (as Sonnet 38 foregrounds) and around 1600 this definitely included imitating the deity's preconceived archetypal pattern including His numerological finesses. Shakespeare's performance in the latter domain is truly that of a virtuoso.

SHAKESPEARE'S 'ETERNAL NUMBERS': 'WELL-TUNED SOUNDS / BY UNIONS MARRIED'

How can my Muse want subject to invent,
While thou dost breathe, that pour'st into my verse
Thine own sweet argument, too excellent
For every vulgar paper to rehearse?
O give thyself the thanks if aught in me
Worthy perusal stand against thy sight,
For who's so dumb that cannot write to thee,
When thou thyself dost give invention light?
Be thou the tenth Muse, ten times more in worth
Than those old nine which rhymers invoke;
And he that calls on thee, let him bring forth
Eternal numbers to outlive long date.
If my slight Muse do please these curious days,
The pain be mine, but thine shall be the praise.   (Sonnet 38)

Over recent decades a growing consensus has emerged among editors that the sonnets were most likely prepared and sequentially ordered by the author prior to the publication of *Shake-speares Sonnets*, a hypothesis underpinned by the 'numerological finesses' of the collection, indicating 'sophisticated principles of organization at work'.[106] Duncan-Jones' edition foregrounds many instances of deliberate counterpointing between subject and numbering, like Sonnet 66, for example, which rants against worldly corruption in many guises ('Tired with all these', 1), its number simultaneously invoking the beast of the Book of Revelation. In a similar manner, Sonnet 12 appropriately begins 'When I do count the clock that tells the time' (1), evokes the passing of the months, and advocates 'defence' "'gainst Time's scythe' in the form of 'breed[ing] to brave him' (13, 14) – twelve was designated an 'abundant number'. Sonnet 40 about 'Lascivious grace' (13), blame and forgiveness plays on the association of this number with penance and judgement because of the forty days of the deluge, forty days of Christ's temptation, and the forty years spent by the Hebrews in the desert.

Three – 'God's number' – is liberally deployed in Sonnet 105, which opens with the pronouncement, 'Let not my love be called idolatry' (1), claiming, in three-fold fashion, '"Fair, kind and true" is all my argument' (9): 'Three themes in one' (12). Similarly the decad (ten), the number linked to the archetypal pattern of the universe in both Plato and Pythagoras, features obsessively in Sonnet 6 ('ten times happier, be it ten for one: / Ten times thyself . . .', 8–9) and Sonnet 37 ('ten times happy me', 14), and the beloved is meaningfully invoked as the 'tenth Muse, ten times more in worth / Than those old nine which rhymers invocate' (9–10) in Sonnet 38, then appropriately called upon to inspire the poet's 'Eternal numbers' (the divine pattern of the universe contained in the decad will thus be mirrored in the poet's verse). The number one hundred denoted a return to unity – to the One or God – and it is significant that the sonnet in the sequence with this number chides:[107]

> Where art thou, Muse, that thou forget'st so long
> To speak of that which gives thee all thy might?
> Spend'st thou thy fury on some worthless song,
> Dark'ning thy pow'r to lend base subjects light?
> Return, forgetful Muse, and straight redeem
> In gentle numbers time so idly spent.   (Sonnet 100, 1–6)

The return of the tenth Muse is needed to beat Time (to achieve unity and thus eternity) and Sonnet 101 upbraids the 'truant Muse' further for the 'neglect of truth' (1–2) – Christ is both love and truth in spiritual alchemy.

Sonnet 27 is interesting from the symbolic number perspective too. Twenty-seven was linked to St John's vision of the Heavenly Jerusalem and Shakespeare's sonnet of this number is a deeply meditative one – about a 'zealous pilgrimage' taken by the 'soul's imaginary sight' presenting 'thy shadow to my sightless view' (lines 6, 9, 10). In inner alchemy meditation is associated with procreation of the soul as Ficino's *De amore* describes:

The love of procreation which is assigned to the cognitive part of the soul causes the soul to desire truth as its proper food, by which, in its own way, it is nourished and grows. And if anything escapes the soul through forgetfulness, or lies inert through inactivity or neglect, by diligence in recall and meditation, the love of procreation regenerates it, so to speak. (p. 131)

Further, Sonnet 27's 'jewel (hung in ghastly night)' (11) evokes the light in darkness trope of alchemical poetry, associated with the eye of the mind and with sparks of divinity in the black soul (see Chapter 3).

While symbolic numbers encode religious and philosophical meanings into the sequence – functioning as an 'allegory by numbers' – they do not perform the crucial unifying work of alchemy.[108] As Norton's *Ordinall* proclaims, it is the 'conjunctio' or joining by numbers and the subsequent creation of 'musicke' and 'harmony' which achieve this. In fact, spiritual alchemy's perception of the unifying effect of harmony was completely orthodox, as this passage from St Augustine's *De vera religione* testifies: 'In all the arts that which pleases is harmony, which alone invests the whole with unity and beauty. This harmony requires equality and unity, either through the resemblance of symmetrical parts, or through the graded arrangement of unequal parts.'[109]

Indeed, as Røstvig has foregrounded, a similar conception can even be found in Calvin's *Institutes*.[110] As she argues, Augustine's treatise on 'true religion' is dominated by the idea of a need and drive in the individual to return to unity from multiplicity: 'We worship one God by whom we were made and his likeness by whom we are formed for unity, and his peace whereby we cleave to unity' (*De vera religione*, I. v. 113).[111] Through loving God we can return to the eternal One from the mutable Many and Augustine (followed by Ficino, Pico and Giorgio) repeatedly affirms that the arts – poetry and music centrally – can lead us back to unity. This is undoubtedly the understanding that is motivating Shakespeare's speaker's quest for the eternal through 'numbers': 'eternal Numbers' might smack of mysticism to us, but viewed through the lens of St Augustine's teachings they are perfectly orthodox.[112]

Ficino's Hermeticism was thoroughly informed by Augustine's marriage of Pythagoras and Plato with Christian teaching and his unifying religio-aesthetics was similarly based on multiple philosophical systems drawn together into agreement ('the consonance of diverse things').[113] These passages from Ficino's letter 76 to the poet Benivieni suggest the seminal importance of unity in his understanding of music:

We must ask why all musicians make especial use of . . . ratios . . . They acknowledge them in different ways on different occasions – in the size of pipes, in the mass or weight of other instruments, in the tension and length of strings, and finally in the vehemence of action and the speed of motion . . . The followers of Pythagoras and Plato consider the one itself the most perfect and the most pleasing of all . . . At the other extreme, they consider disconnected multiplicity the least perfect and most distressing.[114]

Hearing indeed longs for unity, since it itself is also one and arises from one, but it desires a unity perfectly blended from the many and composed in the same proportion as that by which it itself is also naturally brought to a unity from the many . . . it readily welcomes a number of notes when they are brought perfectly into one note and into harmony. (*Letters*, vol. VII, Letter 76, p. 85)

Music resolves 'disconnected multiplicity' by combining notes into harmony and through its musical sounds poetry can tune and thus heal the soul:

Obviously the soul cannot return to One unless it itself becomes one . . . The whole soul is filled with discord and disharmony. Therefore first there is need for the poetic madness which, through musical sounds, arouses those parts of the soul which are asleep, through harmonious sweetness calms those which are perturbed, and finally, through the consonance of diverse things, drives away dissonant discord and tempers the various parts of the soul. (Ficino, *De amore*, p. 170)

It is the forging of 'the consonance of diverse things' through 'musical sounds' that is so crucial to soul making and the soul must be tuned to the harmony of the octave. Following Boethius's teaching in *De Musica*, John Case's *The Praise of Musick* (1586) even describes the human soul as divided into intervals of the fourth and fifth, thus making reason, the highest note, to sound an octave with desire, the lowest.[115]

Music was imagined to connect everything in the universe: thus heavenly or divine music, music of the spheres, music of the human soul and instrumental and voice music constituted an interconnected whole. It was music's imagined facility in linking extremes and antitheses within both conceptual-ideal and physical-mundane worlds that made it invaluable to the alchemical process. As the physician-alchemist Robert Fludd describes, there can be no inner alchemy in the absence of the Pythagorean study and application of

harmonic ratios: 'the true and profound music of the wise'.[116] Further, as his
Tractus Apologeticus (1617) explains, without knowledge of the mysteries of
music it is 'impossible for anyone to know himself. And without this he will
be unable to reach a perfect knowledge of God, for he who understands
himself truly and intrinsically perceives in himself the idea of the divine
Trinity.'[117] That Shakespeare was aware of this Hermetic wisdom is evident
from the outstandingly beautiful passage in *The Merchant of Venice*.[118]

> There's not the smallest orb which thou behold'st
> But in his motion like an angel sings,
> Still quiring to the young eyed cherubins;
> Such harmony is in immortal souls,
> But whilst this muddy vesture of decay
> Doth grossly close it in, we cannot hear it.   (v. i. 60–5)

> The man that hath no music in himself,
> Nor is not moved with concord of sweet sounds,
> Is fit for treasons, stratagems, and spoils.
> The motions of his spirit are dull as night.   (v. i. 83–6)

'Mark the music' this lyrical passage concludes: the man with no music
simply cannot be trusted.

In this context it is deeply significant that, as Fred Blick has foregrounded,
the majority of Shakespeare's sonnets 'exhibit the rhyming concord of unison'
in their rhyme scheme and Sonnet 8 exploits this to 'an extraordinary
degree'.[119] This is appropriate because the number eight denotes the octave
or diapason in music described by Francis Bacon as 'the sweetest Concord: in
so much as it is in effect an Unison'.[120] Giorgio had argued that because Christ
rose on the eighth day the world was made perfect by the octave and that
pursuit of the octave leads to a return to God.[121] But what, in mathematical
terms, is the diapason? According to the Pythagorean tuning system, the
relations among one, two, three and four produce a scale of eight notes and
the diapason comprises eight notes: it is derived mathematically from the
ratios between the first four integers. The 2: 1 proportion can be repeated an
infinite number of times along the open-ended continuum of sound, thus
music constitutes an excellent way of relating the finite to the infinite and
reconciling opposites. Boethius declared, 'Not without cause is it said that all
things, which consist of contraries, are conjoined and composed by a certain
harmony. For harmony is the joining together of several things and the
consent of contraries.'[122] The ratio 12:6 is equivalent to 2:1, the diapason
with a double proportion, and the ratio 12:8 is equivalent to 3:2, giving a one
and a half proportion – the diapente.[123] As we shall see, Shakespeare's Sonnets

126 and 128 play upon the meanings of the diapason with double proportion and the diapente respectively.

Helen Vendler has highlighted how Sonnet 8's strategies for unifying its parts into a concord – 'well-tuned sounds / By unions married' (5–6) – are immensely varied and ingenious.[124] Fred Blick, too, has admirably demonstrated how through doubled use of words and chiasmus, word chimes, flurries of puns, as well as visual and musical rhymes, Sonnet 8 achieves this effect.[125] However, his analysis falters when he attempts to marry the poem's substantive concerns to the intricacies of its formal patterning. Echoing Wisdom 8:1 ('and sweetly doth she order all things'), this is how the sonnet 'sweetly chide[s]' the youth, urging him to marry:

> If the true concord of well-tuned sounds
> By unions married, do offend thine ear,
> They do but sweetly chide thee, who confounds
> In singleness the parts that thou shouldst bear.
> Mark how one string, sweet husband to another,
> Strikes each in each by mutual ordering;
> Resembling sire, and child, and happy mother,
> Who all in one, one pleasing note do sing:
> Whose speechless song being many, seeming one,
> Sings this to thee, 'Thou single wilt prove none.'
>
> (Sonnet 8, 5–14)

Read literally this simply does not make musical sense. As Blick points out, such a family, because of 'age and sex', is unlikely to 'sing on one note at one pitch in unison'.[126] However, if, as I am proposing, the sonnet is read in the light of its alchemical implications the riddle is solved: the union of two would result not in three separate bodies, but one hermaphrodite ('all in one' 'seeming one') and thus 'one pleasing note'. Obviously the three in one of the Trinity is evoked here too. Additionally, the final line resonates with the popular Pythagorean and alchemical paradox – one is no number ('In things of great receipt with ease we prove / Among a number one is reckoned none', Sonnet 136, lines 7–8) – effectively affirming that after 'conjunctio' he will be one (he will have achieved desirable unity). Being single in the alchemical sense (but only after marriage or union) is positive: one is none – 'no number' yet perfect unity, as Otto Vaenius's emblem on the topic (*Amorum Emblemata*, 1608) renders clear. At the same time, the youth's resistance to harmony is not propitious; as Ficino observed: 'Our Saint Augustine writes in his books on music that a man is not harmoniously formed who does not delight in harmony; nor is that unjust . . . he who takes no pleasure in concordant sounds in some way lacks concord within'.[127] This is obviously the philosophy echoed in Shakespeare's *Merchant of Venice* (v. i. 6–86). Read from this angle, the beautiful youth's discordant soul is definitely in need of spiritual 'tuning'; however, his resistance to multiplicity (implied by his reluctance to marry) also points, from the perspective of unifying philosophy, to his desire for oneness: Shakespeare is revelling in this play of paradoxes.

Shakespeare's pyramids

While repeatedly affirming the 'insistently secular' nature of the Bard's sonnets, Katherine Duncan-Jones highlights the 'pioneering analysis' of the collection's pyramidal structure by Alastair Fowler, analysis which has profound religious implications.[128] In *Triumphal Forms*, Fowler illuminated the geometrical patterning of Shakespeare's sequence.[129] His erudite study locates a range of further mathematical-substantive intricacies, but it is his finding of a significant pyramidal structure within the sequence that is crucial in the context of this study: as Emblem 21 of Maier's *Atalanta Fugiens* suggests, the triangle or pyramid is a key form in the alchemical *opus*.

Commencing with the axiom that any self-referring sonnets should be taken seriously as commenting on their own form, and that structural analysis must examine the pattern created by any irregular sonnets (in this case 99, 126 and 145), Fowler proceeds to unravel an elaborate structural symmetry. If the self-referring Sonnet 136 ('Then in the number let me pass untold') is counted out, a total of 153 sonnets emerges – 'one of the best known of all symbolic numbers'.[130] The religious significance of 153 resided in this being the total catch of fish in John 21: 11, fulfilling prophecies in Ezekiel and Matthew 13: 47–9 : 'the kingdome of heaven is like unto a draw net cast into the sea, that gathereth of all kinds of things. Which, when it is full, men draw to land, and fit and gather the good into vessels, and cast the bad away. So shall it be at the end of the world.' But why 153 fish? St Augustine explains that '153 is the sum of the first seventeen numbers, and 17 in its turn is the sum of 10 (the commandments) and of 7 (the gifts of the Holy Ghost)'.[131] In fact, 153 had kept the Church Fathers especially busy, attracting many interpretations, but the dominant recurring theme was that of the elect – of 'believers risen in Christ and endowed with the spirit'.[132]

Furthermore, among Shakespeare's contemporaries, Fowler suggests, the especial importance of 153 resided in its triangularity. Set out in

Pythagorean manner, 153 forms an equilateral triangle with a base of seventeen; and when the irregular stanzas, 99, 126 and 145, are located in the sequence pattern 'each is denoted by a triangular number within the greater triangle 153'.[133] Thus 145 commences a culminating ten-sonnet triangle and 126 begins a twenty-eight-sonnet triangle and both these numbers were profoundly significant: ten was the principle of divine creativity and twenty-eight of moral perfection, eternity and 'the perfect bliss in heaven towards which saints yearn'.[134] Twenty-eight was the number of verses used by Ezekiel to describe his vision of the divine chariot: thus the number of perfection is employed to depict a vision of perfect creation.[135] Additionally, if we take heed of Sonnet 136's instruction, 'Though in thy store's account I one must be' (line 10) we have twenty-eight dark lady sonnets; yet if we let 136 'pass untold' in this collection we have twenty-seven – one of the cubes that concludes the *lambda* series which constitutes the world soul. It is also the number associated with St John's Vision of the Heavenly Jerusalem, and Guy Le Fèvre de la Boderie's preface to his translation of Pico's *Heptaplus* links twenty-seven with the three-fold structure of the world.[136] A Trinitarian interpretation of 153 took the triangular faces to represent the three-fold creative principle: we might recall here the speaker's repetitive insistence on 'Fair, kind and true' being all his 'argument'.

Symbolic pyramids thus abound in Shakespeare's sequence. No wonder Sonnet 123 declares, 'No! Time' (1), 'Thy pyramids built up with newer might, / To me are nothing novel, nothing strange' (2–3). No wonder, too, that Milton, 'On Shakespeare' (1630), alludes to Shakespeare's building of a 'live-long monument' (8) in 'easy numbers' (10) comparing this, with meaningful irony, to 'a star-ypointing Pyramid' (4).[137] Shakespeare had built eternal pyramids in his sonnet sequence and thus had no need of a material monument: 'What needs my Shakespeare for his honoured bones, / The labour of an age in piled stones' (1–2)? His eternal numbers and his poem are monuments enough; 'piled stones' would, by comparison, be 'weak witness of thy name' (6). If, as I have been arguing, Sonnet 126 forms the 'great base' of a pyramid leading to 'eternity' (alluded to in Sonnet 125); the triangle demanded by the alchemical adept in *Atalanta Fugiens* has been inscribed in the sequence through divine mathematics. In fact, pyramids with Trinitarian, eternalizing significances abound in alchemical texts. Fludd described how light 'streaminge from the presence of God shining out of darkenes may be reduced into a formall pyramis' linking the spiritual with the material world and vice versa.[138] Significantly, too, Puttenham's *Art of English Poesy*, commenting on the form of 'the Spire or Taper called

Pyramis', likens it to a flame which is always pointed 'and naturally by his form covets to climb'.[139]

A base of a 'pyramis' or triangle leading to 'eternity'; 'a flame ... coveting to climb'; Sonnet 126, whose number suggests the Pythagorean 12: 6 – the whole diapason with a double proportion – would appear to warrant closer scrutiny from the perspective of spiritual alchemy. Twelve and six are, in fact, the extremes of the diapason made consonant in the harmonic mean nine so that opposites are joined in stable concord. The number 126 is also the sum of two grand climacterics, and sonneteers often used sixty-three symbolically to indicate a crisis or culminating point in a sequence. We should observe, too, that the musicologist Hildemarie Streich maintains that in Maier's alchemical sequence the 'double octave ... symbolizes the constellating of a new wholeness, the spiritual child or fruit, and also the stone of the Wise which is yet to be achieved'.[140]

Sonnet 126

Shakespeare's Sonnet 126 is a particularly strange sonnet, which puzzles editors; indeed, it only makes sense in the light of the alchemical lexicon and *opus*. It is short – twelve lines – and composed of rhyming couplets. Two odd parentheses mark the two absent lines: we might recall how Michael Drayton compared the final couplet of a stanza to an architectural base and illustrated this with sickle, or parenthetical shaped marks.[141] The significant repetition of 'o's, as long vowel sounds slowing down the opening lines, seems to enact 'power' over time and is appropriate for relating the slow growth of 'lovely Boy' – the spiritual 'babe' or child. Beginning with the ejaculated cry 'O', they also seem to register the poet-alchemist's pleasure and success; he is almost crooning over his creation:

> O thou my lovely Boy, who in thy power
> Dost hold Time's fickle glass, his sickle hour;
> Who hast by waning grown, and therein show'st
> Thy lovers withering, as thy sweet self grow'st.   (1–4)

The uncanny line, 'Thy lovers withering, as thy sweet self grow'st', is inexplicable outside the alchemical context: through repeated operations of the *opus* – incorporating union, death of the lovers and regeneration – 'my' (signifying proud ownership) 'sweet' distillation has 'grown'. The power to stay the destructive effects of Time is now within the 'lovely Boy's' 'power'. However – a warning comes next, 'fear' Nature:

> If Nature (sovereign mistress over wrack)
> As thou goest onwards still will pluck thee back,
> She keeps thee to this purpose, that her skill
> May Time disgrace, and wretched minute kill.
> Yet fear her, O thou minion of her pleasure:
> She may detain, but not still keep, her treasure!
> Her audit (though delayed) answered must be,
> And her quietus is to render thee.   (5–12)

This 'sovereign mistress' might 'pluck thee back' as a 'minion of her pleasure' (to 'kill' minutes), but she can't keep you: you must eventually be 'render[ed]' – fired again and/or handed over. The second line here captures the ebb and flow of the alchemical opus – the 'still' *will* hold him back. It would seem that Mistress Nature's purposeful 'skill' is necessary at this stage in the *opus* in order to 'disgrace' time (to achieve eternity). The sonnet is abruptly terminated and two coffin-like parentheses mark the spot (suggestively two grand climacterics).

From now on, we should note, Time ceases to appear: lovely boy's distilled beauty appears to have stopped time. The terminating parentheses, 'lunulae' or little moons (as Erasmus called such curved brackets), form the base of a pyramid introducing a moon phase of twenty-eight sonnets dominated by the fickle, cunning dark lady. It is interesting that in the Hermetic ascent (described as to the moon), the philosopher reaches a stage in which he gives up the 'force which works increase and decrease' and then has to overcome 'the machinations of evil cunning'; 'the lust whereby men are deceived'; 'domineering arrogance'; 'unholy daring and rash audacity'; 'evil strivings after wealth'; and 'the falsehood which lies in wait to work harm'.[142] Are these, perhaps, our poet-speaker's struggles with his dark lady? Darkness is a function of innerness, of interiority – predominantly feminine as Elizabeth Harvey points out and 'the matrix of poetic creation'.[143] Further, in Fludd's famous image of personified Nature and the cosmos (*Integrae Naturae Speculum. Artisque Imago*) the moon on Nature's *mons pubis* signifies the creative mercurial spirit, the Spirit of the Moon or Urania.

CHAPTER 3

The dark mistress and the art of blackness

PART I IN PRAISE OF BLACKNESS

In the old age black was not counted fair,
Or if it were it bore not beauty's name;
But now is black beauty's successive heir.

(Sonnet 127, 1–3)[1]

Thy black is fairest in my judgement's place.

(Sonnet 131, 12)

When nature made her chief work, Stella's eyes,
In colour black why wrapped she beams so bright?
(Sidney, *Astrophil and Stella.* 7, 1–2)[2]

Shakespeare's enigmatic dark lady makes her abrupt entrance in Sonnet 127, immediately compelling the question, why is she 'black'? This is, of course, a witty strategy, 'cocking a snook' at Petrarchan norms and allowing the poet to demonstrate his considerable prowess, subverting the usual blazon with 'dun' breasts and 'black wires' (Sonnet 130, 3, 4) and shaping novel beauty in his lines. In his fashioning of Stella's hybrid black and white excellence, Sidney had dipped his toes into these dusky female waters somewhat before, inaugurating a tradition of poetic play around a black–white dichotomy. In her seminal study, *Things of Darkness*, Kim Hall has argued that the latter preoccupation was a direct consequence of 'concerns' and 'fears' bred by 'increased travel abroad' and 'colonial/imperial encounters with the twin otherness of culture and gender'.[3] In Hall's reading, cultural anxieties about racial difference and miscegenation were subdued or even effaced through the mediation of a textual poetics that rendered black women 'fair', and also by visual artefacts like the fashionable jewelled miniatures bearing sardonyx busts of black ladies. According to Hall, white male artists, poets and colonialists were empowered by such manoeuvres, which effectively controlled and mastered their exotic, attractive, but threatening female subjects.[4]

While aspects of this 'exoticism' thesis are plausible, it is by no means an exhaustive explanation – early modern black–white manoeuvres were simply more complex than this.[5] For one thing the dynamic could operate in the reverse direction, or, indeed dialectically, as in Spenser's *Amoretti* sequence, where the dark speaker is initially 'enlumind' by his lighter mistress:

> for now your light doth more it selfe dilate,
> and in my darknesse greater doth appeare.
> Yet since your light hath once enlumind me,
> with my reflex yours shall encreased be.

> (*Amoretti*, 66, 11–14)[6]

Then, too, such operations were not the sole prerogative of male poets and artists. A recent biography of John Whitgift is interesting in this respect: it appears that, in a type of reverse strategy, Elizabeth I strangely transformed her archbishop of Canterbury from her 'White-gift' to 'her little black husband' through the witty deployment of affectionate sobriquets.[7] A fascination with dark exoticism hardly seems to explain Whitgift's royal blackwashing, although it could certainly account for the queen's decision to adorn the exterior of the jewelled pendant present she gave to her leading seaman and explorer, Sir Francis Drake, with a cameo of a handsome black man – often designated an emperor – in profile. Such matters may seem rather trivial – after all, black and white were the queen's colours – but, as I shall demonstrate, they are significant in this endeavour to understand Shakespeare's and Sidney's preoccupation with dark ladies and the poetic tradition of praise of blackness that ensued.

Far from ceasing with Elizabeth's reign, the vogue for black–white contrasts in art forms escalated in the Jacobean period; indeed, the first court masque in 1605 was Ben Jonson's *Of Blackness*. Here, twelve masquers, 'nymphs, Negroes and the daughters of Niger' (lines 42–3) – actually Queen Anne and her ladies painted black – were drawn before the court in a 'great concave shell, like mother of pearl' (46).[8] Chevron lights adorning the shell 'struck a glorious beam upon them' (49), spotlighting their thick black hair that was 'curled upright in tresses, like pyramids' (57) and dressed with 'orient pearl, best setting off from the black' (60) (we might recall Shakespeare's 'jewel' in 'ghastly night' image in Sonnet 27). The queen had instructed Ben Jonson to create herself and her entourage as 'blackamoors' of 'Fair Niger's' 'beauteous race' (79, 81), who 'though but black in

face' are 'bright, / And full of life and light' (82, 83–4). Jonson presents
something curiously 'faithful' (126), constant ('firm'), and divine about their
illumined blackness:

> Though he – the best judge, and most formal cause
> Of all dames' beauties – in their firm hues draws
> Signs of his fervent'st love, and thereby shows
> That in their black the perfect'st beauty grows,
> Since the fixed color of their curled hair,
> Which is the highest grace of dames most fair,
> No cares, no age can change.   (116–22)

Perfectly beautiful they might be; nevertheless, these black ladies have
travelled in despair to the English court hoping to be whitened by
Albion's temperate rays. It seems that, much to their dismay, they have
heard rumours of the poets' story that 'negroes' like themselves were
actually 'fair' before Phaeton's disastrous accident with his father's chariot,
which careered out of control, hurtling too close to earth and burning the
inhabitants of Ethiopia black. Blackness may be God-made 'perfect'st
beauty' but it is simultaneously in this construction an aberration wrought
by chaos. Of course, in this masque representation only the English court
can put things right, restoring whiteness as the valued symbolic norm.

What do we make, then, of Queen Anne's desire to play a blackamoor's
part? The answer lies in 'his fervent'st love' and in the masquers' fans
decorated with 'mute hieroglyphics' (238), which, Jonson's text tells us,
'the Egyptians are said first to have brought from the Ethiopians' (241); in
this context the black nymphs' curious pyramid hairstyles are noteworthy
too. Thomas Browne's cumulative reflections on the blackness of 'Negroes'
in his encyclopaedic *Pseudoxia Epidemica* (1646) are revealing:

We that are of contrary complexions accuse the blackness of the Mores as ugly: But
the Spouse in the Canticles excuseth this conceit, in that description of hers, I am
black, but comely: And howsoever Cereberus, and the furies of hell be described by
the Poets under this complexion, yet in the Beauty of our Saviour blacknesse is
commended, when it is said his locks are bushie and blacke as a Raven. So that to
infer this is a case, or to reason it as a deformity, is no way reasonable. ('Of the same'
['Of the Blacknesse of Negroes'])[9]

Browne's analysis helps to illuminate the masque's highly ambivalent
representation of blackness: 'his fervent'st love' in Jonson's masque
construction refers to 'our Saviour' as depicted in the *Song of Solomon*
(the divine right monarch, King James I, is a type of Solomon too).
'The Argument' preceding 'An Excellent Song Which was Salomans' in

the Geneva Bible explains: 'In this Song Salomon by most sweete and comfortable allegories and parables describeth the perfite love of Jesus Christ, the true Salomon and king of peace, and the faithfull soule or his Church.' In the early modern period, the *Song* was read allegorically as the love between Christ and the godly soul or Christ and his Church, and in Browne's tract the comely black bride (the soul and/or the Church) is beautiful in the eyes of Solomon/Christ who, significantly, has black, 'Raven' locks. Most contemporary commentators insisted that the *Song* should be read spiritually and mystically, not literally and carnally. Joseph Hall's 1609 'plaine Paraphrase' of the *Song* proclaims, 'O my deare Church: for, behold; in mine eies, thus clothed as thou art with my righteousnesse, oh how faire and glorious thou art; how above all comparison glorious and faire.'[10]

The spouse/Church/soul is, thus, a 'faire' blackamoor. Furthermore, as Elias Ashmole explains in *Theatrum Chemicum Britannicum*, in the Hermetic tradition Solomon was a noted alchemist who wrought 'wonders', building his temple with the aid of the philosopher's stone: 'After Hermes had once obtained the knowledge of this Stone, he gave over the use of all other Stones, and therin only delighted: Moses, and Solomon (together with Hermes were the only three that) excelled in the knowledge therof, and who therewith wrought Wonders.'[11]

It seems that increasing encounters with foreign others were not the sole motivating force behind the strange and often ambivalent representations of black beauty in this period. In fact, art forms preoccupied with black–white transformations and blackamoors were thoroughly informed by Hermetic philosophy (the ancient repository of which was thought to be Egyptian hieroglyphs and 'dark' allegories) and by the intimately related biblical *Song of Solomon*.

YOU *CAN* WASH A BLACKAMOOR WHITE

Riddles and seemingly nonsensical paradoxes lay at the heart of the 'dark' alchemical imagination and perhaps the most common of these was associated with the popular emblem image of a 'blacke More' being furiously 'skowre[d]' – 'Æthiopem lavare'.[12] Apprehended literally, this emblem seems to depict the impossible: no amount of washing can transform a person's skin colour. However, the alchemist and, indeed, the mercurial poet could work 'wonders', like Solomon: they could, as we shall see, wash a blackamoor white. Indeed, black was highly valued as the essential starting point of the alchemical 'work':

But White and Black, as all men maie see,
Be Colours contrary in most extremetie:
Wherfore your worke with Black must begin,
If the end shulde be with whitenes to winn.

(Thomas Norton, *The Ordinall of Alchimy*, 1477)[13]

In the base metals or chaotic dark soul (the *prima materia* of the process) resided a mystery which had to be consciously experienced as a spark or light in darkness before the process of regeneration or transformation could begin. Read from the Neoplatonic perspective, Stella's bright 'beams' in 'colour black' (*Astrophil*, Sonnet 7) thus signal Astrophil's spiritual awakening – 'thy beauty draws the heart to love' (*Astrophil*, Sonnet 71) – and the *Masque of Blackness*'s negro nymphs lit by chevron lights similarly allude to this divine mystery. But Edward Herbert's 'Sonnet of Black Beauty' provides the most comprehensive poetic account of the Hermetic significance of blackness:

Black beauty, which above that common light,
Whose Power can no colours here renew
But those which darkness can again subdue,
Do'st still remain unvary'd to the sight,
And like an object equal to the view,
Art neither chang'd with day, nor hid with night;
When all these colours which the world call bright,
And which old Poetry doth so persue,
Are with the night so perished and gone,
That of their being there remains no mark,
Thou still abidest so intirely one,
That we may know thy blackness is a spark
Of light inaccessible, and alone
Our darkness which can make us think it dark.[14]

This paean to 'Black beauty' is thoroughly informed by the Hermetic myth of origins – 'the beginning of things, following the theology of Hermes Trismegistus' – in dark formless 'Chaos', with Love/God residing in its 'bosom' (*De amore*, pp. 37, 37–40).[15] Ficino's *De amore* waxes particularly lyrical about this singular wonder, drawing constant analogies between Love in chaos and the spark of divinity in the dark soul: 'Love accompanies chaos, precedes the world, wakens the sleeping, lights the dark, gives life to the dead, gives form to the formless, perfects the imperfect. Greater praises than these can hardly be expressed or conceived' (p. 40).

As another of Edward Herbert's poems, 'To Her Hair', renders clear (again following Ficino's account of the Orphic mysteries), the spark of divine light in blackness is inaccessible to those rendered blind by their downward vision:

> That shining light in darkness all would find,
> Were they not upward blind
> With the Sun beams below.

While in Herbert's 'Another Sonnet to Black Itself' we learn of a 'hidden power' in darkness and this, according to the alchemists, was the 'spiritual fifth element' – the *Quinta Essentia*. This divine quintessence, William Bloomfield explains,

> Is not in sight, but resteth invisible:
> Till it be forced out of Chaos darke,
> Where he remaineth ever indivisible.
> This Chaos darke the Mettalls I do call.[16]

This was the true transforming work of the spiritual alchemist: to reproduce God's macrocosmic creation in the microcosm of man, extracting the quintessence out of 'Chaos darke' – the black metal of the soul – and lightening darkness. In this manner the soul could be regenerated, repairing the ravages of man's fallen condition and enabling enhanced spiritual vision. Edward Herbert's preoccupation with such matters is given pronounced visual expression in a miniature portrait of him by Isaac Oliver in which Herbert strikes a melancholic-philosophical pose and the shield at the centre of the image adorning his prostrate body bears the inscription *Magica Sympathiae* with a scarlet heart rising from golden flames. Roy Strong has decoded the emblem as a reference to the doctrine of sympathetic magic and to the ascent of the soul to heavenly wisdom.[17] Sir Thomas Browne's words capture something of this divine mystery in far more familiar terms than Herbert's: 'The smattering I have of the Philosopher's stone (which is something more then the perfect exaltation of gold) hath taught me a great deale of Divinity, and instructed my beliefe, how that immortall spirit and incorruptible substance of my soule may lye obscure, and sleepe a while within this house of flesh.'[18]

Alchemists, deriving their symbolism from Acts 8 of the Bible, employed the image of the Ethiopian or black man to represent the blackened matter of the soul or stone before purification and restoration to a state of purity and whiteness known as the *Albedo*. Blackamoor poems such as Henry Rainold's 'A Black-Moor Wooing a Fair Boy' indicate how black tropes linked to allusions of 'Love' (or Christ) in Solomon's *Song* could combine to produce witty and humorous alchemical conceits:

> Stay lovely Boy, why fly'st thou mee
> That languish in these flames for thee?
> I'm black 'tis true: why so is Night,
> And Love doth in dark Shades delight.
> The whole World, do but close thine eye,
> Will seem to thee as black as I.[19]

In Henry King's response to this poem – 'The Boyes Answer to the Blackmoor' – the extended conceit draws further on the 'conjunctio', eclipse and death associated with the *opus*:

> Black Maid, complain not that I fly,
> When Fate commands Antipathy:
> Prodigious Night and day together move,
> And the conjunction of our lips
> Not kisses make, but an Eclipse;
> In which the mixed black and white
> Portends more terrour than delight
> Yet if my shadow thou wilt be,
> Enjoy thy dearest wish: But see
> Thou take my shadowes property,
> That hastes away when I come nigh:
> Else stay till death hath blinded mee,
> And then I will bequeath my self to thee.[20]

Alchemical poems involving blackamoors were not, however, solely playful. Soul regeneration (or washing the blackamoor white) necessitated immersion in a *Nigredo* phase which corresponded to dark but productive (and therefore to be welcomed) melancholia, as these lines from Henry Vaughan's poem, 'Affliction', render clear:

> O come, and welcom! Come refine;
> For *Moors* if wash'd by thee, will shine.
> Man *blossoms* at thy touch; and he
> When thou draw'st blood, is thy *Rose-tree*.   (1–4)[21]

In George Herbert's 'To the Right Hon. The L. Chancellor' (Francis Bacon), religious devotion, wit and obsequious praise rub shoulders in a rather strange little 'Blackamore' poem:

> My Lord. A diamond to mee you sent,
> And I to you a Blackamore present.
> Gifts speake their Givers. For as those Refractions,
> Shining and sharp, point out your rare Perfections;
> So by the Other, you may read in mee
> (Whom Schollers Habitt & Obscurity

Hath soild with Black), the colour of my state,
Till your bright gift my darknesse did abate.
Onely, most noble Lord, shutt not the doore
Against this meane & humble Blackamore.
Perhaps some other subject I had tryed
But that my Inke was factious for this side.   (1–12)[22]

Here Bacon is the light in darkness, the diamond set off by Herbert's blackness. In the verbal currency of the time, Herbert, as a representative of the Church, could qualify as a blackamoor to Solomon/Christ (in the manner of Archbishop Whitgift in relation to Elizabeth I/Solomon). A 'Divine Epigram' by Richard Crashaw called 'On the baptized Aethiopian' indicates how the popular whitewashing conceit, linked to Solomon's *Song*, could also be used in a deeply serious way to embrace religious conversion:

Let it no longer be a forlorne hope
  To wash an Æthiope:
He's washt, His gloomy skin a peacefull shade
  For his white soule is made:
And now, I doubt not, the Eternall Dove,
  A black-fac'd house will love.[23]

These sophisticated, multi-layered alchemical conceits were operative in visual texts too, notably in the field of miniature art, as an examination of the enigmatic Drake Jewel will serve to reveal.

'BY THE GATE OF BLACKNES' TO 'PARADYCE'

And thus by the Gate of Blacknes thou must come in
To light of Paradyce in Whytenes yf thou wylt wyn.
            (George Ripley, *The Compound of Alchymie*)[24]

After Sir Francis Drake's successful circumnavigation of the globe (1577–80), Elizabeth I's chief explorer presented his royal mistress with a composite jewel gift appropriately bearing an ebony boat and boasting an African diamond.[25] A few years later, possibly to reward Drake for his part in defeating the Spanish Armada in 1588, the queen reciprocated with another composite jewel, embellished not this time with a solitary diamond set in black ebony but with a bust in profile of a black man surrounded by precious gems. This was a blackamoor gift, although unlike George Herbert's later offering to the Lord Chancellor, it was far from 'humble'. The Drake Jewel is dense with symbolic meanings, all ultimately designed to celebrate the queen's divine powers. As we shall see, by the late 1580s the lexicon of alchemy was central to these.

The Drake Pendant or Jewel is a magnificent affair of gold enamelled in white, pale green, blue, translucent red and green. The jewel is set with table-cut rubies and diamonds and suspended from the case is a cluster of small pearls and one larger one. The centrepiece is a two-layer, sardonyx cameo, the bulk of which presents a black male bust in left profile almost covering a left profile of a white female face (see Fig. 8(a)). The reverse opens to reveal a miniature painting of the queen by Nicholas Hilliard and an image of a phoenix on parchment (see Fig. 8(b)).[26] Karen Dalton has argued that the pendant's symbolism centres on a key theme of Elizabeth's icon-ography: the return of the Golden Age of peace and plenty under her rule, as prophesied in Virgil's Fourth Eclogue.[27] Thus she aligns the black emperor with Saturn and the white profile with Astraea, while Elizabeth, the phoe-nix, embodies the 'renovatio'.[28] As Dalton points out, the queen herself was sometimes likened to an alchemist, as in Sir John Davies's *Hymnes to Astraea*:

> R udeness it selfe she doth refine,
> E ven like an Alychymist divine,
> G rosse times of Iron turning
> I nto the purest forme of gold:
> N ot to corrupt, till heaven waxe old,
> A nd be refin'd with burning.[29]

Certainly, the return of the Golden Age is one aspect of the Jewel's symbolic refractions. However, others are discernible if we refuse to stabilize the black–white, male–female transforming image embellishing the case of the pendant and approach it more allusively – more alchemically.

Artistic evocations of blackness and black–white conjunctions would undoubtedly have pointed an elite audience in the closing decades of the sixteenth century towards alchemical meanings; indeed, Elizabeth's gift to Drake seems literally to capture and enact an important maxim of one of the most popular English alchemical poems of the period: 'And thus by the Gate of Blacknes thou must come in / To light of Paradyce in Whytenes yf thou wylt wyn' (Ripley, *Compound*, p. 150). Quite simply, Elizabeth the phoenix embodies the 'light of Paradyce' revealed on opening the pendant case, which is faced with a blackamoor – 'the Gate of Blacknes'. Elizabeth I's gesture of proffering a blackamoor gift was by no means unique. Sardonyx cameos with alchemical resonances provided talented artists with a wonder-ful opportunity to harness the natural dark–light colours of the onyx meaningfully, and busts and heads of black people fashioned in onyx poured from the studios of sixteenth-century Italian craftsmen.[30] Many,

Image Unavailable

8(a) The Drake Jewel, front cameo view: ornate gold and coloured enamel, rubies, diamonds, pearls, sardonyx and cameo of a man and woman in profile.

Image Unavailable

8(b) The Drake Jewel, back view: opened to show miniature painted in watercolour on vellum of Elizabeth I and a phoenix by Nicholas Hilliard.

like the Gresley Jewel bearing the head of a black woman on its outer case and a portrait of a white man and woman inside, seem designed to celebrate the marriage of aristocratic couples. The 'chemical wedding', or union of male and female forces to produce pure love or the stone (the philosophical child) was, of course, a key alchemical theme.

The crafting of the black–white, male–female cameo fronting the Drake Jewel is highly suggestive of a 'conjunctio' or marriage of black and white forces. Viewed from this angle, Solomon's *Song* is the refracted image, especially if we recall how the queen designated the head of her Church, her 'little black husband'. Significantly in this context, Sir Francis Drake was involved in another type of marriage between black and white forces. In 1576 he had formed an alliance with the 'cimarrones' – runaway African slaves – in order to capture a Spanish train loaded with treasure crossing the Panama.[31] The raid was successful, Drake won a reputation as a liberator of slaves and the productive 'conjunctio' resulted in real, as opposed to spiritual, gold and riches for Drake and his men. Spurred on by this success, in 1585–6 he planned to rebuild this black–white alliance, ostensibly with a more spiritual goal in mind this time. His design was none other than to increase English power in the West Indies, thereby liberating Spanish America from tyranny and popery. His stated ambition, undoubtedly one shared with his queen, was thus to extend the English church in the Americas, converting black souls to Protestantism and purifying existing Catholicism there of its papal, Spanish, 'dark' corruptions.[32] In relation to this there is an interesting passage in Joseph Hall's 1609 *Open and Plaine Paraphrase, upon the Song of Songs* about the reason for the 'blackish . . . hew' of the 'comely bride':

Looke not therefore disdainefully upon me, because I am blackish, and darke of hew: for this colour is not so much naturall to be; as caused by that continuall heat of afflictions wherewith I have bene usually scorched: . . . their idolatrous religions, and superstitious impieties. (p. 5)

By the early seventeenth century, the *Song* had clearly been appropriated in the service of reform and conversion. From the alchemical perspective, Drake's was truly a whitewashing 'renovatio' enterprise of deep significance. It is hardly surprising, therefore, that Elizabeth's pendant gift to her leading seaman takes us through a gate of blackness, to a paradise of whiteness: to herself as divine monarch (an alchemist like Solomon) and head of the English Church – the true, renovated Church regenerated by her powers (she is the healing stone) and symbolized by the phoenix with red wings (the *Rubedo* phase of the alchemical process). It is politically significant, how-ever, that it is a 'conjunctio' or alliance of black and white forces that is figured in this piece of royal propaganda as the first step in achieving the imperial-religious goal. In alchemy white is concomitant upon black ('Now as to colours, that which does not make black cannot make white', *The Secret Book of Artephius*): they exist in a continuum and it is only the uniting of ostensible binary forces (male–female, black–white) that can result in the ultimate, perfect *Rubedo* phase.[33] Repeated 'conjunctios' with the reconciliation and integration of opposing forces is, we should recall, the work-in-progress of the *opus*.

This way of thinking about contraries is rather different, we should note, from conceptualizing in terms of irreconcilable binaries. In traditional Christian teaching, black and white are moral opposites with black signifying evil. Indeed, it has been asserted that blackness and evil 'ran so deep that it was impossible to extirpate, and to praise things dark inevitably sounded sophistical'.[34] However, as I have demonstrated, in the early modern 'chymical' imagination – which was by no means limited to a handful of erudite minds – blackness could resonate with perfection and divinity. Thus, in a letter to the chemist Robert Boyle dated 28 October 1658, Johann Morian described one of Samuel Hartlib's attempts to produce the philosopher's stone: 'All succeeded favourably, and [the material passed] through various inconstant colors, arriving then at perfect blackness'; and, as we have seen, poets even wrote paeans to blackness itself.[35] Furthermore, Queen Anne and her ladies insisted on blacking themselves up for a court entertainment. Little wonder, then, that Shakespeare could glibly assert in Sonnet 127 'now is black beauty's successive heir' (3). Blackness was definitely in vogue.

LITERARY DARK LADIES

The biblical *Song of Song*'s 'comely black bride' (the soul and/or the Church) was by no means the only mysterious dark lady of alchemical significance in the Renaissance. The highly complex and notably ambivalent Greek mythic figure, Medea, was of major importance. The myth of Jason and the Argonauts underwent many permutations throughout ancient history but the basic components are persistent. Jason set out on a long sea voyage in his ship, the Argo, along with the chief Greek heroes, including the poet Orpheus, to win the golden fleece. The latter was in the possession of King Aeetes of Colchis, and was guarded by an ever-watchful dragon. With the assistance of the enchantress, princess Medea, and her magic herbal potions, Jason won the fleece and returned home to Iolcus with his lover and bride, Medea. But things went disastrously wrong for the couple and their children in Corinth when Jason deserted Medea in order to marry the king of Creon's daughter. Medea retaliated by poisoning her rival and murdering her own offspring by Jason. In all her contradictions she challenged the classical imagination, and both Greek and Roman writers present her with mingled admiration and horror: as a lovely 'helper-maiden' princess, but also a famous witch and a wrathful, dark, 'foreign' woman (she was not Greek) whose love and lust for vengeance drove her to commit multiple cruel murders.[36] In modern analytical accounts, she is said to resemble the type of female reproductive demon productive of enormous anxiety throughout the ancient and modern world and also – of especial interest from the perspective of this study – to be a nexus of conflicting desires, evoking the disturbing possibility of 'otherness lurking within self'.[37] Medea's story seems to have been old and famous by the eighth century BC and to have occupied a special place in Greek mythology: Homer's *Odyssey* refers to it as 'of interest to everyone'.[38]

It was certainly of interest to Renaissance Hermeticists. Like Solomon's *Song*, the entire story of Jason and the Argonauts could be interpreted alchemically, as Sir Walter Raleigh's *The History of the World* points out:

Some there are, that by this journey of *Jason*, understand the mysterie of the Philosopher's Stone, called the golden Fleece; to which also other superfine Chymists, draw the twelve labours of *Hercules*. *Suidas* thinkes, that by the golden Fleece, was ment a booke of Parchment, which is of sheepeskinne, and therefore called golden, because it was taught therein how other mettals might be transmuted. ('Of the Expedition of the Argonauts', Book II, Ch. 13)[39]

The golden fleece becomes none other than the philosopher's stone – the goal of the *opus*. Titus Burckhardt's study of alchemy quotes at length from an anonymous work entitled the *Purissima Revelatio*, which explains the analogy, calling nature a book that only the divinely illumined may read. Nature is, furthermore:

A very thick wood into which many have penetrated in order to try and wrest its holy secrets from it. But they have been swallowed up, because they did not have the light weapons which alone could conquer the terrible dragon protecting the golden fleece. And those who were not killed, had to retrace their steps, gripped by terror and covered in shame and disgrace. Nature is also that measureless sea on which the Argonauts set out. Woe to sailors who do not know our art! For they may travel their whole life long without ever reaching harbour. They will find no refuge from the frightful storms. Burnt by the sun and frozen by icy winds they will undoubtedly perish, unless they implore the help of the most high and mighty Lord . . . For it is not given to many to reach the shore of Colchis . . . Only the wise Argonauts, who strictly observe the laws of nature and are completely devoted to the will of the almighty, can win the precious golden fleece, which Medea, the personification of nature, will yield up, against the order of her darksome father and to the great anger of the surprised dragon.[40]

The treatise proceeds to explain how the happy winners are those who, affianced to wisdom, know how to seduce the sorceress Nature, enabling them to obtain her secrets, but who subsequently return home, possessing the golden fleece and true to their virtuous bride wisdom. However, 'woe to him who, like Jason, having conquered with the help of Medea, lets himself be seduced by his dangerous conquest and submits to nature the sorceress, instead of remaining constant and true to his divine bride, wisdom'.[41] These are the twin faces of universal Nature – likened to Medea (mistress) and Sophia (bride) – and in alchemy they are both present in human nature too; both are feminine in relation to the human will.[42] Dark Nature is actually an enchanting force with an element of compulsion about her; dangerous and seductive she might be, but she is essential to the divine quest, for it is only she who possesses the power to release the soul from its arid sterility.[43] The alchemist's spiritual labours thus necessitate a type of Herculean struggle involving passions and reason, will and wit, often associated both in classical times and in the early modern period with a relation of Medea's, another very dark lady indeed, Circe (Medea's aunt).

In many early modern texts, Circe and her analogues (notably Acrasia in Spenser's *Faerie Queene*) emerge in a very one-sided way – nothing but trouble, these witch-types use a cocktail of wily seduction and magic to entrap and brutalize men. Increasingly associated in the sixteenth century with Babylon and the notorious whore of the Book of Revelation, they also come to signify false religion in an entirely negative way.[44] However, Homer's Circe in the *Odyssey* was a far more light and dark creation: although she turns Odysseus's men into pigs, the wise hero manages to overcome her charms with, notably, the counter magic of 'Moly' or Hermes. Tamed by her lover, Circe even shows concern for the well-being of Odysseus and his men and eventually assists them. Homer's Circe resembles the equally ambiguous Ishtar of the Gilgamesh Epic – a fearsome, accomplished seductress who threatens to transform her lovers. According to Charles Segal, both Homer's Circe and Ishtar have attributes of the *potnia theron* connecting them 'with the Great Mother, goddess of sexuality, death, and rebirth in the cycles of vegetation, who holds the key to both love and death'.[45]

Assiduously eschewing one-sidedness (in favour of the union of contraries), Renaissance Hermeticists tended to create complex Circes of the latter type, preserving both positive and negative poles of nature in one form (as in the French Academy's *Ballet Comique* outlined in Chapter 1). Giordano Bruno's Circe in *De gli eroici furori* (1585) (hereafter, *The Heroic Frenzies*) – 'Daughter and mother of darkness and horror'– is particularly complex and noteworthy.[46] This densely philosophical work, written during his stay in London (1583–5), is a compendium of argument, dialogues, sonnets, allegories and emblems, which illustrate the progress of the soul towards God through love. It self-consciously aligns itself both with the Petrarchan literary tradition and – extremely significantly – with the *Song of Solomon*. Bruno's 'Argument', dedicated to Sir Philip Sidney, rather audaciously declares that he had wished, in fact, to call his book 'Canticle', after the *Book of Solomon* which, 'under the guise of lovers and ordinary passions, contains similarly divine and heroic frenzies, as the mystics and cabbalistic doctors interpret'.[47] A truly syncretic work, it also invokes ancient Egyptian religion and extols Hermes Trismegistus's 'prophetic wisdom' (p. 182) in relation to the necessary 'mutations', from good to evil and evil to good, of all things. In a key allegory of the book, nine men who appear to be lustily pursuing one beautiful woman, Giulia, are declared actually to be 'rivals in the shadows and vestiges of the divine beauty'. While in that state they decide to seek out Circe, who, the reader is instructed,

represents the generative matter of all things. She is called the daughter of the sun, because from the father of forms she has inherited the possession of all those forms which, by a sprinkling of waters – that is to say by the act of generation and by the power of enchantment – that is by reasons of a secret harmony – she transforms all beings, making those who see become blind. For generation and corruption are causes of oblivion and of blindness, as the ancients explain by the figure of souls who bathe and inebriate themselves in the waters of Lethe. (p. 75)

Bruno's Circe appears to resemble Ficino's conception of 'Nature': 'when we say Nature, we mean the power placed in the Soul's faculty of procreation' (p. 49). In the *Heroic Frenzies*, blindness is a crucial part of the affliction that the individual soul must experience in its pursuit of divine illumination and it is conferred by this confluence of Circe/Nature. Crucially, Circe blinds, but she provides the means for cure too: she gives the newly blinded men a 'fatal vase' (the Hermetic vase of the alchemical *opus*) which, she makes clear, she is 'powerless to open' (p. 26). They must wander far and wide on a pilgrimage of the world seeking the one who can: 'for destiny wishes that this vase remain closed until lofty wisdom and noble chastity and beauty apply their hands to it; all other labours are fruitless to pour this water' (p. 261). When they find their 'Diana' they will be cured by healing waters, experience 'divine virtue', and, notably, see 'everything as one' (p. 261). Bruno's 'Argument' renders clear that 'men carry with themselves the decree and destiny of a new metamorphosis': Circe can only 'entrust the vase to them' (p. 76). The resounding message is that men's desires might be projected on to female forms like Giulia in *The Heroic Frenzies* and the enchantress Circe, but the latter's transforming powers actually reside within men themselves. Again, this corresponds with Ficino's philosophy where 'the mind (in its own nature dark) . . . is forced to receive according to the capacity of its own nature' (p. 100).

Importantly, for Bruno, inner harmony or 'Diana, the Monad', who enshrines the Platonic virtues, 'beauty, truth and goodness', is achieved through the perfect integration and balancing of body and spirit – the material and the spiritual (pp. 37, 43, 45). This is a significant departure from the *stil novisti* tradition in which responding to the body's natural instincts is completely at odds with the pursuit of divine love. In Bruno's philosophy, eschewing the sensual self entirely is equally as unhelpful as blindly pursuing passions at the expense of spirit: 'lofty' and 'profound' thoughts should join with 'the maternal bonds of the afflicted soul' – with the 'domestic fires' (pp. 37, 130). Dichotomies and cleavages are antithetical to harmony: Bruno thus advocates a middle path towards the ideal (pp. 48–9). Indeed, the sonnet 'Annosa quercia' expresses the lover's joy in this ability to unite these contrary natures of the soul: 'Ancient oak, which spreads its branches to the air, and fixes its roots in the earth; neither the trembling earth, nor the powerful spirits which the sky lets loose from the bitter wind . . . can ever uproot you from the place where you stand firm' (p. 162). Recovering 'natural beauty' is thus construed as the 'conjunctio' and balancing of the soul's contraries. The soul's regeneration is achieved through the 'furnace of Vulcan' (p. 166):

Therefore, as the soul desires to recover its natural beauty, it seeks to purge itself, heal and reform itself; and for this purpose the soul uses fire, for like gold mixed with earth and shapeless, it wishes by a vigorous trial to liberate itself from impurities, and this end is achieved when the intellect, the true smith of Jove, sets to work actively exercising the intellectual powers. (p. 166)

This is, of course, inner alchemy.

Another notable, and not dissimilar representation of Circe occurs in Aurelian Townshend's masque, *Tempe Restored*, which derives from the French *Ballet Comique*. In the 1632 English production both Lord Herbert and Mr Philip Herbert participated as 'Influences'. Here we are told, Circe embodies 'Desire in general, the which hath power on all living creatures, and being mixed of the divine and sensible, hath diverse effects, leading some to virtue and others to vice'.[48] The message of this masque is that men bind their own minds, not Circe: they become slaves to the enchantress through their own 'sloth' and lust' (p. 156). Indeed, this resonates with the wisdom of Shakespeare's Enobarbus of *Antony and Cleopatra*, who confirms that 'Herculean' Antony's problem is not Cleopatra's cunning and charms – she is, of course, another notable literary dark lady – but that of allowing his effeminate will to dominate his reason. Townshend's Circe seems also to enshrine the two loves or Venuses – divine and reproductive – described in Plato's *Symposium*. Corresponding in many ways to Nature's dual faces, both spiritual and sensible loves were construed as essential to human life and, in Ficino's *De amore*, both are characterized as 'daemons'.

PART II WILL'S DARK MISTRESS

Is she an idealized Petrarchan goddess, above good and evil? Is she a natural essence, like the ocean? Or is she a calculating accumulator of goods?[49]

Who, or what, is the dark lady? Mysterious mutability is the hallmark of alchemical writing and just as the speaker's 'friend' dissolves in and out of material existence, sometimes seeming a 'he', sometimes a 'he-she', sometimes an aspect of the poet's psyche, occasionally resembling a 'she', and possibly even God,[50] so the dark mistress defies our inevitable attempts to stabilize her. Suggestively, in Sonnet 127 she is even 'beauty's successive heir' – the 'bastard' offspring of 'lovely boy', his 'successor' in the *opus*. A 'cunning', whimsical tyrant in love, who also has maternal aspects (as when she is called upon to comfort blubbering Will in Sonnet 148), she is certainly a complex and ambivalent literary creation. But one of her most dominant – though neglected – guises is that of Mistress Nature herself – a literary cousin, to be sure, of the type of Ishtar, Medea and Circe described above. This does not entirely, however, rule out rather more material contenders for some aspects of Shakespeare's dark muse – 'Mary Fitton, or Lucy Negro, Jacqueline Field, Emilia Lanier, or [even] ... Mistress Winifred Burbage' – for in Hermeticism nature's inward power could be awakened by the contemplation of Dame Nature in the beauty of the female body.[51]

We should recall that in Sonnet 126 the poet's 'lovely boy' appears to have come to something of a fruition: through repeated operations of the *opus* – incorporating union, death of the lovers and regeneration – his 'sweet' distillation has 'by waning grown'. The power to stay the destructive effects of time is now within 'lovely boy's' 'power'. However, a warning is issued: 'fear' Nature. It would seem that 'mistress' Nature's purposeful 'skill' is necessary at this stage in the *opus* to achieve eternity. The sonnet is abruptly terminated, two rather threatening coffin-like parentheses mark the spot and 'black beauty' makes her debut. In the alchemical context this is entirely appropriate for her 'skill' as 'Kind' [Nature] is essential in order to engender 'kindness' (the third aspect of the triangle or trinity – 'Fair, kind and true') and to complete 'Will's' – the artist's – spiritual transformation. As Burckhardt explains, alchemists frequently asserted that 'covetousness' – defined rather strangely as 'attachment to one's limited ego in thrall to passion' – was the key obstacle to the soul's Hermetic ascent and this is a crucial aspect of inner nature that Will is striving to control in the last twenty-eight sonnets.[52] Exercising his higher powers, the artist must now eradicate Will in 'overplus', tame his sensual self and lighten his dark spiritual nature. He must in fact negate himself – 'Myself I'll forfeit' (Sonnet 134), 'For nothing hold me' (Sonnet 136) – and bring his will into conformity with God's. Alchemists insisted that a too dominant 'I' could be overcome only by kindness – 'compassion alone delivers us from the artfulness of the ego' and Nature's 'skill' in engendering this was crucial.[53] Not surprisingly, therefore, Elias Ashmole introduces his collection of alchemical poetry with the promise that readers will encounter the 'wooing' of Dame Nature: '[Here] you may meet the Genii of our Hermetique Philosophers, learne the language in which they woo'd and courted Dame Nature.'[54]

The final stage of the alchemical *opus*, which culminates in the liberation of the spirit with heightened powers of perception, can be achieved only 'by means of a natural vibration of the soul' when Nature comes to the aid of the art, according to the alchemical adage: 'The progress of the art pleases nature greatly.'[55] Always dark and female, she is both the 'power of desire and longing in man' and a potent force that 'develops all the capacities hidden in the soul, against or in keeping with the desires of the ego, depending on whether the latter assimilates the power of nature, or becomes its victim'. As Sophia or 'wisdom' she is a positive, nurturing power but as extreme passion she binds the soul and blocks spiritual progression.[56] Her ambivalent, shifting nature – actually a reflection of her lover's conflicting desires – and her spiritually improving potential, help us to understand seemingly ironic Shakespearean lines such as the close of Sonnet 141 and the opening of 142: 'Only my plague thus far I count my gain, / That she that makes me sin awards me pain' (13–14). 'Love is my sin, and thy dear virtue hate, / Hate of my sin, grounded on sinful loving' (1–2). Affliction and pain are considered a crucial and unavoidable part of the regeneration process. Importantly, though, the outcome of this 'fear'[ful] encounter with his 'sovereign mistress' is by no means assured. Like the alchemists' Medea described above, she will present a dangerous challenge for her Herculean-type victim; the *Shake-speare* of the *Sonnets'* title page (a spear is featured on his coat-of-arms) is playfully suggestive in this context. Can he tame her dark powers and harness them productively, or will he become her slave, collapsing into lust and sin? Another outcome is possible: will he, like Hercules (and indeed, like Spenser's Redcross Knight), emerge strengthened and victorious after a period of enslavement to his Omphale? Whatever happens she cannot 'keep' him: in the end he must be 'rendered' and face the ultimate test – divine judgement.

THE FALL AND RISE OF WILL

The lover of the body is content with sight alone. Thus the desire to touch is not a part of love, nor is it a passion of the lover, but rather a kind of lust and perturbation of a man who is servile ... he who loves the beauty of the soul is content with the perceiving of the Intellect alone. (Ficino, *De amore*, p. 58)

The 'test' certainly does not get off to a promising start. Indeed, the beautifully sensual musical Sonnet 128 positively jangles with alarm bells. As the speaker contemplates his mistress-muse – 'my music' – playing the virginal she becomes reduced synecdochically to 'sweet fingers' tickling the 'dancing chips': 'those jacks that nimble leap / To kiss the tender inward of thy hand' (5–6). Envying the 'saucy jacks'' intimacy with her hand, the music 'confounds' his ear disharmoniously, desire to touch dominates, and the sonnet concludes anticipating kissing lips. The descent from sight to erotic touching via 'delicate and playful' music could not have been more rapid and, measured against the strictures of Ficino's *De amore*, this is 'vulgar', not 'heavenly' love:

But there are said to be two kinds of musical melody. For one is ponderous and steady. The other is delicate and playful. Plato, in the books on the Republic and Laws, judges the former to be beneficial to users and the latter harmful. In the Symposium he assigns to the former the Muse Urania, to the latter Polyhymnia. Some people love the first type; others, the second. The love of the former people should be tolerated, and the sounds which they desire should be permitted; but the appetite of the latter people should be resisted. For the love of the former is heavenly; of the latter, vulgar. (p. 67)

Those contemporary readers of the sonnets trained in Pythagorean musicology would have detected further troubling signs. Fred Blick argues that the number 128 is significant: it suggests a twelve-note sequence of semitones followed by the octave note, known as the 'Eight'.[57] Interestingly, it therefore indicates dissonance and concord simultaneously. In a letter to the poet Domenico Benivieni on musical harmony, Ficino describes how 'the twelfth' – 'allotted to hidden enemies and to prison' – expresses 'the dissonant falling away of the second note from the first'.[58] Invoking the octave, it would be usual to anticipate 'wiry concord' – harmony – as the instrumentalist 'sway'st'; however, the rendition of a sequence of twelve semitones 'with gentle gate' would, according to Blick, 'confound' the ear with its disharmony. Through its evocation of the 'eight' and of music, this sonnet is linked to number 8 in the sequence; indeed, according to the Pythagorean 2:1 octave ratio principle, 128 is in unison with but four octaves lower than the number 8, rendering it bass or, perhaps, base in this context. Both sonnets notably feature 'conjunctios' – a marriage and a kiss respectively. However, the 'conjunctio' of 128 is associated with a disharmony that anticipates the jarring rant of the next poem.

Sonnet 129 suggests that touching proceeded well beyond lips, resulting in the speaker's vehement disgust at his wasteful 'lust' – 'Th'expense of spirit in a waste of shame' (1) – and a rapid descent into a compelling sexual madness: 'Past reason hated as a swallowed bait / On purpose laid to make the taker mad' (7–8). Here, then, is something new in the English sonnet tradition: a representation of consummated passion with a 'shame'[ful] mistress, complete with all the 'bliss', 'woes', 'blame' and fascinating erotic detail that entails. While Sidney's Astrophil manages to secure one brief kiss from his dark-eyed but vehemently chaste muse as she sleeps, leaving his desire crying 'Give me some food' (Sonnet 71), Shakespeare's Will is consumming his desire in 'overplus' and still craving more. His 'music' is far from chaste and Sonnet 130 even appears to foreground and celebrate its sensual earthiness: 'My mistress when she walks treads on the ground' (12). There is undoubtedly an element of poetic brinkmanship in this.

It is as if Shakespeare has taken up the bait laid down by writers against 'Circean' entrapments, including Giordano Bruno and Marsilio Ficino. For, although the representation of erotic passion was novel in respect to the English sonnet tradition, it had been extensively described in Hermetic treatises on love. Ficino's *De amore* depicts this 'infection' of the blood in a particularly graphic manner, detailing its symptoms – such as 'foul stains' on the skin and 'itchiness' (we might recall Will's 'plague' here) – the way it is caught ('frequent gazing ... eye to eye', 166) and its frenzied progress: 'As long as the love lasts, they are afflicted first by the burning of the bile, then by the burning of the black bile, and they rush into frenzies and fire, and as if blind do not know where they are being precipitated . . . by this madness man sinks back to the nature of beast' (*De amore*, p. 168). The speaker of this passage, Ficino's friend Giovanni Cavalcanti, also suggests (citing Lucretius as his authority) some surprising cures including 'frequent coitus' (p. 168).

As Bruno's 'Argument' prefacing *The Heroic Frenzies* makes clear, pro-creative love is desirable in moderation but definitely *not* in excess:

Most illustrious knight [Sir Philip Sidney], it is indeed a base, ugly and contaminated wit that is constantly occupied and curiously obsessed with the beauty of a female body! What spectacle, oh dear God, more vile and ignoble can be presented . . . than a rational man afflicted, tormented . . . melancholic . . . hot . . . cold . . . confused . . . resolute; one who spends most of his time and the choice fruits of his life letting fall drop by drop the elixir of his brain by putting into conceits and in writing . . . those persuasive speeches, those laborious complaints and most bitter labours inevitable beneath the tyranny of an unworthy, witless, stupid and odoriferous foulness!

What a tragicomedy! . . . which with surface appearance, a shadow, a phantasm, a dream, a Circean enchantment put to the service of generation, deceives us as a species of beauty. (pp. 59–60)

'What a tragicomedy!' It is exactly this that we witness in the witty depiction of Will's 'fall'. In Sonnet 130, 'My mistress' eyes are nothing like the sun' (1), 'black wires grow on her head' (4), we learn that she is ugly, 'reeks' and speaks poorly – but he loves her. Self-irony abounds and Will's 'enchantment' progresses textbook style. Here is *De amore* for example: 'Venereal madness leads to intemperance, and therefore to disharmony. Therefore it likewise seems to lead to ugliness, whereas love leads to beauty' (p. 41). This is how men are 'ensnared' (p. 167): 'By very frequent gazing, directing their sight eye to eye, they join lights with lights and drink a long love together, poor wretches . . . the whole cause and origin of this illness is certainly the eye . . . drives people mad' (p. 166). And this is what ensues: 'For lovers, blinded by the clouds of love, often accept false things for true . . . They contradict themselves on account of the vehemence of love, for reason considers one thing, and concupiscence pursues another. They change their counsels at the command of the beloved; they oppose themselves in order to comply with others' (p. 126).

Notably, 'they oppose themselves in order to comply with others'; it is as if Will has read *De amore* and is playing the stereotypical part of the 'ensnared' lover:

> Yet in good faith some say, that thee behold,
> Thy face hath not the power to make love groan;

> To say they err I dare not be so bold,
> Although I swear it to myself alone.   (Sonnet 131, 5–8)

And again:

> Past cure I am, now Reason is past care,
> And, frantic-mad with ever more unrest,
> My thoughts and my discourse as madmen's are,
> At random from the truth vainly expressed.
>
> (Sonnet 147, 9–12)

To some extent the poet's evident confusion might be apprehended as a rational response to such treatises on love which, certainly, under Ficino's polyvalent penmanship (there are five speakers, who introduce seven commentators on Plato), appear contradictory at many points and profoundly confusing: both the eye and the intellect have sight, for example, and how you distinguish which one is doing the seeing at any one moment (and therefore the truth or deception of the vision) is largely a matter for conjecture. Thus, Will's frustration at his lack of perspicuity even begins to seem reasonable:

> Thou blind fool love, what dost thou to mine eyes
> That they behold and see not what they see?
>
> (Sonnet 137, 1–2)

Viewed through the perplexing lens of the Renaissance manuals and emblem books on love as a route to the divine, it is, in fact, impossible to work out what is true and whether his 'eye' is 'perjur'd' or not.[59]

Overwhelmingly, however, to adopt Bruno's words, this appears to be a 'spectacle' of a poet 'letting fall drop by drop the elixir of his brain', under the spell of an 'odiferous foulness' (Argument, pp. 59–60). Katherine Duncan-Jones is only one of a range of commentators to find such representations offensive and deeply misogynistic: an 'elaborate mockery of a woman who is no more than a sexual convenience'.[60] But what if the 'reeking' foulness described in Sonnet 130 is the speaker's own? In one of the most popular alchemical poems of Shakespeare's day, Thomas Norton's *The Ordinall of Alchimy*, discussed in Chapter 1, 'stinkinge' smells feature prominently in the description of the process whereby 'All proud appetites' are brought to 'equalitie': 'when Evill substance shall putrifie / horrible Odour is engendred thereby'.[61] If the 'dark lady' is sometimes an aspect of the speaker's dark inner nature – of 'otherness lurking within the self (Medea),[62] this would be a clever and humorous way of signifying the purifying phase of the alchemical process. Indeed, Bruno wrote a sonnet on this odiferous theme beginning, 'I hoist my sails to the wind, which pulls me toward the odious good and leads me to sweet tempestuous damnation' (*Heroic Frenzies*, p. 113). The ensuing dialogues of

Bruno's *Heroic Frenzies* proceed to depict the 'rise and fall' of the inferior and superior powers of the soul, likening them to the 'inconstant moon': 'Our soul in its entire substance is symbolized by the moon. It shines through the hemisphere of the superior potencies when turned toward the light of the intelligible world; and it is darkened on the side of the inferior potencies when occupied with the government of matter' (p. 61).

As Burckhardt describes, the third stage of inner alchemy is dominated by the moon (associated in the Renaissance with Urania, the divine Muse) and is finished when all the soul's potentialities are developed and unified, producing perfect whiteness – Diana.[63] The numerological emphasis on twenty-eight dark lady sonnets in Shakespeare's sequence undoubtedly symbolizes the moon which, with her characteristic changes and influences, is always personified as female and, as William Basse's contemporaneous poem 'Urania' (1612) explains, is simultaneously 'Mistress' of the 'mind'.[64] In an illuminating passage Basse declares:

> Where from her influence succeeds some ill
> To any, 'tis their faults and not her will,
> And where 'tis sayd she favours doth bestow,
> 'Tis their good natures help to make it so.
> For as the Bee and spider from one flower
> Honey and poison sayd are to devoure,
> Her guifts all prove according to the frame
> Of those capacities receive the same.
> She being ill with ill, and good with good,
> No harm can doe; and would not if she cou'd. (pp. 313–14)

Moon and Nature converge in this poem and she, like the alchemist's Circe combining honey and poison, is responsible for conferring form on the 'good' and 'ill' aspects of the mind/soul but – crucially – ''Tis their good natures help to make it so': Nature is a passive receiver of form. As Alison Shell has demonstrated, Urania was closely associated with a call to the 'creativity of contrition' in this period.[65]

If Shakespeare's mistress sometimes seems to be a projection of the speaker's inner nature – his dark soul – she/he also emerges at points as a type of the church and even as Christ/Solomon. Her 'raven' eyes evoke Solomon's 'raven' locks in the *Song* and the prominence given to her black beauty is suggestive of the bride's comeliness. Sonnet 143 is particularly interesting in this respect:

> Lo, as a careful housewife runs to catch
> One of her feathered creatures broke away,

> Sets down her babe and makes all swift dispatch
> In pursuit of the thing she would have stay,
> Whilst her neglected child holds her in chase,
> Cries to catch her whose busy care is bent
> To follow that which flies before her face,
> Not prizing her poor infant's discontent;
> So runn'st thou after that which flies from thee,
> Whilst I, thy babe, chase thee afar behind.
> But if thou catch thy hope, turn back to me
> And play the mother's part: kiss me, be kind.
> So will I pray that thou mayst have thy Will,
> If thou turn back and my loud crying still.   (Sonnet 143)

The tone is surprisingly psalm-like and Duncan-Jones notes how it contains echoes from Psalm 68.[66] The latter's allegorical focus is mercy and redemption, as the Geneva Bible annotation explains: '[In this Psalm] David expresseth the wonderfull mercies of god towards his people, who by all meanes and most strange sort, declareth himself unto them. Gods Church therefore by reason of his promises, grace and victories, doth excel all worldy things: wherefore all men are moved to prayse God for ever.'[67]

The version 'Set forth and allowed to be sung in all Churches' in the 1599 Geneva Bible begins: 'Let God arise, and then his foes will turne themselves to flight: his enemies then will runne abroad, and scatter out of sight. And as the fire doth melt the waxe, and winde blowes smoake away, so in the presence of the lord, the wicked shall decay' (p. 37). It promises, rather engagingly, that women who remain at home instead of fleeing will partake of the 'spoyle' and:

> Though yee were as blacke as pots,
> Your hew shall passe the Dove:
> Whose wings and feathers seeme to have
> Silver and gold above.   (p. 38)

Then, we hear:

> The Mores most blacke shall stretch their hands
> unto their Lord and king.   (p. 39)

If we read Shakespeare's sonnet allusively and allegorically, in the light of this psalm and the Geneva Bible annotations and our knowledge about blackamoors (the darkened soul and Church that *can* be washed white), it becomes possible to see how the speaker might be engaging in a meditative exercise (veiled in 'amorous deceits')[68] in which the soul's, the Church's and ultimately Christ's fall and rise – the Resurrection – feature prominently. We might consider, too, that in the Hermetic ascent one of the areas that must be encountered and successfully grappled with for spiritual progress to occur is 'unholy daring and rash audacity'.[69] Viewed from within these contexts, the prior sonnet's accusation – 'those lips of thine / That have profaned their scarlet ornaments / And sealed false bonds of love as oft as mine' (Sonnet 142, 5–7) (invoking Isaiah 1. 18 and Revelation 17. 30) – begins to resonate with new meaning; and Sonnet 151's plea, 'No want of conscience hold it that I call / Her "love", for whose dear love I rise and fall' (13–14) becomes far less bawdy than a surface reading suggests. Indeed, my extended discussion in Chapter 5 of Sonnet 151 in the light of the Geneva Bible marginalia to Romans 7: 19 – 'the flesh stayeth even the moste perfect to runne forwarde as the spirit wisheth' – further amplifies the spiritual meanings of this sonnet.[70] This allegorical context is the correct one for understanding the deeply serious and explicitly religious Sonnet 146, 'Poor soul, the centre of my sinful earth, / Spoiled by these rebel powers that thee array' (1–2), which urges, 'Buy terms divine' (11) – that is, spiritual 'store' – at the expense of 'dross' – earthly riches.

But who or what are these 'rebel powers'? Certainly, the troubled ménage à trois – 'him, myself and thee', 'A torment thrice threefold' (Sonnet 133, 7, 8) – seems implicated. The entry on 'Meditatio' in Martin Ruland's *A Lexicon of Alchemy* is illuminating here: 'The name of an Internal Talk of one person with another who is invisible, as in the invocation of the deity, or communion with one's self, or with one's good angel.'[71] 'Communion with one's self' is the means whereby the contrary and warring aspects of the soul are reconciled in inner alchemy. Thus, in Bruno's treatise we witness 'the sufferings of the soul' under the 'turbulent republic' (*Heroic Frenzies*, p. 69) 'of the diversity of the inclinations which are in his [man's] several parts' (p. 68). This leads to a 'variety of dispositions', which cause the individual to 'rise and fall' (like Shakespeare's speaker in Sonnet 151), to go 'forward and backward', so that he 'withdraw[s] himself from himself and also withdraws into himself' (p. 68). Indeed, as Bruno's formulations reveal, alchemical meditation led to an obsessive awareness of a fractured, troubled inner psychic space: the 'self' was acknowledged as a multiplicity of different, mutable selves. No wonder, then, that Shakespeare's speaker rather torturously laments, 'Me from myself thy cruel eye hath taken, / And my next self thou harder hast engrossed' (Sonnet 133, 5–6), and in the next sonnet offers, 'Myself I'll forfeit, so that other mine / Thou wilt restore to be my comfort still' (Sonnet 134, 3–4). The 'covetous' and the 'kind' (6) are aspects of one will or 'I', which is why 'I, being pent in thee, / Perforce am thine, and all that is in me' (Sonnet 133, 13–14). Furthermore, they seem to correspond to Plato's and Ficino's 'two . . . loves':

These two eternal loves in us are daemons which Plato predicts will always be present in our souls, one of which raises us to things above; the other presses us down to things below. One is a kalodaemon, that is, a good daemon; the other is a kakodaemon, that is an evil daemon. In reality both are good, since the procreation of offspring is considered to be as necessary and virtuous as the pursuit of truth. But the second is called evil because, on account of our abuse, it often disturbs us and powerfully diverts the soul from its chief good, which consists in the contemplation of truth, and twists it to baser purposes. (*De amore*, p. 119)

It is this Ficinian-style drama within the alembic of the 'head' which is given such vivid expression in Sonnet 144, resembling a *psychomachia*:

> Two loves I have, of comfort and despair,
> Which like two spirits, do suggest me still.
> The better angel is a man right fair;
> The worser spirit a woman coloured ill.
> To win me soon to hell my female evil
> Tempteth my better angel from my side,
> And would corrupt my saint to be a devil,
> Wooing his purity with her foul pride.
> And whether that my angel be turned fiend
> Suspect I may, yet not directly tell,
> But being both from me, both to each friend,
> I guess one angel in another's hell.
> Yet this shall I ne'er know, but live in doubt,
> Till my bad angel fire my good one out.

Read literally, the speaker is apparently conjecturing that his absent 'friends' have embarked on a sexual relationship, which will be confirmed only when 'my female evil' gives 'my saint' a dose of venereal disease; however, as might be anticipated, the alchemical allegory inscribes 'double-speak'. Read alchemically, the anticipated 'conjunctio' (facilitated by 'I', 'myself', the mercurial mediator who has brought these contraries together) might not be as disastrous as the bawdy sense of this sonnet implies. On the contrary, a 'firing' might be exactly what these opposing and turbulent dispositions of the soul require. As, when male sulphur and female quicksilver are 'married' in the alembic, mutual 'penetration' leads to 'generation', so spiritual regeneration might result from this union.[72] However, the outcome is by no means assured because 'a one-sided conjunction of heat and humidity', resembling the 'condition of consuming passion', can lead to a 'wrapping up of the ego-consciousness in itself' – 'a mortal condition of the soul'.[73] Mutual 'penetration' is crucial then: will Will succeed in harmonizing his 'rebel powers'?

His descent into unreason, confused discourse, madness and seeming blindness through the course of the sequence is usually cited as incontrovertible evidence that the speaker's obsessions are entirely lecherous and that any quest for the higher reaches of his 'self' is merely ironical or has, in any case, been lost.[74] This is by no means clear, however. As Edgar Wind's *Pagan Mysteries in the Renaissance* argues, in this period 'on the authority of Plotinus, sustained in this instance by Epicurus, a noble "voluptas" was introduced as the *summum bonum* of Neoplatonists'.[75] Plotinus maintained:

that the mind has two powers ... The one is the vision of the sober mind ... the other is the mind in a state of love ... for when it loses its reason by becoming drunk with nectar ... then it enters into a state of love, diffusing itself wholly in delight ... and it is better thus to rage than to remain aloof from that drunkenness. (*Enneads*, VI, vii, p. 35)[76]

Incorporating this belief into Hermetic philosophy, both Ficino and his pupil, Pico, disseminated the view that the very highest form of love *is* blind, passionate and frenzied – above reason (Ficino, *De amore*, p. 168).[77] Pico thus declared 'Love is said by Orpheus to be without eyes because it is above the intellect' (*Commento II*, iii).[78] Quoting Pico, Reynolds' *Mythomystes* describes how the man pursuing the road to 'celestial love' often appears 'extaticke' and 'ravisht', leading to the loss of 'the use of ... corporall eyes': like 'Tyresias', the 'eyes of his understanding are thereby granted higher powers of vision'.[79] Similarly, for Thomas Campion, 'Love in the bosome is begot, Not in the eyes.'[80] Furthermore, as Ficino's *De amore* renders explicit, because amatory love (divine love) is frenzied and blind (it sees with the mind), it is very easy to confuse it with other 'adulterous emotions' which also culminate in madness (p. 172), crucially, that is, with venereal passion. It is precisely these two 'loves' – *Eros* (venereal) and *Anteros* (divine) – that we meet in the concluding sonnets.

TWO CUPIDS AND DIANA

The last two sonnets of Shakespeare's sequence, featuring Cupid and based on a fifth-century Greek epigram, have been descried as 'early work', 'frivolous', 'silly', 'anticlimactic', 'loose[ly]' related to the rest; 'tagged on' to finish the job – 'a rutted and pointless recital'.[81] Furthermore, for Thomas Roche, as for the majority of recent editors and commentators, it is patently obvious that 'Shakespeare is telling us that his Will has failed'.[82] According to Vendler, Sonnet 154 'envisages no cure at all' – 'passion wins' – and for De Grazia, 'the ungodly denial involved in counting black "fair" allows for no such conversion': despite 'his awareness of his moral demise' Will is simply unable to change.[83] As Sonnet 153 proclaims, he knows he is 'sick' but he can only keep returning to his mistress's 'eye[s]'; suggestively her sexual organ too – the source of his venereal infection. Read literally, pox-ridden Will remains his 'mistress' thrall' (slave), and is condemned to seeking out a 'remedy' for his disease in the form of a 'healthful' 'bath' (Sonnet 154): 'hot houses' with their 'sweating' tubs were the unpleasant and ineffectual early modern 'cure' for syphilis.[84] This is surely a 'fitting conclusion' to Will's obsessive rutting and incessant 'babbling'?[85]

According to this widely accepted critical tradition, even to the very last line wicked Will is echoing and thus parodying – in ironic and ungodly fashion – lines from the Bible (*Song of Solomon* 8: 6–7). Although broadly adhering to this view, Roche's voluminous and erudite study, *Petrarch and the English Sonnet Sequences*, injects a note of caution: 'we have not yet learned the rules of the game ... and we still need to know more about the meaning of individual words. Historical criticism has foundered in the cul-de-sac of biography without adequate sociological or religious information or interest'.[86] Yet for Roche, Egyptian hieroglyphs, the Hermetic tradition and emblem books were 'no go', forbidden areas and Frances Yates' famous forays in those directions – particularly in relation to Giordano Bruno and sixteenth-century religious controversies – were 'totally unwarranted'.[87] Roche's pronouncement here seems oddly prejudiced. As I have been arguing in this chapter, a rich but perplexing double vision is maintained throughout Shakespeare's sequence. Spiritual meanings are frequently present in the intertwined vocabularies of late sixteenth-century Neoplatonism, Hermeticism and alchemy – a lexicon widely disseminated in the Renaissance through all the art forms and royal propaganda discussed above and additionally by the highly popular emblem books pouring off the sixteenth-century presses. It is to the latter tradition that I now wish to turn in order to unravel the tangled web of allusion that constitutes Shakespeare's final sonnets.

The sixteenth-century emblematist Andrea Alciati translated a fascination with Ficino's rendering of the *Symposium*'s two loves into emblem book format (*Emblematum liber*, Augsburg, 1531) and thus commenced what John Manning has rather nicely described as a 'theatrical *erotomachia*' or contest between *amor divinus* and *amor humanus*.[88] In the emblem, *Anteros, id est amor virtutis* (*Anteros*, the love of virtue) we meet a chastened, virtuous Cupid – wings clipped and without bow and arrow – and in *Anteros, Amor virtutis, alium Cupidinem, Anteros*, the love of virtue, overcomes *amor humanus*. Interestingly, as Manning points out, the emblems sometimes 'sceptically interrogate' Cupid's traditional iconography: if, for example, Cupid cannot see, why does he require a blindfold?[89] The hackneyed and clichéd philosophical discourses of love have thus begun to be a resource for playful satiric treatment. In 1586 Geoffrey Whitney adapted Alciati's emblem of *Anteros* overcoming *Eros* for his own book, *A Choice of Emblems*. His free adaptation of Alciati's Emblem III depicts not two Cupids but an inverted burning torch accompanied with the inscription, 'Who nourishes me, extinguishes me' and the lines:

> Even as the waxe dothe feede, and quenche the flame,
> So, love gives life; and love, dispaire doth give:
> The godlie love, doth lovers croune with fame:
> The wicked love, in shame dothe make them live,
> Then leave to love, or love as reason will,
> For lovers lewde doe vainlie languishe still.[90]

Two loves of comfort and despair – 'wicked love' and 'godlie love' – were explicitly juxtaposed here for English consumption; and then, just a year before Shakespeare's sonnets are published, what by now constitutes something of a tradition explodes into the 'erotic polyglottism' of Otto Vaenius's *Amorum Emblematum* (Antwerp, 1608).[91] As Manning describes, this volume functioned as a sort of 'pattern book' for the age, 'suggest[ing] a whole linguistic universe ruled by Love, which is investigated by the poet in an effort to map its interconnectedness by means of visual puns, textures and physiognomies'.[92] This is exactly the 'linguistic universe' that Shakespeare's sonnets inhabit. Indeed, it is noteworthy that Vaenius's trilingual edition was dedicated to the Pembroke brothers, the same dedicatees as the first folio.[93]

As we saw in Chapter 2, in Vaenius's playful volume we discover many of the themes and preoccupations of Shakespeare's sonnets, including 'Love is not perfect unless it is directed towards one'; 'the end of love, is that two might become one'; and Cicero's adage on friendship, 'one soul in two bodies'.[94] Indeed, Vaenius's emblem, 'Love's fyre is unquenchable', is remarkably close to Shakespeare's Sonnet 153 (Vaenius, pp. 170–1) and 'love blyndeth' confirms the possibility of a 'stumbling' but forward trajectory of confused blind love (such as Shakespeare's speaker's): 'thogh starck blynd hee bee hee stumbling forward goes / Because his wisest way hee neither sees nor knowes' (Vaenius, pp. 60–1). Apparently at the urging of Queen Isabella of Spain and the Jesuits, Vaenius was persuaded in the next decade (1615) to render his emblems more explicitly 'divine', making them into spiritual allegories in which Cupid as *Anteros*, now unmistakable with his halo, is the companion and guide of a chastely garbed female *Anima*; in the 1609 volume, however, the two loves mingle far more promiscuously in eyebrow-raising fashion.[95] The *Eros–Anteros* topos was clearly popularized by these engaging emblem books and, for an educated early modern readership, the presence of the two Cupids in Shakespeare's final sonnets would not have been difficult to discern.[96] Peggy Munoz Simonds has established the presence of *Eros* in Sonnet 153 and *Anteros* in Sonnet 154 and, to her observations, I wish to add my own about the invocation of 'the fairest votary' – Diana – in the final sonnet.[97] Their dual presence and Diana's evocation in 154 is deeply significant and must lead us to question the critical consensus that Will leaves the sonnet stage in 154 poxed, unrepentant, unregenerate and doomed. The double vision of the concluding sonnets must be brought into focus – they end on a highly ambiguous note.

SEEING DIANA

The domination of the Moon in the operation begins when the Matter, after putrefaction, changes its colour ... into that of white. When the Sages speak of their Moon in this state they call it *Diana Unveiled*, and they say that happy is the man who has beheld Diana naked, that is to say, the Matter at the Perfect White Stone.[98]

Another secret is that you need the mediation of the Virgin Diana (a quintessance, most pure silver): otherwise the mercury and the regulus are not united. (Isaac Newton)[99]

At the close of Sonnet 153, the poet-speaker, 'a sad distempered guest' (12), finds no cure in the 'seething bath' and announces his return to 'my mistress' eyes' (14) – the 'bath for my help' (13). But the 'eyes' are not necessarily his mistress's genitals. As Ficino teaches, 'the eye ... drives people mad': it is the source of other 'strange maladies'; namely, both venereal and divine madness (*De amore*, p. 166). Which of the three infections (venereal pox is always a third possibility) Will is suffering from at this stage is unclear but in Sonnet 154 the potential for cure is announced by the appearance of 'the fairest votary' who takes up 'the little Love-god's' 'heart-inflaming brand' – the 'fire' that 'many legions of true hearts had warmed' (6) (possibly Christian believers). The 'cool well' (9) in which chaste Diana plunges it produces 'heat perpetual' (10) and a 'healthful remedy / For men diseased' (11–12). The language here is suggestive of divine love, constancy and healing and, as Simonds has observed, 'the flaming heart is a familiar baroque religious image that expresses the yearning for a love union with divinity'.[100]

Has the speaker triumphed in his painful quest for soul regeneration and the philosopher's stone? The alchemical *opus*, we should recall, involves repeated 'conjunctios' facilitating the balanced integration of male and female, black and white oppositions within the soul. As Isaac Newton recorded (see epigraph above), 'the mediation of the Virgin Diana' was essential in the production of the philosopher's stone. A mediating Diana certainly emerges in Sonnet 154 and her role in the alchemical-spiritual process, together with the significance of water, is illuminated by Giordano Bruno:

In that river are the nymphs . . . which assist and administer to the first intelligence, similar to Diana among the nymphs of the wilderness. She alone among all the others has by her triple virtue the power to open every seal, untie every knot, uncover every secret and bring to light whatever is hidden. By her unique presence, by her double splendour of goodness and truth, benevolence and beauty, she pleases all wills and intellects, sprinkling them with the salutary waters of purgation. (Bruno, Argument, *Heroic Frenzies*, p. 76)

Humbled and the servant now of his soul – 'my mistress' thrall' – Will has recourse to the waters of purgation 'for cure', and 'prove[s]' the paradox: 'Love's fire heats water; water cools not love' (Sonnet 154, 14). The double-speak continues, of course: the bawdy meaning points to the burning water (urine) of venereal disease; however, to those adepts with privileged understanding – like Newton – the 'bath' would have an additional meaning. As Abraham's *Dictionary* reveals, 'The bath, submersion, drowning and baptism are synonymous, and symbolize the breaking down and cleansing of the old outmoded state of being, leading to the birth of the rejuvenated, illumined man.'[101]

Michael Maier's Emblem 34 (see Fig. 6) illustrates this healing 'bath' with the accompanying Epigram proclaiming: 'Resplendent glows the bath when he's conceived . . . A stone he is, yet not; a gift from Heaven.'[102] Furthermore, Shakespeare's final line resonates with the ancient biblical/alchemical wisdom of Solomon: 'Set me as a seale on thine heart, *and* as a signet upon thine arme: for Love *is* strong as death . . . the coales therof *are* fiery coales, *and* a vehement flame. Much water cannot quench love, neither can the floods drowne it' (*Salomons Song*, VIII: 6).

The Geneva Bible's marginal annotation declares, 'the spouse desireth Christ to be joined in perpetual love with him': divine love is eternal – a fire which cannot be extinguished. Fiery water is a key spiritual paradox. Furthermore, Solomon's 'seale' – two intersecting triangles – is a symbol of the integration and stabilization of elements within the soul, the desired end of spiritual alchemy. In this final sonnet the speaker contemplates Diana and it seems most fitting to allow the words of a noted adept, Bruno, to encapsulate this mystery: 'Very few are the Actaeons to whom destiny gives the power to contemplate Diana ... he no longer sees his Diana as through a glass or window ... And now he sees everything as one' (Bruno, *Heroic Frenzies*, pp. 225–6).

As in the *Song of Solomon*, the poet of the sonnets weaves a sacred thread into the profane sense. Apparent contraries meet and blur into one, and the product is a densely rich tapestry of verbal play about desire – divine and venereal – together with all the conflicted emotions, joyous and tortured, that involves. As the next two chapters will serve to amplify, Shakespeare has taken us deep inside the poet's alchemical 'head' to illuminate creative process and, crucially, both types of desire are shown to be legitimate, operative and even crucial. But the 1609 quarto of poetry does not finish here; if we turn the page after reading Sonnet 154 we encounter *A Lovers Complaint* on its verso.

CHAPTER 4

A Lovers Complaint *by William Shake-speare*

Love *is* strong as death ... the coales therof *are* fiery coales, *and* a
vehement flame. Much water cannot quench love, neither can the
floods drowne it.

(Salomons Song, VIII: 6)

And I saw as it were a glassie sea, mingled with fire, and them that had
gotten victorie of the beast ... stand at the glassie sea, having the
harpes of God.

(Revelation, XV: 2)

We left diseased Will at the close of the sonnet sequence desperately returning to his mistress's 'eyes' in search of a water 'cure' – a 'bath for my help'
(Sonnet 153, 13–14); and finally Diana's 'cool well' provides a glimpse of hope
in Sonnet 154 (9). Bawdy meaning acknowledged ('eye' as female genitalia),
this is also suggestively a 'healthful remedy' for his burning sexual infection
and/or a spiritual one; the latter is evoked by the submerged religious paradox
contained in the final line, 'Love's fire heats water; water cools not love'
(Sonnet 154). Resonating with the fiery-water biblical passages above about
the strength of 'Love' and attaining 'victorie of the beast', the concluding
sonnet thus cleverly hints at the successful completion of an alchemical *opus*
culminating in the Seal of Solomon – 'fluid fire' and 'fiery water' – with the
integration of all opposing elements of the soul including religious love and
desire for sex.[1] Furthermore, if we recall the numerology built into the
sequence, our poet has produced 153 sonnets (if 136 is counted out as
instructed) symbolizing 'believers risen in Christ and endowed with the
spirit', with a culminating twenty-eight-sonnet triangle implying a quest
for moral perfection, and incorporating a ten-sonnet pinnacle signifying
imitation of the principle of divine creativity.[2]

All this amounts to a consummate but potentially disturbing display of
wit and craftsmanship. To those readers unaware of the alchemical allegory
playing throughout the sequence and engaging solely with the ribald level of
meaning (perhaps hearing the troubling biblical echoes too), the final
sonnets confirm Will's hubristic, unregenerate nature – his physical and

moral demise. However, for those interpreting the 'chymical' layer of meaning, and aware that sex and the sacred were legitimately united in alchemical discourses and symbolism, the philosophical and spiritual contexts will be pronounced and thought-provoking – the interpretation far less black *or* white. Michael Maier's reflections 'To the Reader' accompanying *Atalanta Fugiens* should serve as a caution against too literal an approach:

> If the other arts were to give emblems of morals, or other things such as the secrets of nature, they would be thought to be alien to their scope and end, because they want to be, and should be, understood by all. Chemistry is not thus, but like a chaste virgin behind a lattice, and like Diana, is not to be seen without a veil of various colors.[3]

'Chemistry', at the turn of the seventeenth century, prides itself on being an intellectually elite pursuit, only fitted for the ears and eyes of worthy initiates; and 'a veil of various colors' necessitates the deployment of a deliberately deceptive, 'color[ed]', rhetoric, a kind of double speak.[4] Confusingly and troublingly, then, any morally upstanding account of an alchemical *opus*, even the process of spiritual alchemy, *will* entail 'craft' (and a perjured eye/I). This is *serio ludere* at its most profound.

Alchemical poetry should, therefore, be approached with a heightened sceptical consciousness and a preparedness to look (and listen) from oblique perspectives, which were considered more suited in this period to discerning spiritual truths. It is notable that Shakespeare's writing always validates 'awry' perspectives as more honest (notably in *Richard II*, where the queen tends to interpret correctly through prisms of tear drops and eavesdropping from the sidelines, hidden behind bushes in the court gardens). Indeed, problems of proper discernment – intimately related to 'seeming' and 'being', to rhetorical modes, hypocrisy and to devils masquerading as angels – are constant Shakespearean preoccupations and the sonnets obsessively interrogate the philosophical-ethical-religious questions surrounding these issues when they are caught up in the complicating fog and din of urgent, burning desire.[5] Read in the light of alchemy, when their spiritual perspectives come most into focus, the sonnets leave the reader 'burning' to know for certain (intensely desirous to understand) the conclusion of this perilous personal quest to which he/she has been a privileged eavesdropper. The effect on the reader is intended and crucial in a collection of poems so interested in rhetorical affect: self-reflection is in order as the interpreter is thoroughly caught up by the sequence's seductive plot (conveyed through the medium of deceitful language), longing for narrative closure which is withheld; the concluding 'finis' is a let-down, disconcertingly anticlimactic.

Has the sonnets' speaker 'gotten victorie of the beast' (Revelation xv)? Has the burgeoning 'Babe' – the philosopher's child – grown to fruition? Is it angel or devil? Does the quest end, as Bruno says it should, by its protagonist seeing 'everything as one', and what exactly might that mean anyway?[6] The reader desires answers.

The 1609 quarto does not, however, end with Sonnet 154 but with a 329-line complaint in rime royal. If *A Lovers Complaint* is read as a coda to *Shake-speares Sonnets* – as most recent editors have suggested it should be – there is the potential for further insight into the outcome of this 'craft of will' (*Complaint*, 126). Shakespeare was by no means the first sonneteer to include a narrative poem featuring a female complainant at the end of his collection of sonnets. A translation by George Turbeville of Ovid's *Heroides* in 1567 produced a late sixteenth-century vogue for complaints by jilted women which, as in Ovid, are voiced by distracted lovers caught between the imperatives of public morality and private desires and who often give vent to their distractions in curiously legalistic language. Indeed, recent studies have convincingly argued that the rhetorical figure of *prosopopoeia* utilized by complaint (in the construction of tragic masks) was understood to be particularly affective, complicating readers' responses and, crucially, encouraging ethical re-evaluation.[7] Samuel Daniel attached *A Complaint of Rosamond* to the authorized edition of *Delia* in 1592, Thomas Lodge published *The Tragic Complaint of Elstred* with *Philis* in 1593, and Edmund Spenser appended *Epithalamion* to his *Amoretti* in 1595. By 1609 something of an English tradition had been established of authors positioning a narrative poem meditating on desire from the female perspective beside their sonnet sequences (producing a questioning effect); we might, therefore, expect Shakespeare to compete with his fellow wits in this genre.[8] *A Lovers Complaint* is, however, frequently given short shrift or ignored completely by critics because its diction and imagery are so strange ('ornate, stylized, dense and contorted', 'inventive but sometimes opaque in imagery') and its slight-seeming jilted lover plot appears insufficiently rewarding of the considerable interpretive challenge the poem seems to represent.[9] John Kerrigan, characterizing the *Complaint* as 'This extreme, rewarding poem', certainly rose to the challenge, returning it to its original position at the end of the sonnets in his edition, while pointing out that 'the editor of *A Lover's Complaint* finds himself with no real tradition to draw on'.[10] Ilona Bell, another admirer of the poem, alludes, too, to its 'abstruse and virtually unexplicated poetry'.[11]

This lack of a strong interpretive tradition is partly a consequence of intermittent attempts to excise it from the canon as un-Shakespearean.

Indeed, a recent study by Brian Vickers constitutes the lengthiest re-evaluation of the poem to date.[12] Arguing that *A Lovers Complaint* lacks the stylistic and imaginative qualities associated with Shakespeare, and utilizing electronic word searches to establish alternative authorship, Vickers reassigns the poem to a contemporary he designates as a 'mediocre', 'derivative' writer – John Davies of Hereford (not Sir John Davies). Vickers' assertions are, however, compromised in three important areas. First, by the compelling evidence from linguistic computing submitted by MacDonald P. Jackson and others that *A Lovers Complaint* exhibits 'an overwhelming preponderance of vocabulary links with Shakespeare's seventeenth-century plays', especially *Cymbeline*.[13] Vickers' counter suggestion that Shakespeare 'had read *A Lover's Complaint* and recalled it while writing the play' is not persuasive – why would Shakespeare borrow from a 'mediocre' poet?[14] Vickers uses an inverse argument to explain why 'the author of *A Lover's Complaint* modelled many of his rhymes on *The Rape of Lucrece*': John Davies's 'magpie mentality' led him to steal from Shakespeare.[15] We might be forgiven for concluding that it is just as likely that Shakespeare wrote both poems himself.

A second major problem is that Vickers is unaware of the allegorical nature of the *Complaint* and, reading literally, he declares it to be uninventive and 'misogynistic', possessing a bluntly moralistic and didactic plot about 'how seducers catch their prey'.[16] As this chapter will demonstrate, this is far from the case: *A Lovers Complaint* is a philosophical and ethically complex work about erotic and spiritual desire – indeed, it deploys rhetoric ingeniously to undermine naive didacticism. As, in Vickers' estimation, the work of John Davies of Hereford exhibits 'a didactic insistence unmatched by any other Jacobean poet', he is highly unlikely to have penned the *Complaint*.[17] Finally, most of the passages that Vickers' book singles out as 'grotesque', strained, 'archaic', 'irredeemably vague and confused' – and therefore un-Shakespearean – owe their obscurity to a very precise alchemical lexicon.[18] This chapter will analyse these episodes in detail, but it is important to stress that currently the balance of scholarship remains in favour of this being 'an authentic work of Shakespeare', with stylistic similarities to *The Rape of Lucrece* and sharing the vocabulary of the latter part of his career.[19]

Indeed, the majority of editors, including Duncan-Jones, Kerrigan and Burrow, argue that *A Lovers Complaint* was intended to be read and published with the sonnets and that these were most likely prepared and ordered by the poet himself prior to publication. Not only does the first page of *A Lovers Complaint* begin on the verso of the last page of

Shake-speares Sonnets but it proudly proclaims its authorship at its head – '*A Lovers Complaint* by William Shake-speare'. This attribution appears never to have been contested by Shakespeare; nor did he rush out and publish an alternative authentic collection as his friend, Samuel Daniel, found necessary when his sonnets were pirated. Daniel had been dismayed, as the dedication makes clear, to discover his 'secrets bewraide to the world, uncorrected'.[20] However, the central argument in my chapter – that this is a philosophical poem with an alchemical plot which rewords ('reworded', 1) and echoes elements of *Shake-speares Sonnets*' themes and episodes allowing them to be reflected upon from additional perspectives – stands independently to proof of authorship. *A Lovers Complaint* has never before received critical attention in this light: as an alchemical poem firmly yoked to the sonnets, which puts spiritual as well as sexual desire (and desire involved in the act of reading too) climaxing in ecstatic passion/Passion, glaringly and interrogatively under the spotlight.

Colin Burrow's perceptive account of *A Lovers Complaint* describes its language as 'so full of innovation that it is difficult even to penetrate its literal sense let alone to grasp what the objects which are being described mean to the participants in the story'.[21] Further, he declares, its objects are 'darkly laden with hidden significance'; this is a poem that 'actively seeks enigmas'.[22] If the *Complaint* is a work with an alchemical narrative as I am suggesting, Burrow's observations confirm that the poet-adept has performed his task well. In such a poem the literal meaning of the plot is not the important one but intended only to lead gullible fools astray and, to adopt Maier's phrasing, the poet has succeeded in using a 'veil of colours' and enigmas to obscure its spiritual allegory from all but the worthy initiated. In fact, *A Lovers Complaint* employs a very precise alchemical lexicon, which gives rise to its bizarre literal constructions. While Shakespeare's witty peers would no doubt have been fairly familiar with many of the terms and symbols that I am about to unravel, to modern eyes they appear extremely odd and even alienating, particularly if the sonnet sequence immediately preceding it is imagined to be about the poet's intimate relations with actual people. Read through a chemical lens, however, as a seriously playful theosophical poem, *A Lovers Complaint* is rich with Shakespearean wisdom and, to echo Kerrigan, immensely 'rewarding'.

THE 'CONCAVE WOMB' AND ITS 'FICKLE MAID'

From off a hill whose concave womb reworded
A plaintful story from a sist'ring vale,

My spirits t'attend this double voice accorded,
And down I laid to list the sad-tuned tale;
Ere long espied a fickle maid full pale,
Tearing of papers, breaking rings a-twain,
Storming her world with sorrow's wind and rain.

(*A Lovers Complaint*, 1–7)

Hill settings are quite usual in complaints and emblems from this period but *A Lovers Complaint*'s 'concave womb' immediately hints at a very specific alchemical place – the alembic or vessel in which all the 'chymical' activities take place. The 'Lymbecks warme wombe' (John Donne, 'The Comparison', 36) is the site of the philosopher's stone's conception, growth and birth.[23] In psychic alchemy the 'womb' [or 'head'] holds the blackened *prima materia* from which the purified matter of the imaginative soul emerges, whitened. The refining of base matter occurs in the *opus alchymicum*, we should recall, through repeated operations of the *solve et coagula* (dissolve and congeal) process, in which the chaotic form of the matter is dissolved into the original stuff of creation, the *prima materia* (necessitating death – the *Nigredo*), and coagulated into a new, purer form. Each time this cycle of separation and conjunction is repeated, the substance in the alembic-womb becomes purer. The 'triumphant' moments in the cycle occur when opposing qualities are chemically joined – sulphur and mercury, hot and cold, dry and moist, fixed and volatile, spirit and body, form and matter, active and receptive, male and female – resulting in loss of strife and reconciliation and thus, optimistically, pure love and peace.[24]

The aim of the process is gradually to purify and free the soul from its imprisonment in the turmoil of matter which occurs when the spirit rises as a volatile vapour to the top of the womb-vessel (as the material is heated by fire), where it condenses and falls as 'rain' from heaven on to the 'carcass' at the bottom of the alembic.[25] If the alembic is not sufficiently well sealed, some of the spirit inevitably escapes. Katherine Philips used this alchemical analogy to great effect in this elegy 'On her Son':

Too promising, too great a mind
In so small room to be confin'd:
Therfore, as fit in Heav'n to dwell,
He quickly broke the Prison shell.
So the subtle Alchimist,
Can't with Hermes Seal resist
The powerful spirit's subtler flight.

(Katherine Philips, EPITAPH. On her Son H. P. at *St Syth's*
Church where her body also lies Interred, 11–17)[26]

In its final purified form the spirit-soul can be illumined by the 'Mind' above and gain knowledge of its own true nature. Theoretically, if it survives this perilous process (unlike Philips' son), the soul-spirit eventually unites in a final conjunction with the cleansed base matter (its body) below, which gives it agency to put into action the understanding it has been granted in this elevated level of consciousness.[27] John Donne's 'The Extasie' is another poetic evocation of this process. Here, two lovers lying on a bank, with intertwined eyes are 'so by love refin'd' (21) that they undergo a 'dialogue of one' (75) (compare Bruno's 'and now he sees everything as one'):[28]

> Our soules, (which to advance their state,
> Were gone out,) hung 'twixt her, and mee.
> And whil'st our soules negotiate there,
> Wee like sepulchral statues lay.
>   . . .
> Wee then, who are this new soule, know,
> Of what we are compos'd, and made
>
> ('The Extasie', 15–18, 45–6)

As Donne characteristically makes clear, the body is essential to this 'refin-ing' process; erotic love is validated as the route to spiritual improvement:

> But O alas, so long, so farre
> Our bodies why doe wee forbeare?   (49–50)

Bodies are not 'drosse' to us but are crucial, 'Else a great Prince in prison lies' (68):[29]

> Loves mysteries in soules doe grow,
> But yet the body is his booke.   (71–2)

Reading the opening lines of *A Lovers Complaint* from within this context and as a coda to *Shake-speares Sonnets*, and with the knowledge of their Hermetic plot-line, the 'thought might think' (10) – an extraordinary but very Shakespearean construction that functions to promote questioning – that our poet's 'spirits' (3) have been sufficiently refined to escape the 'womb' (1) of the alembic so that he is able to access something significant and improving in an elevated state of consciousness. But what the 'spirits' see and hear initially is not particularly promising: who is this dishevelled 'fickle maid' (5) whose words are echoing pitifully around the 'womb'?

The 'spirits' tell us that the 'thought might think' (some imagi-nation is clearly required) it sees the 'carcass' of one partially 'scythed' by 'Time' but who retains some 'beauty' in spite of 'seared age' (10–14). Her eyeballs are shooting up to heaven – 'the spheres'

(23) – and down to earth, then 'right on' uncontrollably: 'nowhere fixed, / The mind and sight distractedly commixed' (26, 27–8). It is noteworthy that Ripley's *Compound* describes the 'Phylosophers Chyld' as a soul flying 'betwyxt Hevyn and Erth' (the Hermetic quest seeks to link them together). As Ilona Bell has foregrounded, the *Complaint* contains 'pervasive and insistent links to the sonnets' and this is the first of them.[30] Indeed, the 'thought might think' that there are parallels with Will's distracted 'frantic-mad' state (Sonnet 147, 10), in which he is unable to see and know clearly, in the latter dark lady sonnets (especially Sonnets 147–52). But the strongest verbal connection occurs in Sonnet 119: 'How have mine eyes out of their spheres been fitted / In the distraction of this madding fever?' (7–8). There are pronounced echoes from another Shakespearean work here, too. This is Theseus's description of the poet's frenzy in *A Midsummer Night's Dream*:

> The poet's eye, in a fine frenzy rolling,
> Doth glance from heaven to earth, from earth to heaven,
> And as imagination bodies forth
> The forms of things unknown, the poet's pen
> Turns them to shapes, and gives to airy nothing
> A local habitation and a name.   (v. i. 12–17)[31]

Love madness and poetic frenzy seem to blur in these accounts and the sonnets' poet likewise appears to merge at points with the *Complaint*'s 'maid' – boundaries are porous and subjectivities overlap.[32] Personified Time is reaping havoc in the *Complaint*, as in the sonnets (12), and why is the maid's peculiar 'seared' (14) quality remarked upon (*OED* 4, 'to burn, scorch')? Again 'the thought might think' (if it has been reading alchemical tracts) that this is a maid who has had a firing in a 'womb'-alembic: she is burnt and resembles a 'carcass' – a dead body (*OED* 1). Carcass is the precise alchemical term for the 'spent' matter left in the alembic after copulation. This fanciful 'thought' (10) is strengthened later on in the poem when the maid tells the 'reverend man' (57) that he is looking upon 'the injury of many a blasting hour' (72) (a blast-furnace is used in metalwork). As spent matter she is *prima materia*, also known as 'burning water' and the mercurial solvent or sea which dissolves matter but which has no 'form' of its own – it is chaotic, unstable and maleable. Alchemists referred to this female *materia* in derogatory terms ('menstruum', 'common')[33] – hence the designation of the unkempt, changeable maid as 'fickle' (5). Given the blurring of subjectivities at play here, we might just make a connection at this point in our reading with the imaginative female side of Will: the creative matrix residing in the fertile *prima materia*.

Putting that thought to one side for the moment, what should we make of those 'fluxive eyes' (50) 'Laund'ring' in 'brine' her napkin covered in 'conceited characters' (17, 16); and of her tearing up papers and letters 'Enswathed and sealed to curious secrecy' (49)? Why is she throwing gem 'favours' – 'amber crystal' (37) – into a river? Arguing that this poem is un-Shakespearean because of its strange metaphors, Vickers finds 'Laund'ring' (17) particularly illustrative of this – 'hardly an appropriate metaphor in this context'.[34] Read literally, this passage is highly melodramatic and the verb choice is odd but, once again, 'laundering' has precise alchemical meanings – it is a key term. Ruland's *Lexicon* describes the circulation of the matter in the alembic, with its ascent of vapour and descent of rain, as 'like a shower upon new linen at the fullers'.[35] We know that Shakespeare was familiar with this idea because he used it to humorous effect in *The Merry Wives of Windsor*; Sir John complains, 'And then, to be stopped in, like a strong distillation with stinking clothes . . . think of that . . . that am as subject to heat as butter, a man of continual dissolution and thaw' (III. iv. 104–8).

At the dissolution phase of the *opus* the wet, cold, feminine aspect dominates and 'tears' and rain threaten to drown everything as they wash the blackened stone lying in the 'womb-alembic', removing its impurities.[36] The *Aurora Consurgens* (attributed to Thomas Aquinas) says of the circulatory distillation: 'the waters are sublimed and rise like birds over the earth, which remains below as if dead [a 'carcass'], then drops down again like living rain or dew'.[37] In fact, laundering, prodigious tears and drowning become quite common literary tropes. Thus *The Golden Tract* (1678) describes how a bride sealed with her husband in the 'prison' of the vessel dissolved into endless tears as she saw her husband being melted: 'she wept for him, and, as it were, covered him with overflowing tears, until he was quite flooded and concealed from view'.[38] There are numerous alchemical emblem book representations of women doing their washing, scrubbing at soapy tubs and hanging out their sheets to dry. The dissolution phase was known as 'women's work' and Ruland's *Lexicon* relates alchemists' advice about mastering it: 'Go and look at the women who are employed over the washing and fulling of linen; see what they do, and do what they are doing.'[39] Michael Maier's Epigram 3 of *Atalanta Fugiens* declares: 'You see a woman, washing stains from sheets, / As usual, by pouring on hot water? / Take after her, lest you frustrate your art, / For water washes the black body's dirt' (see Fig. 4).[40] It would seem that the alchemist had to undertake menial 'laundering' – putting his female domestic side to work – as an essential part of the transforming process.

The description of the maid's eyes as 'fluxive' is significant too. In metalwork and chemistry a 'flux' is 'any substance that is mixed with a metal, etc., to facilitate its fusion'.[41] It also means 'fluctuating'; mercury is a fluxive substance. In spiritual alchemy, 'laundering' results in the white *Albedo* phase of the *opus* when the material in the alembic (the cleansed body) is pure enough to be reunited with the separated spirit. At this white stage, when flowing, mutable matter is fixed into a state of permanence, crystals are said to be produced.[42] John Donne employs many of these alchemical ideas in his 'Elegie on the Lady Marckham':

> So at this grave, her limbecke, which refines
> The Diamonds, Rubies, Saphires, Pearles, and Mines.   (23–4)

Lady Marckham's 'limbecke' tomb is also the womb of new life associated with precious gems. Which brings me to *A Lovers Complaint*'s 'favours' of 'amber crystal'. Another poem is helpful here: Richard Crashaw's 'The Weeper' contains the idea of amber gold ('Not the soft Gold which / Steales from the Amber-weeping Tree', 80).[43] Amber and crystal grow on alchemical trees – they are spiritual gold and the fruits of the *opus*. In the *Complaint*, such gems are notably the gifts to the beautiful youth from his former lovers: 'trophies of affections hot' (218). The fickle maid throws these, together with odd letters 'enswathed and sealed to curious secrecy', into the river 'Bidding them find their sepulchres in mud' (49, 46). 'Sepulchre' is a specific alchemical term referring to the alembic at the *Nigredo*, which results, we should recall, in the death of the lovers with the birth of one 'hermaphrodite'.

The 'conceited characters' on the napkin that the maid reads in her desperation, and the mysterious, secret papers from the former lovers, evoke the sense of secrecy surrounding Hermeticism. As Lyndy Abraham describes, in Michael Maier's *Symbola aureae mensae*, a Sibyl tells an alchemist that if he can learn to understand her hieroglyphical narrative he will be made 'a witness of the mysteries of God and the secrets of nature'.[44] The maid brings to mind the frustrated, disturbed Hermetic philosopher in Henry Vaughan's poem, 'Vanity of Spirit', pondering 'broken letters' and 'Hyerogliphicks quite dismembred', and breaking up 'seales' (24, 23, 10).[45] Yet, on the literal level, the *Complaint's* maid is simply a jilted, frustrated lover – hardly a philosopher. What should we make of all this? And why is she 'set' very specifically at the 'weeping margin' (39) of a river 'Like usury applying wet to wet' (40). Another strong parallel with the sonnets emerges here: in Sonnet 134 the dark lady is a 'usurer that put'st forth all to use' (10). In Sonnet 135 she is likened to the capacious sea:

> The sea, all water, yet receives rain still,
> And in abundance addeth to his store;
> So thou, being rich in Will, add to thy Will
> One will of mine to make thy large Will more.   (9–12)

In this sonnet Will wants to hide his will in the dark lady and become one with her. Bawdy this is, but if we study the verbal parallels operating here, the *Complaint's* maid begins to bear a strange resemblance to Will's mistress – dark nature – with whom he seeks to merge and deflate his own burgeoning troublesome will (an aspect of his soul as well as his male member). Subjectivities are extraordinarily fluid in the entire 1609 volume of poems and *Shake-speares Sonnets* and *A Lovers Complaint* appear to 'dialogue' with one another: the *Complaint* frequently gives the impression of 'rewording' lines from the sonnets. What effect is this having on the reader? Are we – possibly – beginning to 'see everything as one':[46] are all the participants in these strange alchemical plots seeming 'one'?

A master of ambiguity, Shakespeare clearly recognized the crucial involvement of the reader in the construction of meaning, and in this difficult poem he is stretching his reader's imaginative – 'the thought might think' – and interpretive skills to their limits. This is an immensely sophisticated volume of poetry rich with intriguing emblematic representations that invite decipherment. *A Lovers Complaint* is written in a style that demands the active participation of its coterie audience and among those there would undoubtedly be 'blusterer[s]'

> that the ruffle knew
> Of court, of city, and had let go by
> The swiftest hours observed as they flew.   (58–60)

These types of men, drawn towards 'this afflicted fancy' – both the intriguing woman and Shakespeare's poem (61) – are not unlike the 'reverend man' whom Colin Burrow has described in his gloss to these lines as 'an example of a figure, popular in the period 1590–1610, who has withdrawn from court life in order to retreat into a life of philosophical contemplation'.[47] This narrative moment surely stimulates some self-reflexive amusement. Shakespeare is playing with his sophisticated readers, inviting their participation and guesswork with such phrases as 'And controversy hence a question takes' (110), and 'nice affections wavering stood in doubt' (97), 'But quickly on this side the verdict went' (113). This poem was written for a select audience of wits – those with privileged access to turn of the seventeenth-century philosophical conundrums.

The *Complaint* then proceeds to recount the maid's confidences to the reverend man, which ventriloquize the youth's utterances, which incorporate his former lovers' desires as 'reworded' by the poet-speaker's 'spirits'. The absence of quotation marks emphasizes the blurring of subjectivities. Further, the maid resembles Will and the dark lady while, as we shall now see, her youthful seducer bears an uncanny resemblance to the sonnets' lovely boy. Subjectivities and voices blur into one.

THE PHOENIX YOUTH: 'OUR MERCURY'

> too early I attended
> A youthful suit – it was to gain my grace;
> O one by nature's outwards so commended
> That maidens' eyes stuck over all his face.
> Love lacked a dwelling and made him her place,
> And when in his fair parts she did abide
> She was new lodged and newly deified.
>
> . . .
>
> Each eye that saw him did enchant the mind.   (78–84, 89)

The introduction of the beautiful youth warrants close scrutiny: on the surface this is about secular love and desire and inevitably this is how editors gloss it. The boy is so well endowed by 'nature' that he is subject to 'sycophantic adoration';[48] the 'suit' was to win the maid's favour. 'Love' takes up residence in him and somehow this renders her newly 'deified'.[49] The choice of diction is troubling. 'Grace', 'Love' and 'deified' all potentially have spiritual-religious associations and Duncan-Jones draws attention to a biblical echo too: 'the eyes of all that were in the synagogue were fastened on him', Luke 4: 20.[50] There is certainly an unsettling hint of Christ in the presentation of this seducer, which continues throughout the *Complaint*. The 'fickle' maid, like the sonnets' Will, is guilty, perhaps (depending on your perspective), of idolatrous love. If, however, we bear in mind Ficino's rendering of the pathway to spiritual transcendence as being through the eyes of a beautiful man, and recall the Neoplatonic plot-line of the sonnets, the possibility emerges that the *Complaint*'s youth is, like the lovely boy, a route (via spiritual alchemy) to 'attain . . . grace' – religious grace.

Intriguingly, as Kerrigan points out, the formulation 'Love . . . place' is 'a commonplace of Renaissance poetry, but . . . one usually applied to women, not men'.[51] As the maid's account continues, the youth's androgynous qualities are foregrounded: his chin grows 'phoenix down' not bristles and his skin is oddly 'termless' (immortal like a phoenix); he has curly brown 'locks' that notably hang 'crooked[ly]' kissing his lips and he is 'maiden-tongued' (93–4, 85, 100). Yet he is skilled in the masculine arts of horse-manship and 'subduing' eloquence – 'He had the dialect and different skill, / Catching all passions in his craft of will' (120, 125–6). He seems to share Will's rather dubious rhetorical talents while possessing the sonnets' young man's hermaphroditic qualities together with his enchanting eyes and charisma (we might recall Sonnet 96: 'How many gazers mightst thou lead away, / If thou wouldst use the strength of all thy state?' 11–12). Like lovely boy of Sonnet 20 he controls all 'hues' (all 'hes, shes, theys'):[52] 'Of young, of old, and sexes both enchanted' (128). However, those who observe him, like the sonnets' speaker pondering his beautiful muse, find it difficult to discern his true nature. They question if it is he who governs his horse, or his horse him and whether his 'livery' is false (111–12, 105). Might his inside not match his outside? Is he 'like a canker in the fragrant rose' (Sonnet 95)? We might also recall Sonnet 93's reflection, 'How like Eve's apple doth thy beauty grow, / If thy sweet virtue answer not thy show' (13–14). He seems rather king-like (and/or Jesus-like): 'reign[ing]' in the 'general bosom', commanding 'duty' from all his followers (127, 130). But more troublingly he 'enchants', 'haunts', 'bewitches', possessing 'charmed power' in the manner of a demonic spirit (128, 130, 131, 146). Indeed, he appears 'crooked' like the hang of his curls. He is given to 'foul beguiling' and seems randomly to impregnate those whom he seduces: his 'plants (suggestively "bastards") in others' orchards grew' (170, 171). He is a master of 'deceit' and 'gilding' ('deceits were gilded in his smiling', 172), evoking the 'gilding' 'alchemy' of Sonnet 33 and thus, like lovely boy of the sonnets, his love appears to teach others 'this alchemy' – to make 'cherubins' of 'monsters and things indigest' like himself (Sonnet 114, 5–6). The phoenix youth is a 'false jewel', yet the general 'verdict' is – paradoxically – that he is 'Accomplished in himself, not in his case' (154, 116).

Further, his lovers continuously send him 'tributes', including 'deep brained sonnets' (197, 209) – like Shakespeare's. Also objects, 'with wit well-blazoned' (217) and precious stones, but these are all undervalued, recalling Sonnet 48's 'thou, to whom my jewels trifles are'. Then we hear that Nature has 'charged' him (recalling Sonnets 4, 11, and 126) 'to yield them up where I myself must render' to the *Complaint*'s maid for 'audit' (221, 230). She is strangely designated 'my origin and ender' (222), resonating with 'Alpha and Omega, the beginning and the ending' of Revelation 1: 8. This is an 'oblation' and he is 'their altar' (123, 124). As in Sonnet 125, a holy offering is suggested, but in the *Complaint* it is 'Hallowed with sighs that burning lungs did raise' (line 228 echoing the Lord's Prayer and Sonnet 108's 'hallowed'). The 'burning lungs', the 'broken bosoms' of former conquests – these 'trophies of affection hot' (254, 218) – now all belong to the 'phoenix' youth. This evokes Sonnet 31 addressed to the lovely boy:

> Thy bosom is endeared with all hearts
> Which I by lacking have supposed dead   (1–2)

> Thou art the grave where buried love doth live,
> Hung with the trophies of my lovers gone,
> Who all their parts of me to thee did give;
> That due of many, now is thine alone.   (9–12)

The phoenix youth, like the lovely boy, is an uncanny compound of former lovers: they and their tributes are 'combined sums' (*Complaint*, 231).

Heather Dubrow is one of a number of recent commentators who have expressed puzzlement about why the youth's former victims are apparently egging him on, 'according' ('Lending soft audience to my sweet design', 278), or speaking in one voice, with the seducer of the 'fickle maid'.[53] Read literally, their complicity is frankly odd; however, read alchemically it makes perfect sense. 'Their distract parcels' (231) are now constituents of the hermaphroditic phoenix lover (they have been chemically combined with him through fire, hence the 'burning lungs') and their future is his: 'Now all these hearts that do on mine depend', 'supplicant their sighs to you extend' (274, 276). It should now be obvious that, as Ilona Bell has stressed, there are 'countless parallels' not only 'between the sonnet speaker and the female complainant' but between the *Sonnets*' beautiful androgynous youth and the *Complaint*'s seducer.[54] The links among the poems are 'pervasive and insistent', and any attempt to render *A Lovers Complaint* un-Shakespearean must address these sustained and pronounced verbal echoes and thematic connections.[55]

It is predominantly *A Lovers Complaint*'s frustrating diction and obscurity, its 'grotesque' and 'inappropriate' metaphors, which periodically provoke the unease of interpreters leading to questions about authorship.[56] Lines like these do, indeed, verge on the surreal:

> [prior lovers have] emptied all their fountains in my well,
> And mine I pour your ocean all among.
> I strong o'er them, and you o'er me being strong,
> Must for your victory us all congest,
> As compound love to physic your cold breast. (255–9)

The maid has given in to her lover's 'suit', doffed her white gown and been 'poisoned' by the phoenix youth's 'drops', while he has been 'restored' (300–1). Why do his eyes contain 'infected moisture' (323)? Why are his lungs 'spongy' (326)? Read literally this is little more than melodramatic nonsense. However, as I have been arguing, this is an alchemical allegory and these lines contain a description of a 'chymical' copulation – of a union between 'common mercury' or *prima materia* (the *Complaint*'s maid) and the burgeoning philosopher's stone, 'our mercury' (the youth with, notably, 'phoenix' down and 'termless skin', whose face is reminiscent of 'paradise', 94, 91). Mercury has cold and wet qualities, hence the watery epithets. I am suggesting that *A Lovers Complaint* contains a look-alike portrait of 'our Mercury', or Mercurius – the developing philosopher's stone – and this is why he double-talks, dissimulates, but commands worship. Mercury was renowned for his contradictions: he was a consummate multiplicity in one.

The phoenix youth thus corresponds to the growing 'babe' of the sonnets produced by rhythmical cycles of dissolution and 'congelation', with repeated unions of male and female 'lovers' necessitating the death of one to produce an ever purer 'stone'. The mercurial waters are likened to a deadly poison – 'infected moisture' (323) – 'killing' the material in the alembic, putrefying it until they rain down on to the matter, like the dew of grace, resurrecting it into new life. Interpreted as a spiritual allegory this means that the understanding of the nature of the lower self – which comes through the grace of divine knowledge – at first acts like a deadly poison upon the alchemist-artist. As the lower nature is overcome, this knowledge should act as a harbinger of new life.[57] The following passages from the writings of adepts help to clarify the very precise use of an alchemical lexicon in the Shakespearean lines above:

The waters of mercury (also called the never-failing fountain, or the water of life, which nevertheless contains the most malignant poison).[58] (*The Sophic Hydrolith*)

This blessed Tincture, which expelleth all Poyson, though it self were a deadly Poyson before the Preparation, yet after it is the Balsam of Nature, expelling all Diseases.[59] (*Ripley Reviv'd*)

'Well' (the vessel in which the purifications take place), 'fountain' (the mercurial water of generation), 'congest' and 'poison' were common alchemical terms, while protean Mercury (our phoenix youth) – the king of paradoxes – was the key player in the 'theatre' of the alembic and in the early seventeenth century he was famous in elite circles.[60]

Mercury even starred in several court masques including, most famously, Ben Jonson's *Mercury Vindicated from the Alchemists at Court* (1614) acted by the King's Men and featuring Mercury, Vulcan, Prometheus, Cyclope and Nature, as well as male and female masquers. Stephen Orgel succinctly characterizes this masque as about 'false and true artists, and the proper use to which Mercury – wit and learning – may be put'.[61] Opening with a scene in an alchemist's laboratory, Mercury appears thrusting his head out of a furnace while the audience hears about 'Soft subtile fire, thou soul of art', which can improve 'weaker Nature, that through age is lamed' (4–6). 'Precious golden Mercury' has a long, comic speech which sets out his multiple contradictory roles and guises:

Mercury. Save Mercury and free him ... The whole household of 'em are become alchemists ... Howsoever they may pretend under the specious names of Geber, Arnold, Lully, Bombast of Hohenheim to commit miracles in art and treason again' nature. And as if the title of philosopher, that creature of glory, were to be fetched out of a furnace, abuse the curious and credulous nation of metal-men throughout the world, and make Mercury their instrument. I am their crude and their sublimate, their precipitate and their unctuous, their male and their female, sometimes their hermaphrodite; what they list to style me. It is I that am corroded and exalted and sublimed and reduced and fetched over and filtered and washed and wiped; what between their salts and their sulfurs, their oils and their tartars ... my whole life with 'em hath been an exercise of torture; one, two, three, four and five times an hour ha' they made me dance the philosophical circle. (27–57)

A little later he declares: 'Health, riches, honors, a matter of immortality is nothing' (84) and the audience learns that:

In yonder vessels ... they have enclosed materials to produce men ... Not common or ordinary creatures, but of rarity and excellence. (124–5)

These 'rare men' are clearly developing philosopher's stones. A 'fencer i'the mathematics' is alluded to as well; we should recall how central divine mathematics was to this golden game. It would seem that at the Jacobean court the activities of alchemists and their prime subject, Mercury, were notorious. As *Mercury Vindicated* makes clear, Mercury is not only the 'crude' beginning of the work – the *prima materia* or the mother of metals – but the goal of his own transformation, too, as *ultima materia* or the hermaphroditic philosopher's stone. In Jonson's hands London's budding alchemists, together with these curious Mercurian paradoxes, were some-times – though not always – the butt of amusement, but in many Jacobean masques Mercury-Hermes featured in more serious ways. He was certainly topical and fashionable.

In Francis Beaumont's *The Masque of the Inner Temple and Grays Inn* (1613), Mercury appears dressed in 'doublet and hose of white taffeta, a white hat, wings on his shoulders and feet, his caduceus in his hand'.[62] A helper, messenger god who transcends boundaries, having power through his rod to 'search the heavens, or sound the sea' (notably, recalling Theseus's description of the poet's imagination flitting between heaven and earth), conducting souls to and from lower and upper worlds, he is, nevertheless, addressed by Iris negatively here as 'Dissembling Mercury' (p. 91). Mercury's contradictions were well known in the Renaissance and they had a long heritage: while the Roman god had to do with merchandise and profit (warranting persuasive speech and cunning), the Greek god Hermes (with whom he was regularly conflated) was closely associated with art, learning and eloquence and with the role of the psychopomp conducting souls between worlds. It was Hermes who prevented Odysseus from suc-cumbing to the wiles of Circe through his gift of moly (a magic plant), and it was Hermes who accompanied Orpheus on his journey to the underworld to collect Eurydice. It is significant that the helpful palmer-guide in Spenser's *Faerie Queene* carries a protective Mercurian wand – a caduceus. The two intertwined serpents around the rod symbolize the harmony of antithetical elements achieved through spiritual alchemy. The caduceus had the power to raise the soul to wisdom.

In Ben Jonson's *Lovers Made Men* (1617) Mercury stars in his role as psychopomp, conducting the ghosts of love's ravages to river Lethe and the fields of rest; it is Hermes, spectators are instructed, who teaches men to love with wit instead of folly. The following year Jonson presents him crowning Hercules in *Pleasure Reconciled to Virtue* for having mastered the conjunc-tion and thus ended 'all jars' ''Twixt Virtue' and her noted opposite Pleasure (171–2). In these years Mercury-Hermes was arguably the most popular god of court festivities and, as Douglas Brooks Davies has shown, in spite of his equivocal reputation as 'Tongue's man of the Universe',[63] it was still considered decorous to flatter both Prince Henry and King James in Mercurian terms: 'Lighten the eyes, thou great Mercurian Prince, / Of all that view thee'.[64]

But why was Mercury so central to English Renaissance intellectual and court culture? It would seem that once again the Florentine academy and

Ficinian Hermeticism is implicated. Ficino had done much to elevate the status of this patron god of the arts; in several of his published letters he extols the particular wonders of Mercury:

Mercury is the bestower of intelligence as well as the maker of the lyre. Thus we see that when Mercury looks down on a man's birth without much favour, that man often seems like an ass with both lyre and letters. On the other hand, those who are regarded favourably by Mercury, the master of lyre and letters, have an ability for both.[65]

The successful artist must, it seems, be mercurial; crucially, it is Mercury who facilitates inner contemplation and 'transformation':

Through the wonderful grace of intelligence and eloquence Mercury turns men to himself, especially those who practice contemplation, and fires them with love of divine contemplation and beauty. Indeed, understanding does not usually transform us into what we understand but love does transform us into what we love. For this reason our Plato considers that it is by this very yearning for divine beauty rather than by the pursuit of knowledge or by any other power that the mind, regaining its wings, flies back to its true home.[66]

It is no wonder in this context, therefore, that Shakespeare's fellow-countryman, the poet Michael Drayton, saw fit to select a markedly mercurial coat of arms featuring a winged hat and a unicorn surrounded by 'pelleted' tears (symbols of mercury).[67]

Participating in divine and material worlds, and increasingly associated in the Renaissance with Hermes Trismegistus (priest, magician, king) and pristine religion, our Mercury – the philosopher's stone, the phoenix – was also a type of Christ and he symbolized, too, the spiritual light in the dark soul ('like a jewel (hung in ghastly night)', Sonnet 27) awaiting illumination and resurrection. However, because of his participation in the dark world as well as the light, Mercury consorted with the devil and was thus also tinged with evil: he was Janus-faced, a bundle of conjoined antithesis – a multiplicity in unity. Thus Mercury poisons and kills, but he heals and regenerates too, like his chemical namesake: 'it is the water that killeth and reviveth ... It is the water which dissolveth and congealeth' (*The Rosary of the Philosophers*).[68] Such a close association of alchemy (and its copulating couples) with the central Christian mystery of Christ's resurrection and the redemption might suggest troubling unorthodoxy, but one of the fathers of Protestantism, Martin Luther, even commended the art and its spiritual allegories:

The science of alchemy I like very well ... I like it not only for the profits it brings in melting metals ... I like it also for the sake of the allegory and secret signification, which is exceedingly fine, touching the resurrection of the dead at the last day. For, as in a furnace the fire extracts and separates ... and carries upward the spirit, the life, the sap ... while the unclean matter, the dregs, remain at the bottom, like a dead and worthless carcass; even so God, at the day of judgment, will separate all things through fire. (*Table Talk*)[69]

With Luther's words to the fore, we should ponder the climactic image of *A Lovers Complaint*, which the maid describes as the phoenix youth's 'passion' (295).

THE *RUBEDO* AS CHRIST'S PASSION

> This said his wat'ry eyes he did dismount,
> Whose sights till then were leveled on my face,
> Each cheek a river running from a fount,
> With brinish current downward flowed apace:
> O how the channel to the stream gave grace!
> Who glazed with crystal gate the glowing roses
> That flame through water which their hue encloses.
>
> . . .
>
> What rocky heart to water will not wear?
> What breast so cold that is not warmed here?
>
> (*Complaint*, 281–7, 291–2)

Again, in this passage the poet is deploying a very exact alchemical lexicon; one that is unfamiliar to modern eyes but that would have been extremely redolent with meaning to an elite Renaissance readership.[70] The 'crystal gate' of the alchemical *opus* (the stages of the process were known as 'gates') is the climactic point which occurs at both the *Albedo* and the *Rubedo* when spirit is crystallized. The reddening of the white matter ('glowing roses') during the very last conjunction of the cycle is highly significant. This is how Norton's *Ordinall* describes the *Rubedo*:

> Then is the faire White Woman
> Married to the Ruddy Man.
> Understandinge therof if ye would get,
> When our White Stone shall suffer heate,
> And rest in Fier as red as Blood,
> Then is the Marriage perfect and good.[71]

The alchemist, Petrus Bonus, urged caution in the choice of the body at the final *Rubedo* union:

When the Anima Candida is perfectly risen, the Artist must joyn it, the same moment, with its body: For the Anima without its body cannot be held. But such an Union must be made by mediation of the Spirit ... And such an Union and Conjunction is the end of the Work. The Soul must be joined with the First body whence it was, and with no other.[72]

His specification – 'The Soul must be joined with the First body ... no other' – is important in relation to the youthful seducer's designation of the maid as 'my origin and ender' (222): she is the *prima materia* or 'first mercury' and he is the combined sums of prior unions between sulphur and mercury. She is material and without form, he is spirit-soul. This is, as it were, a body being put back together again after the separation and 'laundering' of its parts; hence the prior female lovers' positive support for the phoenix youth's 'sweet design'. Further, as Heather Dubrow has highlighted, the referent of 'Lending soft audience' (278) is 'tellingly ambiguous', syntactically collapsing the earlier women with the 'fickle maid'.[73] Dubrow is unaware of the alchemical allegory pervading the poem, but read from within that context the curious syntax of these lines beautifully anticipates and enacts the fickle maid's dissolution (her 'poisoning') and incorporation into the hermaphroditic compound that is the phoenix youth. The 'glowing roses' passage of the *Complaint* is, in fact, an allegory of Christ's Passion and the Resurrection, and of spiritual rebirth. This is why this passage, which has caused editors enormous difficulty, resonates with the biblical book of Revelation: 'And I saw as it were a glassie sea, mingled with fire, and them that had gotten victorie of the beast ... stand at the glassie sea' (xv: 2); 'And he sayd unto mee, It is done, I am Alpha and Omega, the beginning and the end: I will give to him that is athirst, of the well of the water of life freely' (xxi: 6). This culminates in a vision of holy Jerusalem, 'shining ... like unto a stone most precious, as a jasper stone clear as chrystall' (xxi: 10, 11). The ultimate triumph of religious love is thus captured by the *Complaint*'s image of 'glowing roses / that flame through water' evoking Christ's Passion.

Shakespeare was by no means alone in his choice of alchemical imagery – for example, the symbolism of the *Rubedo* – to evoke the mystery of the Crucifixion and Resurrection and thereby inscribe a spiritual level of meaning in poetry. Indeed, passages from Drayton and Marvell suggest that it was not an unusual seventeenth-century literary trope. Drayton used it in *Endimion and Phoebe*: 'She putteth on her brave attire, / As being burnisht in her Brothers fire ... Which quickly had his pale cheeks over-spred, / And tincted with a blushing red'.[74] While in Marvell's 'The Nymph Complaining for the Death of her Faun' the white 'false' fawn folds itself 'In whitest sheets of lilies cold' (90) and feeds on roses 'Until its lips e'en seemed to bleed': 'Lilies without, roses within'. It is slain by the troopers, shedding its purple blood over its whiteness, and it yields the healing balsam of the sages (84–97).[75] The divine red tincture (recalling Christ's blood) flushes the white stone and the *ultima materia* – philosopher's stone, phoenix or fifth essence, the ultimate healing balsam – is achieved.

The *Rubedo* climax of *A Lovers Complaint* might appear to signify the poet-philosopher's 'triumph' – his achievement of the stone (the trans-formation of the earthly man into the illumined philosopher) – but once again the poet manages to leave the reader dangling in a frustrating web of uncertainty; there is no closure. Why does the poet have the fickle maid end her tale in such a perplexing way by describing her phoenix lover as a 'concealed fiend', a 'tempter', 'which like a cherubim above them hovered' (319)? Shakespeare is presenting us with yet another enigmatic puzzle requiring our active intellectual engagement with his poem.

HUMAN NATURE REVEALED

And now he sees everything as one. (Bruno, *Heroic Frenzies*, p. 225)

Readers are free to impose their own meaning on the end of the narrative, but the task is daunting: a variety of interpretations are possible because, rather like a medieval sermon (strange as that may seem), and in the manner of Spenser's *Faerie Queene*, which also contains alchemical imagery, this poem operates on several levels simultaneously and demands that the reader approach it as a hermeneutic contest over ways of seeing. Potentially, we have a literal plot, an alchemical allegory and anagogical (spiritual) as well as tropological (moral-philosophical) dimensions to decipher. Indeed, critical attempts simply to read the plot literally have resulted in markedly anti-thetical responses. For some readers the fickle maid is simply that – a product of early modern gender stereotyping in its most severe form. This gullible, careless and wavering female has been seduced by a duplicitous cad and such is her stupidity and malleability in the face of his persuasive rhetoric that she would do it all again given half the chance. Vickers argues, for example, 'The poem is in effect an indictment of female sexuality and an attack on the pleasure principle, simultaneously moralizing and misogyn-istic.'[76] In contrast, Bell and Dubrow have been acute observers of the web of interconnections among the sonnets and *Complaint* and of the pro-nounced blurring of subjectivities that I have outlined above.[77] Simple gendered interpretations are obviously invalidated by the recognition that clear male–female boundaries are deliberately confounded by our poet's relentless games. This is Shakespeare in his element – revelling in a consummate display of rhetorical and philosophical skill and wisdom.

A fascinating recent essay about 'The Enigma of *A Lover's Complaint*' by Catherine Bates makes a particularly shrewd observation about the poem's depiction of 'masochistic subjectivity and desire' as androgyne:

> It seems to me that *A Lovers Complaint* is best understood if it is seen as a text that looks ahead to recent developments in psychoanalytic theory – developments which suggest that an originary masochism is constitutive of all human subjectivity. Indeed, the poem begins to make sense when it is seen to anticipate recent suggestions that the figure of the seduced girl might, perhaps, be the prototype of all human sexuality, 'male' no less than 'female' . . . the fundamental point of origin in the psychic history of all human beings. In this account, the figure of the seduced girl comes to exemplify the foundation of all psychic development, in men as well as women.[78]

If *Shake-speares Sonnets* and *A Lovers Complaint* are read as containing parallel alchemical plot lines dramatizing a process of psychic and spiritual integration ('oneing'), the fickle maid as *prima materia* is the chaotic prototype of all human desire. But also, as we shall see in the next chapter, she is the fertile creative matrix of the male poet's psyche. Interpreted metaphysically, the lovely boy and dark lady, the fickle maid and phoenix youth, are fragmented, overlapping, contesting aspects of one psyche: distinct male and female qualities which, like all other antitheses in the soul-body, must be united and dissolved in the alchemist's 'head' and reconstituted as an integrated, hermaphroditic unity – the goal of the alchemical *opus*.

At an advanced stage in the alchemical cycle the spirits are sufficiently purified to be granted what amounts to an out-of-body experience, which is illuminating of human nature. We might recall Donne's lines: 'Wee then, who are this new soule, know, / Of what we are compos'd, and made' ('The Extasie', 45–6). Suggestively, the reader of *A Lovers Complaint* is a privileged eavesdropper of just this. The 'thought might think' that, like the poet-alchemist whose 'spirits' are hovering above the alembic, we readers are peering over the poet's shoulder, listening in to a privileged visionary experience – 'seeing things as one', as Bruno put it. Certainly many critics have commented on the omnipotent poet-speaker who is – effectively – ventriloquizing a diversity of voices in one narrative stream in *A Lovers Complaint*. This effect is heightened, as Heather Dubrow has pointed out, by the absence of quotation marks.[79] Our witty poet has, it seems, masterminded his constructions so as to give a playful literal form to a profound Hermetic mystery: what we are witnessing here is a multiplicity of voices in unity.[80]

But what is revealed about how 'we are compos'd and made'? The fickle maid, suggestively an aspect of Will the poet, seems remarkably un-illumined and confused (distractedly tearing up symbolic artefacts) throughout the poem, but then she is *prima materia* or first mercury; as such she is changeable, malleable, lacks form and (being mercurial) is capable of deception too – we cannot trust her account. Likewise, the phoenix youth, Mercurius, is two-faced: he is both divine and devilish, crafty and honest. We cannot trust him either. Furthermore, whenever the poem seems on the verge of being sententious or didactic (and its rime royal form gives plenty of opportunity for this), it pulls back. It refuses to offer moral guidance: precedent, forced examples and counsel are consistently undermined. In addition, it presents the very strength of burning desire as rendering public statements of morality no more than a sham:

> When thou impressest, what are precepts worth
> Of stale example? When thou wilt inflame
> How coldly those impediments stand forth
> Of wealth, of filial fear, law, kindred fame.
> Love's arms are peace 'gainst rule, 'gainst sense, 'gainst shame,
> And sweetens in the suff'ring pangs it bears
> The aloes of all forces, shocks and fears. (267–73)

Didactic and narrowly moralistic, this poem most certainly is not.[81] Indeed, the *Complaint* goes out of its way to undercut the use and validity of such an approach. Rather, it deploys all its narrative energies to present a sceptical 'examination of the power of rhetoric and exemplary wisdom' and – cru-cially – as Colin Burrow has so aptly described, in this poem 'desire and moral aversion are not opposites but intimate interdependents'.[82] As described earlier, in the Renaissance the complaint genre's use of *prosopo-poeia* (involving tragic personae) was understood to be particularly affective, complicating readers' responses and, crucially, encouraging ethical re-evaluation – Shakespeare's poem excels at this. A complex understanding of human desire is at work in *A Lovers Complaint*. Furthermore, the poet is alchemically marrying antitheses again; desire and moral aversion are made to co-exist. This is, we should remember, a serious game and there is certainly some profound Shakespearean wisdom for us to ponder. The power of love in the face of adversity – 'Love's arms are peace 'gainst rule, 'gainst sense, 'gainst shame' (271) – and the co-existence of consummated erotic love and religious desire are inscribed into the 1609 volume of poems by the alchemical allegory.

Sex and the sacred are a seeming antithesis (though not in the *Song of Solomon*) which must be united by our alchemist-poet and, as in Donne, the body's passions are not denied: human nature is corporeal and sensual as well as intellectual and spiritual; to deny the body's needs is ultimately to imprison the soul. Giordano Bruno's sonnet sequence similarly abandoned the Petrarchan ideal of complete denial of one's corporeal nature in order to achieve unity with the Deity. Significantly, the lover who strives to deny the body's needs in Bruno's *Heroic Frenzies* is rendered blind. He cannot move on spiritually and thus regain his sight until he acknowledges his body's needs. Bruno's Diana is, notably, a symbol of the synthesis between the corporeal and the spiritual, the material and the formal.[83] We should recall that the desire to unite with a beautiful body is a key route to spiritual and intellectual enhancement in Ficinian Neoplatonism, but while Ficino appears to reject actual physical union, Shakespeare, Donne and Giordano Bruno do not. These poets are manipulating the Petrarchan vehicle and engaging in a highly philosophical debate about the nature of desire (spiritual and sexual), the body's passions and spiritual growth.

Shakespeare takes this debate to its bodily, erotic limits and he manages to do this through his skilful deployment of the blatantly sexual imagery of Renaissance alchemy. Interpreted from this perspective, the phoenix youth's 'plants' that grow in 'others' orchards' (171) are not only bastard children as the bawdy level of meaning suggests; they are also philosophical ones. The alchemical physician Paracelsus declared:

Gold, through industry and skill of an Alchymist may bee so far exalted that it may grow in a glass like a tree, with many wonderful boughs and leaves ... which the Alchymists call their Golden hearb, and the Philosopher's Tree.[84]

In *Atalanta Fugiens*, Michael Maier described how 'philosophers call their stone vegetable, because it grows and multiplies like a plant'.[85] Plants, trees and orchards are symbolic of spiritual growth and fruition. It seems that the phoenix youth's sexual proclivities do not preclude development. Indeed, 'copulation' is essential to the successful *opus*. Through the deployment of alchemy's overt sexual lexicon, Shakespeare reunites erotic love with the sacred. The biblical *Song of Solomon* undoubtedly provided some justification for this and we should recall how the final line of the sonnets, 'Love's fire heats water; water cools not love', resonates with the *Song*.

But why the syntactically compounded cherubim-fiend at the close of this surreal vision? The first answer might be that the *opus circulatorium* has gone horribly wrong. Alchemists cautioned against just this outcome:

> For if your minde be vertously set,
> Then the Devil will labour you to lett;
> In three wises to let he woll awaite,
> With Haste, with Dispare, and with Deceipte.
>
> (Norton, *Ordinall*, 30)

In this reading the alchemist has not been virtuous and vigilant enough and his angel has turned devil – a constant anxiety of the sonnets.[86] Furthermore, the devil was a noted 'master of facsimile and its paradoxes' concealed, as one French Bishop put it, by 'the cloak of verisimilitude' – resembling our concealed fiend's 'garment of a grace' (*Complaint*, 316).[87] However, another look reveals the fiend in Shakespeare's odd syntactical construction blurring into a guardian angel:

> Thus merely with the garment of a grace
> The naked and concealed fiend he covered,
> That th'unexperient gave the tempter place,
> Which like a cherubim above them hovered.   (316–19)

Such is the strength of her desire for this 'spongy lung[ed]' (326) seducer that the 'reconciled maid' (329) – suggesting spiritual reformation or reconciliation – would give in to this fiend-angel and do it all again and again and again (the alchemical process is circular and repetitious): 'Ay me, I fell; and yet do question make / What I should do again for such a sake' (321–2). Once again, desire and moral aversion clash head on and join, but this odd syntactical construction also begs the question – a profound religio-philosophical one – about the nature of good and evil. Is any quest for complete spiritual perfection simply wrongfooted? Do good and evil always coexist in human nature as in Mercurius?

   This should not be taken to mean that the poet is undermining the value of the alchemical quest: rejecting Aristotle's and Scholasticism's dualistic view of the universe and embracing Nicholas of Cusa's coincidence of opposites, Renaissance alchemy strove obsessively to unite contraries, and dark and light aspects of the psyche had to be made fruitfully to coalesce. Indeed, the Hermetic teachings underpin this vision of human nature: *Corpus Hermeticum X* declares, 'the human is not only good, but because he is mortal he is evil as well' and, further, 'the human soul – not every soul, that is, but only the reverent – is in a sense demonic and divine'.[88] Significantly, in his sermons, John Donne located 'a bosom devil' tempter – a *spontanaeus daemon* – in each of us; while Robert Fludd's writings talk in more heterodox fashion of the light–dark, Apollonian–Dionysian, 'two-fold differing' paradox of God.[89] The key Hermetic imperative, 'Know thyself', entailed the acknowledgement of conjoined good and evil in all human kind. We might recall Prospero's recognition of Caliban – 'This thing of darkness I / Acknowledge mine' (v. i. 278–9). *A Lovers Complaint* is, indeed, a very Shakespearean poem.

Brilliantly and wittily capturing the paradoxical, mysterious and seductive character of the alchemical quest, the poem ends with the maid's repeated equivocal exclamations of wondrous desire, of suffering and joy, significantly (given the *opus circulatorium* of alchemy) a sequence of 'O's or circles upon the page ('Just as in the beginning there was One, so also in this work everything comes from One and returns to One'[90]). *Anaphora* (repetition) is a figure which, according to Henry Peacham, denotes a word 'of importance and effectual signification'.[91] The five 'O's foregrounded in the last stanza of *A Lovers Complaint* might function, too, to evoke the five wounds of Christ at the Passion – a familiar image in Renaissance paintings.[92] We are certainly meant to note this Shakespearean climax of ejaculated 'O's, of conjoined divine and sexual passion – of ecstasy.

CHAPTER 5

Inner looking, alchemy and the creative imagination

PART I THE INWARD TURN: DOING 'MIND'
IN 'CHARACTER'

If there be nothing new, but that which is
Hath been before, how are our brains beguiled,
Which, labouring for invention, bear amiss
The second burden of a former child?
O that record could with a backward look,
Even of five hundred courses of the sun,
Show me your image in some antique book,
Since mind at first in character was done. (Sonnet 59, 1–8)

Doing 'mind . . . in character' had a long and distinguished heritage by the time Shakespeare took up his pen at the turn of the seventeenth century. Indeed, the 'backward look' that the words of Sonnet 59 prompt might help to establish the limits of his introspective innovation. How distinctive is Shakespeare's poetic 'child'? The Bard appears to have set himself a challenge of 'invention', and readers are invited to consider whether or not he has laboured successfully. Is this poet's brain 'beguiled' or original? It is time to take that 'backward look'.

For the Renaissance, Petrarch was, of course, a towering landmark along this particular literary pathway and his famous 'Letter IV' describing his ascent of Mount Ventoux implicitly reveals his own profound indebtedness to 'antique' models, prime among them the colossus St Augustine. 'Driven by the sole desire to see the famous altitude of this place' and assisted by the 'vigour of [his] will', Petrarch attempts to ascend the highest of the peaks, which the forest dwellers call 'The Son'.[1] However, a 'tortuous path' repeatedly takes him to 'lower ground' and clouds obscure his sight; in fact he cannot make progress until, in a state of exhausted frustration, he sits down and 'Rising on the wings of thought from bodily things to spiritual things' he reproaches himself and begins to meditate (pp. 99, 97). His painful bodily movements have, in fact, led to a psychic inward turn, which prompts him to consider the two opposed wills (a 'perverse and wicked' one and 'another') warring on the 'battlefield of [his] . . . mind'. His is clearly a fragmented mind-soul requiring urgent unifying work.

As the narrative foregrounds, Petrarch's mountain climb is a 'pilgrimage', simultaneously an allegory of spiritual awakening involving much pain (resonating with the suffering of Christ) and culminating in clearer vision. At the summit he marvels at the mountains, shores and rivers about him and then takes out the little book he just happens to be carrying with him, 'Augustine's book of *Confessions*', and immediately opens it, reading aloud: 'And men go to marvel at the heights of mountains, the mighty waves of the sea, the vast flowing rivers, the immensity of the ocean and the revolutions of the stars, and yet they neglect themselves' (p. 105). Augustine's words immediately preceding this, about 'the power of memory', are worth quoting in full:

Great is this power of memory, exceeding great, O my God, a spreading limitless room within me. Who can reach its uttermost depth? Yet it is a faculty of my soul and belongs to my nature. In fact I cannot totally grasp all that I am. Thus the mind is not large enough to contain itself: but where can that part of it be which it does not contain? (*Confessions*, Book 10, viii)[2]

Augustine is 'overcome' as he ponders this question, while Petrarch is 'stunned' as he reflects on the significance and relevance of this passage, proclaiming:

I swear I was astonished . . . I was angry with myself that I should have been marvelling at earthly things at that very point. I should have learnt a long time before, even from non-Christian philosophers, that nothing except the soul is wondrous and that, compared to the soul, nothing is great.

Having had my fill of seeing that mountain, I turned my mind's eyes in on myself. (p. 105)

Having taken the inward turn, Petrarch begins a silent descent as he ponders how the mountain peak seems nothing, merely 'a foot high compared to the loftiness of human contemplation' (p. 107). Commenting on this Letter, Rodney Lokaj observes that in recounting his tortuous climb Petrarch develops a poetics 'based on *imitatio Christi*' 'under the aegis of Augustinian theology . . . but completed by the Franciscan model', in which the writer undergoes a 'mystically silent crucifixion'.[3] Petrarch has clearly discovered 'The Son' within himself. As for those 'antique' models, the ascent of Mt Ventoux is like an 'interweaving dance' in which the prior measured steps of Homer, Cicero, Dante, St Augustine and St Francis mingle harmoniously and sometimes imperceptibly with Petrarch's own.[4]

Turning to the sixteenth century, an extraordinary self-reflexive turn was taken by the essayist Michel de Montaigne when he set out to spy on himself from close-up, boasting 'I study my selfe more than any other subject. It is my supernaturall Metaphisike, it is my naturall Philosophy' ('Of Experience').[5] Acknowledging 'two or three former ancients' who have trodden this 'profitable' way before him (ii, p. 59), Montaigne constantly reveals the novelty and difficulty of his enterprise, his more secular-seeming account nevertheless evoking the 'thorny' pilgrimages of St Augustine and Petrarch:

It is a thorny and crabbed enterprise, and more than it makes shew of, to follow so strange and vagabond a path, as that of our spirit: to penetrate the shady, and enter the thicke covered depths of these internall winding crankes; To chuse so many and settle so severall aires of his agitations: And tis a new extraordinary amusing, that distracts us from the common occupation of the world. (ii, 'Of Exercise or Practice', p. 58)

Certainly, Renaissance poets witnessed Montaigne's labours as innovative and exciting: 'This Prince Montaigne / Hath more adventur'd of his owne estate / Then ever man did of himselfe before' (Samuel Daniel to Florio, i, p. 13). Peering into the murky, agitated pool of his mind ('so bottomlesse a depth, and infinite variety', iii, 'Of Experience', p. 334), Montaigne discovers multiple selves lurking amidst 'extravagant Chimeraes, and fantasticall monsters . . . one hudling upon another' prompting him to 'keepe a register of them, hoping . . . one day to make him ashamed, and blush at himself' (i, 'Of Idlenesse', p. 44). Protean multiplicity, provisionality, and even self-alienation are the finely articulated characteristics of Montaigne's 'soule':

I remove and trouble my selfe by the instability of my posture . . . Sometimes I give my soule one visage, and sometimes another, according unto the posture or side I lay her in. If I speake diversly of my selfe, it is because I looke diversly upon my selfe. All contrarieties are found in her. Shamefast, bashfull, insolent, chaste, luxurious, peevish, prattling, silent, fond, doting, laborious, nice, delicate, ingenious, slow, dull, forward, humorous, debonaire, wise, ignorant, false in words, true-speaking, both liberall, covetous, and prodigall. All these I perceive in some measure or other to bee in mee, according as I stirre or turne my selfe . . . I have nothing to say entirely . . . without confusion, disorder, blending, mingling. (ii, 'Of the Inconstancie of our Actions', pp. 11–12)

The unified self he is seeking can only be found in the frozen-in-time pages of his book – there he concedes he is one, but not the same one as any later versions of his self.

Many have located the origins of modern and even postmodern subjectivity in Shakespeare, but that prize is surely Montaigne's.[6] The Bard is peering over the latter's shoulder (and, indeed, St Augustine's) when he has Achilles plumb the depths of his mind with such profundity: 'My mind is troubled like a fountain stirred, / And I myself see not the bottom of it' (*Troilus and Cressida*, III. iii. 298–9). The most important relation we have in our lives is undoubtedly that between 'I myself' and 'my mind': the continuous dialogue and exchange of views between them, the way we 'personify ourselves on the stage of our imaginations' is, as Nicholas Spice has eloquently argued, the way we 'keep ourselves intact'.[7] Thus we turn things over in our mind and push things out of it continually. In the view of twentieth-century psychology, our inner psychic dramas have therapeutic value and the soul-making techniques of earlier periods certainly have affinities with (as well as marked divergences from) processes of psychic integration outlined by twentieth-century psychoanalysis. We know for sure that the physician and alchemist Michael Maier associated the contemplative techniques of inner alchemy – prompted by the visual emblems and music score of *Atalanta Fugiens* – with health restoring powers. In the early modern period, mental well-being, inseparable from that of the soul, necessitated the inward turn.

It is significant that the language Montaigne selected to articulate the working of the mind was frequently alchemical. Consider this fascinating passage about the confused mind labouring, unsuccessfully, to order itself:

Whosoever hath seene children, labouring to reduce a masse of quick-silver to a certaine number, the more they presse and worke the same, and strive to force it to their will, so much more they provoke the liberty of that generous metall, which scorneth their arte, and scatteringly disperseth it selfe beyond all imagination. (III, 'Of Experience', p. 324)

The 'masse of quick-silver' is mercury, with its malleable, procreative dissolving qualities. That 'generous metall', chaotic *prima materia* with no form of its own, is strangely evocative of Shakespeare's mistress (suggestively his dark creative nature) with her capacious will-absorbing potential, notably in Sonnet 135. Sixteenth-century soul-mind analysis increasingly drew upon a language of metallurgy which assumed a mineral consciousness: alchemy was pre-psychology as well as pre-chemistry and both depended on the fires of Vulcan.

VULCAN AND THE 'REFINER'S FIRE'

God created iron but not that which is to be made of it ... He enjoined fire, and Vulcan, who is the lord of fire, to do the rest ... From this it follows that iron must be cleansed of its dross before it can be forged. This process is alchemy; its founder is the smith Vulcan. What is accomplished by fire is alchemy ... And he who governs fire is Vulcan. (Paracelsus)[8]

He is like a refiner's fire. (Malachi 3: 3)

Post-Cartesian boundaries between spirit and matter, body and mind, render it difficult for us to think about the psyche as a substance, but the Renaissance peered inward differently. Certainly, in the first half of the seventeenth century, nature – internal and external – was frequently perceived as one thing: matter was imagined as infused with spirit. John Milton's writings and those of the Digger, Gerrard Winstanley, bear substantial and notable witness to the extent of this cognitive trend.[9] It was thus possible for Renaissance alchemists to imagine working both the metal of the soul-mind and the minerals in their retorts simultaneously, and this is given interesting visual expression on the title pages of Khunrath's *Amphitheatrum* (1609) and Maier's *Tripus Aureus* (1618), (see Fig. 2, p. 42).[10] Indeed, Robert M. Schuler has drawn attention to a fascinating anonymous manuscript found amongst Sir Hugh Plat's collected materials, which details this 'Parallisme' in two columns – one for material alchemy and the adjacent column for spiritual alchemy. It concludes, 'Chainge of Qualitie is the sure and safest course to obtayne the perfection of Man and Metall; that is, equal and true temper in both.'[11] It seems that the processes of dissolving, cleansing, smelting, distillation and transmutation observed taking place in the refining apparatuses of chemistry could be projected on to mental processes and vice versa. The 'refiner's fire' (Malachi 3: 3), cleansing, purifying and enlightening, could transmute the dark lead of the soul into translucence – letting in more light.

Indeed, it is hard to overestimate the philosophical, scientific and religious weight accorded to transmuting fire and related 'light[s]' by early modern culture. A passage from Cornelius Agrippa's *Occult Philosophy* captures this obsession:

There are two things, saith Hermes, viz., Fire and Earth, which are sufficient for the operation of all wonderful things: the former is active, the latter passive. Fire, as saith Dionysius, in all things, and through all things, comes and goes away bright; it is in all things bright, and at the same time occult and unknown. When it is by itself ... it is boundless and invisible, of itself sufficient for every action that is proper to it ... renewing, guarding Nature, enlightening, not comprehended by lights that are veiled over ... Fire, as saith Pliny, is the boundless and mischievous part of the nature of things ... The Celestial and bright Fire drives away spirits of darkness; also this, our Fire made with wood, drives away the same, in as much as it hath an analogy with and is the *vehiculum* of that Superior light; as also of him who saith, 'I am the Light of the World', which is true Fire, the Father of Lights, from whom every good thing, that is given, comes; sending forth the light of His Fire, and communicating it first to the Sun and the rest of the Celestial bodies, and by these, as by mediating instruments, conveying that light into our Fire.[12]

The Light/Fire of God the Father, the fire of the sun, the fire of the mediating Celestial bodies, the fire within man – this chain of connection is associated by Agrippa with wondrous powers.[13] Symbolic fires feature in a particularly wide range of textual genres in this period. Bruno's *Heroic Frenzies* declares, for example, that

as the soul desires to recover its natural beauty, it seeks to purge itself, heal and reform itself: and for this purpose it uses fire, for like gold mixed with earth and shapeless, it wishes by a vigorous trial to liberate itself from impurities, and this is achieved when the intellect, the true smith of Jove, sets to work actively exercising the intellectual powers.[14]

This is, of course, alchemy applied to inner nature.

Renaissance emblem books, too, are replete with images of heart-shaped furnaces and busy Cupids – both *Eros* and *Anteros* – applying bellows to fires of desire, and Counter-Reformation treatises of religious meditation certainly encouraged this trend.[15] This is Puente's meditation on the Passion, for example:

O that I could enter into his enflamed hart, and see the furnace of infinit fire that burneth therin, and melt in those flames, that issuing forth full of love, I might love as I am loved, and . . . suffer with love, for him who suffered for me, with so great love . . . O infinit love, and immense fire, which the waters of so immense tribulations could not extinguish, but was enkindled the more therewith![16]

We might, of course, connect the fiery water image here with the Song of Solomon and the final line of Shakespeare's sonnet sequence – 'Love's fire heats water; water cools not love'.

Robert Southwell's famous poem, 'The burning Babe', takes its impetus from such Roman Catholic manuals of devotion:

> As I in hoarie winter's night
> Stoode shivering in the snow,
> Surpris'd I was with sodaine heate,
> Which made my hart to glow;
> And lifting up a fearfull eye,
> To view what fire was neare,
> A pretty Babe all burning bright
> Did in the ayre appeare;

> Who, scorched with excessive heate,
> Such floods of teares did shed,
> As though his floods should quench his flames,
> Which with his teares were fed.   (1–12)[17]

Meditating on the infant Jesus, Southwell's breast forthwith becomes a furnace full of the 'metall' of 'defiled soules', while 'Love is the fire' (23, 24, 19). In this manner he re-enacts the refining torments of Christ's Passion within himself:

> For which, as now on fire I am
> To worke them to their good,
> So will I melt into a bath,
> To wash them in my blood.   (25–8)

The meditative inward turn taken by the Counter-Reformation (and particularly advocated by Jesuit manuals such as Puente's) frequently involved passionate contemplation of Christ's Passion – a fixation on His sufferings at the Crucifixion, which should move the emotions and, crucially, be 'felt'.

As we have seen, becoming one with Christ in this way was a feature, too, of Hermetic philosophy and spiritual alchemy. Pico's *Heptaplus* declared, for example, 'Christ, the fullness of all virtues, is formed in us': for Pico, 'Christ, the Word, is born in the contemplative soul'.[18] Significantly, the inscription accompanying an engraving of Michael Maier in *Atalanta Fugiens* proclaims, 'Haec mihi restant. Posse bene in Christo vivere, posse mori.' Hildemarie Streich translates this as 'This remains my task: to be able to live well and to die well in Christ.'[19] We should recall how the apple melody of *Atalanta Fugiens'* fugues has been identified as the 'Christe eleison' of Gregorian Mass IV.[20] Thus Christ, the Logos, the beginning, is the constant theme, the 'golden foundation', underpinning Maier's alchemical scheme for cleansing and regenerating the mind-soul conferring spiritual and mental health. In alchemy, Christ the Son, often symbolized by the Sun, is the creative life power, he is also Love stoking the fires of desire. This encourages a second look at the implications of secular-seeming lines in Shakespeare's sonnets such as these:

> Mine eyes have drawn thy shape, and thine for me
> Are windows to my breast, wherethrough the sun
> Delights to peep, to gaze therin on thee.   (Sonnet 24, 10–12)

Is divine light – the Sun/Son conveying wondrous powers – beginning to enter the poet's soul here courtesy of the lover's memory image?

Spiritual alchemy in fact shares much in common with practices of meditation from this period that are often considered more religiously orthodox; practices which Louis Martz has established as important to understanding Renaissance devotional poetry: 'The art of meditation thus underlies the *ars poetica*: in English religious poetry of the seventeenth century the two arts fuse, inseparably, for both are rooted in . . . charity.'[21] Significantly, given his Hermetic interests, the poetry of Henry Vaughan provides a particularly rich storehouse of exemplars of this 'fusion'; consider, for example:

> 'Tis now cleare day: I see a Rose
> Bud in the bright East, and disclose
> The Pilgrim-Sunne; all night have I
> Spent in a roving Extasie
> To find my Saviour.   (*The Search*, 1–5)[22]

This affective meditation on Christ's Passion is notably characterized as 'a roving Extasie':

> I walke the garden, and there see
> *Idaea's* of his Agonie,
> And moving anguishments.   (37–9)

'DISTILLING . . . THE DELICIOUS HONIE OF DEVOTION': MEDITATION AND CONTEMPLATION

Lift up thyne eies unto that holie roode, and consider all the woundes, and paines, that the Lorde of maiestie suffereth for thy sake . . . Beholde that divine face. (Luis de Granada, *Of Prayer and Meditation*, 1612)[23]

In my meditation is the fire kindeled, sayth the prophet David. For to kindle the fire of Gods love in thy will, and to have the more perfect knowledge of God, meditation, and Contemplation, be both most necessarie. (Diego de Estella, *The Contempte of the World*, 1584)[24]

Martz's seminal study, *The Poetry of Meditation*, argued convincingly that the art of meditation 'constituted one of the great developments in European culture; its influence penetrated to the center of European consciousness'.[25] Further, he stressed that English poets would not have needed to read any particular treatise because the latter had become part of 'the popular culture of the era'.[26] That does not mean they did not read them though, and Martz demonstrates a complex textual interplay among the works of the poets and the devotional manuals. Of particular note to this study are the verbal similarities and grim humour that punctuate Fray Luis de Granada's meditation on a 'grave maker' and the levelling effects of death

in *Of Prayer and Meditation* and Hamlet's famous 'chop-fallen' speech (v. i.
179–91). As Martz remarks, this treatise would have been available to
Shakespeare in many editions.[27] A substantial number of the treatises,
frequently written by Jesuits, were translated and even printed in
Protestant England; thus one of the most influential, Scupoli's *Spiritual
Combat*, seems to have been translated by John Gerard, a Jesuit, and printed
secretly in England even though it declares itself 'Printed at Antwerp,
1598'.[28]

   Diego de Estella's treatise was published in English as *The Contempt of the
World* in 1584 and it draws interesting distinctions between 'Meditation',
which is more 'paynefull and difficult', and 'contemplation', which 'is more
easie and sweete' to the initiated. Easier it might be, but it is also much more
mystical and elevating:

Contemplation is more then meditation, and as it were the end therof . . . For the
understanding having attentively . . . meditated the mystery, and gathered divers
lights together, doth frame unto her self a cleere knowledge, wherof without further
discourse, one way or other, she enjoyeth (as I may say) a vision which approacheth
to the knowledge of Angells, who understand without discourse. (Jesuit, Louis
Richeome, *The Pilgrime of Loreto*, 1604)[29]

'Visions' and the 'knowledge of Angells' link the highest reaches of spiritual
experience to the contemplative soul, and meditation is the route to
contemplation:

When we thinke of heavenly things, not to learne but to love them, that is called to
meditate: and the exercise therof Meditation: in which our mynd, not as a flie, by a
simple musing, nor yet as a locust, to eate and be filled, but as a sacred Bee flies
amongst the flowers of holy mysteries, to extract from them the honie of Divine
Love . . . Meditation is an attentive thought iterated, or voluntarily intertained in
the mynd, to excite the will to holy affections and resolutions . . . Briefly, devotion,
is nothing els but a spirituall swiftnesse and nimblenesse of love. (St François de
Sales, *A Treatise of the Love of God*, 1616)[30]

De Sales' imagery of flies, bees, and his emphasis on the singular significance
of love to achieving 'oneness', notably takes us into the domain of
Renaissance emblem books – alchemical and others; there is considerable
cross-fertilization between the two genres. In his analysis, while 'Meditation
considereth by peecemeale the objectes proper to move us', contemplation
is unity: 'contemplation beholdes the object it loves, in one simple and
recollected looke, and the consideration so united, causeth a more lively and
strong motion' (*Love of God*, p. 336). Again, strong, affective emotions are
associated with effective contemplation. De Sales notably employs

alchemical imagery to describe the devotional process: 'with a spirit of mildenesse, charitie, humilitie: distilling as much as thou maiest (as it is said of the spouse in the Canticles) the delicious honie of devotion'.[31] The focus on unifying the soul through love is central to Puente's influential treatise, too, and here it is possible to decipher the same connection between soul-making and healing the distressed mind that we uncovered in Maier:

Thou art troubled and perplexed with many thoughtes, affections, and cares, but the most necessary point is, that thy soule be one, that is to say, united and recollected within it selfe … one in her sensuall affections, reducing them to union with the spirit … one in hir will, referring hir whole will, entirely to the will of almightie God … One in her thoughts, gathering them all together … one finally in love, placing it wholly in one only infinit good.[32]

Love is the key to everything, it would seem; no wonder late sixteenth-century European Renaissance culture is possessed, as Manning describes, by an '*erotomachia*', in which 'the profane supported the sacred'.[33] Puente explains why 'provocation to love' is so crucial to devotion:

For the memorie and the understanding only love when they remember, thinke and ponder the things that provoke to love. The imagination, and the appetites of the soule doe likewise love, when they budde forth imaginations and affections, which doe awaken and give life to love … And in resisting the temptations which divert them from loving: that charitie may in such sort be rooted in the soule, that nothing created can separate it from the same, nor the waters of manie tribulations extinguish it. (*Meditations*, vol. 1, p. 596)

Effectively, these treatises were guides to attaining self-knowledge as well as mystical experiences and Lorenzo Scupoli's 'extraordinarily popular' *Spiritual Combat* – the 'supreme achievement' of the sixteenth-century Italian schools – confirms how thoroughly a popular manual of devotional exercises could embrace fashionable currents of Platonism.[34] Here for example:

When the beauty of mankind impresses you, you should immediately distinguish what is apparent to the eye from what is seen only by the mind. You must remember that all corporeal beauty flows from an invisible principle, the uncreated beauty of God. You must discern in this an almost imperceptible drop issuing from an endless source, an immense ocean from which numberless perfections continually flow. (*The Spiritual Combat*, p. 65)

The Spiritual Combat is a fairly eclectic manual and also advises more traditional, medieval-style internal battles with imagined enemies – 'that particular vice or disorderly passion that you are trying to conquor' (p. 46) – and urges the acknowledgement of one's own strong tendency to evil.[35]

Thus, it would seem that these books were an accessible and acceptable source of theosophical ideas. Indeed, the constant theme of the earlier, highly admired *Theologia Germanica* (which was edited by Martin Luther) was the return to Platonic 'oneness'. It preached further that with the termination of the Old Law, God descended into man in the figure of Christ and thereby could 'deify' man if he renounced his own will and imitated the life and sufferings of Christ (we might recall how 'Love' was 'newly deified' when 'lodged' in the phoenix youth in *A Lovers Complaint*, 82–4).[36]

Importantly in such texts, the body and senses were by no means always eschewed and derided: as in Florentine Platonism sensual desires and even passions could be a route to the divine and, as illuminated by Petrarch's Letter IV, bodily exercise and pain could provide a wake-up call for the spirit, encouraging meditation. In fact, *The Imitation of Christ*, probably written by Thomas à Kempis sometime before 1426 (notably translated by Henry VII's wife, Margaret Beaufort, with English editions published in 1530 and 1585),[37] contains many similar currents to Girolamo Savanorola's, *De Simplicitie Vitae* (1496), which taught, 'let us begin with corporal things, in order to understand more easily spiritual things' (lib 2, concl 1).[38] Indeed finding a constructive middle way between the intellectual and the affective, balancing and unifying these two aspects of human nature, was, Martz argues, a central aim of late sixteenth-century Catholic spirituality.[39] In this respect, then, Bruno's sonnet sequence, which insisted on finding a middle way, a marriage between soul and body rather than denial of the latter, was in line with late sixteenth-century Catholic devotional teaching. Interestingly, too, in relation to Shakespeare's sonnets, Ciceronian-style love for a friend and 'intimate' colloquies with Christ as best friend are advocated in *The Imitation of Christ*:

> If through neglicence of thy selfe thou loose him [Christ], what freende shalte thou then have? Without a freende thou mayest not long endure, and if Jesu be not thy freende moste before all other, thou shalt be verie heavys and desolate, and be lefte without all perfect frendship.[40]

This manual encouraged 'wondrous familiaritie' with Christ and advised that Christ should be questioned 'as a lover is wont to speake to his beloved, and a freende with his beloved freende'.[41] This is the poetic-devotional territory of George Herbert, and the work of Southwell and Donne is evoked too. Sacred parody – including the erotic playfulness of Renaissance emblem books – surely took its cue from such popular treatises of devotion, and this is an important additional lens through which we should examine Shakespeare's sonnets.

'A POET, A LOVER AND A LIAR': 'STRANGE' TRUTH

> Most true it is that I have looked on truth
> Askance and strangely.   (Sonnet 110)

The blasphemous quality of Shakespeare's sonnets has been widely and vehemently stressed by critics in recent decades at the same time as speculation about the Bard's sexuality has spiralled. If, however, the sonnets are resituated amidst the emergent theosophical-aesthetic currents of his own moment, the inevitability of both his blasphemous intentions and his 'homosexuality' (premised on his erotic attraction to lovely boy) recedes, and a space is opened up for alternative readings.[42] It becomes possible, as I have been arguing, to interpret the sequence as a veiled record of spiritual experience – though not necessarily an authentic history. The latter point is significant and I will return to it shortly. In his important study of subjectivity in the sonnets, Joel Fineman correctly observes that Shakespeare employs 'all the standard, well-known arts of language so as not to mean the things he seems most to say'.[43] What the poet-speaker most seems to say for the majority of modern commentators is that he is erotically obsessed with both lovely boy and the more dubious dark lady (who are sexually entangled with one another) and that his just reward for his inability to control his bodily passions is a dose of fiery venereal disease. Granted, this seems to be the literal meaning. However, allegorical and anagogical interpretations are also available throughout the sequence courtesy of the philosophical lexicon woven into the sonnets. Shakespeare's 'eye'/'I' might not be quite as unredeemably 'perjured' as it may initially seem to be.

In employing allegory in his sequence, Shakespeare was in fact drawing on 'antique' models. In the Middle Ages, Dante's *Convivio* had inaugurated a tradition of transforming a love song through allegory into a philosophical poem, which 'had opened the way for every sort of abstruse interpretation of what were ostensibly songs of courtship and complaint'.[44] Effectively, he applied the method employed by the Church Fathers to interpret Scripture, to the conventional *canzone* of love, producing the potential for allegorical, anagogical and moral meanings to be hidden under the 'beauteous fiction' of poetry.[45] With developments in Italy initially by the thirteenth-century poet Guido Cavalcanti, ostensible love songs could become densely philosophical. This is especially apparent in Bruno's late sixteenth-century *Heroic Frenzies*. As I have been arguing throughout this book, we should definitely take more notice of the numerous Shakespearean hints and prompts and look less 'head on' in order to uncover the spiritual and philosophical meanings playing beneath the 'strange' literal layer of his sonnets.[46] For Renaissance culture, truth was always hiding in askew ('askance', Sonnet 110) perspectives.

We have established that Shakespeare was hyper-alert to the poetic traditions to which he was contributing. Further, two lines in Sonnet 59 foreground the philosophical context with which he is most preoccupied: 'O that record could with a backward look, / Even of five hundred courses of the sun.' The Platonic or Pythagorean Great Year is alluded to here: as Pythagoras's speech in Ovid's *Metamorphosis* describes, the cycle of the phoenix was 500 years.[47] Plato's and Ovid's 'antique' books are definitely at the forefront of the poet's recollection of the 'wits of former days' then, and it is interesting in this context that Renaissance Hermeticists read Ovid's *Metamorphosis* as an alchemical allegory. Dante's *Vita Nuova* had, of course, harnessed Platonic ideas to describe the poet's progress toward the absolute through focusing on the ideal of his beloved Beatrice; her frequent denials spur his spiritual progress. Petrarch's interventions captured a new, more intimate subjectivity; in his *Rime*, the poet's personal plight, his inner conflict, expressed in his characteristic antithetical style, becomes the principal focus. In these 'antique books', scholasticism had notably ensured that Plato's *Symposium*'s male lovers were replaced by beautiful but remote female guides: corporal urges had in the end to be conquered – the soul disentangled from the body – to enable spiritual transcendence. There are many other stops along this particular generic pathway prior to Sir Philip Sidney, but in *Astrophil and Stella* we certainly find the poet kicking against the ascetic Petrarchan bricks: Astrophil desires 'food' – which for him means sex – but he does not secure it; however, neither does he appear to make spiritual progress.

Sidney was undoubtedly familiar with the anti-Petrarchanism trend that was flourishing on the Continent, especially in France. Humanists writing in Latin, notably Théodore de Bèze and Marc-Antoine Muret, had started this movement and in 1533 Joachim Du Bellay published 'À Une Dame', subsequently known as 'Contre les Petrarquistes', in which the poet self-consciously turns away from the favourite Petrarchan conceits advocating, instead, 'jouyssance'. Then the great Pierre de Ronsard takes up the gauntlet, breaking with Petrarch in his 'Elégie à son livre' (1556), which makes explicit reference to Catullus, Tibullus and Ovid.[48] Of particular interest in relation to Sidney is Ronsard's *Sonnets pour Hélène* (1578), supposedly about the poet's love for a 'demoiselle d'honneur' at the court of Charles IX. Like Stella, Hélène is steeped in the philosophy of ascetic Neoplatonism and maintains a virtuous chastity while her lover attempts seduction in his pursuit of hedonistic enjoyment; he ends up morose and unfulfilled, rather like Sidney's Astrophil.[49]

Indeed, by the late sixteenth century, to many on the Continent and in England, too, love poetry seemed to have become detached from its divine roots. As the Jesuit Southwell's epistle prefatory to 'Saint Peter's Complaint' (1595) renders clear, a campaign was on to wrench love from the pen of the devil and reunite it with God:

> Poets by abusing their talent, and making the follies and faynings of love the customary subject of their base endeavours, have so discredited this facultie, that a Poet, a Lover, and a Liar, are by many reckoned but three wordes of one signification. But the vanity of men, cannot counterpoyse the authority of God, who delivering many parts of Scripture in verse, and by his Apostle willing us to exercise our devotion in Himnes and Spirituall Sonnets, warranteth the Arte to be good, and the use allowable ... But the Divell as he affecteth Deitie, and seeketh to have all the complements of Divine honor applied to his service, so hath he among the rest possessed also most Poets with his idle fansies. For in lieu of solemne and devout matter, to which in duety they owe their abilities, they now busie themselves in expressing such passions, as onely serve for testimonies to how unworthy affections they have wedded their wils. And because the best course to let them see the errour of their workes, is to weave a new webbe in their owne loome, I have here layd a few course threds together, to invite some skillfuller wits to goe forward in the same, or to begin some finer peece, wherein it may be seene how well, verse and vertue sute together. ('The Author to his loving Cosen')[50]

This notorious preface was printed in London eleven times between 1595 and 1636 and went through many continental editions.[51] What a challenge for the Bard searching around for 'new invention'! In the early seventeenth century, as John Manning describes, 'Christianity thoroughly appropriated erotic images and allegories'; a new synthesis did indeed emerge and our 'skillfuller wit', Shakespeare, is prime among those who weave a 'strange' new 'webbe'.[52] He takes up the gauntlet in a rather mischievous manner, succeeding in being 'Poet, Lover and Liar' while reconnecting Petrarchan verse with the Divine – surely, the height of 'skill'. This poet's eye 'in a fine frenzy rolling' (*A Midsummer Night's Dream* v. i. 12) moves repeatedly and dizzyingly from earth to heaven and back again. Not only does he renew the link between upper and lower spheres but he also reconnects Platonism with Plato: as we saw in Chapter 2, the *Symposium*'s emphasis on male beauty as the key to spiritual and intellectual growth is obviously very much to the fore in Shakespeare's sequence.

Further, the poet-speaker's male friend is sometimes the vehicle for intimate conversations with Christ in the manner advocated by *The Imitation of Christ* and occasionally, after 'oneing' with his friend, he even seems to be blending with Christ, presumably having found the Son/Sun within himself:

> For bending all my loving thoughts on thee:
> The injuries that to myself I do,
> Doing thee vantage, double vantage me.
> Such is my love, to thee I so belong,
> That for thy right myself will bear all wrong.
>
> (Sonnet 88, 10–14)

It is likely no mere coincidence that this meditation on and as the friend, Jesus, occurs in Sonnet 88, since the number 888 was symbolic of the name of Jesus. Sonnet 89 might be read, literally, as addressed to the earthly friend or devotionally as spoken intimately to love/Christ:

> Say that thou didst forsake me for some fault,
> And I will comment upon that offence.
> Speak of my lameness, and I straight will halt,
> Against thy reasons making no defence.
> Thou canst not (love) disgrace me half so ill,
> To set a form upon desired change,
> As I'll myself disgrace, knowing thy will.   (Sonnet 89, 1–7)

Knowing whose will – the friend's or Christ's? Does this colloquy on 'Thy sweet beloved name' (Sonnet 89) suggest to the poet-speaker that he must 'vow debate' against his male friend associated with the 'fault' and profanity? Consider the concluding couplet:

> For thee, against myself [his friend and his self] I'll vow debate;
> For I must ne'er love him whom thou dost hate.

Sonnet 90's 'cross', 'loss', 'make me bow', 'sorrow', 'woe' evoke a meditation on Christ's suffering at the Crucifixion which culminates in the couplet,

> And other strains of woe, which now seem woe,
> Compared with loss of thee, will not seem so.

Is this loss of the friend, his own self/soul or Christ (or all three)? Sonnet 91 continues the theme: worldly goods and themes are 'not my measure': 'All these I better in one general best'. Is this the Neoplatonic divine 'one'?

In this group of sonnets, the radical improvisation associated with Ciceronian friendship discourses blends with the demands of Christian meditation. Sonnet 108 takes this further, even 'hallowing' 'thy fair name'. Indeed, this manner of rhetorical play with the divine calls to mind a passage in one of Ficino's published letters which recounts a dialogue between God and the repentant soul (echoing John 14:11 and 20): 'God: it is no stranger who speaks to you but one who is your very own . . . Indeed, I am both with you and within you. I am indeed with you, because I am in you; I am in you, because you are in me. If you were not in me you would be in yourself, indeed you would not be at all.'[53]

Shakespeare's fellow countryman, Michael Drayton (who commissioned an alchemical coat of arms for himself), certainly seems to have been aware of such Ficinian formulations when he wrote his sonnet sequence, *Idea*. Sonnet 11 (1619 edition) begins:

> You are not alone, when You are still alone,
> O God from You, that I could private be,
> Since You one were, I never since was one,
> Since You in Me, my selfe since out of me.   (1–4)[54]

Such fluid poetic inscapes are a strange manifestation of the traditional belief that we are made in the likeness of Christ. While Petrarch had built on this, foregrounding the notion that man's inner life is a constant process of spiritual creation, Ficino and his followers took it a step further, promulgating the belief that the divine image in man could actually be regenerated to a pre-lapsarian purity – especially, as we shall see, through creative activities. It is precisely this mentality that is underpinning Edmund Spenser's lines in 'A Hymne in Honour of Love' (1596):

> Such is the power of that sweet passion,
> That it all sordid basenesse doth expel,
> And the refyned mynd doth newly fashion
> Unto a fairer forme.   (190–3)[55]

This was inevitably a way of thinking not shared by all and, if Jonson's response to Donne's 'First Anniversary' (discussed below) is anything to go by, many among Shakespeare's contemporaries probably did look 'askance' at his sequence. In the manner of an accomplished Hermetic philosopher and poet, the Bard dissolves antitheses, 'marrying' the sacred and the profane, the lewd and the divine, in an innovative and potentially shocking distillation.

The most pronounced example of this is the verbal play around 'nothing' and none: 'In things of great receipt with ease we prove / Among a number one is reckoned none' (Sonnet 136). 'Nothing' can be a woman's genitals or God – 'One' 'no number', 'none' – the ultimate transcendent something and container of everything. As Macrobius reported of the mysterious 'One': 'although the monad is itself not numbered, it nevertheless produces from itself, and contains within itself, innumerable patterns of created things'.[56] It is 'both male and female, odd and even, itself not a number, but the source and origin of numbers. The monad . . . refers to the supreme God.'[57] Thus 'nothing' carries immense symbolic weight in Sonnet 109, 'For nothing this wide universe I call / Save thou, my rose; in it thou art my all', and Sonnet 20's famous line, 'By adding one thing to my purpose nothing' is freighted with spiritual as well as bawdy meaning. Similarly, to those in the know around 1600, 'the master-mistress of my passion', would have suggested both erotic and divine desire that would lead to an inner 'passion'.

Shakespeare was not alone in his constant play of 'knowing lasciviousness' in relation to sacred things. Vaenius's *Amorum Emblemata* (1608) takes us into similar lewd territory. In one emblem, for example, a winged Cupid is rubbing together two large crossed sticks in front of his genitals producing fire. The emblem is ostensibly illustrating the Horatian 'golden mean' (the crossed sticks) but this is playfully centred on the genitals with the fire hinting at venereal 'burning' as well as religious desire. As Manning succinctly points out, the Jesuits were keen to use such popular sources in the cause of religion: 'the fashion was ripe for exploitation as a means of using human lusts to lead one to God'.[58]

But to return to the 'truth' question: are Shakespeare's sonnets a true record of spiritual experience? It is illuminating to consider John Donne's statement about lines such as these from 'The First Anniversary':

> Shee tooke the weaker Sex, she that could drive
> The poysonous tincture, and the staine of *Eve*,
> Out of her thoughts, and deeds; and purifie
> All, by a true religious Alchymie;
> Shee, shee is dead.   ('An Anatomy of the World', 179–83)[59]

Ben Jonson apparently objected to the terms of eulogy of a young girl in 'The First Anniversary', declaring it 'profane and full of blasphemies' and bluntly telling Donne 'if it had been written of the Virgin Mary it had been something'. According to Drummond's account, Donne's rebuttal was that 'he described the Idea of a Woman and not as she was'.[60] After all, he might have added, Dante's Beatrice and Petrarch's Laura were 'Ideas' too. Attempting to establish poetic 'sincerity' in this period is a particularly hazardous enterprise. Peter Sharrat's discussion of French humanist love poetry succinctly sets out the parameters of the 'sincerity' problem:

There are many different ways in which love-poetry is related to experience. Sometimes poets admit that they have invented the loved one . . . sometimes, as . . . in the case of Ronsard, a poet may write on someone else's behalf, or choose a real person as a 'passion-pretexte'. In none of these kinds of poetry is it possible to talk of sincerity, though in the last two there may in the end be a real emotional experience. Love poetry may be generalized and unfocussed, without reference to a particular person; it may, on the other hand, call for a multiplicity of loves, addressing more than one woman in the same collection as Marot and Ronsard sometimes did. Finally, it may be the account of a real lived experience.[61]

Lovers were frequently figments of the imagination or part real and a bit made up: wit and invention ruled, it seems. Indeed, I feel inclined to rehearse Helen Wilcox's stance on this matter when she asks in relation to Donne's rhetorical self-presentation, 'Is autobiography written to express selves, or to create them?'[62] Certainly, Michael Drayton's 'To the Reader of These Sonnets' highlights what might be described as the 'true' fictionality and playful ingenuity of his sequence, 'Idea':

> My verse is the true image of my Mind,
> Ever in motion, still desiring change;
> And as thus to Varietie inclin'd,
> So in all Humors sportively I range.[63]

Against this turn-of-the-seventeenth-century philosophical-aesthetic back-drop our modern conceptions of truth, applied to early seventeenth-century poetry, are simply anachronistic. Shakespeare is certainly a consummate 'liar', but this is to miss the point: a 'perjured eye' might be very 'phantasti-call' but 'true'.

PART II THE ALCHEMICAL 'MAKING' MIND

And this fantasy may be resembled to a glass . . . There be again of these glasses that show things exceeding fair and comely, others that show figures very monstrous and ill-favored. Even so is the fantastical part of man (if it be not disordered) a representer of the best, most comely, and beautiful images or appearances of things to the soul and according to their very truth. If otherwise, then doth it breed chimeras and monsters in man's imaginations, and not only in his imaginations, but also in all his ordinary actions and life which ensues. Wherefore such persons as be illuminated with the brightest irradiations of knowledge and of the verity and due proportion of things, they are called by the learned men not *phantastici* but *euphantasiotie*, and of this sort of fantasy are all good poets, notable captaines stratagematic, all cunning artificers and engineers, all legislators, politicians, and counselors of estate, in whose exercises the inventive part is most employed. (George Puttenham, 1, 8, 110) (my underlining)[64]

The key traditions – old and new around 1600 – in which Shakespeare's sonnets are imbricated are now established, and prior chapters have unravelled the alchemical thread woven into the 1609 collection of poems. We have, in fact, uncovered a complex drama of 'working the mind': in the sonnet sequence the poet's alembic-head is his stage and the plot is driven by love, nature and time. However, an important question remains: how exactly did inner alchemy connect with creativity in this period? In Chapter 2, I explored the crucial place of numerology in Renaissance invention: numbers were construed as bridging the gap between matter and Ideas; as 'an accessible route to knowledge of absolute truth', 'directing upward the faculties'.[65] Once the artist had discovered these truths or Ideas – the archetypes in the mind of God the 'Maker' – he had to replicate them in his own work. It is highly significant, therefore, that Shakespeare imposes a complex geometrical scheme redolent with symbolism upon his sequence. As we shall see in this section, the retrieval of truths or Ideas that have their origins in the Mind of the heavenly maker was not restricted to numbers. In the view of Ficino's *De amore*, accomplished artists following the footsteps of the divine craftsman carried a weighty responsibility on a par with that accorded to 'governor[s]'. 'Love', diligence and exactitude in replicating archetypes in art forms were crucial:

For, whoever greatly loves both works of art themselves and the people for whom they are made executes works of art diligently and completes them exactly. In addition to these points there is the fact that artists in all the arts seek and care for nothing else but love.[66]

The earthly maker had to replicate the ways of God the maker and, in the Hermetic aesthetic paradigm, desire could never be extricated from creativity. Indeed, Ficino construed strong desire (perceived as dangerous passion by some) as heightening the artist's imaginative power. Shakespeare's productions suggest he was sympathetic to this view; *A Midsummer Night's Dream* famously declares of the transforming power of love, for example: 'Things base and vile, holding no quantity, / Love can transpose to form and dignity' (I. i. 232–3).

As we began to see in the introduction to this book, late sixteenth-century poetic treatises reveal how thoroughly steeped in Neoplatonic-Hermetic philosophy notions of creativity were in the late sixteenth century. Thus Puttenham describes how the 'good' poet's fantasy should be like a clear mirror, well ordered so that it receives the brightest illuminations of 'knowledge', truth ('verity') and correct ('due') proportion of things (p. 110). Indeed, any occupation necessitating originality ('the inventive part') required a particularly well-ordered fantasy (p. 110). The ultimate 'good poet' for this period was Old Testament David and for Sidney his Psalmes are: 'a heavenlie poesie, wherein almost hee sheweth himselfe a passionate lover of that unspeakable and everlasting beautie to be seene by the eyes of the minde, onely cleared by fayth'.[67] The poet with a clear eye of the mind can even go beyond Nature in inventiveness, 'disdayning to be tied to any ... subjection, lifted up with the vigor of his owne invention, [the poet] dooth growe in effect another nature, in making things either better then Nature bringeth forth, or, quite a newe, formes such as never were in Nature' (*Apology for Poetry*, p. 156) – he can create golden worlds. Indeed, those with the most perceptive inner vision – like David – are prophets, imitating and borrowing nothing, 'of what is, hath been, or shall be: but range, onely rayned in with learned discretion, into the divine consideration of what may be, and should be' (*Apology for Poetry*, p. 159).

The key message of the Hermetic writings was of the necessity of striving for heightened vision, of cleansing and ordering the brain, enabling the soul's eye to see more truly and clearly. Puttenham's treatise is aware of this; not for nothing, it would seem, did a copy of the Hermetic writings sit in his library alongside the works of Ficino.[68] In his enthusiasm about the heightened powers of the good poet, Puttenham even touched (with some trepidation) on the *Hermetica*'s *alter deus* theme:

And this science in his perfection cannot grow but by some divine instinct – the Platonics call it *furor* – or by excellence of nature and complexion, or by great subtlety of the spirits and wit, or by much experience and observation of the world and course of kind, or peradventure by all or most part of them ... How could he so naturally paint out the speeches, countenance, and manners of princely persons and private ... It is therefore of poets thus to be conceived, that if they be able to devise and make all these things of them selves ... that they be (by manner of speech) as creating gods. (I, I, p. 94)

It is through capturing the 'speeches, countenance, and manners' of ideal 'princely and private persons' in their 'speaking pictures', which 'styrreth and instructeth the mind', that poets teach virtue (*Apology for Poetry*, p. 179). 'Fayn[ing]' is essential because it 'may bee tuned to the highest key of passion' and passion moves the soul (*Apology for Poetry*, p. 169). As we saw in Chapter 2, memory is construed as absolutely crucial to the creative process too: 'There is nothing in man of all the potential parts of his mind (reason and will except) more noble or more necessary to the active life than memory; because it maketh most to a sound judgement and perfect worldly wisedom' (Puttenham, I, 19, p. 128).

Order and proportion associated with subtle and refined spirits, a well-maintained fantasy and clear inner eye, together with a well-stocked memory store, are key to the understanding of creativity in this period, and this necessitates the 'work' of spiritual alchemy. There can be no invention without the purifying and remaking of inner nature: in the words of Paracelsus, 'This work of bringing things to their perfection is called "alchemy"'.[69]

NATURE MENDING NATURE: SOUL REMAKING

> This is an art
> Which does mend nature – change it rather; but
> The art itself is nature   (*The Winter's Tale*, IV. iv. 95–7)

In this Philosophical work, Nature and Art ought so lovingly to embrace each other, as that Art may not require what Nature denies nor Nature deny what may be perfected by Art. (Arthur Dee, *Fasciculus Chemicus*, 1631, liv)

As we have seen, in *The Civilization of the Renaissance in Italy*, Burckhardt foregrounded the 'lofty myth' that facilitated the birth of Renaissance man. As expressed by Pico della Mirandola, man was a protean 'molder and maker' of himself; he could degenerate into a 'brute' or become 'divine' according to his will and actions.[70] The source of this belief was the Hermetic text *Asclepius*: 'A human being is a great wonder'.[71] As I argued in Chapter 1, such a heroic conception of man thoroughly captured the Renaissance imagination. But how might man achieve his god-like potential? As the *Asclepius* expounds, this is largely through the intensive study and contemplation of nature (p. 74).

According to the Florentine academy's interpretation of the *Hermetica*, the book of nature was a work of divine revelation and the devout Renaissance philosopher was thus duty bound to study her works (as a companion to the Book of the Word) and seek out the treasures which were believed to have become hidden after man's expulsion from the Garden of Eden. The paramount work of nature was the microcosm – man – and 'know thyself' was the Hermetic philosopher's most important maxim. In Ficino's appealing, if tautologous, formulation, this philosophy applied to art is like a carpenter working inside the wood: 'For what after all is human art? It is a sort of nature handling matter from the outside. And what is nature? It is art moulding matter from within, as though the carpenter were in the wood' (*Platonic Theology*).[72]

According to this optimistic rendition, nature's internal shaping of nature is capable of producing stupendous (God-like) workmanship:

But if human art, though it is outside the matter, is nevertheless so well attuned and so close to making the work that it can bring definite works to completion in conformity with definite ideas, how much more then will art of nature be able to achieve this, the art which does not touch the outer surface of matter with hands or other external tools in the way the geometer's soul touches the dust as he traces figures on the ground, but rather the geometer's mind fashions imaginary matter within? (*Platonic Theology*, p. 253)

In Hermeticism, the celestial bodies are a link between God and mankind (the doctrine of sympathy and antipathy): they are capable of infusing their powers into terrestrial matter, and thus natural entities like flowers, stones, liquids, herbs and the matter of man's mind can acquire the same occult virtues imparted to them by heavenly bodies – they possess divine efficacy which the skilled natural philosopher might access. Processes such as alchemical distillation (inner and outer) could eventually lead to the recovery of divine 'signatures'. As John Cotta's treatise explains, in this manner the 'true artist' can better nature: 'Nature cannot decoct, infuse, compound, mix or prepare her rootes, metals, or other drugs and simples, in number and nature infinite; but Art is unto her benefite and service theirin accurate.'[73]

The artist-philosopher follows Nature's footprints to detect her 'secrets' then harnesses and speeds up her processes. This is the phenomenon that Francis Bacon describes as 'natural magic': 'I . . . understand it as the science which applies the knowledge of hidden forms to the production of wonderful operations; and by uniting (as they say) actives with passives displays the wonderful works of nature' (*De Dignitate et Augmentis Scientarum*, Sp. 1.573).[74] In the early seventeenth century this notion of natural magic (which drove Baconian science) is definitely informing the theories of the artists' 'powers' of invention that we have met in poetic treatises and it is highly operative in Shakespeare's sonnets too.[75] We should recall how it is our artist's meditation upon nature ('When I consider everything that grows'), and of man as mutable nature ('When I perceive that men as plants increase'), as well as the 'secret influence' of the 'stars' which 'comment' on the 'shows' of the world, which sets in train the entire 'engraft[ing]', distillation process (Sonnet 15). The poet has, furthermore, to get in touch with the rhythms of Nature (growth, decay, copulation, birth, death, the sun rising and setting, the passage of the moon) so that she will come to his aid as Mistress Nature – the dark, fertile female side of his psyche, aligned with *prima materia* – and complete the regenerative cycle.

The artist-philosopher had first to cleanse his soul in order to let in more heavenly light and thus recapture traces of divinity lying tarnished within himself if he wanted to progress and reach the dizzying innovative heights of 'alter deity'. He had to rekindle the Sun/Son within himself: it was Christ's incarnation that made possible the restoration of humanity to its prelapsarian state. This is why Edmund Spenser's 'A Hymne in Honour of Love' (1596) dwells on the significance of the 'sweet passion' to the microcosmic creative paradigm – 'Such is the power of that sweet passion, / That it all sordid basenesse doth expel' (190–1)– only 'the refynd mynd' can 'dwell / In his high thought' (192, 193–4), admiring 'heavenly light' (196). The poet's 'deepest wit' and 'hungrie fantasy' (197, 198) are illumined by this refinement or inner 'passion'.[76]

Shakespeare's poet of the *Sonnets* knows this too: he is deeply involved in the troubled business of remaking himself and, in accordance with Hermetic philosophy, it is love that drives the project. More specifically it is Platonic-style desire for a man that sets him on his lofty path to truth.[77] Indeed, apostrophes such as 'O, change thy thought, that I may change my mind' (Sonnet 10) and 'Make thee another self for love of me' (Sonnet 10) can be read (on one level) as attempts on the part of the speaker to engage the lovely youth (and/or his own self) in his enterprise: literally, 'changing' or transmuting his mind through intellectual procreation which generates pure love – the philosophical 'babe' or infant. The beautiful youth – the tenth Muse – functions to 'give invention light' (Sonnet 38).

We might at this point pause to reconsider those fascinating Shakespearean lines which invoke another type of craftsman, the 'dyer', who works with 'colours' – though not rhetorical ones – like the poet : 'my nature is subdued / To what it works in like the dyer's hand' (Sonnet 111). The poet's creative matrix is shaped and restricted by 'what it works in' – the state of his soul or his inner nature (also perhaps the breast of the beloved with whom he is 'one') – as well as by the limited 'means' that determines the social context of his writing and the public 'nature' of his occupation. The analogy is apposite because the 'dyer's hand' is stained, like his soul. This is, of course, why our poet seeks to cleanse it; to cure his infection with 'potions of eisel', 'penance' and 'correction' and thus to amplify his creative powers. Significantly, 'Pity me, then, and wish I were renewed' (Sonnet 111) resonates, as Duncan-Jones points out, with the biblical lines 'thy youth is renewed like the eagle's', Psalms 104.5; and 'though our outward man perish, yet the inward man is renewed day by day', 2 Corinthians 4.16.[78] In Shakespeare's hands poetic making – the major preoccupation of the sequence – cannot be disentangled from soul remaking and divine considerations.

The central sonnets of the sequence reward consideration from this perspective. They reflect directly upon the 1609 book of poetry: 'When thou reviewest this, thou dost review / The very part was consecrate to thee'; the poet's 'spirit' in the beloved's breast is reflected in the lines of the volume (Sonnet 74). Since the poet and his beloved are one, and the poet is seeking Christ within himself, it is a mistake to try to wrench the threesome apart in such lines as these:

> So are you to my thoughts as food to life,
> Or as sweet seasoned showers are to the ground;
> And for the peace of you I hold such strife
> As 'twixt a miser and his wealth is found.   (Sonnet 75, 1–4)

The desired 'peace' – his soul's harmony – might be the speaker's, which requires a 'piece/peace' of the beloved (his friend/Christ), his image in his breast, as 'food' to refresh (like 'showers') his 'thoughts' or contemplation. As we have seen, spiritual alchemy is strife-ridden, involving the continuous integration of opposed and warring elements within the self. The goal is to secure spiritual harmony and rejuvenating intellectual 'store', so the simile is pertinent. Sonnet 76 proclaims his verse simple ('barren of new pride') and constant – all about 'one' – humble ('in a noted weed'), capturing the rhythms of the sun ('daily new and old') to write about 'sweet love', the beloved/Christ. The exact halfway point in the sequence – Sonnet 77 – is of especial significance:

> Thy glass will show thee how thy beauties wear,
> Thy dial how thy precious minutes waste,
> The vacant leaves thy mind's imprint will bear,
> And of this book this learning mayst thou taste:
> The wrinkles which thy glass will truly show
> Of mouthed graves will give thee memory;
> Thou by thy dial's shady stealth mayst know
> Time's thievish progress to eternity.
> Look what thy memory cannot contain,
> Commit to these waste blanks, and thou shalt find
> Those children nursed, delivered from thy brain,
> To take a new acquaintance of thy mind.
> These offices, so oft as thou wilt look,
> Shall profit thee, and much enrich thy book.   (Sonnet 77)

These lines are usually glossed by editors as addressed to the lover, but they are equally instructions to 'thee', my self, and they are about inner looking – divine, profitable meditation (hence 'offices') prompted by a 'glass' (mirror), the dial (time passing) and the paper memory of the book. The poet is communing with his self (who is 'one' with the lover) and the incremental repetition, underpinned by the reiteration of 'th' sounds, is appropriate for suggesting the gradual procreation of thought and soul and book enrichment or growth too. The couplet tie, 'look' and 'book', linked to 'profit' highlights the spiritual and creative significance of such inner looking – of 'oft' repeated 'offices'. Spurred by the influence of the beloved's 'eyes', and the subsequent memory image 'sealed' on the poet's mind, the speaker has advanced (humbly speaking) 'as high as learning' (Sonnet 78).

But where are fantasy and invention in this scheme? George Puttenham's treatise is significant here. He describes the 'well affected' brain as 'very formal, and in his much multiformity uniform, that is well proportioned, and so passing cleare, that by it, as by a glass or mirror, are represented unto the soul all manner of beautiful visions, whereby the inventive part of the mind is so much helped, as without it no man could devise any new or rare thing' (1, 8, p. 109). Puttenham, like Shakespeare, employs the word 'glass' (mirror), but in this passage it is used very precisely to describe the refined brain's formal powers to present visions to the soul which are essential for 'invention'. Puttenham shortly repeats the glass simile and this time it is quite clear that he is referring, in particular, to 'fantasy': 'And this fantasy may be resembled to a glass' (1, 8, p. 110). The analogy was quite commonplace around 1600; Fulke Greville uses it in *A Treatie of Humane Learning*:

> Knowledges next organ is Imagination;
> A glasse, wherin the object of our Sense
> Ought to reflect true height, or declination,
> For understandings cleare intelligence. [79]

It is deployed very precisely in Sir John Davies's *Nosce Teipsum* too:

> The *wit*, the pupil of the *Soules* cleare eye,
> And in mans world the onely shining *Starre*,
> Lookes in the mirrour of the phantasie,
> Where all the gatherings of the *Senses* are.
>
> From thence this power the shapes of things abstracts,
> And them within her *passive part* receives,
> Which are enlightened by that part which *acts*,
> And so the formes of single things perceives.   (lines 1157–64) [80]

From the 'grosse matter' (541) of the senses the soul 'drawes a kind of Quintessence' (542) of 'formes' through a process of 'sublimation' (538), which gives them 'celestiall wings' (544). Then, '*Reason*' '*rates*' these 'formes' while '*Understanding*' passes '*Judgement*' (1169–76). This is how intellectual memories are made and, when they are relegated to the 'Store-house', 'no Lethean Flud' can wash them away (1224). As the higher powers of the soul contemplate these it reconnects with the divine forms or Ideas languishing in its midst and establishes 'universall kinds'. The mind itself then becomes a 'mirror' reflecting back 'truly' and thus enabling a glimpse of the '*Soules*' eternitie':

> But who so makes a mirror of his mind,
> And doth with patience view himselfe therin;
> His *Soules* eternitie shall cleerly find,
> Though th'other beauties be defac't with sinne.   (lines 1300–3)

In line with this, Sir Philip Sidney's *Apology for Poetry* speaks tantalizingly of Ideas as the 'fore-conceite' of the poet's 'work', 'Which delivering forth . . . is not wholie imaginative' (p. 157). Ideas captured in a work of art are construed as more than figments of the imagination: they mysteriously enable man to 'learne aright why and how that Maker made him' (p. 157).

If we now substitute fantasy for 'glass' in Shakespeare's Sonnet 77, its rich layers of potential meaning begin to emerge. Consider these lines again: 'The wrinkles which thy glass will truly show / Of mouthed graves will give thee memory'. In a meditation upon 'mouthed graves' – death – his phantasy and/or soul will reflect 'truly'; this is healthy imagination, then, enabling the soul's eye contemplating fantasy images to maximize 'true' invention (with the aid of the higher powers of the soul). We can extrapolate with the assistance of the above lines from *Nosce Teipsum* that this will increase the 'store' of intellectual memory which, as we saw in Chapter 2, is immortal, and the book will give the poet (as well as his beloved) 'memory' too. It should now be apparent that this important sonnet, significantly exactly midway in the sequence, reflects upon the brain's 'remaking' process and this is inextricable from the making of poetry – Shakespeare's 'book'. Writing poetry – doing art – is integral to soul remaking, to mending inner nature. It is intriguing in this respect that when the Irish symbolist poet W. B. Yeats was asked why he rewrote his early ornate poems, his lyrical response was:

> The friends that have it I do wrong
> Whenever I remake a song
> Should know what issue is at stake:
> It is myself that I remake.[81]

Of note, too, is that while Yeats was seeking to achieve a 'witty simplicity', Shakespeare celebrated his 'noted weed', 'barren of new pride' (Sonnet 74). I'll return to this connection later.

THE 'DOTING TRUMPERIE' OF IMAGINATION[82]

> My selfe am *Center* of my circling thought,
> Onely *my selfe* I studie, learne, and *know*.
>
> (*Nosce Teipsum*, 167–8)

In the early years of the seventeenth century every wit (and his devout neighbour) was, it seems, seeking to 'know himself' and at the same time the potential of man's imagination to access divine 'truths', Ideas and 'universalls' was being liberally celebrated, especially by poets. Besides Florio's 1603 English translation of Montaigne's *Essays*, multiple English editions of Pierre de la Primaudaye's *The French Academie* between 1586 and 1618 encouraged this trend by presenting a highly accessible version of the 'Platonicall Academy's' understanding of 'the body and soule of man'.[83] The latter volume, notably sympathetic to the resurgence of Platonism, provides crucial insights into gathering anxieties in the minds of some about the potential of the Hermetic study of Nature to compromise God:

They will make an iddle of Nature . . . They will rather put out their owne eyes then follow this Nature, which they forge unto themselves as a soveraigne Mistresse, whereas she is but the meanes to leade them to God . . . and their Creator, of whom she is but a servant, and very small image. (*The Second Part of the French Academie*, 1605, p. 425)

'Mistresse' Nature (and we should, in my view, be considering Shakespeare's dark Circean 'mistress' in this light) was leading philosophers into dangerous territory aside from idolatry and this had to do with the flip side of the fantasy coin – in Drayton's words, the 'doting trumperie' of imagination.

It was, I suggest, the fantasy's chemical synthesizing quality, its transforming potential, its innovatory powers – its very strength – that disturbed people. Consider *The French Academie*'s description:

'Fantasie': it staieth not in that which is shewed unto it by the sences that serve it, but taketh what pleaseth it, and addeth thereunto or diminisheth, changeth & rechangeth, mingleth and unmingleth, so that it – asunder and secureth up againe as it listeth. (*The Second Part of the French Academie*, p. 155)

In the alchemy of the mind imagination joined contraries, often uniting things that were not usually lawfully matched. Sometimes it wrenched things apart and made new marriages. It was a promiscuous custom breaker, then, as well as the source of all originality. We can see why it required constant scrutiny.

The French Academie proceeds:

In trueth, fantasie is a very dangerous thing. For, if it bee not guided and brideled by reason, it troubleth and moveth all the sence and understanding, as a tempest doeth the sea. For it is easily stirred up not onely by the externall sences but also by the complexion and disposition of the body. Heerof it proceedeth that even the spirits both good and bad have great accesse unto it, to stirre it either to good or evill, and that by meanes unknowen to us. (*The Second Part of the French Academie*, p. 156)

The external senses, humoral make-up ('complexion and disposition') and evil spirits are all implicated in stirring tempests that can send the unstable ship of 'fantasie' dangerously off course.

Further amplification of how the fantasy mechanism was construed will help to illuminate this troublesome power. La Primaudaye's detailed description of the role of the external and internal senses is a helpful starting point:

Corporall things are the subject and objects of the corporall senses, and ... the bodily senses receive and know them corporally, even such as they are presented unto them ... But they cannot receive or perceive any more then that which is laied open unto them, and manifesteth it selfe outwardly. Now after the outward senses have thus received them and their matter covered with their qualities, the internall senses, to which the externall are serviceable, conceive the images without the matters and qualities of those things wherof they are images. For the eye cannot see either the Sunne or the light of it, nor yet any other creature discovered by the light, except it be present before it. But the *Fantasie* and imagination receive and conceive the images of things, even in darkenesse ... Wee see then already how these images are separated from the matter of which they are images, and how the internal senses behold them. (*The Second Part of the French Academie*, p. 559)

This amazing eye which sees, 'even in darkenesse' is, of course, implicated in Shakespeare's poet's ability to look 'on darkness which the blind do see' (Sonnet 27). Importantly, inner vision is purer because it does not involve 'corporall matter' and is accessible to the understanding 'spirit':

Then having received them thus purged from their corporall matter, the spirit receiveth them yet more pure, and goeth further in the knowledge and understanding of them then all the senses do, comprehending other things, of which the senses can have no knowledge or apprehension. (*The Second Part of the French Academie*, p. 560)

Eventually, in their divested of matter state, 'fantasie' images viewed by the soul can lead to the knowledge of 'infinite thinges':

The soule is of another nature and substance ... Likewise by this, that it is capable of the knowledge of infinite thinges, of which it retaineth the memorie, and that it inquireth into secret thinges separated from all corporal matter, which can not be perceived by any sense. (*The Second Part of the French Academie*, p. 560)

In this way, the sonneteer's night-time contemplation of lovely boy's memory image constitutes a 'zealous pilgrimage' (Sonnet 27). His 'soul's imaginary sight' – his fantasy – presents a 'shadow' to his 'sightless view', which is more intensely pure and beautiful than the original. Thus this 'jewel (hung in ghastly night)' contains the ultimate potential to lead the poet to the understanding of infinite things in his own soul ('When most I wink, then do myne eyes best see', Sonnet 43) and, as we saw earlier, this was construed as the route to immortality: 'meditation or reminiscence is a recovering, as it were, of lost knowledge . . . Certainly by this remedy mortal things are rendered like immortal ones' (Ficino, *De amore*, p. 131).

Imagination or fantasy is a sort of bridge, then, between the soma and the soul but it also links the microcosm with positive influences in the macrocosm and heavens. Katherine Park has illuminated its important role in natural astral magic – the phenomenon that Shakespeare calls the 'secret influence' of the 'stars' (Sonnet 15). The fantasy is the highest power of the human soul to work through corporeal organs and as such it is susceptible to physical celestial influences transmitted by the *spiritus mundi*.[84] Ficino provides an elaborate explanation of how the upper and lower worlds, form and matter, are reconnected and restored creatively through fantasy and reason:

The Soul of [a human being], which is affected by the individual impulses of individual bodies through its earthly body, receives these images of the Ideas maculated by the matter of the universe through perception, but collects them through fantasy, cleans and refines them through reason, and connects them at last with the universal Ideas of the mind [Mens]. So the celestial ray that had descended to the lowest things returns to the higher beings, because the images of Ideas, formerly dispersed in matter, are collected in the fantasy, and, formerly impure, they are purified in reason, and formerly particular, they are lifted in the mind [Mens] to universality. In this way the Soul of [mankind] restores the world that had already been shaken.[85]

Furthermore, angels, when minded to inspire man to prophecy, can only work through the physiological manipulation of the imagination.[86] We should recall how Sidney's *Apology* celebrates the relation between poetry and prophecy. Used correctly, the fantasy is thus truly wondrous. However, because it relies on the input from external sight, smell, touch, taste and hearing it can be easily contaminated by the body's drives and excesses; additionally, bad spirits and the devil access the imagination in the same manner as good spirits and angels – fantasy is thus an intensely ambivalent power around 1600.[87] This helps us to understand Edmund Spenser's strangely equivocal representation of fantasy's chamber in *The Faerie Queene*, with its 'swarth[y]' complexioned, 'crabbed', melancholic occupant who seems 'mad' (II. ix. 52) – *Phantastes*. His room buzzes with 'flies' of 'idle thoughts and fantasies, / Devices, dreames, opinions unsound, / Shewes' as well as 'tales, and lies' (II. ix. 51); however, it simultaneously contains the 'shapes of things . . . such as in the world were never yit' (II. ix. 50).[88] It is left to the occupant of the next soul chamber – meditating 'goodly reason' – to sift through this buzzing soup, judging and separating the wheat from the chaff, wisdom and prophecy from nonsense, before consigning the best to memory for remembrance and contemplation by *Eumnestes* 'tossing and turning them withouten end' (II. ix. 58). Phantasy, Reason and Memory are all, notably, valuable counsellors, 'of greatest powre' to Alma, the soul (II. ix. 47). Imagination is thus apprehended as dangerous but essential and a powerful force for good if correctly maintained and utilized.

It was, however, readily disordered by anything which compromised humoral balance: ill health, gluttony and old age were construed as particularly corrupting states, leading to fantastical delusions being delivered higher up the soul chain and these, in common with madness or frenzy, could readily undermine Reason and Understanding, leading to cognitive errors and consequent immoral behaviour. Thus Sir John Davies declares:

> But if a *Phrensie* do possesse the braine;
> It so disturbes and blots the formes of things,
> As phantasie proves altogether vaine,
> And to the wit, no true relation brings;
>
> (*Nosce Teipsum*, 1649–52)

Furthermore, melancholy – the humoral state associated with Saturn and dark meditation and thus with inner alchemy – was termed the 'devil's bath'. For many non-Hermeticists the intense imagination deemed essential by alchemists for the production of the stone (*Zoroaster's Cave* urged, for example, 'first exercise thyself in a diuturnity of Intense Imagination') was tantamount to bathing in the devil's waters.[89] The melancholic alchemist's 'laundering' and 'bathing', crucial for attaining *Albedo* whiteness and purity – 'the seething bath' discovered in Shakespeare's Sonnets 153 and 154 – was thus a double-edged phenomenon linked both to negative influences and to spiritual cleansing. Hence the profound dangers to the soul associated with inner alchemy: the potential for evil distortions (devils masquerading as angels), delusions and subversion of the *opus*, was huge. As Thomas Wright expressed it, 'a false imagination corrupteth the understanding, making it believe that thinges are better than they are in very deede'; 'passions' put 'greene spectacles before the eyes of our witte'.[90]

Shakespeare wittily captures these topical anxieties and paradoxes in slippery lines like the following:

> If that be fair whereon my false eyes dote,
> What means the world to say it is not so   (Sonnet 148)

and, reflecting on alchemy more directly,

> Your love taught it this alchemy,
> To make of monsters and things indigest
> Such cherubins as your sweet self resemble.   (Sonnet 114)

Additionally, as we saw in Chapter 3, intense passion was given higher credence by some Neoplatonists than Reason in achieving the final goal of the opus. Ficino declared: 'For we achieve neither poetry nor mysteries, nor prophecy without vast zeal' (*De amore*, p. 172); indeed, Orphic 'madness' was construed as essential for tempering 'the unharmonious and dissonant' qualities of the soul (*De amore*, p. 171–2). Puttenham mentions this: 'this science in his perfection can not grow but by some divine instinct – the Platonics call it *furor* [heroic frenzy]'; and Sidney celebrates 'fayning' because it 'may bee tuned to the highest key of passion' (*Apology for Poetry*, p. 169). Passion (especially 'amatory' passion), even frenzy, were clearly not always negative states in Renaissance culture. This is undoubtedly why Shakespeare's Theseus in *A Midsummer Night's Dream* reminds the audience, no doubt with a gleam in his eye, that the lunatic and the poet have much in common: 'The lunatic, the lover and the poet are of imagination all compact' (v. i. 7–8).

Caveats aside, then, bathing in melancholy in association with 'frenzy' was considered crucial to originality by many philosopher-wits at the turn of the seventeenth century.[91] Viewed from within this discursive network we can begin to see why treatises of melancholy, including Robert Burton's weighty tome, proliferated in this period, delivering messages such as this: 'Some ascribe all vices to a false and corrupt imagination . . . deluding the soul with false shews and suppositions' ('Of the Force of Imagination').[92] Thomas Nashe warned even more alarmingly, 'And even as slime and durt in a standing puddle, engender toads and frogs, and many other unsightly creatures, so this slimie melancholy humor still thickening as it stands still, engendreth many misshapen objects in our imaginations.'[93]

Yet, on the upside, Burton notes how lengthy ruminating on fantasy images leads to invention – 'making new of his own' – to the 'feigning' and 'forging' associated with the creative imagination (*Anatomy of Melancholy*, p. 159). Further, none of this would be possible without initial sense impressions – fantasy depends on matter, on the body. No wonder our sonneteer seeks to incorporate and foreground the body and its passions in the soul-remaking, poetry-making process of the *opus*. 'Madding fever', 'frantic mad'[ness] – 'reason' has left the poet – is associated in Shake-speare's sonnets with the creative process (Sonnets 119, 147, 148) but in a characteristically ambivalent way. It would seem that the master of inven-tion, around 1600, is acknowledging the crucial role of matter and the senses and of Orphic madness in creativity: 'My mistress when she walks treads on the ground' (Sonnet 130). Kissing and touching actually stimulate his muse; as in Daniel's poetic treatise 'incounters of touch', an idea of language rooted in the body, which has 'pulse, life, and energie', is validated.[94]

Certainly, other contemporary poets were associating Orphic 'rage' and 'rapture' with heightened creativity, for example Thomas Campion, in the *Lords Maske* (1613), where it is mistaken for 'Mania':

Orpheus:

Alas, good Entheus, hast thou brook't this wrong;
What? Number thee with madmen? O mad age,
Sencelesse of thee, and thy celestiall rage.
For thy excelling rapture, ev'n through things
That seems most light, is borne with sacred wings.[95]

Incorporating Hermetic philosophy, Bruno's *Heroic Frenzies* had argued that the ascent towards the divine had to involve the body and acknowl-edging its sensual drives and their need for temperate fulfilment (the 'unity' of body and soul); without the 'fires' of the body – 'the natural instincts of human love and generation' – it is impossible to become a fully integrated soul (*Heroic Frenzies*, pp. 37, 130). Shakespeare takes this a daring step further: uniquely at this time, he associates creative frenzy with the agonized union of sensual bodily and divine desire. Phallic rising and falling is not a 'want of conscience' but an urgent necessity: the 'whole' man (body and soul) is involved in love (Sonnet 151) and Love-Christ (who also rose and fell as a man) is the supreme good in Shakespearean philosophy. It is note-worthy that Henry Vaughan used the 'rise' and 'fall' imagery (without bawdy connotations) in relation to 'Tuning' the 'brest' of 'disorder'd man' in his poem 'Affliction': rising and falling is a 'sacred, needful art' to 'stretch ev'ry part/Making the whole most Musicall' (39–40).[96] Shakespeare's serious play is, in fact, rendered highly complex by the presence of an echo of the Geneva Bible annotation to Romans 7: 19: 'the flesh stayeth even the moste perfect to runne forwarde as the spirit wisheth'. Beatrice Groves convincingly argues that

The wit of the Pauline allusion . . . resides in the fact that flesh betrays the spirit not in the normal, Pauline, sense of doing the opposite of what it desires . . . but by being in absolute accordance with it. The flesh is so obedient to the 'nobler part' that it reveals the desires of the mind through an erection. Shakespeare punningly transforms Paul's martial metaphors in which the body's 'membres' (7: 23) are at war with the spirit into an account of a member which is an entirely obedient little soldier: standing, falling and pointing with military precision.

The whole sonnet can, indeed, be read as a 'playful disavowal' of the Pauline dichotomy between flesh and spirit: tuning and harmonizing the Shakespearean subject (re-)incorporates the 'flesh'.[97] We might ponder the sermonizing words of a kindred spirit at this point: 'In the constitution and make of a natural man, the body is not the man, nor the soul is not the man, but the union of these two makes up the man.'[98] We might recall, too, the string of meaningful 'o's in 'The Extasie' (which seem to resonate with the ejaculatory 'o's at the end of *A Lovers Complaint)*: 'But o alas, so long, so farre / Our bodies why doe wee forbeare ?' (49–50).[99] Donne is certainly insistent that 'Love must not be, but take a body too' ('Aire and Angels', 10): 'Love sometimes would contemplate, sometimes do' ('Love's growth', 14).

But perhaps it was with Montaigne's pithy reflections, his eloquent carrying of the banner for the body's cause, that the sixteenth-century project of bodily incorporation began in earnest (in the face, perhaps, of the mutterings of impending Cartesianism); he proclaimed in 'Of Experience': 'My selfe who but grovel on the ground, hate that kinde of humane Wisedome' – the inhuman wisdom which eschewed the body and its needs for sensual gratification – and, further, 'I hate that we should be commanded to have our minds in the clouds, whilst our bodies are sitting at the table.'[100] Shakespeare, like Montaigne, Donne and Herbert (Herbert's speaker is told he 'must sit down' and 'eat' at the close of 'Love III') and unlike Sidney, sat down to eat. He certainly brought refreshing 'food' to the Petrarchan table; his brain was not 'beguiled'.

DESIRE, ABSENCE AND TRUTH

The desire for abundance . . . arises and grows from poverty, as if that were a loss . . . Desire . . . is always poverty-stricken. (Ficino, Letter 88)[101]

O let me true in love but truly write. (Sonnet 21)

As should now be clear, the central concern of Shakespeare's densely philosophical sonnet sequence is with creative 'making' – a process inseparable from soul remaking and which is couched in the language and rhythms of alchemy. Love and desire – for men, for God and for sensory and sensual gratification (linked predominantly to the female body) – are presented as key to the speaker's creativity. But the sequence explores other less central aspects of the 'making' process. For example, it ruminates in a fascinating way on the relations between desire, absence and creativity and, more broadly, on emotional states and a writer's productivity. The following lines are not necessarily just about absence and the seasons:

> How like a winter hath my absence been
> From thee, the pleasure of the fleeting year!
> What freezings have I felt, what dark days seen,
> What old December's bareness everywhere!   (Sonnet 97, 1–4)

Indeed, this is the sonnet replete with pathetic fallacy that so inspired Keats' 'Ode to Melancholy', for obvious reasons. It describes 'dark days' of absence from the beloved object, connected with emotional 'freezings' that make it seem December rather than summer. 'And yet' this melancholic time of darkness has been productive, 'Bearing the wanton burden of the prime'. 'This abundant issue', can be construed as 'issue' of the pen as well as 'teeming autumn's' fruit. The 'leaves' that 'look pale, dreading the winter's near' are the pages of a poetry book as well as nature's leaves. This is reminiscent of writer's block, a 'freezing' feared perhaps by all writers even amidst a productive surge. Because it is the contemplation of the soul's memory images (collected in the 'prime') that leads to invention, desire and longing in absence can obviously function to heighten creativity. This is precisely the philosophical point stressed by Ficino's important Letter 88 'Divinitas animi ab inventione' ('Divinity of soul from invention'):

The desire for abundance, as if it were a possession, arises and grows from poverty, as if that were a loss . . . Desire . . . is always poverty-stricken . . . the human soul is never impoverished, for it creates abundance even from poverty, weaves invention from its absence, and digs up gleaming silver and glittering gold from the darkest corners of the earth . . . this is the eternal land of the soul, whose fruit is inexhaustible . . . The letter therefore implores us a thousand times to cultivate this land; for it offers us incorruptible fruits, most abundant and most sweet.[102]

For Ficino, and as I have been arguing here for Shakespeare, too, 'invention' was a crucial aspect of soul regeneration. As for Shakespeare's poet's 'abundant issue' (Sonnet 97), though, they seem to the writer unsatisfactory, 'orphan' births, the product of unmet desires, 'unfathered fruit'. Absence, longing, suffering has stirred his pen but his mood state renders him far from content with the result.

Sonnet 98 dwells further on the material absence of his muse and 'play [ing]' with the lover's memory image – his 'shadow' as well as with images drawn from the natural world – 'the deep vermilion in the rose'. The couplet tie, 'You away', 'I did play', conveys a certain relish, nevertheless, at this sensual feast of absence, which is represented in the lines of this sonnet and even more playfully and abundantly in Sonnet 99. Memory images were frequently referred to as 'flowers' and 'shadows' of the beloved and colourful blooms mingle and transmute in the poet's fantasy, producing particularly rich and sensuous combinations – 'figures of delight' (Sonnet 98).

But I must end this section by turning once again to troublesome 'truth' – the conundrum of how to write 'truly'. This was, of course, a common sixteenth-century Petrarchan topos, and we might expect Shakespeare to contribute to the intellectual debate. Sidney's *Astrophil and Stella* had raised the paradoxical issue of how to 'feign' truly in its very first sonnet. How might the poet capture the 'heart'['s] feelings in words? 'O let me true in love but truly write' (Sonnet 21), as Shakespeare phrased it. Even more problematically, how might a writer capture Ideas and Universals, garnered through the inner distillation process, in his creation? Divine geometry, not reliant upon material signs, was imagined to offer an additional, more accessible route to truth. Words were stumbling blocks. Florentine theorists such as Ficino had insisted, we should recall, on the importance of 'diligent' and 'exact' works of art, which captured the divine archetypes to which the refined mind of the lover-artist had privileged access (*De amore*, p. 66). For some, like Sir Philip Sidney, the daunting issue of 'prophecy' was at stake too.

Significantly, the frustrated expression of the inexpressible ideal is a recurring feature of Shakespeare's sonnets, as in Sonnet 101 (the lines anticipate the spoken response of the muse):

> 'Truth needs no colour with his colour fixed,
> Beauty no pencil beauty's truth to lay,
> But best is best if never intermixed'?
> Because he needs no praise, wilt thou be dumb?
> Excuse not silence so, for't lies in thee
> To make him much outlive a gilded tomb.   (Sonnet 101, 6–11)

While others undertake 'gross painting' in 'strained touches' (Sonnet 82), our poet claims to be (undoubtedly tongue-in-cheek) 'tongue-tied' (Sonnet 85): 'Finding thy worth a limit past my praise' (Sonnet 82). The urge is always to add something more: 'So all my best is dressing old words new, / Spending again what is already spent' (Sonnet 76). However much a poet might extend himself, broadening the range of his medium, deploying his virtuosity to its limits, he finds himself locked into a process of accumulation of epithets and rhetorical figures and tropes, celebrating his subject through 'cultivated excess'. The influential French poet Ronsard had foregrounded and, nevertheless, praised this technique in *Odes* (1550): 'it is the true aim of the lyric poet to celebrate to the extreme the subject whose praise he undertakes'.[103] Shakespeare's poet suggests he is trying to resist the urge towards *copia* and ornamentation: 'I love not less, thou less the show appear' (Sonnet 102). The effort to praise more, truly, without show is captured here: 'And to the most of praise add something more; / But that is in my thought' (Sonnet 85). Paradoxically, of course, the aimed for simplicity and constancy – a 'noted weed' – manifest themselves as repetition and excess: 'Fair, kind and true, varying to other words'. Ultimately language is insufficient; it cannot embody the transcendent which must remain imprisoned in 'dumb thoughts, speaking in effect' (Sonnet 85). Nevertheless, paradoxically again, 'feigning' truth is superior to silence, 'dumb thoughts'. Indeed, this sonnet may well be toying with the Aristotelian proposition that human thoughts ordered into spoken, written and mental propositions, can indeed, when mixed, present a whole truth that is half spoken and half thought. The struggle to figure forth true thoughts in words continues.

Reflecting on the meditative poet's 'discipline', Louis Martz concluded, 'Toward the union of "the powers of the soul", Herbert's "simplicity", or Yeats's "Unity of Being" – toward such a principle, by disciplined effort, the meditative poet makes his way, while creation of the poetry plays its part in the struggle. There is, as Yeats has said, a close correspondence between this discipline and the creative imagination.'[104]

I would like to add Shakespeare to the list of writers Martz includes in his study of the poetry of meditation. Like George Herbert, John Donne, Robert Southwell, Henry Vaughan and Andrew Marvell, Shakespeare would have understood only too well what Yeats meant when he declared that remaking a song was remaking his self:

> The friends that have it I do wrong
> Whenever I remake a song
> Should know what issue is at stake:
> It is myself that I remake.[105]

Striving for greater simplicity of expression as well as unity of being, Yeats insisted that there was an inseparable bond between disciplined inner looking, self-remaking and poetic making and, furthermore, that a strong dramatic sense was crucial to the enterprise: 'If we cannot imagine ourselves as different from what we are and assume that second self, we cannot impose a discipline upon ourselves ... Active virtue as distinguished from the passive acceptance of a current code is therefore theatrical, consciously dramatic, the wearing of a mask.'[106]

Impressed by these insights, Louis Martz defined the meditative poem quite loosely as 'a work that creates an interior drama of the mind'. Shakespeare would undoubtedly have agreed. It is significant that Yeats practised methods of meditation with the 'Hermetic students of the Golden Dawn', 'the Cabbalistic Society, which taught me methods of meditation that had greatly affected my thought'.[107] This apparently involved intense concentration upon visual symbols, cleansing the mind of impurities, and a step-by-step progress towards purer and more powerful and arcane knowledge.[108] In the 1890s Yeats even planned an Irish Mystical Order that would buy an island castle:

Where its members could retire for a while for contemplation, and where we might establish mysteries ... and for ten years ... I had an unshakable conviction, arising how or whence I cannot tell, that invisible gates would open as they opened for Blake ... Swedenborg ... Boehme, and that this philosophy would find its manuals of devotion in all imaginative literature.[109]

A central aim was to 'reunite the perception of the spirit, of the dream, with natural beauty': ancient mystical traditions together with their early modern developments, through figures like Jacob Boehme (1575–1624), contemplation, myth, ritual, natural beauty – these are the ingredients of his vision.[110] Although God and Christ seem starkly absent, it is not difficult to see the similarities between Yeats' 'effort to evoke and discipline the natural powers of the mind' and the technique of spiritual alchemy nurtured by a resurgence of Neoplatonism and Hermeticism in the Renaissance and, again, in Romanticism.[111]

In 1975, the psychologist-philosopher James Hillman asked a crucial question of the Renaissance:

Just how was this efflorescence in art, literature, music, politics, science, discovery – this new vision of man and the world, to which we still turn today for our sources and models – how was this Renaissance *psychologically* possible? That era, in terms of economic and political history and history of art and science, has been thoroughly surveyed, but ... We must ask what interior ferment made possible such a revival in so many fields. I believe that psychology is missing from Renaissance studies because it is their very content, the latent unconscious ground upon which all else has been erected.[112]

He concluded that it was an obsession with soul remaking or 'care of soul' and a willingness to confront one's dark inner shadow that ignited this intellectual ferment. It is, indeed, striking that so many luminaries from this period identified themselves as prone to deep melancholia: it shadowed the lives of Dürer, Savonarola, Machiavelli, Ficino, Leonardo, Michelangelo and Petrarch. It is no coincidence that the first three operas to emerge in the early seventeenth century, including Monteverdi's *Orfeo* (1607), rehearsed the myth of the descent of the lover Orpheus into the realm of the under-world to retrieve his lost love: this was a culture obsessed with desire and the dark caverns of the mind, with plumbing the depths and remaking the soul.[113] The 'Rebirth' (Renaissance) alluded to by humanists surely had something to do with the soul – with fantasies about its *renovatio* – as well as with the revival of ancient texts. 'Renaissance humanitas' was, predom-inantly in Hillman's view, 'a care for the contents of the intellectual imagination' and its extraordinary debt to Petrarch was that he pioneered the project to demonstrate the way in which literary expression, philosophy and care of souls were related. For Petrarch, writing eloquently could not be dissociated from the condition of the soul – 'right expression and right psyche were one'.[114] In this schema, nurtured and developed by the Florentine and Parisian academies, soul making, creative making and eloquence (rhetoric) cannot be teased apart, and this is the fertile territory of Shakespeare's 'interior drama of the mind'.

CHAPTER 6

Conclusion: Shakespeare's poetics of love
and religious toleration

> But stay, I see thee in the *Hemisphere*
> Advanc'd, and made a Constellation there!
> Shine forth, thou Starre of Poets, and with rage,
> Or influence, chide, or cheere the drooping Stage;
> Which, since thy flight from hence, hath mourn'd like night,
> And dispaires day, but for thy Volumes light.[1]
>
> (Ben Jonson, 'To the memory of my beloved, The Author
> Mr William Shakespeare: And what he hath left us')

In the first prefatory poem of the 1623 Folio, Ben Jonson pays homage
'To ... my beloved, The Author Mr William Shakespeare', significantly
likening Shakespeare's power 'to charme' to that of Mercury, and his
'influence' to that of a 'Starre'. In this witty deployment of the terms of
Ficinian natural magic, Shakespeare shines forth as a 'Constellation' in the
heavens and is urged to project his powers on to the 'drooping Stage'.[2] His
'Volume', meanwhile, radiates spiritual 'light' in darkness. Interestingly,
Jonson's lines allude, very specifically, to the Shakespearean 'art' of poetic
making:

> Yet must I not give Nature all: Thy Art,
> My gentle *Shakespeare*, must enjoy a part.
> For though the *Poet's* matter, Nature be,
> His Art doth give the fashion. And, that he,
> Who casts to write a living line, must sweat,
> (Such as thine are) and strike the second heat
> Upon the *Muses* anvile: turne the same,
> (And himself with it) that he thinkes to frame.

The poet in this construction fashions Nature's 'matter' from within,
producing inspired art through a process of distillation (hence the 'sweat')
and 'heat / Upon the ... anvile' – metalwork.[3] Both the poet and the poem
are fashioned in this process: 'A good Poet's made, as well as borne', Jonson

affirms. Seven years later in 'On Shakespear', the young John Milton playfully eulogizes Shakespeare's 'live long Monument' in 'easie numbers' (lines 8, 10). These are the feet of Shakespeare's poetic monument, of course, but additionally, as I suggested in Chapter 2, the 'Star-ypointing Pyramid' comparison (4) is probably an ironic and witty allusion to the divine numbers and geometry in the *Sonnets*, which are far more efficacious and enduring ('live-long') than a pile of material 'Stones' (1–2).[4] In fact both Jonson and Milton pay homage to Shakespeare as an artist influenced by the intellectual currents nurtured by the Italian and French academies – as an inspired poetic maker. Milton's 'Il Penseroso' notably associates inspiration with dark contemplation, a 'prophetic strain', and with 'Thrice great Hermes' ('Il Penseroso', line 88). A passage in Henry Vaughan describing a 'true *Hermetist*' is illuminating:

I call them *Hermetists*, who observe nature in her workes, who imitate her, and use the same method that she doth, that out of nature, by the mediation of nature, and the assistance of their owne judgements, they may produce and bring to light such rare effectual medicines, as will safely, speedily, and pleasantly cure … the most deplorable diseases. These are the true *Hermetists*. (*Hermetical Physick*)[5]

There is, I suggest, a self-conscious healing 'influence' in Shakespeare's writing – one targeted at the 'disease' of religious extremism and persecution that was blighting his age. In seeking to uncover, via biography, a Shakespeare dominated by Roman Catholicism or Lutheranism scholars are, ironically, missing the persistent drive enshrined in the texture of his art, especially his late works – that towards the promotion of religious toleration and unity.[6]

Literary criticism's disinclination for prejudicial reasons (Hermeticism is associated with a retrograde mysticism and occultism) to engage in depth with a major intellectual current around 1600 has meant that it is overlooking a crucial facet of Shakespeare. It is interesting in this respect that while critics have been comfortable discussing alchemy as a prominent frame of reference in Donne's works, it has provoked unease in relation to Shakespeare. This is perhaps because Donne is seen as largely 'of his time' – a colourful character on the cusp between magic and science – while Shakespeare is heavily burdened by the idea of being 'for all time', standing outside history, and has even been appropriated for modernity:[7] in Joel Fineman's words, 'Shakespeare's sonnets inaugurate and give a name to the modernist literary self'.[8] However, time and again Renaissance Hermetic-alchemical philosophy shapes the structure, form and content of Shakespeare's creations including their religiosity and politics. Read in historical context, the desiring, divided self of the sonnets which Fineman reads as 'modernist', is a poetic persona undergoing the painful throws of alchemical soul work but its 400-year-old lexicon is unfamiliar and frequently perplexing to modern eyes.

Indeed, the play which heads up the First Folio, *The Tempest*, depicts, as Frank Kermode's edition foregrounded in 1954, a Hermetic Magus with 'the power to manipulate stellar influences and to contribute to the course of earthly events',[9] and Prospero, for the majority of commentators, resembles the creative artist, Shakespeare himself. Their mutual endeavour – Prospero's and his creator's – is to bring about moral and spiritual reform, harmony and peace through 'potent art' and thus to help to perfect nature.[10] *King Lear*, too, is a 'master-piece' of 'chemical theatre', according to Charles Nicholl: an alchemical parable unfolding a chemical-spiritual process of dismemberment, dissolution, separation and conjunction.[11] Lear's purgatorial journey on the stormy heath from rage and spiritual blindness to self-knowledge and love accompanied, significantly, by a 'wise fool', entails suffering 'Upon a wheel of fire' (IV. vi. 40).[12] This is a complex image invoking Ixion and the torture of heretics but also the type of spiritual 'cross' celebrated by true alchemists (as opposed to false 'coiners') as bringing about inner regeneration:

> Materiall Crosses then, good physicke bee,
> And yet spirituall have chiefe dignity.
> These for extracted chimique medicine serve,
> And cure much better, and as well preserve;
> Then are you your own physicke, or need none,
> When Still'd, or purg'd by tribulation.
>
> Let Crosses, so, take what hid Christ in thee,
> And be his image, or not his, but hee.
>
> (Donne, 'The Crosse', 25–30, 35–6)[13]

Shakespeare's romances have been particularly associated with the alchemical cycle and the affirmation of the 'possibility of regeneration'.[14] In Scene xii of *Pericles*, for example, we encounter a charitable Paracelsian-type physician called Cerimon who proclaims 'virtue and cunning' to be 'endowments greater / Than nobleness and riches': 'immortality attends the former, / Making a man a god' (xii. 24–5, 27–8). As Mebane has pointed out, there are echoes here from the Hermetic text *Asclepius* and Pico's *Oratio*, and the former reverberates in *The Winter's Tale*, too, in the episode in which the mysterious statue of Hermione is brought miraculously to life.[15] Leontes notably declares, 'If this be magic, let it be an art / Lawful as eating' (V. iii. 110–11). Repeatedly in Shakespearean

drama, and emphatically in the late plays, tyranny and destructiveness are
reformed and corrected through the healing associated with suffering and
the regenerative power of love and art. Catherine M. Dunne has argued that
the world of the romances operates 'largely according to Neoplatonic
principles. This world is like a gigantic instrument upon which the gods
play. When it is in tune, there is peace.'[16] Harmonious music characteristically accompanies a love match between male and female representatives of
opposing factions. As Hymen proclaims in *As You Like it*:

> Then is there mirth in heaven
> When earthly things made even
> Atone together.   (*As You Like It*, v. iv. 106–8)

'Marriages' are crucial to the alchemical *opus* but, as this book has shown,
other 'conjunctions' are advocated too: music, numerology and rhetoric are all
implicated in the unifying process outlined in Norton's *Ordinall*.[17] It is thus
extremely significant that Shakespeare's rhetoric works tirelessly to juxtapose
and marry seeming binaries producing the balanced antitheses and paradoxes
for which he is critically renowned. T. G. Bishop, for example, has described the
'fitting together of contraries' as 'a preoccupation and a sensibility that manifests
itself at all levels of his writing', leading this poet to 'push apparent difference
towards some deeper reciprocal unity, sometimes imagined beyond language
itself, as in "The Phoenix and the Turtle"'. Interestingly, Bishop singles out
'incarnation' as the principal trope for all kinds of unification in Shakespeare's
'theatre of wonder'.[18] In Ficinian philosophy, such as we have witnessed in
Shake-speares Sonnets, 'oneing' with one's beloved is a route to discovering
Christ within the self – the ultimate incarnation – facilitating inner resurrection
with enlightened spiritual vision which is essential to poetic inspiration. Helen
Vendler, too, has declared of the *Sonnets* that 'Shakespeare's strategies for
unifying sonnet-parts into a true *concord . . . by unions married* are enormously
varied'.[19] To modern eyes, Shakespeare is a master of paradox, but he probably
saw himself as a consummate rhetorician of unification. If we are prepared to
address formal concerns in the context of the major philosophical currents
influencing creative writing at the turn of the seventeenth century, it is clear that
Hermetic alchemy shapes the intellectual texture of Shakespeare's poetry and
plays (especially his later work) on many levels.

Love drives the alchemical *opus* and even in relatively early plays, notably
Love's Labour's Lost (1595), it is the most formidable enlightening, harmonizing, reforming and civilizing 'power' as Biron explains:

> But love, first learned in a lady's eyes,
> Lives not alone immured in the brain,

But with the motion of all elements
Courses as swift as thought in every power,
And gives to every power a double power
Above their functions and their offices.
It adds a precious seeing to the eye.

And when love speaks, the voice of all the gods
Make heaven drowsy with the harmony.
Never durst poet touch a pen to write
Until his ink were tempered with love's sighs.
O, then his lines would ravish savage ears,
And plant in tyrants mild humility.
From women's eyes this doctrine I devise.
They sparkle still the right Promethean fire

(*Loves Labours Lost*, IV. iii. 303–9, 319–26)

Here, as in Ficino's *Letters* and *De amore*, creation is sustained and civilized through the flow of love and the creation of art and no distinction is made between earthly and divine love: 'creation is so ordered that there is no true love that is not religious nor is there any true religion but that sustained by love'.[20]

But what about erotic love of the body such as we find in Shakespeare's sonnets? Interestingly, in an important recent essay, 'Libertinism and Toleration: Milton, Bruno and Aretino' (2007), James Grantham Turner has argued a link between Milton's and Bruno's philosophy of religious toleration, which manifests itself partly as an emphasis upon embracing the 'promiscuous' body along with 'promiscuous' reading, such as that found in the pornographic philosophical creations of the Italian writer Pietro Aretino, for example.[21] Crucially, Grantham Turner argues, 'Bruno assumes, like Milton later, that "wicked" material becomes the site of a hermeneutic contest over ways of seeing. The good observer "gazes and regazes" through a special optic lens that converts turpitude into philosophical insight, while the "ribald" turns everything into obscenity.'[22] Notably, *Areopagitica* uses alchemical language to describe this process: 'a wise man like a good refiner can gather gold out of the drossiest volume'.[23] As we have seen throughout this book, it is just this type of 'hermeneutic contest over ways of seeing' that many of Shakespeare's sonnets invite, but *A Lovers Complaint* is a particularly consummate production in this mode. Quoting from Bruno's *Spaccio de la Bestia Trionfante* (1584),[24] Grantham Turner demonstrates how in both Bruno and Milton 'growth and perfecting, come from experiencing the clash of passions that include the most powerful erotic feelings ... The dynamic, mutually maximising, exchange of "contraries" requires ... the full range of passions and gut reactions from delight to revulsion.'[25] I would argue that Donne and Shakespeare undoubtedly shared this philosophy and even inaugurated a turn-of-the-seventeenth-century English poetics in which the erotic body was actively inserted into divine discourse. A poetics of 'incorporation' is being aligned in this period with religious inclusiveness (incorporation) and toleration.

Shakespeare's 1609 quarto of poetry is infused with such a poetics. *A Lovers Complaint*, for example, contains the intriguing line, 'religious love put out religion's eye', relating to a nun who has broken free from the confines of her convent (the confining bricks and mortar of Roman Catholicism) in order to offer herself body and soul to the beautiful phoenix youth with whom she is in love. One of the available meanings of this ambivalent line in which there is bawdy play on 'eye', is certainly that established religion's 'eye'/I (egotism) has been displaced and replaced by passionate 'phoenix' love. Intriguingly, in *Areopagitica* Milton seems to be meaningfully echoing the philosophy underpinning this representation of the nun, declaring, 'Banish all objects of lust, shut up all youth into the severest discipline that can be exercis'd in any hermitage, ye cannot make them chaste, that came not thither so.'[26] This may seem like an implicit critique of sexual promiscuity, but Grantham Turner argues that promiscuity is a positive quality in Milton's tract, aligned with broad, inclusive reading and with a philosophic-religious stance of toleration.

A little later in *A Lovers Complaint* we hear that 'Love's arms are peace 'gainst rule, 'gainst sense, 'gainst shame' (line 271). This is very much in keeping with Shakespeare's magnificent paean to love, Sonnet 124:

> If my dear love were but the child of state
> It might for Fortune's bastard be unfathered,
> As subject to time's love, or to time's hate,
> Weeds among weeds, or flowers with flowers gathered.
> No, it was builded far from accident,
> It suffers not in smiling pomp, nor falls
> Under the blow of thrilled discontent,
> Wherto th'inviting time our fashion calls.
> It fears not policy, that heretic,
> Which works on leases of short-numb'red hours,
> But all alone stands hugely politic,
> That it nor grows with heat, nor drowns with show'rs.
> To this I witness call the fools of Time,
> Which die for goodness, who have lived for crime.

Duncan-Jones finds a 'love transcending the operations of time' here, while Helen Vendler observes how in this sonnet love 'has ... removed itself utterly from the biological ... and from the expedient ... and has constructed itself as a Platonic form, virtual, biologically uninhabitable, and aloof, all alone'.[27] In fact, our poet's 'hugely politic' love is steeped in cultural meaning in the context of the early seventeenth century.[28]

It is productive to juxtapose Shakespeare's Sonnet 124 to Donne's Holy Sonnet XVIII (probably written between 1609 and 1611):[29]

> Show me deare Christ, thy spouse, so bright and clear.
>   ...
> Dwells she with us, or like adventuring knights
> First travaile we to seeke and then make Love?
> Betray kind husband thy spouse to our sights,
> And let myne amorous soul court thy mild Dove,
> Who is most trew, and pleasing to thee, then
> When she is embrac'd and open to most men.   (lines 1, 9–14)[30]

Christ's promiscuous church is 'most trew' when 'open to most men'. Crucially, this is not a religion of tyranny; it is a 'mild Dove' keen to 'embrace'.

Donne's biographer suggests that he described himself as a member of the 'sect' of 'the philosophy of love' and David Wootton has argued that Donne's preoccupation with love and the religion of love identifies him as a likely member of the Family of Love.[31] Donne's true church, Wootton argues, 'is not on seven hills, like that of Rome, or on one hill, like that of Geneva, but on no hill': Donne's is a spiritual, invisible church founded on love.[32] While I would hesitate to relegate Donne specifically to the Familism camp (which seems to be against the spirit of inclusiveness that he extols) I would agree that his poetry and sermons preach a spiritual religion of love and contemplation in which the boundaries between sexual and divine desire often dissolve and combine in startlingly 'explosive' ways.[33] Donne frequently, as we have seen, uses a 'chymical' lexicon not dissimilar to Shakespeare's and this is significant: in the period in which they were writing, alchemical rhetoric conveyed important cultural meanings, especially amongst the London elite intellectual community that both men inhabited. As we have established, from the time of Hermeticism's resurgence in the Florentine academy, it was associated with a pristine, ancient theology that was free from the anatagonisms of latter day Christianity. The *Hermetica*'s stress on one religion and on the importance of self-knowledge and spiritual purification suggested a peaceful route to truth: here was the basis of a universal religion that could reconcile all teaching.[34]

This insight was assisted in the same era by Nicholas of Cusa's novel assertion that 'all oppositions are united in their infinite measure, so that which would be logical contradictions for finite things, can exist without contradiction in God'.[35] It was this unifying spirit that encouraged the development of Florentine academy philosophy in the context of the religious strife in France in the next century; indeed, Baif's academy of poetry and music brought Catholics and Huguenots together in the 1560s to heal divisions through the incantatory influences of poetry and music.[36] As we have seen, too, in 1581 Du Plessis Mornay clearly saw in Hermes Trismegistus's 'one' an antidote to the warring extremes of Christianity in his own 'miserable times' (Dedication, *De la Verite*).[37] Frances Yates finds in Mornay's work a reflection of the circumstances 'in Antwerp in 1581 where William of Orange was trying to establish the Southern Netherlands ... as a state in which religious toleration should be practiced'.[38] It was at this stage, she suggests, that the Erasmian tradition of toleration joined the Hermetic-Cabalist tradition amidst mounting intellectual interest in the *prisca theologia*.[39]

It was in this context that alchemy's lexicon of conjunctions and 'chymistry's' refusal of binaries became charged with significance. Robert Bostocke's version of Paracelsian medicine for the English public makes this clear: 'The difference between the auncient Physicke, first taught by the godly forfathers, consisting in unitie, peace and concord: and the latter Phisicke proceeding from Idolaters, Ethnickes and Heathen: as Gallen, and such other, consisting in dualitie, discorde and contrarietie.'[40] Alchemical medicine, which in Bostocke is a revival of ancient Egyptian medicine, is symbolic of unity and peace, while the Aristotelian–Galenic doctrine of contraries and dualism is quite simply evil discord. Significantly, in Paracelsianism 'like cures like' while contrary medicines are construed as producing and prolonging morbidity. George Puttenham's *Art of English Poesy* happily extends this belief to the aesthetic domain:

Therefore, of death and burials, of the adversities by wars, and of true love lost or ill-bestowed, are the only sorrows that the noble poets sought by their art to remove or appease, not with any medicament of a contrary temper, as the Galenists use ... but as the Paracelsians, who cure *similia similibus*, making one dolor to expel another, and in this case, one short sorrowing the remedy of a long and grievous sorrow.[41]

'Lamenting' is thus construed as 'a very necessary device of the poet and a fine': poetry plays the physician 'making the very grief itself (in part) cure the disease' (1: 24, pp. 135–6).

There was Pauline authority for the alchemical aversion to binaries. St Paul to the Ephesians, II: 14–19, in the words of the Geneva Bible, is a key text:

14 For hee is our peace, which hath made of both one, and hath broken the stoppe of the partition wall.

15 In abrogating through his flesh the hatred, that is, the Law of commaunde-ments *which standeth* in ordinances, for so to make twaine one new man in himselfe, *so* making peace,

16 And that hee might reconcile both unto God in one bodie by *his* crosse, and slay hatred therby.

17 And came, and preached peace to you which were afarre off, and to them that were neere.

18 For through him we both have an entrance unto the Father by one Spirit.

19 Now therefore ye are no more strangers and forreiners: but citizens with the Saints, and of the household of God.

The Geneva Bible marginalia aligns this 'household of God' with the holy temple, one Spirit, with 'grace' and the true 'Catholique Church'. The Pauline holy temple embraces 'strangers and forreiners' – 'most men' – and abhors 'partition wall(s)'.

In the same manner The Family or Household of Love, led from the middle of the sixteenth century by the Dutch mystic Hendrick Niclaes (H. N.), embraced Catholics and Protestants alike: 'Let every Nation then have among them, so many-maner of Groundes, Beleefes, Religions, Ceremonies, and Services, as they will wherin they love Gods Trueth, and the Righteousness.'[42] As Christopher Marsh has described, H. N.'s message was about transcendence of conflict, 'the shedding of innocent blood was to cease as Christians, Jews, Muslims, Turks and heathens responded to the call. The service of love was to be incorporated within established religious systems.'[43] Importantly, you could be Catholic, Calvinist, Lutheran or Presbyterian (or, according to Niclaes, even non-Christian) and also belong to the Family. Within this community there was, furthermore, a stress on obedience to governors, and on general peaceableness. In order to maintain social harmony and not attract persecution (martyrdom was unnecessary bloodshed) it was also perfectly acceptable, indeed preferable, to dissemble one's religion.[44] We might look again in this context at the line in Shakespeare's Sonnet 124, which seems to designate religious martyrs (those who 'die for goodness'), rather unheroically, as 'fools of Time'. One's inner spiritual state was crucial, outward appearance was mere show (it is intriguing to recall the line in Shakespeare's Sonnet 102, 'I love not less, though less the show appear', in relation to this). H. N. believed that through Christ and the Resurrection every man could become spiritu-ally regenerated and godded with god or 'deified' (an odd word, which appears in *A Lovers Complaint*, line 84). Two works that we met in the last chapter, *The Theologia Germanica* and *The Imitation of Christ*, were seminal texts for The Family, as also were biblical texts on the 'wise fool'.

One prominent Familist, John Everard, translated the *Hermetica* while another, John Pordage, also promoted the writings of the German mystic Jacob Boehme, whose works employ a pronounced alchemical symbolism.[45]

There are obvious crossovers here with the form of spiritual alchemy practised and advocated by Michael Maier,[46] but he was closely associated, along with John Dee and Robert Fludd in England, with another highly secretive Christocentric spiritual community advocating religious toleration known as the Fraternity of the Rosy Cross or Rose Cross (Rosicrucianism). Frances Yates has, of course, written extensively on this movement.[47] While the Family of Love seems to have initially attracted more Catholics, Rosicrucianism possibly had a greater affinity with Protestantism.[48] Alastair Hamilton suggests that Familist spirituality in the Low Countries may well have merged in the early seventeenth century, briefly at least, with the Fraternity of the Rosy Cross.[49] The spiritual faith practised by both minimalized the significance of external forms – ceremonies, vestments and bricks and mortar – and emphasized the Resurrection of Christ within the self and the building of a spiritual temple – a brethren of love. In the words of the Familist John Etherington, 'All the stones of this building are his brethren, reborn and made anew, not in show but in very truth, not for a time but forever . . . this universal church of Christ, consisting of stones of life.'[50]

We know that these spiritual movements appealed to several prominent humanist intellectuals desirous of tolerant religious settlement. Christopher Plantin's printing enterprise in Antwerp, Abraham Ortelius's cartography workshop, the De Bry engraving studio and Justus Lipsius's circle in Leiden appear to have been associated with the dissemination of this late sixteenth-century message of toleration.[51] In 1589 an anonymous tract, possibly published in Leiden, entitled *Temporis filia veritas* declared that tolerance and true godliness were embarked on a 'troublesome travel' but they would eventually prevail 'to the glory of God, the preservation of Princes, and to an everlasting peace among all people'.[52] The research of Hamilton and Marsh has established that in England several men allowed particularly close to Queen Elizabeth's person identified with the Household of Love, raising interesting questions about the sympathies of the *via media* monarch herself (who, as we have observed, incorporated alchemical symbolism into the centre of her symbolic portfolio in the latter part of her reign).[53] Several of the London Yeomen of the Queen's Guard – Robert Seale, Thomas Mathewe, Anthony Enscombe, Lewes Steward – were identified by hostile contemporaries in 1578 as being members of the Family.[54] The Privy Council nevertheless found that 'they [were] in all pointes of Religion verie sound' and discharged them. However, two years later they were under suspicion again and during inter- rogation three of them confessed that they believed themselves 'deyfyed' ('deified') and regenerated spiritually through Christ's Resurrection in them. Although, in 1580, the Privy Council drew up a 'set abjuration to which suspected Familists were ... required to assent', most of them, as Hamilton points out, 'suffered no further consequences'.[55] In fact, the brethren's key message of religious toleration and peace, coupled with firm allegiance to rulers who believed in divine right, probably made them particularly trustworthy individuals to surround the queen's body.[56]

Indeed, this context might lead scholars to research further the biography of John Salusbury, who was Esquire of the Body of the Queen from 1595. Although enmeshed in a prominent recusant family associated with the Babington Conspiracy, John was staunchly loyal to the queen and knighted in 1601 for helping to foil the Essex rebellion.[57] Salusbury's personal motto was 'To be able [to do harm] and abstain from doing it is noble', which resonates strikingly with Shakespeare's line in Sonnet 94: 'They that have pow'r to hurt, and will do none'.[58] Most significantly from the perspective of this study, Salusbury is the dedicatee of a very mysterious volume containing a long, seemingly inconsequential poem by Robert of Chester – *Loves Martyr: or Rosalins Complaint. Allegorically Shadowing the Truth of Love, In the Constant Fate of the Phoenix and Turtle* (1601) – to which 'Ignoto' (possibly Donne), Shakespeare, John Marston, George Chapman and Ben Jonson appended newly written 'poeticall Essaies' 'consecrated by them all generally, to the love and merite of the true-noble Knight, Sir John Salisburie' (title page).[59] Shakespeare's purported contribution to these poems, known as 'The Phoenix and Turtle', is often printed and read in isolation but Katherine Duncan-Jones and Henry Woudhuysen's recent important editorial decision to provide a facsimile appendix of all the verses serves to foreground the appropriateness of reading the baffling Shakespearean lines in context. In fact, this seems crucially important because within these dedicatory verses 'consecrated' to Salusbury (and this does not include Chester's poem), the poets intermittently claim to be speaking together as a 'vatum chorus', as one: '**we** bring / **Our** owne true Fire, Now **our** thought takes wing' (my emphasis, p. 178). In keeping with this, it is frequently impossible to be certain which poetic voice is speaking – the boundaries between them are sometimes indi- cated by attribution but at other times identities seem 'chymically' fluid and indistinct with 'I' and 'my' merging apparently seamlessly into 'we' and 'our'. Indeed, the lines beginning, 'Let the bird of lowdest lay', usually attributed to Shakespeare, do not have a name ascribed and might well be by the 'compounded' chorus of poets. To date, the perplexing 'Phoenix and Turtle' has been read variously as an allegory about Elizabeth I and the Earl of Essex, for example, or as an elegy for Catholic martyrs and, for those critics who eschew biography, it has been understood as a meditation on an abstract idea or as perhaps about poetry itself.[60] The phoenix is, of course, the prime alchemical symbol; we should delve a little deeper into these intriguing 'essaies'.

Significantly, the opening invocation of this distinguished 'vatum chorus' is to a conflation of God and the Sun ('bright God, whose golden Eies'), and the poets' request is to 'propagate / With your illustrate faculties / Our mentall powers' so that 'holy waters' inspire their verse (p. 167). These are the terms of creative astral magic and alchemy. 'Infusde in our retentive braine' and 'distild thence', from a 'true Zeale, borne in our spirites' the chorus of poets will celebrate Salisburie's 'high Merites' with 'an Invention, freer then the *Times*' (p. 168). Their divinely inspired collective prophetic voice claims it is about to break out of the confining political shackles of its moment – we should listen attentively.

The perplexing riddles of the verses that follow pivot around a lexicon of the two birds (the phoenix and the turtle (dove)), 'Fire', 'Time', 'devinest *Essence*', and 'Quintessance', '*Ens*' (an active principle or influence in Paracelsian medicine), 'Contemplation' and '*Ideas*'.[61] The lines about the phoenix and turtle attributed to Shakespeare are particularly paradoxical, continuously evoking and refuting binaries:

> So they loved as love in twaine,
> Had the essence but in one,
> Two distincts, Division none,
> Number there in love was slaine.
>
> Hearts remote, yet not asunder;
> Distance and no space was seene.   (25–30)

It seems that 'Division grow[s] together'; the two are 'compounded' and 'concordant'. The *Threnos* that follows, notably with Shakespeare's name following it, opens with 'Beautie, Truth, and Raritie' (evoking 'Three themes in one, which wondrous scope affords', Sonnet 105). We are certainly enmeshed in the same Hermetic-Neoplatonic territory of inspired artistry encountered in Shakespeare's 1609 poems and examined in detail in Chapter 5. The lines that follow, which may be by Marston, take us even deeper into the '*Metaphysicall*' realm of the 'making' mind:

> Now yeeld your aides, you spirites that infuse
> A sacred rapture, light my weaker eie:

> Raise my invention on swifte Phantasie,
> That whilst of this same *Metaphysicall*
> God, Man, nor Woman, but elix'd of all
> My labouring thoughts with strained ardor sing,
> My Muse may mount with an uncommon wing. (p. 173)

'Sacred rapture', the eye of the mind, inner light, phantasy and a notable authorial divine androgyny ('God, Man, nor Woman, but elix'd of all') are all evoked as essential to genius and prophecy. The verses culminate in a collective *Epos:* 'To deepe eares we sing' (p. 178). The *Epos* begins with a familiar warning about 'the Mind' misled by 'subtill traines' that enable 'severall Passions' to 'invade':

> Of which usurping ranke ['severall Passions'], some have thought
>   *Love*
> The first, as prone to move
> Most frequent Tumults, Horrors, and Unrests,
> In our enflamed brests.
> But this doth from their cloud of Error grow,
> Which we do overblow.
> The thing they here call Love, is blind *Desire*,
> Arm'd with Bow, *Shafts*, and *Fire*;
> Inconstant like the Sea, of whence 'tis borne,
> Rough, swelling, like a Storme:
> With whome who sailes, rides on the surge of *Feare*,
> And boiles as if he were
> In a continuall Tempest. (pp. 178–9)

Such tyrannical, persecuting 'Love' is delusion and 'Error' (suggesting a religious context). The passage on 'true *Love*' that follows is crucial:

> Now true *Love*
> No such effects doth prove:
> That is an *Essence* most gentle, and fine.
> Pure, perfect; nay divine:
> It is a golden Chaine let downe from Heaven
> Whose linkes are bright, and even
> That fals like Sleepe on Lovers; and combines
> The soft and sweetest *Minds*
> In equal knots: This beares no *Brands* nor *Darts*
> To murder different harts,
> But in a calme and God-like unitie,
> Preserves *Communitie*. (*Epos*, pp. 179–80)

Thus the poets' divinely inspired chorus – a multiplicity in one – extols a gentle, simple 'true *Love*' of unity and community free from rage and strife. It is distilled purity – a 'fine' '*Essence*' or 'elixir' – constant and sober, transcending 'Time' (p. 180). This is entirely consistent with the Love extolled in Sonnet 124. Further, the enigmatic lines of the 'Let the bird of lowdest lay' verses (which are by either Shakespeare or the 'vatum chorus') are illuminated by the surrounding poems and by *Shake-speares Sonnets*. Their 'riddle' has been succinctly summarized as 'what is simultaneously simple and complex, and in this way contains and reveals the fact of its own nothingness?'[62] This part of the poem undoubtedly alludes to the divine 'One', the mysterious multiplicity in unity, the rare 'nothing', 'no number' and 'none' ('Among a number one is reckoned none', Sonnet 136) – the phoenix or philosopher's stone and Christ in alchemy. This is also the 'true *Love*' '*Essence*' of the *Epos*.

The concluding dedicatory verse is ascribed to Jonson and, fittingly for this poet, it is a tongue-in-cheek eulogy ('let no man / Receive it for a fable, / If a Bird so amiable, Do turne into a woman') to the earthly woman-phoenix of state propaganda *c.* 1601, Elizabeth I.[63] Ironically, of course, situated within Time and politics she cannot be the transcendent Love described above. She (or more accurately her body politic) is, however, the phoenix encountered at the end of Shakespeare and Fletcher's *King Henry VIII* (1613) or *All is True*, a play which puts so much iterative pressure on the words 'true' and 'grace' that they seem almost emptied of meaning. In this drama of reformation politics and persecution, religion is pulled this way and that by a luxurious greed for power and possessions. Disastrously caught up in these machinations masquerading as religion, Queen Katherine exclaims (to egotistical, self-serving Wolsey):

> Is this your Christian counsel? Out upon ye!
> Heaven is above all yet – there sits a judge
> That no king can corrupt.   (*King Henry VIII*, III. i. 97–9)

Amidst these 'sad ... troubles' (III. i. 1) Katherine notably seeks comfort in Ficinian-style Orphic music recalling – for intellectuals in the know at least – the activities in Baif's academy aimed at healing religious divisions.[64] The play emphasizes the showy pomp of the Roman prelates and the French and English kings' costly cavorting on the Field of the Cloth of Gold. But all that glitters is not true gold. Any sincere truth and grace that emerges in *All Is True* resides in the 'mingled yarn, good and ill together'[65] of flawed but virtuous spirits rather than in the persuasive rhetoric, bricks and mortar and exterior trappings of either showy Roman Catholicism or 'spleeny' Lutheranism. It is notably Cranmer, the most positively presented churchman in this play, whose *Book of Common Prayer* and *Thirty-Nine Articles* shaped Anglicanism, who issues the phoenix prophecy at its close. Elizabeth's *via media* settlement and accent on religious toleration made her body politic an acceptable 'type' of the Phoenix love which was undoubtedly the dramatists' hope for a more peaceful English future.

CODA

> Beauty consists in colours; and that's best
> Which is not fixt, but flies, and flowes;
> The settled *Red* is dull, and *whites* that rest
> Something of sickness would disclose.
>
> (Vaughan, 'Affliction', 25–8)[66]

The modern mindset is captivated by binaries, and discussions of early modern English religio-politics seem all too often to pivot around the strident voices of intemperate extremes. Ameliorating undercurrents are more difficult to detect, especially when they involve dark 'parables' and obfuscation and, for reasons of safety, dissimulation. Such strategies are inevitably met with suspicion by modern readers and given short shrift by those critics who associate mystical religious currents with a retrograde occultism incompatible with Christian orthodoxy, or who link a spiritual turn with a concomitant withdrawal from social and political life. Identified as *prisca theologia*, Egyptian religion was not incompatible with Christianity around 1600.[67] Further, the Hermetic god was the ultimate 'unmoved mover' ('moving others' yet 'Unmoved', Sonnet 94);[68] Hermeticism did not preach apathy: 'Chymistry's' drive to recapture Eden was a dynamic enterprise affecting many areas of social and intellectual life in the first part of the seventeenth century and, as historians have demonstrated over recent decades, it was a prime impetus in the establishment of the Royal Society. Yet, while Ficino's *De amore* is experiencing something of a revival, it is strangely rare to meet literary scholars who have glanced at the *Hermetica* or read Pico's *Oratio*, let alone alchemical poetry or the writings of French intellectuals with whom we know figures like Puttenham and Sidney interacted and shared ideas. In a situation in which engagement with important Renaissance philosophical trends is prejudiced and selective the voices of the middle ground are not being sufficiently heard.[69] For this reason, Christopher Marsh asks in his study of The Family of Love whether researchers should 'pay more attention to the mental habits, spiritual beliefs and cultural mechanisms which enabled many local societies to survive periods of major religious or political upheaval without tearing themselves apart'.[70] The answer is surely

'yes'. The Christocentric spiritual-philosophical movements that flourished in the late sixteenth and early seventeenth centuries, informing
intellectual currents and doing important cultural work, clearly appealed
to many mainstream creative writers including Shakespeare. The voices of
toleration, peace and social cohesion deserve to be encountered on their
own terms.

Notes

INTRODUCTION

1. J. Starkie Gardner, *Ironwork: Part 1. From the Earliest Times to the End of the Medieval Period* (London: Victoria and Albert Museum, 1927), pp. 3–4.
2. Gardner, *Ironwork*, proceeds, 'many metals, including iron, on being released from an amalgam of mercury, are left in such an extraordinary state that they take fire' (p. 4). Seven metals were associated with the sun, the moon and the five known planets. Lead was analogous to Saturn, the slowest moving planet.
3. Esther Leslie, *Synthetic Worlds: Nature, Art and the Chemical Industry* (Harmondsworth: Reaktion, 2005), p. 13.
4. Leslie, *Synthetic Worlds*, p. 21. Alchemical texts poured off the presses in the middle of the seventeenth century.
5. See Frank Whigham and Wayne A. Rebhorn (eds.), *The Art of English Poesy by George Puttenham: A Critical Edition* (Ithaca and London: Cornell University Press, 2007), p. 233.
6. George R. Potter and Evelyn M. Simpson (eds.), *The Sermons of John Donne*, 10 vols. (Berkeley and Los Angeles: University of California Press, 1953–62), vol. IV, p. 110.
7. Donne, 'Divine Poem XIV', in Herbert J. C. Grierson (ed.), *The Poems of John Donne* (Oxford: Oxford University Press, 1912), p. 328. All references to Donne's poetry are to this edition.
8. Potter and Simpson, *The Sermons of John Donne*, vol. VI, p. 41.
9. All references to Shakespeare's plays are to Stanley Wells and Gary Taylor (eds.), *The Complete Works*, compact edition (Oxford: Oxford University Press, 1988) and are hereafter cited parenthetically in my text. All references to Shakespeare's sonnets and poems are to Colin Burrow (ed.), *The Complete Sonnets and Poems* (Oxford: Oxford University Press, 2002).
10. Thomas Tymme, *The Practise of Chymicall and Hermeticall Physicke, for the Preservation of Health* (London, 1605), sig. G4v.
11. See Burrow's gloss to these lines, *Complete Sonnets*, p. 442.
12. George Ripley, *The Epistle of George Ripley written to King Edward IV*, in Stanton J. Linden (ed.), *The Alchemy Reader: From Hermes Trismegistus to Isaac Newton* (Cambridge: Cambridge University Press, 2003), p. 146.
13. Joel Fineman, *Shakespeare's Perjured Eye* (Berkeley: University of California Press, 1986), p. 269.

14. I have used the 1609 quarto's versions of the titles: the lack of an apostrophe in 'Lovers' leaves open the question of whether this is one or many (or a multiplicity in one).

15. *A Lovers Complaint* line 219 refers to 'deep-brained sonnets'.

16. Dympna Callaghan, 'Confounded by Winter: Speeding Time in Shakespeare's Sonnets', in Michael Schoenfeldt (ed.), *A Companion to Shakespeare's Sonnets* (Oxford: Blackwell, 2007), p. 115; Burrow, *Complete Sonnets*, p. 113.

17. For a fuller account of this, and an analysis of Francis Bacon's *New Atlantis* in this light, see Margaret Healy, 'Protean Bodies: Literature, Alchemy, Science and English Revolutions', in Margaret Healy and Thomas Healy (eds.), *Renaissance Transformations: The Making of English Writing, 1500–1650* (Edinburgh: Edinburgh University Press, 2009), pp. 161–77.

18. Charles Webster, *The Great Instauration: Science, Medicine and Reform, 1626–1660* (London: Duckworth, 1975) and Webster, *From Paracelsus to Newton: Magic and the Making of Modern Science* (Cambridge: Cambridge University Press, 1982); Paulo Rossi, 'Hermeticism, Rationality and the Scientific Revolution', in M. L. Bonelli and William R. Shea (eds.), *Reason, Experiment and Mysticism in the Scientific Revolution* (Basingstoke: Macmillan, 1975), pp. 247–75 and Rossi, *Francis Bacon: From Magic to Science*, trans. Sacha Rabinovitch (London: Routledge, 1968). See also Ingrid Merkel and Allen G. Debus (eds.), *Hermeticism and the Renaissance: Intellectual History and the Occult in Early Modern Europe* (Washington DC: Folger Library and Associated University Presses, 1988) and Allen G. Debus and Michael T. Walton, *Reading the Book of Nature: The Other Side of the Scientific Revolution* (Kirksville, Mo.: Sixteenth Century Journal Publishers, 1998).

19. See, for example, Brain Vickers, *Shakespeare, 'A Lover's Complaint' and John Davies of Hereford* (Cambridge: Cambridge University Press, 2007). Vickers argues that the *Complaint* is by John Davies of Hereford.

20. Katherine Duncan-Jones (ed.), *Shakespeare's Sonnets* (London: Arden Shakespeare; Thomson Learning, 2004); John Kerrigan, *The Sonnets and A Lover's Complaint* (London: Penguin, 1986); Burrow, *Complete Sonnets*; Helen Vendler, *The Art of Shakespeare's Sonnets* (Cambridge, Mass.: Harvard University Press, 1997). Francis Meres, *Palladis Tamia. Wits Treasury. Being the Second Part of Wits Commonwealth* (London, 1598), referred to Shakespeare's 'sugred Sonnets among his private friends', fo. 282r. MacDonald Jackson has recently restated his view that the *Complaint* shares significant vocabulary with *Cymbeline* and the late plays generally; see '*A Lover's Complaint, Cymbeline*, and the Shakespeare Canon: Interpreting Shared Vocabulary', in *Modern Language Review*, 103:3 (July, 2008), 621–38.

21. On this debate see Dympna Callaghan, *Shakespeare's Sonnets* (Oxford: Blackwell, 2007), p. 11; the quote is Thomas Heywood's, cited in Duncan-Jones, *Shakespeare's Sonnets*, p. 34.

22. Frank Erik Pointner, *Bawdy and Soul: A Revaluation of Shakespeare's Sonnets* (Heidelberg: Universitätsverlag, 2003), p. 11.

23. Kerrigan, *The Sonnets*, states 'Shakespeare, of course, was not a neoplatonist', p. 52; while Robert Matz, *The World of Shakespeare's Sonnets: An Introduction* (North Carolina and London: McFarland and Co., 2008) is among the latest voices to find a 'Neoplatonic strain of Petrarchanism' in the sonnets, p. 89.
24. On philosophy as 'contingent construction' see the excellent discussion in William H. Sherman, *John Dee: The Politics of Reading and Writing in the English Renaissance* (Amherst: University of Massachusetts Press, 1995), p. 14.
25. Richard Strier, 'The Refusal to be Judged in Petrarch and Shakespeare', in Schoenfeldt (ed.), *Companion*, p. 85; Duncan-Jones, *Shakespeare's Sonnets*, 98; Douglas Trevor, 'Shakespeare's Love Objects', in Schoenfeldt (ed.), *Companion*, p. 240.
26. Heather Dubrow, *Captive Victors: Shakespeare's Narrative Poems and Sonnets* (Ithaca and London: Cornell University Press, 1987), p. 181; Vendler, *Shakespeare's Sonnets*, pp. 5, 25.
27. Beatrice Groves, 'Shakespeare's Sonnets and the Genevan Marginalia', *Essays in Criticism*, 57:2 (2007), 114–28.
28. Thomas P. Roche, *Petrarch and the English Sonnet Sequences* (New York: AMS Press, 1989), p. 461. Helen Hackett's article examining the notion of 'blasphemy' applied to late sixteenth-century poetry asks the important question, 'Donne's clashing together of the erotic and the sacred seems highly unconventional to us; but would it have seemed so at the time?' (p. 31). Her analysis of late sixteenth-century religious imagery in erotic contexts is illuminating; see 'The Art of Blasphemy? Interfusions of the Erotic and the Sacred in the Poetry of Donne, Barnes, and Constable', in *Renaissance and Reformation*, 28:3 (2004), 27–54.
29. Roche, *Petrarch*, p. 461.
30. Alastair Fowler, *Triumphal Forms: Structural Patterns in Elizabethan Poetry* (Cambridge: Cambridge University Press, 1970), p. 190, recalling C. S. Lewis in *English Literature in the Sixteenth Century* (Oxford: Clarendon Press,1954).
31. Burrow, 'Introduction', *Complete Sonnets*, p. 108.
32. James Schiffer, 'The Incomplete Narrative of Shakespeare's Sonnets', in Schoenfeldt (ed.), *Companion*, pp. 55, 54.
33. J. B. Leishman, *Themes and Variations in Shakespeare's Sonnets* (London: Hutchinson University Library, 1963), p. 229.
34. Leishman, *Themes*, pp. 13, 216,
35. Vendler, *Shakespeare's Sonnets*, p. 29.
36. Meres, *Palladis Tamia*, 'his sugred Sonnets among his private friends', fo. 282r.
37. Kerrigan, *The Sonnets*, p. 14.
38. Martin Rulandus, *A Lexicon of Alchemy* (1612), trans. from Latin by A. E. Waite (London, 1892), p. 381.
39. Inga-Stina Ewbank, 'Self and the Sonnets', in *Self-Fashioning and Metamorphosis in Early Modern English Literature* (Oslo: Novus Press, 2003), p. 9.
40. Fineman, *Shakespeare's Perjured Eye*, p. 279.

41. See Michael Schoenfeldt, 'Eloquent Blood and Deliberative Bodies: The Physiology of Metaphysical Poetry', in Healy and Healy (eds.), *Renaissance Transformations*, p. 153.
42. Lyndy Abraham, *A Dictionary of Alchemical Imagery* (Cambridge: Cambridge University Press, 1998); Abraham, *Marvell and Alchemy* (Aldershot: Scolar Press, 1990); Charles Nicholl, *The Chemical Theatre* (London: Routledge & Kegan Paul, 1980); Stanton J. Linden, *Darke Hierogliphicks* (Kentucky: The University Press of Kentucky, 1996); Linden (ed.), *The Alchemy Reader;* Linden (ed.), *Mystical Metal of Gold: Essays on Alchemy and Renaissance Culture* (New York: AMS Press, 2007); John S. Mebane, *Renaissance Magic and the Return of the Golden Age: The Occult Tradition and Marlowe, Jonson and Shakespeare* (Lincoln and London: University of Nebraska Press, 1989); Charles Webster, *The Great Instauration* and *From Paracelsus to Newton*.
43. Frances Yates, *Giordano Bruno and the Hermetic Tradition* (Chicago: University of Chicago Press, 1964) and *Shakespeare's Late Plays: A New Approach* (London: Routledge & Kegan Paul, 1975), are but two in an impressive list. Yates' continuous stress on the occult aspects of hermeticism and alchemy is the least helpful aspect of her research – this over-emphasis has, I suggest, had the unfortunate effect of impeding the serious study of these philosophies.
44. Various scholars have found alchemical resonances in individual sonnets (especially Sonnet 20), most recently Ronald Gray, 'Will in the Universe: Shakespeare's Sonnets, Plato's *Symposium*, Alchemy and Renaissance Neoplatonism', in Peter Holland (ed.), *Shakespeare Survey Volume 59: Editing Shakespeare* (Cambridge: Cambridge University Press, 2006); also Peggy Munoz Simonds, 'Sex in a Bottle: The Alchemical Distillation of Shakespeare's Hermaphrodite in Sonnet 20', *Renaissance Papers* (1999), 97–105. Thomas O. Jones finds hermetic magic in some of the sonnets, *Renaissance Magic and Hermeticism in the Shakespeare Sonnets* (Lampeter: The Edwin Mellen Press, 1995).
45. Key contributions to the debate include, Webster, *From Paracelsus to Newton*; Rossi, 'Hermeticism, Rationality and the Scientific Revolution'; Merkel and Debus (eds.), *Hermeticism and the Renaissance*; Debus and Walton, *Reading the Book of Nature*.
46. On the alchemy of Newton and Boyle, see M. L. Righini Bonelli and William R. Shea (eds.), *Reason, Experiment and Mysticism in the Scientific Revolution* (Basingstoke: Macmillan, 1975); Lawrence Principe, *The Aspiring Adept: Robert Boyle and his Alchemical Quest* (Princeton: Princeton University Press, 1998); and Betty Jo Dobbs, *The Janus Faces of Genius: The Role of Alchemy in Newton's Thought* (Cambridge: Cambridge University Press, 1991).
47. See Sherman, *John Dee*; this book was crucial in demystifying the magus. The John Dee Quartercentenary Conference was held at St John's College, Cambridge, from 21 to 22 September 2009. As Chapter 1 will explore, Paracelsus's persona is currently being similarly revised.

48. For example, Lauren Kassell argues that natural magic in this period was not considered a perversion of religion but a perfection of it; see *Medicine and Magic in Elizabethan London: Simon Forman; Astrologer, Alchemist, and Physician* (Oxford: Clarendon Press, 2005), p. 9. The father of alchemical medicine, Paracelsus, is also undergoing a process of intellectual recuperation; see the following revisionist histories: Charles Webster, *Paracelsus, Medicine, Magic and Mission at the End of Time* (New Haven and London: Yale University Press, 2008); Ole Peter Grell (ed.), *Paracelsus: The Man and his Reputation, his Ideas and their Transformation* (Leiden: Brill, 1998).

49. See, for example, Robert M. Schuler, 'Some Spiritual Alchemies of Seventeenth-Century England', *Journal of the History of Ideas*, 41:2 (1980), 293–318. William R. Newman and Anthony Grafton, 'Introduction', *Secrets of Nature: Astrology and Alchemy in Early Modern Europe* (Cambridge, Mass.: MIT Press, 2001), p. 14, questioned alchemy as a spiritual discipline but this has been robustly countered since, notably by Peter Forshaw, 'Subliming Spirits: Physical-Chemistry and Theo-Alchemy in the Works of Heinrich Khunrath (1560–1605)', in Linden (ed.), *Mystical Metal of Gold*, pp. 255–75.

50. A prime example of this was the interdisciplinary 'Art and Alchemy' colloquium held in Aarhus, Denmark, from 6 to 9 December 2001 organized by Alexandra Lembert from the University of Leipzig and Susanna Akermann from the Swedenborg Library in Stockholm.

51. Ewan Fernie's 'Introduction' to *Spiritual Shakespeare* (London: Routledge, 2005) forcefully makes the point that Shakespearean spituality is a 'distinctive, inalienable and challenging dimension of his plays', p. 2. Laurie Shannon, *Sovereign Amity: Figures of Friendship in Shakespearean Contexts* (Chicago: University of Chicago Press, 2002).

52. See, for example, Neil Rhodes, 'Framing and Tuning in Renaissance English Verse', in Healy and Healy (eds.), *Renaissance Transformations*, pp. 32–47.

53. Sharon Achinstein and Elizabeth Sauer, *Milton and Toleration* (Oxford: Oxford University Press, 2007). See also Andrew Murphy, *Conscience and Community: Revisiting Toleration and Religious Dissent in Early Modern England and America* (University Park, Pa.: Pennsylvania State University Press, 2001).

54. To deride and mock alchemy as practised by covetous and foolish types (called Geber's 'cooks' after a famous alchemist), was not necessarily to register disbelief in the 'science'; on the contrary, adepts did it all the time in their treatises in order to distinguish their own higher pursuits from those of greedy men seeking to transmute gold from base metal.

55. Elias Ashmole, *Theatrum Chemicum Britannicum* (London, 1651), sig. A2r; Thomason Tracts E653, British Library.

56. Thomas Norton, *Ordinall of Alchimy*, in Ashmole, *Theatrum Chemicum Britannicum*, p. 13.

57. For a fuller account of this see Healy, 'Protean Bodies', pp. 170–2.

58. 'Infidel', Entry A.2. *OED* II: 'A Mohammedan, a Saracen'.

59. The copy in the Rosenbach Collection. Duncan-Jones, 'Introduction', *Shakespeare's Sonnets*, associates this comment with the sonnets' lack of spiritual content and the 'blasphemous extremes' of friend worship, p. 49.

1 ALCHEMICAL CONTEXTS

1. John Read, *Through Alchemy to Chemistry* (London: G. Bell and Sons Ltd, 1961), p. 14.
2. Two magnificent recent exhibitions on the culture of the Turks (Royal Academy, 2005) and 'Venice and the Islamic World' (Institut du Monde Arabe, Paris) serve to confirm that this envy was fully justified. See David J. Roxburgh (ed.), *Turks: A Journey of a Thousand Years, 600–1600* (London: Royal Academy of Arts, 2005).
3. Read, *Alchemy*, p. 12. On the origins of alchemy see also John Read, *Prelude to Chemistry* (London: G. Bell and Sons, 1936); E. J. Holmyard, *Alchemy* (Harmondsworth: Penguin, 1957); Jack Lindsay, *The Origins of Alchemy in Graeco-Roman Egypt* (London: Frederick Muller, 1970); Titus Burckhardt, *Alchemy* (Dorset: Element Books, 1986); Allen G. Debus, *The Chemical Philosophy*, 2 vols. (New York: Science Library Publications, 1977); and for a succinct summary see Lyndy Abraham, 'Introduction', *A Dictionary of Alchemical Imagery* (Cambridge: Cambridge University Press, 1998), xv; and Stanton J. Linden, 'Introduction', in Linden (ed.), *The Alchemy Reader: From Hermes Trismegistus to Isaac Newton* (Cambridge: Cambridge University Press, 2003), especially pp. 1–12.
4. See discussion in Stephen A. McKnight, 'The Wisdom of the Ancients and Francis Bacon's *New Atlantis*', in Allen G. Debus and Michael T. Walton (eds.), *Reading the Book of Nature: The Other Side of the Scientific Revolution* (Missouri: Thomas Jefferson University Press, 1998), pp. 91–109, especially p. 100. Also, for a more popularized account see Peter Marshall, *The Philosopher's Stone: A Quest for the Secrets of Alchemy* (Basingstoke: Pan Macmillan Ltd, 2002), especially p. 17.
5. For a detailed analysis of Bacon's *New Atlantis* in relation to Hermeticism and alchemy see Margaret Healy, 'Protean Bodies: Literature, Alchemy, Science and English Revolutions', in Margaret Healy and Thomas Healy (eds.), *Renaissance Transformations: The Making of English Writing, 1500–1650* (Edinburgh: Edinburgh University Press, 2009), pp. 161–77.
6. Read, *Alchemy*, p. 12; Linden (ed.), *The Alchemy Reader*, p. 5.
7. Robert M. Schuler has demonstrated how the understanding of 'spiritual alchemy' in England was particularly culturally specific in the early modern period; see 'Some Spiritual Alchemies of Seventeenth-Century England', *Journal of the History of Ideas*, 41:2 (1980), 293–318.
8. See Read, *Through Alchemy*, pp. 12–22, 58–94 and the introductory texts listed in note 3 above.
9. On Chinese alchemy see Joseph Needham, *Science and Civilisation in China* (Cambridge: Cambridge University Press, 1974), vol. V, p. 104; and E. J. Holmyard, *Alchemy* (Harmondsworth: Penguin, 1957), pp. 31–40.

10. Marshall, *The Philosopher's Stone*, pp. 65, 121.
11. See David Gordon White, *The Alchemical Body: Siddha Traditions in Medieval India* (Chicago: Chicago University Press, 1996); and Linden (ed.), *Alchemy Reader*, p. 7.
12. Abraham, *Dictionary*, p. 100. See also Brian P. Copenhaver, 'Introduction', *Hermetica: The Greek 'Corpus Hermeticum' and the Latin 'Asclepius' in a New English Translation* (Cambridge: Cambridge University Press, 1992), xiii–lix. All references are to this edition.
13. Read, *Alchemy*, pp. 22–3.
14. Cited in Linden (ed.), *The Alchemy Reader*, p. 28, from a translation of a Latin version (originally in Arabic) by Robert Steele and Dorothea Waley Singer, *Proceedings of the Royal Society of Medicine* (1928).
15. Copenhaver, *Hermetica*.
16. On Yates' stress on the occult and on John Dee as a 'magus' see William H. Sherman, *John Dee: The Politics of Reading and Writing in the English Renaissance* (Amherst: University of Massachusetts Press, 1995), especially pp. 12–17. Copenhaver, *Hermetica*, p. xxxii, declares that in those texts translated in his volume, magic was not for the most part a feature; Augustine, however, associated them with magic and the 'snares of demons'.
17. Philippe Du Plessis Mornay, *A Woorke Concerning the Trewnesse of the Christian Religion*, trans. Sir Philip Sidney and George Chapman (London, 1587), p. 27.
18. Mornay's marginalia refer to both the *Pimander* and the *Asclepius*; see Frances Yates, 'Religious Hermetism in the Sixteenth Century', *Giordano Bruno and the Hermetic Tradition* (Chicago: University of Chicago Press, 1964), p. 177.
19. On the rediscovery of the Hermetic writings see John G. Burke, 'Hermetism as a Renaissance World View', in Robert S. Kinsman (ed.), *The Darker Vision of the Renaissance: Beyond the Fields of Reason* (Berkeley: University of California Press, 1974), pp. 95–117; Allen G. Debus, *Chemistry and Medical Debate: Van Helmont to Boerhaave* (Canton, Mass.: Science History Publications, 2001); also, Copenhaver, 'Introduction', *Hermetica*.
20. On the dating of the Hermetic texts see Linden (ed.), *Alchemy Reader*, pp. 10–11.
21. See Burke, 'Hermetism', pp. 95–117.
22. See Yates, *Giordano Bruno*, pp. 176–9.
23. *The Chymist's Key*, in L. C. Martin (ed.), *The Works of Henry Vaughan* (Oxford: Clarendon Press, 1957), p. 600. All references to Vaughan's works are to this edition.
24. Burckhardt, *Alchemy*, p. 19. See also, Burke, 'Hermetism', pp. 95–117.
25. Burckhardt, *Alchemy*, pp. 18–19.
26. Marshall, *Philosopher's Stone*, p. 216. See H. E. Stapleton, R. F. Azon and M. Hidayat Husain, 'Chemistry in Iraq and Persia in the Tenth Century', *Memoirs of the Royal Asiatic Society of Bengal*, 8 (1927), 25–50.
27. *The Mirror of Alchimy* (London: Thomas Creede for Richard Olive, 1597); available in Stanton J. Linden (ed.), *The Mirror of Alchimy Composed by the Thrice-Famous and Learned Fryer, Roger Bachon* (New York: Garland

Publishing, Inc., 1992). See also Charles Nicholl, *The Chemical Theatre* (London: Routledge & Kegan Paul, 1980), pp. 23–4; Holmyard, *Alchemy*, pp. 61–4; and Marshall, *Philosopher's Stone*, pp. 217–18, 259, 304.

28. See Laleh Bakhtiar, *Sufism: Expression of the Mystic Quest* (London: Thames and Hudson, 1976).
29. Marshall, *Philosopher's Stone*, p. 225.
30. Stanton J. Linden, *Darke Hierogliphicks* (Kentucky: The University Press of Kentucky, 1996), p. 15.
31. M. Ruland, *A Lexicon of Alchemy* (1612), translated from the Latin by A. E. Waite (London, 1892), p. 76.
32. R. Patai, *The Jewish Alchemists* (Princeton: Princeton University Press, 1994), pp. 152–69.
33. See Marshall, *Philosopher's Stone*, pp. 242–3.
34. See Healy, 'Protean Bodies', pp. 161–76. In Bacon's *New Atlantis* the laws of Bensalem had been ordained by Moses through a secret cabala, p. 163.
35. Marshall, *Philosopher's Stone*, p. 259.
36. E. J. Holmyard, 'Introduction', *The Ordinall of Alchemy by Thomas Norton of Bristoll* (London: Edward Arnold & Co., 1929), lxii.
37. 'Introduction', p. 13.
38. Deborah E. Harkness, *The Jewel House: Elizabethan London and the Scientific Revolution* (New Haven and London: Yale University Press, 2007).
39. George Ripley, *The Compound of Alchymie*, in Elias Ashmole, *Theatrum Chemicum Britannicum* (London, 1651), pp. 107–86, 186.
40. See Nicholl's discussion of Ripley's 'gates' in *Chemical Theatre*, pp. 32–41.
41. Thomas Norton, *The Ordinall of Alchimy*, in Ashmole, *Theatrum Chemicum*. All references are to this edition.
42. Lauren Kassell, *Medicine and Magic in Elizabethan London: Simon Forman, Astrologer, Alchemist and Physician* (Oxford: Clarendon Press, 2005), p. 54.
43. Thomas Rainold, *A Comendious Declaration of the Excellent Virtues of a Certain Lately Invented Oile* (London, 1551), sigs. B3v–4r.
44. William R. Newman and Anthony Grafton in *Secrets of Nature: Astrology and Alchemy in Early Modern Europe* (Cambridge, Mass.: MIT Press, 2001), p. 14, state that 'early modern alchemy was not a contemplative discipline focusing on internal spiritual development' and that the latter was a nineteenth-century fabrication; however, as Peter Forshaw has subsequently argued, the writings of Heinrich Khunrath and Michael Maier certainly foreground the contemplative dimension of the alchemist's art; see 'Subliming Spirits: Physical-Chemistry and Theo-Alchemy in the works of Heinrich Khunrath (1560–1605)', in Stanton J. Linden (ed.), *Mystical Metal of Gold: Essays on Alchemy and Renaissance Culture* (New York: AMS Press, 2007), pp. 255–75. Norton's treatise, too, strongly suggests an esoteric, spiritual and philosophical dimension to the art. Interestingly, William Sherman has observed that John Dee's 'alchemical annotations are consummately practical', pertaining to the production of a material 'philosopher's stone'; see William Sherman, *John Dee: The Politics of Reading and Writing*

in the English Renaissance (Amherst: University of Massachusetts Press, 1995), p. 90.

45. Holmyard, 'Introduction', *The Ordinall*, iv.
46. See Frances Yates, *The French Academies in the Sixteenth Century* (London and New York: Routledge, 1988), p. 1.
47. 'Introduction', *The Letters of Marsilio Ficino*, trans. Language Dept. School of Economic Science, London, 7 vols. (London: Shepheard-Walwyn Ltd, 1975–), vol. 1, p. 20. All references to the *Letters* are to this edition.
48. 'Introduction', *Letters*, p. 20. See Letter 7, vol. 1, p. 43.
49. Marsilio Ficino, *The Christian Religion*, *Opera Omnia* (Basle, 1561; reprinted Turin: Bottega d'Erasmo, 1959); cited in 'Introduction', *Letters*, vol. 1, pp. 22–3.
50. Yates, *Academies*, p. 2, n. 1.
51. Yates, *Academies*, p. 2. On syncretism see also Maren-Sofie Røstvig, *Configurations: A Topomorphical Approach to Renaissance Poetry* (Oslo: Scandinavian University Press, 1994).
52. Ficino, Letter 123, 'Oratorical, Moral, Dialectical and Theological Praise of Philosophy' to Bernardo Bembo, *Letters*, vol. 1, p. 187.
53. Ficino, *The Christian Religion*, cited in 'Introduction', *Letters*, vol. 1, p. 22.
54. On these intellectual contexts see Yates, *Academies*, especially pp. 1–3, and Røstvig, *Configurations* and *The Hidden Sense and Other Essays* (Sarpsburg: Norwegian Studies in English 9, 1963).
55. Ficino's Latin manuscript was translated into Italian in 1474 at the request of Lorenzo de' Medici; see Sears Jayne, 'Introduction', *Commentary on Plato's Symposium on Love*, trans. Sears Jayne (Dallas, Texas: Spring Publications, 1985), pp. 19, 3–4. The Italian version was published in 1544. On Ficino's Plato see Sarah Hutton, 'Introduction to the Renaissance and Seventeenth-Century', pp. 67–76, and Jill Kraye, 'Platonic Love in the Renaissance', pp. 76–86, both in Anna Baldwin and Sarah Hutton, (eds.), *Platonism and the English Imagination* (Cambridge: Cambridge University Press, 1994).
56. Frances Yates, 'Shakespeare and the Platonic Tradition', *University of Edinburgh Journal* (Autumn 1942), 2–12, 9.
57. See Frank Whigham and Wayne A. Rebhorn (eds.), 'Introduction', *The Art of English Poesy by George Puttenham: A Critical Edition* (Ithaca and London: Cornell University Press, 2007), p. 30.
58. Sears Jayne notes that a copy of Ficino's Latin *Opera Platonis* (1484) was housed in the library at Cambridge: Jayne, 'Introduction', *Commentary*, p. 21. See also Stephen Medcalf, 'Shakespeare on Beauty, Truth and Transcendence', in Baldwin and Hutton, *Platonism*, pp. 117–26.
59. The guiding letter titles are Ficino's own. See Preface, *Letters*, vol. 1, p. 17.
60. Sears Jayne, *John Colet and Marsilio Ficino* (Oxford: Oxford University Press, 1963), pp. 18, 5.
61. Cited in Jayne, *De amore*, p. 179.
62. *Euridice* by Jaopo Peri, 1600, *Euridice* by Giulio Caccani, 1600, and *Orfeo* by Claudio Monteverdi, 1607: see Timothy J. McGee, '*Orfeo* and *Euridice*, the

First Two Operas', in John Warden, *Orpheus: The Metamorphosis of a Myth* (Toronto: University of Toronto Press, 1982), pp. 163–79.

63. Cited in Warden, *Orpheus*, pp. 89, 91.

64. Warden, *Orpheus*, pp. 89–91.

65. Warden, *Orpheus*, p. 93.

66. Ficino to Sebastiano Foresi, his beloved fellow priest, Letter 21, vol. v, p. 37.

67. See Copenhaver, *Hermetica*, xlix; Lyndy Abraham, *Marvell and Alchemy* (Aldershot: Scolar Press, 1990), p. 20.

68. Copenhaver, *Hermetica*, xlix.

69. Copenhaver, *Hermetica*, p. 74.

70. Kassell, *Medicine and Magic*, p. 9.

71. Francis Bacon, *De Dignitate et Augmentis Scientarum*, Sp. 1.573; cited in Paulo Rossi, *Francis Bacon: From Magic to Science*, trans. Sacha Rabinovitch (London: Routledge, 1968), p. 21.

72. Bacon, *New Atlantis*, in James Spedding, Robert Ellis and Douglas Heath (eds.), *Collected Works of Francis Bacon*, 12 vols. (London: Routledge, 1996), vol. iii, part i, p. 156.

73. William Shakespeare, *Hamlet*, in Stanley Wells and Gary Taylor (eds.), *The Complete Works*, compact edition (Oxford: Oxford University Press, 1988); all references to Shakespeare's plays are to this edition.

74. John S. Mebane, *Renaissance Magic and the Return of the Golden Age: The Occult Tradition and Marlowe, Jonson and Shakespeare* (Lincoln and London: University of Nebraska Press, 1989), pp. 22–3.

75. Giovanni Pico della Mirandola, 'Oration on the Dignity of Man', trans. Elizabeth Forbes, *Renaissance Philosophy of Man* (Chicago: University of Chicago Press, 1948), pp. 106–8.

76. 'Oration on the Dignity of Man', pp. 104–6. See discussion of Pico in Mebane, *Renaissance Magic*, pp. 36–52, especially pp. 40–1. The Spanish humanist Juan Luis Vives wrote a tract, *A Fable About Man* (Louvain, 1518), which reveals he was very familiar with Pico's *Oratio* and Erasmus's *Praise of Folly* is informed by Pico too. It is interesting that an early work of Thomas More was *The Life of Picus, Earl of Mirandula* (*c.* 1510).

77. Jacob Burckhardt, *The Civilization of the Renaissance in Italy* (New York: Mentor, 1960), p. 257. See Burke, 'Hermetism', p. 95.

78. Bacon, *Redargutio Philosophiarum* (1608), cited in Rossi, *Bacon*, pp. 91–2.

79. John Donne, 'An anatomy of the world: the first anniversary', in Herbert Grierson (ed.), *The Poems of John Donne* (Oxford: Oxford University Press, 1912), pp. 229–45.

80. Martin (ed.), *Works of Vaughan*, p. 418.

81. Cited in Harkness, *The Jewel House*, p. 233.

82. See Harkness, *The Jewel House*.

83. Important revisionist histories of this figure include Charles Webster, *Paracelsus, Medicine, Magic and Mission at the End of Time* (New Haven and London: Yale University Press, 2008) and Ole Peter Grell (ed.),

Paracelsus: The Man and his Reputation, his Ideas and their Transformation (Leiden: Brill, 1998).

84. On the significance of Paracelsus see Walter Pagel, *From Paracelsus to van Helmont: Studies in Renaissance Medicine and Science* (London: Variorum Reprints, 1986); Christopher Hill, *Intellectual Origins of the English Revolution* (Oxford: Clarendon, 1982), pp. 72, 75; Charles Webster, 'Medicine as Popular Protest', in Ole Peter Grell and Andrew Cunningham (eds.), *Medicine and the Reformation* (London: Routledge, 1993), pp. 57–77.

85. Jolande Jacobi (ed.), *Paracelsus, Selected Writings*, trans. Norbert Guterman (New Jersey: Bollingen Series XXVIII, Princeton University Press, 1988). All references to Paracelsus's writings are to this edition unless otherwise stated and are cited by page number in parentheses in the text.

86. See Webster, ' Medicine as Popular Protest', p. 58.

87. On Helmontian medicine see Andrew Wear, *Knowledge and Practice in English Medicine, 1550–1680* (Cambridge: Cambridge University Press, 2000).

88. R. Bostocke, *Auncient and Later Phisicke* (London, 1585), pp. 80, 126. The British Library attributes this to Robert Bostock while the Huntingdon Library copy available on EEBO attributes it to Richard Bostocke.

89. On the hybid physic of turn-of-the-seventeenth-century England see Margaret Healy, *Fictions of Disease in Early Modern England: Bodies, Plagues and Politics* (Basingstoke: Palgrave 2001), especially pp. 18–49.

90. On Mayerne's career see Harold J. Cook, 'Institutional Structures and Personal Belief in the London College of Physicians', in Ole Peter Grell and Andrew Cunningham (eds.), *Religio Medici: Medicine and Religion in Seventeenth-Century England* (Aldershot: Ashgate Scolar Press, 1996), pp. 99–101.

91. Webster, *Paracelsus*, pp. 62–3.

92. Grell, *Paracelsus*, p. 1.

93. I'm thinking particularly of the revisionist accounts by Webster (2008) and Grell (1998).

94. Joseph Glanvill, *Lux Orientalis* (London, 1682), pp. 137–41; John Evelyn, 'Concerning the Millennium' (1688), Christ Church, Oxford, Evelyn Manuscripts 35, 2r–v; cited in Charles Webster, *From Paracelsus to Newton: Magic and the Making of Modern Science* (Cambridge: Cambridge University Press, 1982), p. 40.

95. See Healy, 'Protean Bodies', pp. 161–4, 171.

96. See Webster, *From Paracelsus to Newton*, especially pp. 1–47; see also Allen G. Debus and Michael T. Walton (eds.), *Reading the Book of Nature: The Other Side of the Scientific Revolution* (Kirksville, Mo.: Sixteenth Century Journal Publishers, 1998).

97. On the alchemy of Newton and Boyle see M. L. Righini Bonelli and William R. Shea (eds.), *Reason, Experiment and Mysticism in the Scientific Revolution* (Basingstoke: Macmillan, 1975); Lawrence Principe, *The Aspiring Adept: Robert Boyle and his Alchemical Quest* (Princeton: Princeton University Press, 1998);

and Betty Jo Dobbs, *The Janus Faces of Genius: The Role of Alchemy in Newton's Thought* (Cambridge: Cambridge University Press, 1991).

98. Henry Vaughan, 'The Translator to the Ingenious Reader', *Hermeticall Physick*, in Martin (ed.), *Works of Vaughan*, p. 548; subsequent page references in the text are to this edition.

99. Ashmole, *Theatrum Chemicum Britannicum*, sig. BIV.

100. Joseph Hall, *An Open and Plaine Paraphrase, upon the Song of Songs, which is Salomens* (London, 1609), sig. N2v. All references are to this edition.

101. Ripley, *Compound of Alchymie*, in Ashmole, *Theatrum Chemicum*, p. 186; Ripley, *Cantilena*, verse 37, cited in Nicholl, *Chemical Theatre*, p. 209.

102. On spiritual accounting and meditation, see Marie-Louise Coolahan, 'Redeeming Parcels of Time: Aesthetics and the Practice of Occasional Meditation', *Seventeenth Century*, 22 (2007), 124–43.

103. See Vaughan's poem, 'The Importunate Fortune, written to Doctor Powel of Cantre', in Martin (ed.), *Works of Vaughan*, pp. 634–7 and note 636, p. 758.

104. Baif, *Evvres*, V, 5, cited in Yates, *Academies*, pp. 237–8.

105. Dorat's 'academy' at Coqueret was the forerunner of the official one, Yates, *Academies*, p. 14.

106. See J. Seznec, *La Survivance des dieux antiques* (London: Studies of the Warburg Institute, XI, 1940), pp. 89, 273–5. Yates, *Academies*, pp. 14–15.

107. Yates, 'Shakespeare and the Platonic Tradition', 9.

108. See Ernst Cassirer, *The Platonic Renaissance in England*, trans. James P. Pettegrove (Austin: University of Texas Press, 1953), pp. 42–155; Yates, *Academies*, pp. 15, 3–5.

109. Yates, *Academies*, pp. 236–40.

110. Read, *Alchemy*, p. 62.

111. See Ashmole, 'Prologomena', *Theatrum Chemicum*, sig. A2.

112. There are a large number of copies of *Songe de Poliphile* in various editions in the British Library.

113. Beroalde, *Le Tableau des riches inventions*, in Stanislas Klossowski de Rola, *The Golden Game: Alchemical Engravings of the Seventeenth Century* (London: Thames and Hudson, 1988), p. 12.

114. De Rola, *Golden Game*, pp. 25, 28.

115. Michael Maier, *Atalanta Fugiens,* in *Atalanta Fugiens: An Edition of the Fugues, Emblems and Epigrams*, trans. from Latin by Joscelyn Godwin, Introduction by Hildemarie Streich (Grand Rapids, Mich.: Phanes Press, 1989), p. 103. All references are to this edition.

116. He relays this in *Arcana Arcanissima*, but this exposition is from *Atalanta Fugiens*, p. 79.

117. Godwin, in *Atalanta Fugiens: An Edition*, p. 11.

118. Streich, in *Atalanta Fugiens: An Edition*, pp. 14–15, 21, 23, 36.

119. Streich, in *Atalanta Fugiens: An Edition*, pp. 82, 82, 83.

120. Godwin, in *Atalanta Fugiens: An Edition*, p. 8.

121. Lyndy Abraham, 'Introduction' to Arthur Dee, *Fasciculus Chemicus*, trans. Elias Ashmole (New York and London: Garland Publishing, 1997), xxviii;

R. J. W. Evans, *Rudolf II and His World: A Study in Intellectual History 1576–1612* (Oxford: Clarendon Press, 1973), pp. 196–242; see also Abraham, *Marvell*, p. 2.

122. Peter French, *John Dee: The World of an Elizabethan Magus* (London: Routledge, 1984), especially p. 60; Abraham, *Marvell*, p. 4.

123. A 1698 catalogue (the 'Catalogus Petworthianae') of the Percys' impressive library collection in the late seventeenth century can be consulted today at the West Sussex Record Office in Chichester. It lists Marsilio Ficino's *Plato* (*Platonis Opera Omnia*) and *Le Pimandre de Mercure Trismegiste* (Bordeaux, 1579), and among the alchemical collection are numerous works by Paracelsus in the original Swiss-German, works by Oswald Croll, George Ripley, Conrad Khunrath, and *Theatrum Chemicum*, 3 vols. (Ursellus, 1602). There is also an annotated edition (probably the ninth Earl's hand) of Giordano Bruno's, *Degl' heroici furori* [sic] (1581).

124. See Nicholl, *Chemical Theatre*, p. 17.

125. Abraham, *Marvell*, pp. 2–3. Indeed, Ben Jonson's extensive knowledge of the subject (as displayed in his plays and court masques) suggests that he may have been a visitor too. To deride and mock the type of alchemy practised by covetous and foolish types (Geber's 'cooks') was common among alchemists themselves. See my chapter 'Alchemy, Magic and the Sciences', in Julie Sanders (ed.), *Ben Jonson in Context* (Cambridge: Cambridge University Press, 2010), pp. 322–30.

126. See Betty Jo Teeter Dobbs, *The Foundations of Newton's Alchemy: or The Hunting of the Greene Lyon* (Cambridge: Cambridge University Press, 1975), pp. 62–80.

127. *Gesta Grayorum*, home.hiwaay.net/~paul/bacon/devices/geasta.html, accessed 25 March 2008.

128. Thomas Moffet, *Nobilis*, in Virgil B. Heltzel and Hoyt H. Hudson (trans. and eds.), *A View of the Life and Death of a Sidney* (California: The Huntington Library, 1940), p. 75.

129. Abraham, *Marvell*, p. 5. See Arthur D. Imerti (ed.), 'Introduction', Giordano Bruno, *The Expulsion of the Triumphant Beast* (New Brunswick, N.J.: Rutgers University Press, 1964). In 1576 charges of heresy were drawn up against Bruno by the Inquisition; see p. 4.

130. Yates, 'Shakespeare and the Platonic Tradition', 11.

131. Ronald Gray, 'Will in the Universe: Shakespeare's Sonnets, Plato's *Symposium* and Renaissance Neoplatonism', in Peter Holland (ed.), *Shakespeare Survey Volume 59: Editing Shakespeare* (Cambridge: Cambridge University Press, 2006), pp. 225–38, 228.

132. French, *John Dee*, p. 120.

133. C. H. Josten, 'An Unknown Chapter in the Life of John Dee', *Journal of the Warburg and Courtauld Institutes*, 28 (1965), 234; cited in French, *John Dee*, p. 120.

134. Philippe Du Plessis Mornay, *A Woorke concerning the Trewnesse of the Christian Religion*, trans. Sir Philip Sidney and George Chapman (London, 1587), p. 27.

135. See, for example, John Erskine Hankins, *Backgrounds of Shakespeare's Thought* (Hamden, Conn.: Archon Books, 1978).
136. Francis Bacon, *The Advancement of Learning* (1605), Book I, in Spedding, Ellis and Heath (eds.), *Collected Works*, vol. III, Part I, p. 263.
137. George Puttenham, *The Art of English Poesy* (1589), in Frank Whigham and Wayne A. Rebhorn (eds.), *The Art of English Poesy by George Puttenham: A Critical Edition* (Ithaca and London: Cornell University Press, 2007), I, I, pp. 93–4. All references are to this edition.
138. Sir Philip Sidney, *An Apology for Poetry* (1595), in G. Gregory Smith (ed.), *Elizabethan Critical Essays*, 2 vols. (Oxford: Oxford University Press, 1904), vol. I, p. 156. All references are to this edition.
139. Christopher Marlowe, *The Two Tragicall Discourse of Mighty Tamburlaine, the Scythian Shepheard*, in C. F. Tucker Brooke (ed.), *The Works of Christopher Marlowe* (Oxford: Clarendon Press, 1969), Part I, v. ii, lines 1946–9.
140. John Cleveland (1613–58), 'On the Archbishop of Canterbury', in Brian Morris and Eleanor Withington (eds.), *The Poems of John Cleveland* (Oxford: Clarendon Press, 1967), p. 38, lines 3–4. Cleveland's collected *Poems* were published at the height of the vogue for alchemy, in 1651.
141. The renowned humanist Scaliger spoke of the poet as an *alter deus* (*Poetice*, 1561); see Alastair Fowler, *Triumphal Forms: Structural Patterns in Elizabethan Poetry* (Cambridge: Cambridge University Press, 1970), p. xi.
142. Milton 1644, cited in Mebane, *Renaissance Magic*, p. 15; George R. Potter and Evelyn M. Simpson (eds.), *The Sermons of John Donne*, 10 vols. (Berkeley and Los Angeles: University of California Press, 1953–62), vol. IV, p. 110.
143. Puttenham, *Art of English Poesy*, III, 5, p. 233. The *Art* spells this term 'metall' rather than the 'mettle' substituted by Whigham and Rebhorn. However, as they note, Elizabethans did not distinguish by spelling 'the words for the material substance of metal and mettle as a quality of disposition or temperament', Whigham and Rebhorn, *The Art of English Poesy*, note 7, p. 233.
144. Henry Reynolds, *Mythomystes* (1632), in J. E. Spingarn (ed.), *Critical Essays of the Seventeenth Century* (Bloomington and London: Indiana University Press, 1957), pp. 163–4. All references are to this edition.
145. Francis Meres, *Palladis Tamia, Wits Treasury*, cited in Katherine Duncan-Jones, *Shakespeare's Sonnets* (London: Arden Shakespeare; Thomson Learning, 2004), p. 47.
146. Gabriel Harvey, 'Against Thomas Nash', in Smith (ed.), *Elizabethan Critical Essays*, vol. II, pp. 254, 259.
147. Samuel Daniel, *A Defence of Rhyme*, in Smith (ed.), *Elizabethan Critical Essays*, vol. II, pp. 351–6.
148. Sir Philip Sidney, 'Astrophil and Stella', in Katherine Duncan-Jones (ed.), *Sir Philip Sidney: A Critical Edition of the Major Works* (Oxford: Oxford University Press, 1989), pp. 153–211. All references are to this edition.

2 LOVELY BOY

1. John Manning, *The Emblem* (London: Reaktion Books, 2002), p. 169.
2. Manning, *The Emblem*, p. 169.
3. See Helen Hackett's important article on sacred imagery in erotic poetry in the 1590s: 'The Art of Blasphemy? Infusions of the Erotic and the Sacred in the Poetry of Donne, Barnes, and Constable', *Renaissance and Reformation*, 38:3 (2004), 27–54.
4. This wonderful term is Manning's, *The Emblem*, p. 167. Katherine Duncan-Jones, 'Introduction', *Shakespeare's Sonnets* (London: Arden Shakespeare; Thomson Learning, 2004), describes them as 'virtually never spiritual', p. 70. Most recently Douglas Trevor has pronounced them 'without mediation or qualification of any Christian kind': 'Shakespeare's Love Objects', in Michael Schoenfeldt (ed.), *A Companion to Shakespeare's Sonnets* (Oxford: Blackwell, 2007), pp. 225–41, p. 240.
5. Anon., *The Rosary of Philosophers* (1550), ed. Adam McLean (Edinburgh: Magnum Opus Hermetic Sourceworks, 1980). Cited in Lyndy Abraham, *Marvell and Alchemy* (Aldershot: Scolar Press, 1990), p. 313.
6. Martin Ruland, *A Lexicon of Alchemy* (1612), trans. from Latin by A. E. Waite (London, 1892), p. 394.
7. Mario Praz and Peggy Simonds have noted this. See Peggy Munoz Simonds, 'Eros and Anteros in Shakespeare's Sonnets 153 and 154: An Iconographical Study', *Spenser Studies* 7 (1986), 261–325, 268; and Mario Praz, 'Profane and Sacred Love', in *Studies in Seventeenth-Century Imagery*, 2 vols. (Rome: Edizioni di Storia e Letteratura, 1964), vol. 1, pp. 115–17, especially p. 115.
8. Otto Vaenius (Otto van Veen), Preface (n.p.), *Amorum Emblemata* (Antwerp, 1608). All references are to this edition.
9. Lyndy Abraham, *A Dictionary of Alchemical Imagery* (Cambridge: Cambridge University Press, 1998), p. 176.
10. There are parallels, too, with lines 287 and 292–4 of *A Lovers Complaint*: the 'flame through water' heats 'breasts'.
11. This analysis therefore differs from Joseph Pequigney's in *Such is My Love: A Study of Shakespeare's Sonnets* (Chicago: University of Chicago Press, 1985); Pequigney asserts, 'the interaction of the friends being sexual in both orientation and practice', p. 1.
12. Michel de Montaigne, *Essays*, trans. John Florio, 3 vols. (1603; London: J. M. Dent & Sons Ltd, 1946), vol. 1, p. 199. All references are to this edition.
13. On improvisation and friendship discourses see John Steven McCullough, 'Disputable Friends: Rhetoric and "Amicitia" in English Renaissance Writing 1579–1625', DPhil. thesis, University of Sussex, 2006. See also Laurie Shannon, *Sovereign Amity: Figures of Friendship in Shakespearean Contexts* (Chicago: University of Chicago Press, 2002).
14. Thomas Churchyard, *A Sparke of Friendship* (London, 1588), sig. C1.
15. On male friendship see particularly Rodney Poisson, 'Unequal Friendship: Shakespeare's Sonnets 11–126', in Hilton Landry (ed.), *New Essays in Shakespeare's Sonnets* (New York: AMS Press, 1976), pp. 1–19; Alan Stewart, *Close*

Readers: Humanism and Sodomy in Early Modern England (Princeton: Princeton University Press, 1997); Alan Bray, *Homosexuality in Renaissance England* (London: Gay Men's Press, 1982); Tom MacFaul, *Male Friendship in Shakespeare and his Contemporaries* (Cambridge: Cambridge University Press, 2007).

16. Francis Meres, *Palladis Tamia. Wits Treasury. Being the Second Part of Wits Commonwealth* (London, 1598): 'his sugred Sonnets among his private friends', fo. 282r.

17. Thomas Churchyard, *Churchyard's Challenge* (London, 1593), sig. G3v.

18. On the heart as the place of memory see Mary Carruthers, *The Book of Memory: A Study of Memory in Medieval Culture* (Cambridge: Cambridge University Press, 1990), pp. 44, 48, 172.

19. On these intellectual contexts see Frances Yates, 'Italian Academies and French Academies', in *The French Academies of the Sixteenth Century* (London and New York: Routledge, 1988), especially pp. 1–3; and Maren-Sofie Røstvig, *Configurations: A Topomorphical Approach to Renaissance Poetry* (Oslo: Scandinavian University Press, 1994) and *The Hidden Sense and Other Essays* (Sarpsburg: Norwegian Studies in English 9, 1963).

20. See Ronald Gray, 'Will in the Universe: Shakespeare's Sonnets, Plato's *Symposium*, Alchemy and Renaissance Neoplatonism', in Peter Holland (ed.), *Shakespeare Survey Volume 59: Editing Shakespeare* (Cambridge: Cambridge University Press, 2006), p. 225. See also Stephen Medcalf, 'Shakespeare on Beauty, Truth and Transcendence', in Anna Baldwin and Sarah Hutton (eds.), *Platonism and the English Imagination* (Cambridge: Cambridge University Press, 1994), pp. 117–19.

21. Abraham, *Dictionary*, p. 96.

22. Duncan-Jones, 'Introduction', *Shakespeare's Sonnets*, p. 49.

23. Michael Maier, *Atalanta Fugiens: An Edition of the Fugues, Emblems and Epigrams*, trans. Joscelyn Godwin (Grand Rapids, Mich.: Phanes Press, 1989), p. 147; also in Stanislas Klossowska de Rola, *The Golden Game* (London: Thames and Hudson, 1988), pp. 81, 100.

24. See Thomas Norton, *The Ordinall of Alchimy*, in Elias Ashmole, *Theatrum Chemicum Britannicum* (London, 1651), p. 146; all page references are to this edition. Titus Burckhardt, *Alchemy* (Dorset: Element Books, 1967), p. 149.

25. Abraham, *Dictionary*, p. 37.

26. Marsilio Ficino, *Commentary on Plato's Symposium on Love (De amore)*, trans. Sears Jayne (Dallas, Texas: Spring Publications Inc., 1988), p. 66; cited hereafter as *De amore*.

27. See Dympna Callaghan, *Shakespeare's Sonnets* (Oxford: Blackwell, 2007), p. 12.

28. Helen Vendler, *The Art of Shakespeare's Sonnets* (Cambridge, Mass.: Harvard University Press, 1999), p. 29.

29. Edmund Spenser, *The Ruines of Time*, in William A. Oram (ed.), *The Yale Edition of the Shorter Poems of Edmund Spenser* (New Haven and London: Yale University Press, 1989), pp. 232–61, lines 211–12. See Carruthers, *The Book of Memory*, p. 58. We might think, too, about Milton's words in *Paradise Lost*:

'He took the golden compasses, prepared / In God's eternal store, to circumscribe / This universe'.

30. Carruthers, *Book of Memory*, p. 201.
31. Carruthers, *Book of Memory*, pp. 92, 160, 204.
32. See de Rola, *Golden Game*, pp. 25, 28.
33. De Rola, *Golden Game*, pp. 25–6.
34. Gray, 'Will in the Universe', p. 228.
35. Peggy Munoz Simonds proposed an alchemical reading for Sonnets 19 and 20 in 'Sex in a Bottle: The Alchemical Distillation of Shakespeare's Hermaphrodite in Sonnet 20', *Renaissance Papers* (1999), 97–105, especially 103.
36. De Rola, *Golden Game*, p. 24. See Michael Maier, Emblem 42, 'For him versed in Chemistry, let Nature, Reason, Experience and Reading be his Guide, staff, spectacles and lamp', *Atalanta Fugiens*, p. 189.
37. On flowers and memory images see Carruthers, *Book of Memory*, p. 254.
38. Abraham, *Dictionary*, p. 36.
39. Michael Hattaway (ed.), Ben Jonson, *The New Inn* (Manchester: Manchester University Press, The Revels Plays, 1984).
40. Duncan-Jones, 'Introduction', *Sonnets*, pp. 53–65.
41. Colin Burrow, *The Complete Sonnets and Poems* (Oxford: Oxford University Press, 2002), p. 100.
42. Brian P. Copenhaver, *Hermetica: The Greek 'Corpus Hermeticum' and the Latin 'Asclepius' in a New English Translation* (Cambridge: Cambridge University Press, 1992), pp. 2–3. All references are to this edition.
43. Ruth Gilbert, *Early Modern Hermaphrodites: Sex and Other Stories* (Basingstoke: Palgrave, 2002), pp. 9–32.
44. Lyndy Abraham, *Marvell and Alchemy* (Aldershot: Scolar Press, 1990), p. 92.
45. See Maurice Evans (ed.), Sir Philip Sidney, *The Countess of Pembroke's Arcadia* (London: Penguin Classics, 1987), Book 1, Chapter 12, pp. 129–39, especially p. 131. Pyrocles' description interestingly resonates with that of Shakespeare's Master Mistress. Sir Philip Sidney, *An Apology for Poetry*, in G. Gregory Smith (ed.), *Elizabethan Critical Essays*, 2 vols. (Oxford: Oxford University Press, 1904), vol. 1, pp. 172–3. Stephen Orgel discusses these images in *Impersonations: The Performance of Gender in Shakespeare's England* (Cambridge: Cambridge University Press, 1996), pp. 78–80.
46. See Orgel, *Impersonations*, p. 96, Plate 10. The title page of Michael Maier, *Arcana Arcanissima* (no place of publication, 1614) features Hercules. De Rola, *Golden Game*, claims to have discovered evidence that this alchemical volume – the first by Maier – was actually published in London, p. 60.
47. See Orgel, *Impersonations*, p. 97, Plate 11.
48. In a variation on this royal symbolism, Thomas Campion's *Lord's Masque* represented the marriage of Elizabeth and the Count Palatine as a 'chemical wedding' and Aurelian Townshend's masque, *Albion's Triumph* (8 January 1632) presented Charles and Mary as the alchemical king and queen – the hermaphrodite Mary–Charles.

49. See Anthony Holden, *The Observer Review*, 21 April 2002, front page, with an image of the portrait.
50. James Orchard Halliwell, *Dictionary of Archaic Words* (London: Bracken Books), p. 465.
51. Titus Burckhardt, *Alchemy* (Dorset: Element Books, 1986), p. 27.
52. Cited in Abraham, *Dictionary*, p. 27.
53. Burrow, *Complete Sonnets*, p. 442.
54. Abraham, *Dictionary*, p. 189.
55. See Abraham, *Dictionary*, 189.
56. Quoted from Norton, *Ordinall of Alchimy*, p. 60.
57. Sir Gyles Isham, *Rushton Triangular Lodge* (London: English Heritage, 1986), p. 10.
58. Tresham's adherence to Catholicism in the face of official persecution is often cited as the inspiration for this building; it is said to have been lived in by his warrener: see, for example, Malcolm Airs, *The Tudor and Jacobean Country House: A Building History* (Bridgend: Sutton Publishing Ltd, 1995), p. 9; and Mark Girouard, *Elizabethan Architecture: Its Rise and Fall, 1540–1640* (New Haven and London: Yale University Press, 2009), p. 230.
59. Some commentators have found Cabalistic symbolism here too; see, for example, Maren-Sofie Røstvig, 'Renaissance Numerology: Acrostics or Criticism?', *Essays in Criticism*, 16: 1 (January 1966), 8.
60. An English translation of this epigram appears in Michael Maier, *Atalanta Fugiens: An Edition of the Emblems, Fugues and Epigrams*, trans. Joscelyn Godwin (Grand Rapids, Mich.: Phanes Press, 1989), p. 93.
61. Alastair Fowler, *Triumphal Forms: Structural Patterns in Elizabethan Poetry* (Cambridge: Cambridge University Press, 1970) citing C. S. Lewis, *English Literature in the Sixteenth Century* (Oxford: Clarendon Press, 1954), p. 190.
62. Other notable studies, besides Fowler's, arguing for the significance of numerology to aesthetic theory include: Maren-Sofie Røstvig, *The Hidden Sense and Other Essays* (Sarpsburg: Norwegian Studies in English 9, Sverre Johanson Boktrykkeri, 1963) and *Configurations: A Topomorphical Approach to Renaissance Poetry* (Oslo: Scandinavian University Press, 1994); Alastair Fowler, *Silent Poetry: Essays in Numerological Analysis* (London: Routledge & Kegan Paul, 1970); S. K. Heninger, *Touches of Sweet Harmony: Pythagorean Cosmology and Renaissance Poetics* (California: The Huntington Library, 1974); and Thomas P. Roche, *Petrarch and the English Sonnet Sequences* (New York: AMS Press, 1989).
63. Pietro Bonghi, 'Prefatio', *Mysticae numerorum significationis* (Bergamo, 1585), citing St Augustine, *The City of God* (Bk 11, sept. 30) in Gunnar Quarnstrom, *Poetry and Numbers: On the Structural Use of Symbolic Numbers* (London: CWK Gleerup, 1966), p. 20.
64. St Augustine, *De Trinitate*, in *On the Trinity*, libri 15, trans. Arthur West Haddan (Edinburgh, 1873) IV. vi. p. 10.
65. See Røstvig, *Configuration*, xii.

66. John Dee, Preface, *The Elements of Geometrie of the Most Ancient Philosopher Euclid*, trans. H. Billingsley, with 'a very fruitfull preface made by M. J. Dee' (London, 1570), p. 1. All references are to this edition.

67. Frank Whigham and Wayne A. Rebhorn (eds.), *The Art of English Poesy by George Puttenham: A Critical Edition* (Ithaca and London: Cornell University Press, 2007), II, 1, pp. 153, 154. All references are to this edition.

68. Walter R. Davis (ed.), *The Works of Thomas Campion*, (New York: Doubleday, 1967), p. 48.

69. Samuel Daniel, *A Defence of Ryme*, c. 1603, in Smith (ed.), *Elizabethan Critical Essays*, vol. II, p. 366.

70. Henry Reynolds, *Mythomystes*, in J. E. Spingarn (ed.) *Critical Essays of the Seventeenth Century* (Bloomington and London, 1957), p. 153. All references are to this edition.

71. On this point see Francesco Giorgio, *De Harmonia Mundi Totius Cantica Tria*, trans. Guy Le Fèvre de la Boderie as *L'Harmonie du monde* (Paris, 1579), sigs. E5r, E5 v.

72. Aristotle, *Metaphysica*, trans. Hugh Tredennick, cited in Heninger, *Sweet Harmony*, p. 76.

73. Plato, *Republic*, VII, trans. Paul Shorey in Edith Hamilton and Huntington Cairns (eds.), *The Collected Dialogues of Plato* (Princeton: Princeton University Press, 1961), p. 759.

74. Plato, *Timaeus*, trans. Benjamen Jowett, in *The Collected Dialogues*, pp. 1179–1181.

75. Augustine, *De Musica*, trans. R. C. Taliaferro (Annapolis, 1939), p. 48, cited in Røstvig, *Hidden Sense*, p. 20.

76. Dee, Preface, *Euclid*, p. 1.

77. J. H. Blunt (ed.), *The Myroure of oure Ladye* (London, 1873), Early English Text Society, extra series no. XIX; cited in Røstvig, *Hidden Sense*, pp. 3, 10.

78. Mary Carruthers and Jan M. Ziolkowski (eds.), *The Medieval Craft of Memory: An Anthology of Texts and Pictures* (Philadelphia: University of Pennsylvania Press, 2002), p. 4.

79. Macrobius, *Commentary on the Dream of Scipio*, trans. William H. Stahl (New York: Columbia University Press, 1952), I, vi, pp. 7–8; I, vi, p. 109.

80. Francesco Giorgio, *De Harmonia Mundi Totius Cantica Tria*, cited in Røstvig, *Hidden Sense*, pp. 27–8, 31.

81. Røstvig, *Hidden Sense*, p. 31.

82. Røstvig, *Hidden Sense*, p. 32.

83. Røstvig discusses this preface at length in *Hidden Sense*, p. 28.

84. Cited in Røstvig, *Hidden Sense*, p. 28.

85. Julius Caesar Scaliger, *Poetices libri septem* (Lyons, 1561), p. 3.

86. Guillaume de Saluste Du Bartas, *Devine Weekes and Workes*, trans. Josuah Sylvester (London, 1605), pp. 472–3.

87. Otto Vaenius, *Amorum Emblemata* (Antwerp, 1608).

88. Thomas Masterson, *Third booke of arithmeticke* (London, 1595), sig. A2v.

89. William Ingpen, *Secrets of Numbers* (London, 1624), title page.

90. Michael Drayton, 'Endimion and Phoebe', 1594, in J. William Hebel (ed.), *The Works of Michael Drayton*, 5 vols. (Oxford: Basil Blackwell, 1961), vol. 1, p. 152; and 'Legends', 1619, *Works*, vol. 11, p. 452. All references are to this edition.

91. BL, Addit. MSS. 39830, fo. 191v; cited in Malcolm Airs, *The Tudor and Jacobean Country House: A Building History* (Stroud: Sutton Publishing, 1995), pp. 37, 40, 212. Mark Girouard, *Elizabethan Architecture: Its Rise and Fall, 1540–1640* (New Haven and London: Yale, 2009), pp. 233–7.

92. Airs, *The Tudor and Jacobean Country House*, pp. 37, 40, 212.

93. On the Fletcher link see Girouard, *Elizabethan Architecture*, p. 236.

94. Isham, *Rushton Triangular Lodge*, p. 10. The main theme of Tresham's 'New Bield' house in Lyveden was, similarly, the crucifixion and the salvation of the world that resulted from it.

95. See Maren-Sofie Røstvig, 'Renaissance Numerology: Acrostics or Criticism?', *Essays in Criticism*, 16: 1 (1966), 6–21.

96. Alastair Fowler, *Spenser and the Numbers of Time* (London: Routledge & Kegan Paul, 1964).

97. Plutarch, *Morals*, trans. Philemon Holland (London, 1603), p. 812. Heninger, *Sweet Harmony*, p. 89.

98. See Roche, *Petrarch*, p. 357 and Fowler, *Triumphal Forms*, p. 19.

99. Cited in Fowler, *Triumphal Forms*, p. 18.

100. J. Grundy (ed.), *The Poems of Henry Constable* (Liverpool: Liverpool University Press, 1960), p. 114.

101. Røstvig, *Hidden Sense*, p. 26.

102. Røstvig, *Configurations*, xviii.

103. Tom W. N. Parker, *Proportional Form in the Sonnets of the Sidney Circle* (Oxford: Clarendon Press, 1998), p. 32.

104. Guy Le Fèvre, Preface, *L'Harmonie du monde*, cited in Røstvig, *Hidden Sense*, p. 5.

105. Røstvig, *Hidden Sense*, p. 16.

106. Duncan-Jones, 'Introduction', *Shakespeare's Sonnets*, pp. 100–1.

107. Røstvig, *Hidden Sense*, p. 15.

108. Guy Le Fèvre, Preface, *L'Harmonie du monde*, n.p.

109. Augustine, *De Vera Religione*, cited in Røstvig, *Configurations*, p. 10.

110. J. Calvin, *On the Christian Faith*, in John T. McNeil (ed.), *Selections from the Institutes, Commentaries and Tracts* (New York: The Library of Liberal Arts, 1957), p. 12.

111. Cited in Røstvig, *Configurations*, p. 9.

112. Imbued with the same philosophical ideas, Edmund Spenser's *Shepheardes Calendar* claimed to be atemporal through its reproduction of God's pattern of the cosmos.

113. Marsilio Ficino, *Commentary on Plato's Symposium on Love*, trans. Sears Jayne (Dallas, Texas: Spring Publications Inc., 1988), p. 170.

114. *The Letters of Marsilio Ficino*, translated from Latin by members of the Language Department, London School of Economic Science, 7 vols.

(London: Shepheard-Walwyn, 1975–), vol. VII, Letter 76, p. 84. All references are to this edition.

115. Gretchen Ludke Finney, 'Music: A Book of Knowledge in Renaissance England', *Studies in the Renaissance*, 6 (1959), 36–63, 53. The classical work for Pythagorean music is the *Harmonices Enchiridion* of Nicomachus, which Boethius closely followed in *De Musica*.

116. Robert Fludd, cited in Allen G. Debus, *Robert Fludd and His Philosophical Key* (New York: Science History Publications, 1979), p. 6.

117. Cited in Debus, *Robert Fludd*, p. 9.

118. Stanley Wells and Gary Taylor (eds.), William Shakespeare, *The Complete Works*, compact edition (Oxford: Oxford University Press, 1988). All references are to this edition.

119. Fred Blick, 'Shakespeare's Musical Sonnets: Numbers 8, 128, and Pythagoras', *Upstart Crow* 19 (1999), 152–68, 153.

120. Bacon, *Sylva Sylvarum (1626)*, cited in Blick, 'Musical Sonnets', 154.

121. Røstvig, *Hidden Sense*, p. 31.

122. Boethius, *De Arithmetica*, II, xxxii, cited in Heninger, *Sweet Harmony*, p. 104.

123. On the harmonic ratios see Heninger, *Sweet Harmony*, p. 98.

124. Vendler, *The Art of Shakespeare's Sonnets*, p. 81.

125. Blick, 'Musical Sonnets', 153.

126. Blick, 'Musical Sonnets', 157.

127. Marsilio Ficino to Sebastiano Foresi, *Letters of Marsilio Ficino*, vol. V, Letter 21, p. 37.

128. Duncan-Jones, 'Introduction', *Shakespeare's Sonnets*, p. 97.

129. Fowler, *Triumphal Forms*, p. 190; see also Roche, *Petrarch*, p. 420.

130. Fowler, *Triumphal Forms*, p. 184.

131. Røstvig, *Hidden Sense*, p. 8.

132. Fowler, *Triumphal Forms*, pp. 185, 189.

133. Fowler, *Triumphal Forms*, p. 186.

134. Fowler, *Triumphal Forms*, pp. 186–7.

135. Røstvig, *Hidden Sense*, p. 32.

136. Røstvig, *Configurations*, p. 22.

137. John Milton, 'On Shakespeare', in John Carey (ed.), *Milton: Complete Shorter Poems* (London: Longman, 1968), 123. All references are to this edition.

138. Debus, *Robert Fludd*, p. 152.

139. Whigham and Rebhorn (eds.), '*The Art of English Poesy*', p. 184.

140. Hildemarie Streich, 'Introduction' to Maier, *Atalanta Fugiens*, p. 67.

141. Discussed in Fowler, *Triumphal Forms*, pp. 18–19.

142. See Henry Vaughan, 'The Importunate Fortune, written to Doctor Powel of Cantre', in L. C. Martin (ed.), *The Works of Henry Vaughan* (Oxford: Clarendon Press, 1957), pp. 636, 758 (note).

143. See Elizabeth D. Harvey, 'Flesh Colours and Shakespeare's Sonnets', in Schoenfeldt, *Companion*, p. 325. Interestingly, the moon is associated with Urania and the mind in this period, see, for example, William Basse, *Urania: The Woman in the Moon*, in Foure Cantoes (London, 1612).

3 THE DARK MISTRESS AND THE ART
OF BLACKNESS

1. All quotations from Shakespeare's sonnets are from Colin Burrow (ed.), *The Complete Sonnets and Poems* (Oxford: Oxford University Press, 2002).
2. All quotations from *Astrophil and Stella* are from Katherine Duncan-Jones (ed.), *Sir Philip Sidney: A Critical Edition of the Major Works* (Oxford: Oxford University Press, 1989).
3. Kim F. Hall, *Things of Darkness: Economies of Race and Gender in Early Modern England* (Ithaca and London: Cornell University Press, 1995), pp. 64, 71.
4. Hall, *Things of Darkness*, pp. 62–122.
5. In relation to the poems of Edward Herbert, Michael Morgan Holmes has argued that 'Hall's argument about the "poetics of color" does not explain the decidedly philosophical bent' of the poems; see *Early Modern Metaphysical Literature: Nature, Custom and Strange Desires* (Basingstoke: Palgrave, 2001), p. 62.
6. Edmund Spenser, *Amoretti*, in Ernest De Selincourt (ed.), *Spenser's Minor Poems* (Oxford: Oxford University Press, 1910).
7. William Joseph Sheils, Oxford *DNB*, 2004: http://www.oxforddnb.com/articles/29/29311-article.html, p. 2 of 17.
8. All references to Jonson's masques are to Stephen Orgel (ed.), *Ben Jonson: The Complete Masques* (New Haven and London: Yale University Press, 1969). Lady Herbert was among the blacked-up masquers and her hieroglyph was Diaphane – the figure icosahedron of crystal; the queen's was Euphoris – a golden tree laden with fruit (p. 57). As we shall see in my discussion of *A Lovers Complaint* in Chapter 4, crystal and trees laden with fruit have alchemical-philosophical meanings.
9. Thomas Browne, 'Of the Same', *Pseudoxia Epidemica* (London, 1646), p. 333.
10. Joseph Hall, *An Open and Plaine Paraphrase, upon the Song of Songs, which is Salomons* (London, 1609), p. 14.
11. Elias Ashmole, Prologema, *Theatrum Chemicum Britannicum* (London, 1651), sig. B2r.
12. For example in Geoffrey Whitney, *A Choice of Emblemes* (London, 1586).
13. Thomas Norton, *The Ordinall of Alchimy*, in Ashmole, *Theatrum Chemicum*, p. 56. All references are to this edition.
14. G. C. Moore Smith (ed.), *The Poems, English and Latin, of Edward, Lord Herbert of Cherbury* (Oxford: Clarendon Press, 1923), pp. 37–9, 60. All references are to this edition.
15. Marsilio Ficino, *Commentary on Plato's Symposium on Love*, trans. Sears Jayne (Dallas, Texas: Spring Publications, Inc., 1988). All references are to this edition. This text is most commonly referred to by the shortened title of *De amore*.
16. William Bloomfield, *Bloomfield's Blossoms*, in Elias Ashmole, *Theatrum Chemicum*, p. 313. All references are to this edition.
17. See Holmes, *Metaphysical Literature*, p. 57; Holmes adds that this is in line with Herbert's *De Veritate, De Religione Gentilium*. Roy Strong, *The English Renaissance Miniature* (London: Thames and Hudson, 1983), p. 184.

18. Sir Thomas Browne, *Religio Medici*. Cited in Stanton J. Linden, *Darke Hieroglyphicks* (Kentucky: University Press of Kentucky, 1996), p. 224.

19. In Laurence Mason (ed.), *The English Poems of Henry King* (New Haven: Yale University Press, 1914), p. 16. The poem was apparently sent to King by Rainold.

20. King, *The English Poems*, p. 17.

21. Henry Vaughan, 'Affliction', in L. C. Martin (ed.), *The Works of Henry Vaughan* (Oxford: Clarendon Press, 1957), p. 662.

22. George Herbert, 'To the Right Hon. The L. Chancellor' (Bacon), in F. E. Hutchinson (ed.), *The Works of George Herbert* (Oxford: Oxford University Press, 1941), p. 209.

23. Richard Crashaw, 'On the Baptised Aethiopian', in L. C. Martin (ed.), *The Poems of Richard Crashaw* (Oxford: Clarendon Press, 1957), p. 85.

24. George Ripley, *The Compound of Alchymie*, in Ashmole, *Theatrum Chemicum*, p. 150. All references are to this edition.

25. Omohundro Institute of Early American Culture, http://www.wm.edu/oieahc/uncommon/118/drake.htm, 1 of 2.

26. Mary Edmond, *Hilliard and Oliver: The Lives and Works of Two Great Miniaturists* (London: Robert Hale, 1983), p. 74; Erna Auerbach, *Nicholas Hilliard* (London: Routledge, 1961), p. 187; *Princely Magnificence: Court Jewels of the Renaissance, 1500–1630* (London: Debrett's in association with the Victoria and Albert Museum, 1980), entry 40; Omohundro Institute, 1–2.

27. Karen C. C. Dalton, 'Art for the Sake of Dynasty', in *Early Modern Visual Culture: Representation, Race, and Empire in Renaissance England* (Philadelphia: University of Pennsylvania Press, 2002), p. 186.

28. Dalton, 'Art', p. 186. On Elizabeth I as Mercury, see Douglas Brooks-Davies, *The Mercurian Monarch* (Manchester: Manchester University Press, 1983).

29. Sir John Davies, *Hymnes to Astraea* (London, 1599), 'Hymn I. Of Astrae', in Robert Krueger (ed.), *The Poems of Sir John Davies* (Oxford: Clarendon Press, 1975), p. 71; cited in Dalton, 'Art', p. 201.

30. *Princely Magnificence*, entry 46; Edmond, *Hilliard and Oliver*, pp. 74–5.

31. Omohundro Institute, 1–2; see also Dalton, *Art*, p. 188.

32. Sir Walter Raleigh's *Discoverie of . . . Guiana* (London, 1596) similarly represents Spanish Catholic corruptions as in need of purifying by English interventions.

33. Artephius, cited in Lyndy Abraham, *A Dictionary of Alchemical Imagery* (Cambridge: Cambridge University Press, 1998), p. 27.

34. John Kerrigan, 'Introduction', *The Sonnets and A Lover's Complaint* (London: Penguin, 1986), p. 58.

35. Morian, cited in Abraham, *Dictionary*, p. 27.

36. See James J. Clauss and Sarah Iles Johnston (eds.), *Medea: Essays in Myth, Literature, Philosophy and Art* (New Jersey: Princeton University Press, 1997), especially 'Introduction' by Sarah Iles Johnston, pp. 3–17.

37. Iles Johnston, *Medea*, pp. 5, 14, 6, 8.

38. *Odyssey* 12.70 cited in Iles Johnston, *Medea*, p. 1

39. Sir Walter Raleigh, *The History of the World*, ed. C. A. Patrides (Basingstoke: Macmillan, 1971), p. 209.

40. Cited in Titus Burckhardt, *Alchemy* (Dorset: Element Books, 1986), p. 121, from a French translation: Robert Buchère, *Le Voile d'Isis* (Paris, 1921), p. 183.
41. Cited in Burckhardt, *Alchemy*, p. 122.
42. For the psychoanalyst Jung such dark female types are personifications and archetypes of 'a man's unconscious' or 'anima': 'the anima also stands for the "inferior" function and for that reason frequently has a shady character; in fact she sometimes stands for evil itself . . . She is the dark and dreaded maternal womb, which is of an essentially ambivalent nature'; see H. Read, M. S. M. Fordham and G. Adler (eds.), R. F. C. Hull (trans.), *Collected Works by C. G. Jung*, 20 vols. (London: Routledge, 1979), vol. XII, pp. 150–1. Psychic 'integration' is for Jung the bringing together of chaotic unconscious with consciousness – a synthesis of psychic opposites.
43. Burckhardt, *Alchemy*, p. 122.
44. See William H. Huseman, 'The Entry of Heresy into the Emblem Tradition: Circe and the Great Whore of Babylon', in Alison Adams and Anthony J. Harper (eds.), *The Emblem in Renaissance and Baroque Europe: Tradition and Variety* (Leiden: E. J. Brill, 1992), pp. 181–211.
45. Charles Segal, 'Circean Temptations: Homer, Vergil, Ovid', *Transactions and Proceedings of the American Philological Association*, 99 (1968), 419–42, especially 425; citation from 428.
46. Paul Eugene Memmo (ed. and trans.), *Giordano Bruno's The Heroic Frenzies* (Chapel Hill: The University of North Carolina Press, 1964), p. 76. All references are to this edition.
47. *Heroic Frenzies*, p. 62.
48. Aurelian Townshend, *Tempe Restored*, in David Lindley (ed.), *Court Masques* (Oxford: Oxford University Press, 1995), p. 163. All references are to this edition and are cited by page in the text.
49. Helen Vendler, *The Art of Shakespeare's Sonnets* (Cambridge, Mass.: Harvard University Press, 1997), p. 574.
50. Vendler, *Art of Shakespeare's Sonnets*, p. 574, suggests, for example, that lines 5–10 of Sonnet 135 could be addressed to God: there are pronounced resonances of liturgical prayer and echoes from Ecclesiastes 1: 6–7, 'All the rivers run into the sea; yet the sea is not full.'
51. Kerrigan, 'Introduction', *Sonnets*, p. 10. Burckhardt, *Alchemy*, p. 120.
52. Burckhardt, *Alchemy*, p. 32.
53. Burckhardt, *Alchemy*, p. 32.
54. Ashmole, *Theatrum Chemicum*, sig. A4r.
55. Burckhardt, *Alchemy*, p. 123.
56. Burckhardt, *Alchemy*, pp. 123, 118.
57. Fred Blick, 'Shakespeare's Musical Sonnets: Numbers 8, 128, and Pythagoras', *Upstart Crow*, 19 (1999), 152–68, especially 160–3.
58. *The Letters of Marsilio Ficino*, trans. Language Department, London School of Economic Science, 7 vols. (London: Shepheard-Walwyn Ltd, 1975–), vol. VII, Letter 76, p. 87. All references to Ficino's *Letters* are to this edition.

59. As John Manning has stressed in *The Emblem* (London: Reaktion Books, 2002), 'dark riddles' and 'conceited conundrums' are the very stuff of this linguistic universe of Love (he is reflecting on the period's emblem books and other 'heroic enthusiasms'). In these circumstances, confusion is inevitable and is the source of much playful verbal and visual humour and wit; see pp. 167, 172. For example, Alciato's emblems include one 'On the Statue of Love', which appears satirically to question why Cupid needs a blindfold if he is blind, p. 168.

60. Katherine Duncan-Jones, 'Introduction', *Shakespeare's Sonnets* (London: Arden Shakespeare; Thomson Learning, 2004), pp. 50, 51.

61. Norton, *Ordinall of Alchimy*, in Elias Ashmole, *Theatrum Chemicum*, pp. 67, 71.

62. See discussion of Medea above, pp. 110–12.

63. Burckhardt, *Alchemy*, pp. 187–8.

64. R. Warwick Bond (ed.), *The Poetical Works of William Basse* (London: Ellis and Elvey, 1893). All references are to this edition.

65. On the implications of Urania around 1600 see Alison Shell, *Catholicism and Controversy and the English Literary Imagination, 1558–1660* (Cambridge: Cambridge University Press, 1999), p. 69.

66. Duncan-Jones, *Shakespeare's Sonnets*, p. 400.

67. Gloss, Psalm 68, p. 37, in *The Booke of Psalmes: Collected into English Meeter, by Thomas Sternehold, John Hopkins and Others … with apt notes to sing them withall*, appended to the 1599 Geneva Bible.

68. This is a translation of the French ('couvertes du voile des feintes Amoureuses') by de Rola, from the title page of François Beroalde de Verville's *Le Tableau des riches inventions* (Paris, 1600), reproduced in de Rola, *The Golden Game*, pp. 25–6.

69. See the description in the stages of the Hermetic ascent listed in note on p. 758, Martin (ed.), *The Works of Henry Vaughan*.

70. See Chapter 5.

71. Martin Ruland, *A Lexicon of Alchemy*, 1612, trans. from Latin by A. E. Waite (London, 1892), p. 226.

72. Burckhardt, *Alchemy*, p. 127.

73. Burckhardt, *Alchemy*, p. 127.

74. See, for example, Margreta De Grazia, 'Babbling Will in Shake-speares Sonnets 127 to 154', *Spenser Studies* I (1980), 121–34. Thomas Roche, *Petrarch and the English Sonnet Sequences* (New York: AMS Press, 1989), pp. 429, 439.

75. Edgar Wind, *Pagan Mysteries in the Renaissance* (Harmondsworth: Peregrine, 1967), p. 69.

76. Cited in Wind, *Pagan Mysteries*, p. 60.

77. See extensive discussion in Wind, *Pagan Mysteries*, pp. 53–80.

78. Cited in Wind, *Pagan Mysteries*, p. 79.

79. Henry Reynolds, *Mythomystes* (1632), in J. E. Spingarn (ed.), *Critical Essays of the Seventeenth Century* (Bloomington and London: Indiana University Press, 1957), p. 151.

80. Campion, Poem XV, in Walter R. Davies (ed.), *The Works of Thomas Campion* (London: Faber & Faber, 1969), p. 182.
81. Vendler, *Shakespeare's Sonnets*, pp. 648–9; Roche, *Petrarch*, p. 439; De Grazia, 'Babbling Will', 132; Burrow, *Complete Sonnets*, p. 686.
82. Roche, *Petrarch*, p. 439.
83. Vendler, *Shakespeare's Sonnets*, pp. 649, 648; De Grazia, 'Babbling Will', 132, 129.
84. See Margaret Healy, *Fictions of Disease in Early Modern England: Bodies, Plagues and Politics* (Basingstoke: Palgrave 2001), p. 129.
85. De Grazia, 'Babbling Will', 132.
86. Roche, *Petrarch*, p. 461.
87. Roche, *Petrarch*, p. 96.
88. Manning, *The Emblem*, p. 167.
89. Manning, *The Emblem*, p. 168.
90. Cited in Peggy Munoz Simonds, 'Eros and Anteros in Shakespeare's Sonnets 153 and 154: An Iconographical Study', in *Spenser Studies*, 7 (1986), 261–325, 274.
91. Manning, *The Emblem*, p. 169.
92. Manning, *The Emblem*, p. 169.
93. Otto Vaenius, *Amorum Emblematum* (Antwerp, 1608). All page references cited parenthetically in the text are to this edition. See Simonds, 'Eros and Anteros', 268. Mario Praz, 'Profane and Sacred Love', in *Studies in Seventeenth-Century Imagery*, 2nd edn, 2 vols. (Rome: Edizioni di Storia e Letteratura, 1964), vol. 1, pp. 115–17, especially p. 115.
94. See Manning's detailed description, *The Emblem*, pp. 176–7.
95. Otto Vaenius, *Amoris Divine Emblemata* (Antwerp, 1615). See Manning, *The Emblem*, p. 177.
96. Ben Jonson alludes to *Eros* and *Anteros* in a number of his masques, including *Cynthia's Revels*, *Love Restored* and *Love's Welcome*.
97. Simonds, 'Eros and Anteros'.
98. Ruland, *Lexicon*, p. 400.
99. Isaac Newton, Keynes MS18, 'on the distillation of philosophical mercury – the philosopher's stone', cited in Abraham, 'Diana', *Dictionary*, p. 54.
100. Simonds, 'Eros and Anteros', 263. A 'Well' is featured in Johann Mylius's *Philosophia Reformata* (Frankfurt, 1622): Emblem 16 depicts the philosopher's stone in its silver and gold perfection arising out of the Well of Alchemy.
101. Abraham, *Dictionary*, p. 18.
102. Michael Maier, *Atalanta Fugiens*, in *Atalanta Fugiens: An Edition of the Fugues, Emblems and Epigrams*, trans. from Latin by Joscelyn Godwin, Introduction by Hildemarie Streich (Grand Rapids, Mich.: Phanes Press, 1989), p. 173.

4   A LOVERS COMPLAINT

This is the title as it appears in the 1609 quarto and I have used it throughout because it conveys the possibility of lovers being both one and plural simultaneously – the modern imposition of an apostrophe unhelpfully limits the poem's fluid possibilities. All references apart from the title are to Colin Burrow (ed.), *The Complete Sonnets and Poems* (Oxford: Oxford University Press, 2002), pp. 695–717.

1. On Soloman's Seal see Titus Burckhardt, *Alchemy: Science of the Cosmos, Science of the Soul*, trans. William Stoddart (Dorset: Element Books, 1967), p. 74.
2. See discussion above, Chapter 2, pp. 94–6.
3. Michael Maier, *Atalanta Fugiens*, in *Atalanta Fugiens: An Edition of the Fugues, Emblems and Epigrams*, trans. Joscelyn Godwin, with an Introduction by Hildemarie Streich (Grand Rapids, Mich.: Phanes Press, 1989), pp. 102–3.
4. Quentin Skinner, in a lecture at the University of Sussex, 17 October 2006, argued that in the 1590s Shakespeare was obsessed with 'coloured speech' and its potential for deception, associated particularly with paradiastole.
5. These issues were highly topical in 1609 following the publication in 1608 of George Hakewill's polemical *The Vanitie of the Eie*, which relentlessly explored visual paradoxes and delusions.
6. Paul Eugene Memmo (ed. and trans.), *Giordano Bruno's The Heroic Frenzies* (Chapel Hill: The University of North Carolina Press, 1964), p. 226.
7. See, for example, Jennifer Richards, 'Transforming a Mirror for Magistrates', in Margaret Healy and Thomas Healy (eds.), *Renaissance Transformations: The Making of English Writing, 1500–1650* (Edinburgh: Edinburgh University Press, 2009), pp. 48–63.
8. See Richard Underwood, *Shakespeare on Love: Prolegomena to a Variorum Edition of 'A Lover's Complaint'* (Salzburg: Institut für Anglistik and Amerikanistik, University of Salzburg, 1985); and Shirley Sharon-Zisser and Stephen Whitworth, 'Generating Dialogue on Shakespeare's *A Lover's Complaint*', in *Critical Essays on Shakespeare's 'A Lover's Complaint'* (Aldershot: Ashgate, 2006), pp. 1–53. They point out that thirteen of Thorpe's original 1609 quartos have survived: a surprisingly large number, indicating that the volume's 'first readers were keen to preserve the poetry contained in it', p. 36.
9. Ilona Bell, '"That Which Thou Hast Done": Shakespeare's Sonnets and *A Lover's Complaint*', in James Schiffer (ed.), *Shakespeare's Sonnets: Critical Essays* (New York and London: Garland, 1999), pp. 455–74, 455; John Kerrigan, *The Sonnets and A Lover's Complaint* (London: Penguin, 1986), p. 389. See also Kerrigan, *Motives of Woe: Shakespeare and Female Complaint* (Oxford: Clarendon Press, 1991).
10. Kerrigan, *The Sonnets*, p. 389.
11. Bell, 'That Which Thou Hast Done', p. 455.
12. Brian Vickers, *Shakespeare, 'A Lover's Complaint' and John Davies of Hereford* (Cambridge: Cambridge University Press, 2007) argues that the poem's real author is John Davies of Hereford. Vickers' argument has been countered by MacDonald P. Jackson in '*A Lovers Complaint, Cymbeline*, and the Shakespeare Canon: Interpreting Shared Vocabulary', *Modern Language Review*, 103: 3 (July 2008), 621–38, who re-stresses the links between this poem and Shakespeare's

other works, especially *Cymbeline*. Jackson draws on a word study by G. Sarrazin, 'Wortechos bei Shakespeare', *Shakespeare Jahrbuch*, 33 (1897), 121–65.

13. Jackson, 'A Lovers Complaint', 622.
14. Vickers, *Shakespeare's 'A Lovers Complaint'*, p. 213.
15. Vickers, *Shakespeare's 'A Lovers Complaint'*, p. 203.
16. Vickers, *Shakespeare's 'A Lovers Complaint'*, p. 100.
17. Vickers, *Shakespeare's 'A Lovers Complaint'*, p. 111.
18. Vickers, *Shakespeare's 'A Lovers Complaint'*, pp. 2, 154–93, 232–66.
19. Kerrigan, *The Sonnets*, p. 389. Colin Burrow in the Oxford edition, Walter Cohen in Stephen Greenblatt's Norton edition, Duncan-Jones in the Arden edition and John Roe in the Cambridge edition all believe that Shakespeare is the *Complaint's* author. For a thorough summary of critical views see Sharon-Zisser and Whitworth, 'Generating Dialogue', pp. 1–53.
20. Cited in Bell, 'That Which Thou Hast Done', p. 456.
21. Burrow, 'Introduction', *Complete Sonnets*, p. 141.
22. Burrow, 'Introduction', *Complete Sonnets*, pp. 141, 142.
23. All quotations from Donne's poetry are from Herbert J. C. Grierson (ed.), *The Poems of John Donne* (Oxford: Oxford University Press, 1912).
24. Lyndy Abraham, *A Dictionary of Alchemical Imagery* (Cambridge: Cambridge University Press, 1998) pp. 35, 37.
25. Abraham, *Dictionary*, p. 38.
26. In H. R. Woudhuysen (ed.), *The Penguin Book of Renaissance Verse* (London: Penguin, 1992), p. 662.
27. Abraham, *Dictionary*, pp. 38–9.
28. Bruno, *Heroic Frenzies*, p. 226.
29. See Michael Schoenfeldt, 'Eloquent Blood and Deliberative Bodies: The Physiology of Metaphysical Poetry', in *Renaissance Transformations: The Making of English Writing 1500–1650* (Edinburgh: Edinburgh University Press, 2009), pp. 145–61.
30. Bell, 'That Which Thou Hast Done', p. 456.
31. Stanley Wells and Gary Taylor (eds.), *The Complete Works*, compact edition (Oxford: Oxford University Press, 1998). All references to Shakespeare's plays are to this edition.
32. Heather Dubrow, '"Lending Soft Audience to my Sweet Design": Shifting Roles and Shifting Readings of Shakespeare's "A Lover's Complaint"', *Shakespeare Survey*, 58 (2005) 23–33, has highlighted the porous boundaries between speakers and audience in *A Lovers Complaint*, 26.
33. Abraham, *Dictionary*, p. 155.
34. Vickers, *Shakespeare's 'A Lovers Complaint'*, p. 243.
35. Martin Rulandus, *A Lexicon of Alchemy* (1612), trans. from Latin by A. E. Waite (London, 1892), p. 384. See also Abraham, *Dictionary*, p. 115.
36. Abraham, *Dictionary*, pp. 78–9.
37. Marie-Louise von Franz (ed.), *Saint Thomas Aquinas, Aurora Consurgens*, (London: Routledge & Kegan Paul, 1966), p. 349.

38. In A. E. Waite (ed.), *Hermetic Museum*, 1678 (York Beach, Maine: Samuel Weiser, 1991), p. 47; also cited in Abraham, *Dictionary*, p. 78.

39. Ruland, *Lexicon*, p. 384.

40. Maier, *Atalanta Fugiens* (1618), p. 111.

41. *OED* III. 2.

42. Abraham, *Dictionary*, p. 50.

43. Richard Crashaw, 'The Weeper', in L. C. Martin (ed.), *The Poems of Richard Crashaw* (Oxford: Clarendon Press, 1951).

44. Lyndy Abraham, *Marvell and Alchemy* (Aldershot: Scolar Press, 1990), p. 168.

45. In L. C. Martin (ed.), *The Works of Henry Vaughan* (Oxford: Clarendon Press, 1957). All references are to this edition.

46. Bruno, *Heroic Frenzies*, p. 226.

47. Burrow, *Complete Sonnets*, p. 699.

48. Burrow, *Complete Sonnets*, p. 700.

49. Kerrigan, *The Sonnets*, p. 405; Burrow, *Complete Sonnets*, p. 700.

50. Katherine Duncan-Jones (ed.), *Shakespeare's Sonnets* (London: Arden Shakespeare; Thomson Learning, 2004), p. 437.

51. Kerrigan, *The Sonnets*, p. 405.

52. Definition of 'hue' in James Orchard Halliwell, *Dictionary of Archaic Words* (London: Bracken Books, 1989), p. 465.

53. Dubrow, 'Lending Soft Audience', 30.

54. Bell, 'That Which Thou Hast Done', p. 464.

55. Bell, 'That Which Thou Hast Done', p. 471. Vickers, *Shakespeare's 'A Lovers Complaint'*, simply ignores the web of interconnections between the sonnets and *A Lovers Complaint*.

56. These disparaging epithets are used repeatedly by Vickers to argue that the poem is really by Davies of Hereford.

57. Abraham, *Dictionary*, p. 208.

58. Johann Siebmacher, *The Sophic Hydrolith*, in *Hermetic Museum* (1678), cited in Abraham, *Dictionary*, p. 208.

59. Eirenaeus Philalethes, *Ripley Reviv'd* (1678), cited in Abraham, *Dictionary*, p. 208.

60. For lengthy discussions of these terms see Abraham, *Dictionary*, pp. 214, 81.

61. Stephen Orgel, *Ben Jonson: The Complete Masques* (New Haven and London: Yale University Press, 1969), p. 32. All references to Jonson's masques are to this edition.

62. Herbert Arthur Evans, *English Masques* (London: Blackie and Son, 1929), p. 91. All references to this work are cited from this edition.

63. Richard Davies, *Chester's Triumph in Honour of Her Prince* (St George's Day, 1610), cited in Douglas Brooks-Davies, *The Mercurian Monarch: Magical Politics from Spenser to Pope* (Manchester: Manchester University Press, 1983), p. 90.

64. J. Nichols, *The Progresses, Processions and Magnificent Festivities of King James the First* (London, 1828), II, 291ff, cited in Brooks-Davies, *Mercurian Monarch*, p. 90.

65. *The Letters of Marsilio Ficino*, translated from Latin by members of the Language Department, School of Economic Science, London, 7 vols. (London: Shepheard-Walwyn, 1975–) vol. v, Letter 21 (1479), p. 38. All references are to this edition.
66. Ficino, *Letters*, vol. vi, Letter 42, p. 56.
67. See the illustration in Duncan-Jones, 'Introduction', *Shakespeare's Sonnets*, p. 24.
68. Adam McLean (ed.), *The Rosary of the Philosophers*, 1550 (Edinburgh: Magnum Opus Hermetic Source Works, 1980), p. 18.
69. Martin Luther, *The Table Talk of Martin Luther*, trans. William Hazlitt (London: G. Bell, 1902), DCCCV.
70. Vickers, *Shakespeare's 'A Lovers Complaint'*, p. 254, describes this passage as particularly redolent with 'grotesque' metaphors unworthy of Shakespeare.
71. Thomas Norton, *Ordinall of Alchimy*, in Elias Ashmole, *Theatrum Chemicum Britannicum* (London, 1651), p. 90.
72. Petrus Bonus, *Zoroaster's Cave*, in George Thor (ed.), *Raphael Iconius Eglinus, An Easie Introduction to the Philosopher's Magical Gold* (London: Mathew Smelt, 1667), pp. 85–6.
73. Dubrow, 'Lending Soft Audience', 30.
74. Michael Drayton, 'Endimion and Phoebe', in J. W. Hebel, Kathleen Tillotson and B. H. Newdigate (eds.), *The Works of Michael Drayton*, 5 vols. (Oxford: Basil Blackwell, 1930–41), vol . iv, p. 146, lines 647–52.
75. Andrew Marvell, 'The Nymph Complaining', in Nigel Smith (ed.), *The Poems of Andrew Marvell* (Harlow: Longman, 2003), pp. 69–71. All line references are to this edition.
76. Vickers, *Shakespeare's 'A Lovers Complaint'*, p. 6.
77. Both Bell, 'That Which Thou Hast Done', and Dubrow, 'Lending Soft Audience', focus on these aspects of the *Complaint*.
78. Catherine Bates, 'The Enigma of *A Lover's Complaint*', in Michael Schoenfeldt (ed.), *A Companion to Shakespeare's Sonnets* (Oxford: Blackwell, 2007), p. 437.
79. Dubrow, 'Lending Soft Audience', 29.
80. On this mystery Burckhardt, *Alchemy*, declares: 'In so far as the human intellect, as a result of a more or less complete union with the Universal Intellect, turns away from the multiplicity of things and so to say ascends towards undivided unity, so the knowledge of nature which a man obtains from such a nature cannot be of a purely rational or discursive kind', p. 41.
81. Vickers, *Shakespeare's 'A Lover's Complaint'*, cites the poem's alleged didacticism as making it more likely to be by the lesser poet, John Davies.
82. Burrow, *Complete Sonnets*, pp. 144, 145.
83. On this point see 'Introduction', *Heroic Frenzies*, pp. 40–1.
84. Paracelsus, *Nine Books of the Nature of Things*, cited in Abraham, *Dictionary*, p. 150.
85. Michael Maier, *Atalanta Fugiens*, see Emblem 9 and Epigram 9, depicting an 'old man' eating 'fruits of gold', p. 123.
86. Interestingly, St Augustine had associated alchemists with magic and the 'snares of demons'; see Brian P. Copenhaver, 'Introduction', *Hermetica: The*

Greek *'Corpus Hermeticum' and the Latin 'Asclepius' in a New English Translation* (Cambridge: Cambridge University Press, 1992), p. xxxii.

87. Stuart Clark, *Vanities of the Eye: Vision in Early Modern European Culture* (Oxford: Oxford University Press), p. 168.

88. In Copenhaver, *Hermetica*, pp. 33, 34.

89. George R. Potter and Evelyn M. Simpson (eds.), *The Sermons of John Donne*, 10 vols. (Berkeley and Los Angeles: University of California Press, 1953–62), vol. I, pp. 179, 226; vol. III, p. 121; vol. VI, pp. 150, 187; vol. VII, pp. 217, 446; discussed in David Wooton, 'John Donne's Religion of Love', in John Brooke and Ian Maclean (eds.), *Heterodoxy in Early Modern Science and Religion* (Oxford: Oxford University Press, 2005), pp. 31–58, pp. 48–9. See, for example, Robert Fludd, 'Mosaicall Philosophy', selections in Stanton J. Linden (ed.), *The Alchemy Reader: From Hermes Trismegistus to Isaac Newton* (Cambridge: Cambridge University Press, 2003), pp. 191–8.

90. M. Berthelot, *Bibliothèque des philosophes chimiques* (Paris, 1741); cited in Burckhardt, *Alchemy*, p. 96.

91. Henry Peacham, *The Garden of Eloquence* (London, 1593), pp. 41–2.

92. Shirley Sharon-Zisser foregrounds this in a fascinating essay, applying a Lacanian reading in which the *Complaint's* ending 'speaks not abjection but masochistic jouissance'; see '"True to Bondage": The Rhetorical Forms of Female Masochism in *A Lover's Complaint*', in Sharon-Zisser (ed.), *Critical Essays on Shakespeare's A Lover's Complaint: Suffering Ecstasy* (Aldershot: Ashgate, 2006), p. 187.

5 INNER LOOKING, ALCHEMY AND THE CREATIVE IMAGINATION

1. Francesco Petrarch, 'To Dionigi Da Borgo San Sepolcro of the Order of Saint Augustine, Professor of the Holy Page, on Personal Matters' (26 April 1336, Malaucene), in Rodney Lokaj (trans.), *Familiarum rerum libri. IV. I, Petrarch's Ascent of Mount Ventoux: Familiaris IV* (Rome: Edizioni dell'Ateneo, 2006), p. 101. All page references, cited in parentheses in the text, refer to this edition.

2. Augustine, *Confessions Books I–XIII*, in F. J. Sheed (ed.), Peter Brown (Intro.), *Augustine: Confessions* (Indianapolis: Hackett: 1993), Bk 10, viii, p. 180.

3. Lokaj, 'Introduction', *Petrarch's Ascent*, p. 79.

4. Lokaj, 'Introduction', *Petrarch's Ascent*, p. 95.

5. Michel de Montaigne, *Essays*, trans. John Florio (1603), 3 vols. (London: J. M. Dent & Sons Ltd, 1910), vol. III, p. 331. All references are to this edition in the original English translation by John Florio.

6. Most notably Joel Fineman, *Shakespeare's Perjured Eye: The Invention of Poetic Subjectivity in the Sonnets* (Berkeley, Los Angeles and London: University of California Press, 1988): 'Shakespeare's sonnets inaugurate and give a name to the modernist literary self', p. 29

7. Nicholas Spice, 'I Must be Mad', *London Review of Books*, 8 January 2004, p. 12.

8. Jolande Jacobi (ed.), Norbert Guterman (trans.), *Paracelsus: Selected Writings* (Princeton: Bollingen Series XXVIII, Princeton University Press, 1988), part 1, vol. II, 186–8, p. 93.
9. John Rogers explores the politics of this in *The Matter of Revolution: Science, Poetry and Politics in the Age of Milton* (Ithaca and London: Cornell University Press, 1996).
10. Heinrich Khunrath, *Amphitheatrum Sapientiae Aeternae* (Hanau, 1609). The title page illustrates a spiritual laboratory juxtaposed to a practical laboratory and proclaims Khunrath to be 'a true lover of philosophy and a doctor of both medicines'. The image on the title page of Michael Maier, *Tripus Aureus* (Frankfurt, 1618) juxtaposes a library inhabited by philosophers and a cleric to a practical laboratory. These illustrations confirm that in the early seventeenth century alchemy was construed in inner and outer terms as having both spiritual and material refining implications.
11. Robert M. Schuler, 'Some Spiritual Alchemies of Seventeenth-Century England', *Journal of the History of Ideas*, 41: 2 (April–June, 1980), 293–318, 304–6, 306. Schuler comments on 'the strict schematization of alchemical concepts with corresponding Calvinist dogmas', 306.
12. Willis F. Whitehead (ed.), *Henry Cornelius Agrippa: Occult Philosophy or Magic*, 1651 (London: The Aquarian Press, 1971), pp. 42–3.
13. Ben Jonson's prefatory poem in Shakespeare's First Folio notably associates this same chain of influence with Shakespeare's 'powers'; see Chapter 6.
14. Paul Eugene Memmo (trans. and Introduction), *Giordano Bruno's The Heroic Frenzies* (Chapel Hill: The University of North Carolina Press, 1964), p. 166. All references are to this edition.
15. A rather fine example is Emblem LXXIX in Guillaume La Perriere, *Le theatre des bons engines* (1544) about 'feu de repentence', which ends, 'Voyez amour distiller eau de larmes.'
16. Luis de la Puente, *Meditations upon the Mysteries of our Holie Faith, with the Practise of Mental Prayer touching the same*, trans. John Heigham, 2 vols. (St Omer, 1619), vol. II, pp. 25–6. All references are to this edition.
17. James H. McDonald and Nancy Pollard Brown (eds.), *The Poems of Robert Southwell S.J.* (Oxford: Clarendon Press, 1967), p. 15. All references are to this edition.
18. Giovanni Pico della Mirandola, *Heptaplus*, cited in John S. Mebane, *Renaissance Magic and the Return of the Golden Age* (Lincoln and London: University of Nebraska Press, 1989), p. 49.
19. Hildemarie Streich, Introductory Essay to Michael Maier, *Atalanta Fugiens: An Edition of the Fugues, Emblems and Epigrams*, trans. Jocelyn Godwin (Grand Rapids, Mich.: Phanes Press, 1989), p. 85.
20. Streich, Introductory Essay, p. 11.
21. Louis L. Martz, *The Poetry of Meditation: A Study of English Literature of the Seventeenth Century*, rev. edn (New Haven and London: Yale University Press, 1962), p. 70.

22. L. C. Martin (ed.), *The Works of Henry Vaughan* (Oxford: Clarendon Press, 1957), pp. 405–7.

23. Luis de Granada, *Of Prayer and Meditation*, 1612, trans. Richard Hopkins (Douay, 1612), pp. 288–9.

24. Diego de Estella, *The Contempte of the World, and the Vanitie therof*, trans. 'G.C.' (? Douay, 1584), fo. 213v.

25. Martz, *Poetry*, p. xvi.

26. Martz, Poetry, p. xvi.

27. De Granada, *Of Prayer*, pp. 220–1; Martz, *Poetry*, p. 138.

28. Martz, *Poetry*, p. xvii.

29. Louis Richeome, *The Pilgrime of Loreto*, 1604, trans. 'E.W' (Paris, 1629), p. 50.

30. St François de Sales, *A Treatise of the Love of God*, 1616, trans. Thomas Carre (Douay, 1630), pp. 324–5. All references are to this edition.

31. St François de Sales, *An Introduction to a Devoute Life*, trans. John Yakesley, 3rd edn (Rouen, 1614), p. 357.

32. Luis de la Puente, *Meditations*, vol. 1, p. 430.

33. John Manning, *The Emblem* (London: Reaktion Books, 2002), p. 167.

34. Martz, *Poetry*, p. 125. Lorenzo Scupoli, *The Spiritual Combat*, trans. William Lester and Robert Mohan (Westminster: Newman Bookshop, 1947). The first English translation was printed at Louvain in 1589. All references are to this edition.

35. Martz, *Poetry*, pp. 125–31.

36. See Alastair Hamilton, *The Family of Love* (Cambridge: James Clarke, 1981), pp. 6–7. This text was very influential among members of the Family of Love in England around 1600.

37. Hamilton, *The Family of Love*, p. 6. I am indebted to Brenda Hosington for this information about Margaret Beaufort's translation.

38. Cited in Martz, *Poetry*, p. 285.

39. Martz, *Poetry*, p. 114.

40. Edward J. Klein (ed.), *The Imitation of Christ: From the First Edition of an English Translation Made c. 1530 by Richard Whitford* (New York: Harper, 1941), Bk 2, Ch. 8; cited in Martz, *Poetry*, p. 286.

41. Cited in Martz, *Poetry*, p. 286.

42. Joseph Pequigney has, for example, stressed the homosexual nature of the relationship: 'the interaction of the friends being sexual in both orientation and practice'; see *Such is My Love: A Study of Shakespeare's Sonnets* (Chicago: University of Chicago Press, 1985), p. 1; Joel Fineman, *Shakespeare's Perjured Eye: The Invention of Poetic Subjectivity in the Sonnets* (Berkeley: University of California Press, 1986), p. 272.

43. Fineman, *Perjured Eye*, p. 30.

44. Memmo, 'Introduction', *Heroic Frenzies*, p. 23.

45. Memmo, 'Introduction', *Heroic Frenzies*, p. 24.

46. For example, in relation to the numerology in the sonnets and in Sonnet 59 – the allusion to the Pythagorean Great Year.

47. Katherine Duncan-Jones (ed.), *Shakespeare's Sonnets* (London: Arden Shakespeare; Thomson Learning, 2004), p. 228, draws attention to this, alluding to *Metamorphosis*, 15.66ff, especially lines 431–48.
48. See Peter Sharratt, 'Love-Poetry in the Age of Humanism', in Keith Aspley and Peter France (eds.), *Poetry in France: Metamorphoses of a Muse* (Edinburgh: Edinburgh University Press, 1992), p. 55.
49. On Ronsard's sonnets see Sharratt, 'Love-Poetry', especially p. 56.
50. McDonald and Brown (eds.), *Poems of Robert Southwell*, p. 1.
51. Martz, *Poetry*, p. 184.
52. Manning, *The Emblem*, p. 26.
53. *The Letters of Marsilio Ficino*, trans. Language Department, School of Economic Science, London, 7 vols. (London: Shepheard-Walwyn Ltd, 1975–), vol. 1, Letter 4, To Michele Mercati, 'his beloved fellow philosopher. A theological dialogue between God and the soul', p. 36. All references to the *Letters* are to this edition.
54. Michael Drayton, 'Idea in Sixtie Three sonnets', in William Hebel (ed.), *The Works of Michael Drayton*, 5 vols. (Oxford: Basil Blackwell, 1961), vol. II, Sonnet 11, p. 311.
55. Edmund Spenser, 'Fowre Hymnes, made by Edm. Spenser', in Ernest De Selincourt (ed.), *Spenser's Minor Poems* (Oxford: Clarendon Press, 1910), p. 442.
56. William H. Stahl (trans. and ed.), *Macrobius's Commentary on the Dream of Scipio* (New York: Columbia University Press, 1952), pp. 100–1. On the Monad as God see Plotinus, *Enneads* VI. ix. 6 and V. i. 7.
57. Macrobius, *Dream of Scipio*, pp. 371–3.
58. Manning, *The Emblem*, p. 177.
59. John Donne, 'The First Anniversary', in Herbert Grierson (ed.), *The Poems of John Donne* (Oxford: Oxford University Press, 1958), p. 236. All references are to this edition.
60. 'Conversations with Drummond', in C. H. Herford and Percy and Evelyn Simpson (eds.), *Ben Jonson*, 11 vols. (Oxford: Clarendon Press, 1925–52), vol. 1, p. 133; this incident is recounted in Martz, *Poetry*, p. 228.
61. Sharrat, 'Love-Poetry', p. 59
62. Helen Wilcox, '"The Birth Day of My Selfe": John Donne, Martha Moulsworth and the Emergence of Individual Identity', in A. J. Piesse (ed.), *Sixteenth-Century Identities* (Manchester: Manchester University Press, 2000), p. 173.
63. *Works of Michael Drayton*, vol. II, p. 310.
64. Frank Whigham and Wayne A. Rebhorn (eds.), *The Art of English Poesy by George Puttenham: A Critical Edition* (Ithaca and London: Cornell University Press, 2007), I, 8, p. 110. All references are to this edition.
65. See above, Chapter 2, pp. 83–4.
66. Marsilio Ficino, *Commentary on Plato's Symposium on Love (De amore)*, trans. Sears Jayne (Dallas, Texas: Spring Publications Inc., 1988), p. 66. All references are to this edition.

67. Sir Philip Sidney, *An Apology for Poetry*, in G. Gregory Smith (ed.), *Elizabethan Critical Essays*, 2 vols. (Oxford: Oxford University Press, 1904), vol. 1, pp. 148–207, p. 155. All references are to this edition.

68. See Whigham and Rebhorn, 'Introduction', *The Art of English Poesy*, p. 30.

69. Jolane Jacobi (ed.), Norbert Guterman (trans.), *Paracelsus: Selected Writings* (Princeton: Princeton University Press, 1979), pp. 93, 143.

70. Giovanni Pico della Mirandola, 'Oration on the Dignity of Man', in Elizabeth Forbes (ed. and trans.), *Renaissance Philosophy of Man* (Chicago: University of Chicago Press, 1948), pp. 104–6. Jacob Burckhardt, *The Civilization of the Renaissance in Italy* (New York: Mentor, 1958), p. 257.

71. Hermes Trismegistus, *Asclepius*, in Brian P. Copenhaver, *Hermetica: The Greek 'Corpus Hermeticum' and the Latin 'Asclepius' in a New English Translation* (Cambridge: Cambridge University Press, 1992), p. 69. All references are to this edition. See discussion of Pico's vision in John S. Mebane, *Renaissance Magic and the Return of the Golden Age: The Occult Tradition and Marlowe, Jonson and Shakespeare* (Lincoln and London: University of Nebraska Press, 1989), pp. 36–52, esp. pp. 40–1. The Spanish humanist Juan Luis Vives wrote a tract, *A Fable About Man* (Louvain, 1518), which reveals he was very familiar with Pico's *Oratio*, and Erasmus's *Praise of Folly* is informed by it too. It is interesting that an early work of Thomas More was *The Life of Picus, Earl of Mirandula*.

72. J. B. Allen and John Warden (trans. and ed.), Marsilio Ficino, *Platonic Theology*, Bks I–IV (Harvard: Harvard University Press, 2001), p. 253. All references are to this edition.

73. John Cotta, *A Short Discoverie of Severall Sorts of Ignorant and Inconsiderate Practisers of Physicke in England* (London, 1619), p. 120.

74. Cited in Paulo Rossi, *Francis Bacon: From Magic to Science*, trans. Sacha Rabinovitch (London: Routledge & Kegan Paul, 1968), p. 21.

75. See my discussion of Jonson's and Milton's praise of the deceased poet in the terms of natural magic in Chapter 6.

76. Edmund Spenser, 'An Hymne in Honour of Love', in William A. Oram, Einar Bjorvand, Ronald Bond, Thomas H. Cain, Alexander Dunlop and Richard Schell (eds.), *The Yale Edition of the Shorter Poems of Edmund Spenser* (New Haven and London: Yale University Press, 1989), pp. 691–705. All references are to this edition.

77. See Ficino, *De amore*, p. 108, for example.

78. Duncan-Jones, *Shakespeare's Sonnets*, p. 332.

79. Geoffrey Bullough (ed.), *Poems and Dramas of Fulke Greville*, 2 vols. (Edinburgh: Oliver and Boyd, 1939), vol. 1, p. 156.

80. Sir John Davies, *Nosce Teipsum*, in Robert Krueger (ed.), *The Poems of Sir John Davies* (Oxford: Clarendon Press, 1975), p. 43. All references are to this edition.

81. W. B. Yeats, 'Epigraph to Volume 2', *Collected Works in Verse and Prose*, 8 vols. (Stratford-upon-Avon: Shakespeare Head Press, 1908), cited in Martz, *Poetry of Meditation*, p. 321.

82. Michael Drayton, 'The Tragicall Legend of Robert, Duke of Normandy', *The Works*, vol. 1, p. 262.

83. See A. W. Pollard and G. R. Redgrave, *A Short-Title Catalogue of Books Printed in England, Scotland, and Ireland and of English Books Printed Abroad, 1475–1640*, 3 vols. (London: Bibliographical Society, 1976–81), vol. II, p. 49: First Part, 1586, 1589, 1594, 1602, 1614; Second Part, 1589, 1605. Peter de la Primaudaye, *The Second Part of the French Academie* (London: George Bishop, 1605), title page. All references are to this edition.

84. Katherine S. Park, 'The Imagination in Renaissance Psychology', MPhil thesis, Warburg Institute, University of London, 1974, p. 103.

85. Marsilio Ficino, *Platonis Opera Omnia*, 1:373, cited in Mebane, *Renaissance Magic*, p. 24.

86. See Park, 'Imagination', p. 103.

87. On visual corruptions see Stuart Clark, *Vanities of the Eye: Vision in Early Modern European Culture* (Oxford: Oxford University Press, 2007).

88. A. C. Hamilton (ed.), Edmund Spenser, *The Faerie Queene* (Harlow: Longman, 1977). All references are to this edition.

89. Cited in Lyndy Abraham, *A Dictionary of Alchemical Imagery* (Cambridge: Cambridge University Press, 1998), p. 147.

90. Thomas Wright, *The Passions of the Minde in Generall* (London, 1604), cited in William Rossky, 'Imagination in the English Renaissance: Psychology and Poetic', *Studies in the Renaissance*, 5 (1958), 49–73, 51, 52.

91. William Rossky assumes that passions are always construed negatively in relation to Imagination. This is, as I hope I have demonstrated, not always the case. Reason was being undermined by poet-Hermeticists: poetic imagination was not necessarily exhaustively 'disciplined'; see 'Imagination in the English Renaissance', 73.

92. Robert Burton, *The Anatomy of Melancholy*, ed. Holbrook Jackson (London: J. M. Dent & Sons Ltd, 1932), p. 254. All references are to this edition.

93. Thomas Nashe, *Terrors*, cited in Rossky, 'Imagination in the English Renaissance', 55.

94. Samuel Daniel, *A Defence of Ryme*, in Smith (ed.), *Elizabethan Critical Essays*, vol. II, pp. 362–3.

95. Walter R. Davies (ed.), *The Works of Thomas Campion* (London: Faber and Faber, 1969), p. 251.

96. Henry Vaughan, 'Affliction', in L. C. Martin (ed.), *The Works of Henry Vaughan* (Oxford: Clarendon Press, 1957) pp. 459–60. All references are to this edition.

97. Beatrice Groves, 'Shakespeare's Sonnets and the Genevan Marginalia', in *Essays in Criticism*, 57:2 (2007), 114–128, especially 121–2.

98. George R. Potter and Evelyn M. Simpson (eds.), *The Sermons of John Donne*, 10 vols. (Berkeley and Los Angeles: University of California Press, 1953–62), vol. II, p. 261. For an important discussion of soul–body relations in Donne, see Michael Schoenfeldt, 'Eloquent Blood and Deliberative Bodies', in Margaret Healy and Thomas Healy (eds.), *Renaissance Transformations: The Making of English Writing, 1500–1650* (Edinburgh: Edinburgh University Press, 2009), pp. 145–61.

99. Grierson, *Poems of John Donne*, pp. 53, 22, 33.

100. 'Of Experience', in *Essays*, trans. Florio, vol. III, pp. 374, 375.

101. Ficino, Letter 88, in *The Letters of Marsilio Ficino*, vol. I, p. 138.

102. Ficino, Letter 88, vol. I, p. 138.

103. Ronsard, II, 973–4, in G. Cohen (ed.) *Oeuvres Complètes, Bibliothèque de la Pleiade* (Paris, 1950), cited in Brian Barron, 'Poetry and Imagination in the Renaissance', in Keith Aspley and Peter France (eds.), *Poetry in France: Metamorphoses of a Muse* (Edinburgh: Edinburgh University Press, 1992), pp. 61–83, 70.

104. Martz, *Poetry*, p. 321.

105. Yeats, 'Epigraph to Volume 2', cited in Martz, *Poetry of Meditation*, p. 321.

106. W. B. Yeats, *Autobiography* (New York: Macmillan, 1938), pp. 400–1.

107. Yeats, *Autobiography*, p. 351.

108. See Richard Ellmann, *Yeats, the Man and the Masks* (New York: Macmillan, 1948), p. 87. Martz associates this with a current of Neoplatonism; see *Poetry of Meditation*, p. 328.

109. Yeats, *Autobiography*, pp. 217–18.

110. See Ellmann, *Yeats*, p. 123.

111. Discussed in Martz, *Poetry*, p. 330.

112. James Hillman, *Re-Visioning Psychology* (New York: Harper Colophon Books, 1977), pp. 193–4.

113. See Timothy J. McGee, 'Orfeo and Euridice, the First Two Operas', in John Warden (ed.), *Orpheus, the Metamorphoses of a Myth* (Toronto: University of Toronto Press, 1982), p. 163; Hillman, *Re-Visioning*, pp. 195, 213.

114. E. Garin, *Italian Humanism*, trans. P. Munz (Oxford: Blackwell, 1965), p. 19. On Renaissance rhetoric and psychology see Hillman, *Re-Visioning*, pp. 194–5, 213–26.

6 CONCLUSION: SHAKESPEARE'S POETICS OF LOVE AND RELIGIOUS TOLERATION

1. John Heminge and Henry Condell (eds.), *Mr William Shakespeares Comedies, Histories & Tragedies Published According to the True Originall Copies*, (London: Isaac Iaggard and Ed. Blount, 1623) STC 22273, Prefatory Poem, unpaginated.

2. See the discussion of Ficinian natural magic in Chapter 1, p. 30 and Chapter 5, p. 178.

3. On moulding matter from within see Ficino's *Platonic Theology*, in J. B. Allen and John Warden (trans.), Marsilio Ficino, *Platonic Theology*, Bks I–IV (Harvard: Harvard University Press, 2001), p. 253. This passage is discussed in Chapter 5, pp. 177–8.

4. John Milton, 'On Shakespear', in John Carey (ed.), *Milton: Complete Shorter Poems* (London: Longman, 1968), p. 123. All references to Milton are to this edition. See my discussion in Chapter 2, p. 95.

5. Henry Nollius, Englished by Henry Vaughan, *Hermetical Physick*, in L. C. Martin (ed.), *The Works of Henry Vaughan*, (Oxford: Clarendon, 1957), p. 550.

6. For a summary of critical approaches to religion in Shakespeare see Kenneth J. E. Graham and Philip D. Collington (eds.), *Shakespeare and Religious Change* (Houndmills: Palgrave Macmillan, 2009), especially pp. 1–5 and 238–40. There has been a pronounced trend over the past decade to assert Shakespeare's Roman Catholicism; see, for example, Richard Wilson, *Secret Shakespeare: Studies in Theatre, Religion and Resistance* (Manchester: Manchester University Press, 2004); Stephen Greenblatt, *Will in the World: How Shakespeare Became Shakespeare* (New York and London: W.W. Norton, 2004); Clare Asquith, *Shadowplay: The Hidden Beliefs and Coded Politics of William Shakespeare* (New York: Public Affairs, 2005). By contrast, Katherine Duncan-Jones, *Ungentle Shakespeare* (London: Arden Shakespeare, Thomson Learning, 2001), uncovers a Shakespeare 'habitually indifferent or resistant to public devotion', whose writings are 'notable for their adroit side-stepping of specific religious and ecclesiastical issues', p. 195; in his works 'we find a widespread endorsement of devotion, charity and kindness', p. 196. This would be entirely consistent with the thesis of love and religious toleration expounded in this chapter.

7. I am grateful to Helen Hackett for this insight.

8. Joel Fineman, *Shakespeare's Perjured Eye: The Invention of Poetic Subjectivity in the Sonnets* (Berkeley: University of California Press, 1988), p. 29.

9. This point is made by John S. Mebane, *Renaissance Magic and the Return of the Golden Age: The Occult Tradition and Marlowe, Jonson and Shakespeare* (Lincoln and London: University of Nebraska Press, 1989), p. 181.

10. Mebane, *Renaissance Magic*, p. 181.

11. Charles Nicholl, *The Chemical Theatre* (London: Routledge & Kegan Paul, 1980), pp. 144–5.

12. Intriguingly, biblical texts on the 'wise fool' were particularly admired by the Family of Love.

13. Herbert Grierson (ed.), *The Poems of John Donne* (Oxford: Oxford University Press, 1958), p. 331. All references are to this edition.

14. Mebane, *Renaissance Magic*, p. 175.

15. Mebane, *Renaissance Magic*, p. 186. Jonathan Bate, *Soul of the Age: The Life, Mind and World of William Shakespeare* (London: Penguin Viking, 2008), p. 304, has drawn attention to the fact that the real king of Sicilia at the time was Philip III of Spain and the king of Bohemia, the Emperor Rudolf II, who was obsessed with alchemy, natural magic and Rosicrucianism.

16. Catherine M. Dunne, 'The Function of Music in Shakespeare's Romances', *Shakespeare Quarterly*, 20 (Autumn 1969), 391–405, 394.

17. See the discussion of Norton's advocated alchemical 'conjunctions' in Chapter 2, p. 23.

18. T. G. Bishop, *Shakespeare and the Theatre of Wonder* (Cambridge: Cambridge University Press, 1996), pp. 91, 87.

19. Helen Vendler, *The Art of Shakespeare's Sonnets* (Cambridge, Mass.: Harvard University Press, 1999), p. 81.

20. *The Letters of Marsilio Ficino*, trans. Language Department, London School of Economic Science, 7 vols. (London: Shepheard-Walwyn Ltd, 1975–), vol. 1, Letter 48, p. 92.
21. See James Grantham Turner, 'Libertinism and Toleration: Milton, Bruno and Aretino', in Sharon Achinstein and Elizabeth Sauer (eds.), *Milton and Toleration* (Oxford: Oxford University Press, 2007), pp. 107–25.
22. Turner, 'Libertinism and Toleration', p. 114.
23. *Areopagitica*, in Don M. Wolfe (gen. ed.), *Complete Prose Works of John Milton*, 8 vols. (New Haven: Yale University Press, 1853–82), vol. II, p. 521.
24. On the complex religio-philosophy of this work see the extensive 'Editor's Introduction', in Arthur D. Imerti (ed. and trans.), *The Expulsion of the Triumphant Beast* (New Jersey: Rutgers University Press, 1964), especially pp. 1–63. Imerti states, 'In *Lo spaccio* Bruno reveals his strong attraction to the mysteries of the Egyptian religion, his curiosity in that cult having been aroused by his reading of the Hermetic writings', p. 33. Both Bruno and Milton exalt the 'goddess Isis as the paradigm of active truth-seeking'; see Grantham Turner, 'Libertinism and Toleration', p. 115.
25. Bruno, *The Expulsion*, 89, in Grantham Turner, 'Libertinism and Toleration', p. 115.
26. Milton, *Areopagitica*, p. 527, quoted in Grantham Turner, 'Libertinism and Toleration', p. 121.
27. Katherine Duncan-Jones (ed.), *Shakespeare's Sonnets* (London: Arden Shakespeare; Thomson Learning, 2004), p. 124. Vendler, *Art of Shakespeare's Sonnets*, p. 529.
28. Ewan Fernie's Introduction to *Spiritual Shakespeare* (London: Routledge, 2005) makes the point that Shakespearean spirituality is a 'distinctive, inalienable and challenging dimension of his plays', one that is 'irreducible to any established theory or theology', p. 2. To some extent this is true (it was not reducible to an orthodox theology), but, in the context of the early seventeenth century, spiritual alchemy was steeped in philosophical, aesthetic and political meaning; the liberal deployment of its rhetoric and structures (as in Shakespeare) was indicative of an allegiance to a particular thought system with a collective identity. Shakespearean spiritual-materialism had its feet on the ground; it was certainly not transcendental escapism. See Alan Sinfield's critique of *Spiritual Shakespeare*, in 'Turning on the Spiritual', *Textual Practice*, 20:1 (2006), 161–70. It is important to remember that belief systems are not set in stone but shift in time and culture; my discussion about alchemy's meanings is very much focused on the turn of the seventeenth century.
29. Helen Gardner (ed.), *The Divine Poems*, 2nd edn (Oxford: Clarendon Press, 1978), p. xlix.
30. Grierson (ed.), *Poems of John Donne*, p. 330.
31. Edmund Gosse, *The Life and Letters of John Donne*, 2 vols. (New York: Dodd, Mead, 1899), vol. 1, p. 291; cited in David Wootton, 'John Donne's Religion of

Love', in John Brooke and Ian Maclean (eds.), *Heterodoxy in Early Modern Science and Religion* (Oxford: Oxford University Press, 2005), pp. 31–58, 31.

32. Wootton, 'John Donne's Religion of Love', p. 38.

33. See Helen Hackett, 'The Art of Blasphemy? Interfusions of the Erotic and the Sacred in the Poetry of Donne, Barnes, and Constable', *Renaissance and Reformation*, 28:3 (2004), 27–55, especially 30 and 35, on Donne's 'troublingly unrestricted' use of erotic imagery in religious verse: 'decorum is being not just breached but blasted … things which should be kept apart are being explosively brought together'.

34. Frances Yates has written extensively on this; see Frances Yates, *Giordano Bruno and the Hermetic Tradition* (Chicago: University of Chicago Press, 1964), especially pp. 176–9, and *The Rosicrucian Enlightenment* (St Albans: Paladin, 1972). See also Lyndy Abraham, *Marvell and Alchemy* (Aldershot: Scholar Press, 1990), p. 22. Clearly 'Egyptian religion' (Egypt being the source of the *Hermetica*) was regarded by Hermeticists as a purer, uncorrupted precursor of Christianity.

35. See Ronald Gray, 'Will in the Universe: Shakespeare's Sonnets, Plato's *Symposium*, Alchemy and Renaissance Neoplatonism', in Peter Holland (ed.), *Shakespeare Survey Volume 59: Editing Shakespeare* (Cambridge: Cambridge University Press, 2006), pp. 225–38, especially p. 228.

36. See Ernst Cassirer, *The Platonic Renaissance in England* (Chicago: University of Chicago Press, 1956), pp. 42–155; Frances Yates, *The French Academies of the Sixteenth Century* (London and New York: Routledge, 1988), pp. 15, 3–5.

37. Dedication, *De la Verite de la religion chretienne* (Antwerp, 1581), cited in Yates, *Giordano Bruno*, p. 176.

38. Yates, *Giordano Bruno*, p. 177.

39. Yates, *Giordano Bruno*, p. 178.

40. Robert Bostocke, *Auncient and Later Physicke* (London, 1585), title page.

41. Frank Whigham and Wayne A. Rebhorn (eds.), *The Art of English Poesy by George Puttenham: A Critical Edition* (Ithaca and London: Cornell University Press, 2007), I, 24, pp. 136–7.

42. H. N., *Evangelium regni* (London, 1652), fo. 4r.

43. Christopher Marsh, *The Family of Love in English Society, 1550–1630* (Cambridge: Cambridge University Press, 1994), p. 23. See also Alastair Hamilton, *The Family of Love* (Cambridge: James Clarke, 1981).

44. Marsh, *The Family of Love*, p. 25.

45. Hamilton, *The Family of Love*, pp. 6–10, 138.

46. See the discussion of Michael Maier's alchemical emblem books in Chapter 1.

47. Yates, *The Rosicrucian Enlightenment*.

48. See Hamilton, *The Family of Love*, p. 142.

49. Hamilton, *The Family of Love*, p. 142.

50. J. Etherington, *A Description of the True Church of Christ* (London, 1610), pp. 1–2. Cited in Peter Lake, *The Boxmaker's Revenge: 'Orthodoxy', 'Heterodoxy' and the Politics of the Parish in Early Stuart London* (Manchester: Manchester University Press, 2001), p. 100.

51. See Hamilton, *The Family of Love*, p. 1. Some of The Family's beliefs (such as dissimulation) were incorporated into late sixteenth-century Neo-Stoicism by Justus Lipsius.
52. Anon., *Temporis Filia Veritas* (?Leiden, 1589), sig. B 4v.
53. See the discussion of Elizabeth I and alchemy above, Chapter 3.
54. They were libelled by Puritan divines as dangerous sectarians; see Hamilton, *The Family of Love*, pp. 127–9.
55. Hamilton, *The Family of Love*, p. 127.
56. Hamilton, *The Family of Love*, p. 127.
57. See Katherine Duncan-Jones and H. R. Woudhuysen (eds.), *Shakespeare's Poems* (London: Arden, Cengage Learning, 2007), pp. 91–123. This introduction contains valuable contexts and a helpful discussion for thinking about 'The Phoenix and the Turtle'.
58. Cited in 'Introduction', Duncan-Jones and Woudhuysen (eds.), *Shakespeare's Poems*, p. 100.
59. Robert Chester, *Loves Martyr* (London, 1601). All citations in my text are of the facsimile of the Huntington Library copy in Appendix 3 of Duncan-Jones and Woudhuysen (eds.), *Shakespeare's Poems*.
60. Colin Burrow provides a brief summary of these readings in *Complete Sonnets* and a more extensive compendium of critical views is contained in Richard Allan Underwood, *Shakespeare's 'The Phoenix and the Turtle': A Survey of Scholarship*, Salzburg Studies in English Literature, 15 (Austria: University of Salzburg, 1974).
61. See discussion of *ens spiritual* in Jolande Jacobi, *Paracelsus: Selected Writings* (New Jersey: Princeton University Press, 1979), p. 75.
62. It is not clear that the lines preceding the *Threnos* are by Shakespeare; only the *Threnos* bears his name. The summary of the riddle is from, K. T. S. Campbell, '"The Phoenix and the Turtle" as a signpost of Shakespeare's Development', *British Journal of Aesthetics*, 10 (1970), 167–79.
63. See discussion above, Chapter 3, on Elizabeth as phoenix in the Drake pendant. On Elizabeth as phoenix see Helen Hackett, *Virgin Mother, Maiden Queen: Elizabeth I and the Cult of the Virgin Mary* (Basingstoke: Macmillan, 1995), pp. 9, 27.
64. Katherine's extreme virtue is rendered questionable by her dream: she might be guilty of 'false humility' – 'denying her worthiness while imagining herself attaining a heavenly crown'; see Thomas Healy, 'History and Judgement in *Henry VIII*', in Jennifer Richards and James Knowles (eds.), *Shakespeare's Late Plays: New Readings* (Edinburgh: Edinburgh University Press, 1999), pp. 158–75, 170.
65. *All's Well That Ends Well*, IV. iii. 74–7 is worth quoting in full: 'The web of our life is of a mingled yarn, good and ill together: our virtues would be proud, if our faults whipt them not, and our crimes would despair, if they were not cherished by our virtues'.
66. L. C. Martin (ed.), *The Works of Henry Vaughan* (Oxford: Clarendon Press, 1957), p. 458.

67. Thomas Roche, *Petrarch and the English Sonnet Sequences* (New York: AMS Press, 1989), mistakenly construes 'Egyptian religion' as totally at odds with Chrstianity, p. 81.

68. See *Corpus Hermeticum II* and *Asclepius*, in Brian P. Copenhaver, *Hermetica: The Greek 'Corpus Hermeticum' and the Latin 'Asclepius' in a New English Translation* (Cambridge: Cambridge University Press, 1992), pp. 8–9, 85.

69. The first decade of the twenty-first century has, however, seen a notable rise of interest in religious toleration. See, for example, Andrew Murphy, *Conscience and Community: Revisiting Toleration and Religious Dissent in Early Modern England and America* (University Park, Pa.: Pennsylvania State University Press, 2001), and Sharon Achinstein and Elizabeth Sauer (eds.), *Milton and Toleration* (Oxford: Oxford University Press, 2007).

70. Marsh, *The Family of Love*, p. 69.

Index

253

Lightning Source UK Ltd.
Milton Keynes UK
UKOW07f1158041114

241088UK00011B/528/P